Praise for the First Edition of **Hello! World**

A great book for little kids and big kids alike.
—Gordon Colquhoun, Computer Consultant, Avalon Consulting Services

Python for growing-ups.
—Dr. John Grayson, Author of *Python and Tkinter Programming*

A fun book to read and learn from!
—Dr. André Roberge, President, Université Sainte-Anne

The authors have created a friendly educational programming book that makes learning fun and painless.
—Bryan Weingarten, Software Architect

I highly recommend this book!
—Horst Jens, Python Instructor and Author of *Programming While Playing*

Python is a wonderful language for teaching beginners to program. It is great to see a kid-focused Python book!
—Jeffrey Elkner, Educator

If you teach your child one thing, teach her the golden rule. If you teach her two things, then teach her the golden rule and computer programming. This book is all you need for the latter.
—Josh Cronemeyer, Senior Software Consultant, Thoughtworks

I enjoyed the interaction with Carter in the book … My students are really going to enjoy the Digital Pet program! Reminds me of the Tamagotchi Virtual Pet that I had years ago.
—Kari J Stellpflug, Educator, Rochester Public Schools, Rochester MN

Computer programming is a powerful tool for children 'to learn learning.' … Children who engage in programming transfer that kind of learning to other things.
—Nicholas Negroponte, One Laptop Per Child Project

Advance Praise for the
Second Edition of **Hello! World**

It made programming seem as easy as frying bacon.
—Elisabet Gordon, 10th-grade student, Eagle Harbor High School

A great intro to the world of Python for everyone. This book is so much fun!
—Mason Jenkins, 7th-grade student, Myron B. Thompson Academy

For kids from 8 to 88. The book not only covers programming in Python in a fun way, but also sets the groundwork for good practices that can be used for other programming languages as well.
—Ben Ooms, Software Engineer, Sogeti

If you want to learn programming or teach it to a kid, this is your book.
—Cuberick.com

A very good introduction to programming for anyone, young or old, who wants to start learning this vital and highly enjoyable skill.
—Sue Gee, I-Programmer

Warren and Carter start simply, at the beginning, and take kids or adults all the way to making fun 2D graphical games and simulations. Python is my first choice for a real programming language for new programmers, and using this book is a great way to learn it. I've been recommending this book to my students since the First Edition came out.
—Dave Briccetti, Software Developer and Teacher, Dave Briccetti Software LLC

Hello World!

Second Edition

Computer Programming for Kids and Other Beginners

WARREN SANDE
CARTER SANDE

MANNING

SHELTER ISLAND

For online information and ordering of this and other Manning books, please visit
www.manning.com. The publisher offers discounts on this book when ordered in quantity.
For more information, please contact:

> Special Sales Department
> Manning Publications Co.
> 20 Baldwin Road
> PO Box 761
> Shelter Island, NY 11964
> Email: orders@manning.com

Manning Publications Co.
20 Baldwin Road
PO Box 761
Shelter Island, NY 11964

Development editor:	Cynthia Kane
Copyeditor:	Tiffany Taylor
Proofreader:	Toma Mulligan
Illustrator:	Martin Murtonen
Typesetter:	Marija Tudor
Cover designer:	Leslie Haimes

ISBN 978-1-617290-92-3

Third, corrected printing, August 2014
Printed in the United States of America
6 7 8 9 10 – EBM – 18 17 16

Contents

Preface

The preface is that part at the beginning of a book that you skip over to get to the good stuff, right? Sure, you can skip over it if you want (hey, you're the one turning the pages), but who knows what you might miss…. It's not very long, so maybe you should give it a look, just in case.

What is programming?

Very simply, programming means telling a computer to do something. Computers are dumb machines. They don't know how to do anything. You have to tell them everything, and you have to get all the details right.

But if you give them the right instructions, they can do many wonderful and amazing things.

WORD BOX

An *instruction* is a basic command you give to a computer, usually to do a single, very specific thing.

A computer program is made up of a number of instructions. Computers do all the great things they do today because a lot of smart programmers wrote programs or software to tell them how. *Software* just means a program or collection of programs that run on your computer, or sometimes on another computer yours is connected to, like a web server.

WHAT'S GOING ON IN THERE?

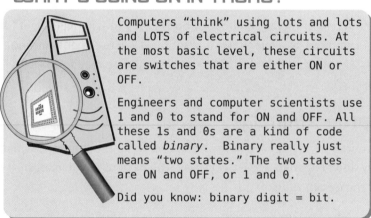

Computers "think" using lots and lots and LOTS of electrical circuits. At the most basic level, these circuits are switches that are either ON or OFF.

Engineers and computer scientists use 1 and 0 to stand for ON and OFF. All these 1s and 0s are a kind of code called *binary*. Binary really just means "two states." The two states are ON and OFF, or 1 and 0.

Did you know: binary digit = bit.

Python—a language for us and the computer

All computers use binary inside. But most people don't speak binary very well. We need an easier way to tell the computer what we want it to do. So people invented programming languages. A computer programming language lets us write things in a way we can understand, and then translates that into binary for the computer to use.

There are many different programming languages. This book will teach you how to use one of those languages—one called Python—to tell the computer what to do.

We highly recommend using the Hello World installer, which installs the correct version of Python you need to use this book. You can find it at **www.helloworldbook2.com**.

Why learn programming?

Even if you don't become a professional programmer (most people don't), there are lots of reasons to learn programming:

- The most important is because you want to! Programming can be very interesting and rewarding, as a hobby or a profession.
- If you're interested in computers and want to know more about how they work and how you can make them do what you want, that's a good reason to learn about programming.
- Maybe you want to make your own games, or maybe you can't find a program that does exactly what you want or need it to do, so you want to write your own.

- Computers are everywhere these days, so there's a good chance you'll use computers at work, at school, or at home—probably all three. Learning about programming will help you understand computers better in general.

Why Python?

With all the programming languages to choose from (and there are a lot!), why did I pick Python for a programming book for kids? Here are a few reasons:

- Python was created from the start to be easy to learn. Python programs are about the easiest to read, write, and understand of any computer language I have seen.
- Python is free. You can download Python—and many, many fun and useful programs written in Python—for free.
- Python is open source software. Part of what open source means is that any user can extend Python (create things that let you do more with Python, or do the same things more easily). Many people have done this, and there is a large collection of free Python stuff that you can download.
- Python isn't a toy. Although it's very good for learning programming, it's also used by thousands of professionals around the world every day, including programmers at institutions like NASA and Google. So once you learn Python, you don't have to switch to a "real" language to make "real" programs. You can do a lot with Python.
- Python runs on different kinds of computers. Python is available for Windows PCs, Macs, and computers running Linux. Most of the time, the same Python program that works on your Windows PC at home will work on the Mac at your school. You can use this book with virtually any computer that has Python. (And remember, if the computer you want to use doesn't have Python, you can get it for free.)
- I like Python. I enjoy learning it and using it, and I think you will, too.

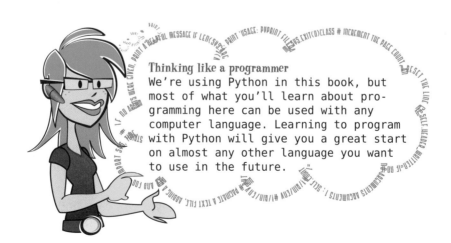

Thinking like a programmer
We're using Python in this book, but most of what you'll learn about programming here can be used with any computer language. Learning to program with Python will give you a great start on almost any other language you want to use in the future.

The fun stuff

There's just one other thing I need to mention now....

For kids especially, one of the most fun parts of using a computer is playing games, with graphics and sound. We're going to learn how to make our own games and do lots of things with graphics and sound as we go along. Here are pictures of some of the programs we'll be making:

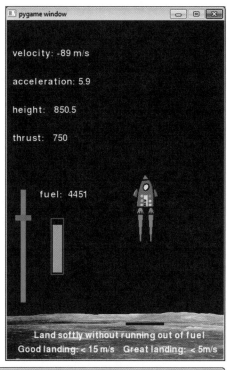

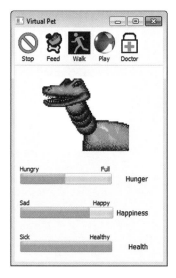

But I think (as least, I hope) you'll find learning the basics and writing your first programs as enjoyable and rewarding as making those spaceships or skiers zoom around the screen.

Have fun!

Acknowledgments

This book would never have been started, much less finished, without the inspiration, initiative, and support of my wonderful wife, Patricia. When we couldn't find a suitable book to feed Carter's keen interest in learning about programming, she said, "You should write one. It would be a great project for you two to work on together." As is often the case, she was right. Patricia has a way of bringing out the best in people. So Carter and I started thinking about what would be in such a book, writing chapter outlines and sample programs, and finding ways to make it fun and interesting. Once we got started, Carter and Patricia made sure we finished. Carter would give up bedtime stories to work on the book. And if we didn't work on it for a while, I would be reminded, "Daddy, we haven't worked on the book for days!" Carter and Patricia reminded me that, if you put your mind to it, you can do anything. And all members of the family, including our daughter Kyra, gave up many hours of family time while the book was in progress. I thank all of them for their patience and loving support, which made this book possible.

Writing a manuscript is one thing; getting a book into people's hands is another. This book would never have been published without the enthusiastic and persistent support of Michael Stephens at Manning Publications. Right from the start, he "got it" and agreed that there was a need for this kind of book. Michael's steadfast belief in the project and his continued patience in guiding a rookie author through the process were immensely valuable and appreciated. I would also like to say a sincere thank you to all the other folks at Manning who helped make this book happen, in particular Mary Piergies for patiently coordinating all aspects of the production process.

This book would not be the same without Martin Murtonen's lively and fun illustrations. His work speaks for itself about Martin's creativity and talent. But what doesn't show is how great he is to work with. It was a pleasure.

One day, I asked my friend and colleague Sean Cavanagh, "How would you do this in Perl?" Sean said, "I wouldn't. I would use Python." So I took the plunge to learn a new programming language. Sean answered many questions when I was learning Python and reviewed early drafts. He also created and maintains the installer. His help is much appreciated.

I would also like to thank the many people who reviewed the book during its development and helped prepare the manuscript: Vibhu Chandreshekar, Pam Colquhoun, Gordon Colquhoun, Dr. Tim Couper, Josh Cronemeyer, Simon Cronemeyer, Kevin Driscoll, Jeffrey Elkner, Ted Felix, David Goodger, Lisa L. Goodyear, Dr. John Grayson, Michelle Hutton, Horst Jens, Andy Judkis, Caiden Kumar, Anthony Linfante, Shannon Madison, Kenneth McDonald, Evan Morris, Prof. Alexander Repenning, André Roberge, Kari J. Stellpflug, Kirby Urner, and Bryan Weingarten

The final result is much better for their efforts.

WARREN SANDE

I would like to thank Martin Murtonen for his exceptional caricature of me, my mom for letting me go on the computer when I was two years old and for coming up with the idea of writing a book, and, most importantly, my dad for all the effort he put into this book with me and showing me how to program.

CARTER SANDE

Acknowledgments for the Second Edition

In updating *Hello World!*, many of the same people contributed who helped with the First Edition. In addition to those people listed previously, we'd like to thank those who helped review the Second Edition during its development: Ben Ooms, Brian T. Young, Cody Roseborough, Dave Briccetti, Elizabet Gordon, Iris Faraway, Mason Jenkins, Rick Gordon, Shawn Stebner, and Zachary Young. Thanks also to Ignacio Beltran-Torres and Daniel Soltis who did a careful technical proofread of the final manuscript shortly before it went into production.

We'd also like to thank all the folks at Manning who helped make this Second Edition of *Hello World!* even better than the original.

About this book

This book teaches the basics of computer programming. It's meant for kids, but anyone who wants to learn how to program a computer can use it.

You don't need to know anything about programming to use this book, but you should know the basics of using your computer. Maybe you use it for email, surfing the Web, listening to music, playing games, or writing reports for school. If you can do the basic things on your computer, like starting a program and opening and saving files, you should have no trouble using this book.

What you need

This book teaches programming using a computer language called Python. Python is free, and you can download it from several places, including this book's web site. To learn programming using this book, all you need are

- This book (of course!).
- A computer with Windows, Mac OS X, or Linux on it. The examples in this book are done in Windows. (There is some help for Mac and Linux users on the book's web site: **www.helloworldbook2.com**.)
- Basic knowledge of how to use your computer (starting programs, saving files, and so on). If you have trouble with this, maybe you can get someone to help you.
- Permission to install Python on your computer (from your parent, your teacher, or whoever is responsible for your computer). ***We highly recommend using the Hello World***

installer, which installs the correct version of Python you need to use this book. You can find it at **www.helloworldbook2.com**.

- The desire to learn and try things, even if they don't always work the first time.

What you don't need

To learn programming with this book, you don't need

- To buy any software. Everything you need is free, and a copy is available on the book's web site, **www.helloworldbook2.com**.
- Any knowledge of computer programming. This book is for beginners.

Using this book

If you're going to use this book to help you learn programming, here are a few pointers that will help you get more out of it:

- Follow along with the examples.
- Type in the programs.
- Do the quiz questions.
- Don't worry, be happy!

Follow along with the examples

When you see examples in the book, they'll look like this:

```
if timsAnswer == correctAnswer:
    print "You got it right!"
    score = score + 10
```

Always try to follow along and type the programs in yourself. (I'll tell you exactly how to do it.) You could just sit in a big, comfy chair and read this whole book, and you'd probably learn something about programming. But you'll learn a whole lot more by doing some programming.

Installing Python

To use this book, you need to have Python installed on your computer. ***We highly recommend using the Hello World installer***, which installs the correct version of Python, plus a few other things you'll need. The Hello World installer is available at the book's web site: **www.helloworldbook2.com**.

If you install Python using some other method, and you don't get the right version of Python and the other modules you need, you might get frustrated when some things don't work like they should.

Type in the programs

The installer program that goes with this book will copy all the example programs to your hard drive (if you want). The installer is on the book's web site: **www.helloworldbook2.com**. You can also view and download individual examples from the web site, but I encourage you to type as many of them yourself as possible. Just by typing the programs, you'll get a "feel" for programming and for Python in particular. (And we can all use more typing practice!)

Do the quiz questions

At the end of every chapter, there are some questions to practice what you've learned. Do as many as you can. If you're stuck, try to find someone who knows about programming to help you. Work through them together—you'll learn a lot by doing that. Don't peek at the answers until you're done, unless you're really, really stuck. (Yes, some of the answers are in the back of the book and on the web site, but like I said, don't peek.)

Carter says

I wanted to make sure this book was good for
kids—fun and easy to understand. Luckily, I had
some help. Carter is a kid who loves computers
and wants to learn more about them. So he
helped me to make sure I got this book
right. When Carter noticed something
funny or unusual, or something that didn't
make sense, we show it like this, at right:

*I'm Carter.
I haven't noticed
anything unusual... yet!
Just wanted to
say hi!*

What's new in the Second Edition

First, let's talk about what didn't change. We decided to stay with Python 2 for *Hello World!,
Second Edition*, rather than switching to Python 3. The reasons for this are explained in
Chapter 1.

Now, here's what's new in the Second Edition, compared to the First Edition:

- Everything is in color! This includes colorized code listings, which should make
  reading and understanding the code even easier.
- We added notes throughout the book explaining the differences between Python 2
  and Python 3.
- We added a section on Python dictionaries in Chapter 12.
- For the GUI programing in Chapter 20, we switched from PythonCard, which is no
  longer supported, to PyQt, which is much more widely used. PyQt is also used for
  the Hangman program in Chapter 22 and the Virtual Pet program in Chapter 24.
- We added a chapter (25) explaining in detail the Skier program, which is presented
  without much explanation in Chapter 10.
- We added a chapter (26) about writing an artificial intelligence (AI) robot that
  competes against other AIs in a simple battle game.
- We added an appendix listing differences between Python 2 and Python 3.
- We added a list of code listings in the back of the book, before the index.

Talk to the authors

You can post comments and ask questions in the book's Author Online forum at **www.helloworldbook2.com**.

Note to parents and teachers

Python is free, open source software, and there is no danger in installing and using it on your computers. You can get the Python software—and everything else you need to use this book—for free at **www.helloworldbook2.com**. The download files are simple to install and use and are free of viruses and spyware.

Books like this used to come with CDs with all the software on them, but now most readers (and publishers) prefer to use the Internet. If you can't download the software from the book's web site, Manning can send you a CD containing the same files available on the web site. There's no cost for the CD, but you'll have to pay the shipping and handling fee based on your address.

To get the CD, send an email to support@manning.com with the subject line "Hello World! 2nd Edition CD." Or you can send a good, old-fashioned letter to:

> Hello World 2nd Edition CD Request
> Manning Publications Co.
> 20 Baldwin Road
> P.O. Box 761
> Shelter Island, NY 11964

Resources for this book and access to the Author Online forum are also available from the publisher's website at **www.manning.com/HelloWorldSecondEdition**.

Getting Started

Installing Python

The first thing you need to do is install Python on the computer you're going to use.

Installing Python is pretty easy. ***We highly recommend using the Hello World installer***, which installs the correct version of Python you need to use this book. You can find it at **www.helloworldbook2.com**. Find the version of the installer that matches your computer's operating system.

IN THE GOOD OLD DAYS

In the early days of personal computers (PCs), people had it easy. With a lot of the first PCs, a programming language called BASIC was built in to the computer. They didn't have to install anything. All they did was turn on the computer, and the screen would say "READY," and they could start typing BASIC programs. Sounds great, huh?

Of course, that "READY" was all you got. No programs, no windows, no menus. If you wanted the computer to do *anything*, you had to write a program! There were no word processors, media players, web browsers, or any of the things we are used to now. There wasn't even a Web to browse. There were no fancy graphics and no sound, except the occasional "beep" if you made a mistake!

There are versions for Windows, Mac OS X, and Linux. All the examples in this book use Windows, but using Python in Mac OS X or Linux is very similar. Just follow the instructions on the web site to run the right installer for your system.

The version of Python that we use in this book is version 2.7.3. If you use the installer on the book's web site, that's the version you'll get. By the time you read this, there might be newer versions of Python out there. All the examples in this book have been tested using Python 2.7.3. They're likely to work with later 2.x versions as well, but we can't see into the future, so there are no guarantees.

If Python is already installed on your computer, and you are not going to use the installer, you will need to make sure that some "extras" that you'll need for this book are also installed. Have a look at the installation section of the web site (**www.helloworldbook2.com**) to find out how to do this. But again, the best way to make sure all the code in the book will work correctly is to use our installer, which you can find at **www.helloworldbook2.com**.

Python 2 vs. Python 3
A few years before this book was written, a new version of Python was released, Python 3. However, it turned out that it wasn't really an "upgrade" so much as a fork in the road. That is, many people did not want to switch to Python 3, so they stayed with Python 2. The folks who develop Python kept making new versions of Python 2 as well as new versions of Python 3. At the time this Second Edition of "Hello World!" was written, the two current versions of Python were Python 2.7.3 and Python 3.3.0. This book uses Python 2.7.3, and the code is likely to be compatible with any future versions of Python 2.x.

For more details on Python 2 vs. Python 3, see appendix B.

Starting Python with IDLE

There are a couple of ways to start using Python. One is called IDLE, and that's the one we'll use for now.

In the **Start** menu, under **Python 2.7**, you'll see **IDLE (Python GUI)**. Click this option, and the IDLE window will open. It should look something like the window below.

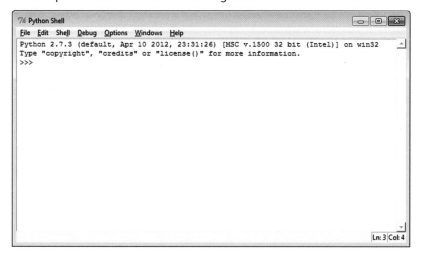

IDLE is a Python *shell*. A shell is basically a way of interacting with a program by typing text, and this shell lets you interact with Python. (That's why you see **Python Shell** in the title bar of the window.) IDLE also happens to be a GUI, which is why it says **Python GUI** in the **Start** menu. IDLE has some other things besides the shell, but we'll get to all that in a minute.

WORD BOX

GUI stands for *graphical user interface*. This means something with windows, menus, buttons, scrollbars, etc. Programs that don't have a GUI are called *text-mode* programs, *console* programs, or *command-line* programs.

The >>> in the previous figure is the Python *prompt*. A prompt is what a program displays when it's waiting for you to type something. The >>> prompt tells you that Python is ready for you to start typing Python instructions.

Instructions, please

Let's give Python our first instruction. With the cursor at the end of the >>> prompt, type

```
print "Hello World!"
```

and press the Enter key. (On some keyboards, this is called the Return key.) You need to press the Enter key after every line you type.

After you press the Enter key, you should get this response:

```
Hello World!
>>>
```

The figure below shows how that looks in the IDLE window.

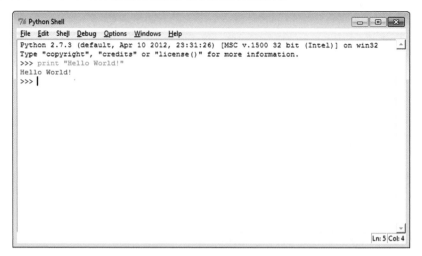

Python did what you told it: it printed your message. (In programming, `print` often means to display text on the screen, instead of printing it on a piece of paper using your printer.) That one line is a Python *instruction*. You're on your way to programming! The computer is under your command!

You are now under my command!

>>> YES MASTERRRRR...

By the way, in learning to program, there is a tradition that the first thing you make the computer do is display "Hello World!" That's where the title of this book comes from. You're following that tradition. Welcome to the world of programming!

Why are there all those fancy colors in IDLE?

Good question! IDLE is trying to help you understand things a bit better. It's showing things in different colors to help you tell different parts of the code apart. (*Code* is just another term for the instructions you give to the computer in a language like Python.) I'll explain what the different parts are as we go through the rest of this book.

If it doesn't work

If you made a mistake, you might see something like this:

```
>>> pront "Hello World!"
SyntaxError: invalid syntax
>>>
```

That error message means you typed something that Python didn't understand. In this example, **print** is misspelled **pront**, and Python doesn't know what to do with that. If that happens to you, try again and make sure you type it exactly like in the example.

Hey, I didn't see the orange color on `pront` like I did on `print`.

That's right. That's because **print** is a Python keyword, and **pront** is not.

WORD BOX

A *keyword* is a special word that is part of the Python language (also known as a *reserved* word).

Interacting with Python

What you just did was use Python in interactive mode. You typed a command (an instruction), and Python *executed* it immediately.

WORD BOX

Executing a command, instruction, or program is just a fancy way of saying "running" it, or "making it happen."

Let's try something else in interactive mode. Type this at the prompt:

```
>>> print 5 + 3
```

You should get this:

```
8
>>>
```

So Python can do addition! That shouldn't be surprising, because computers are good at arithmetic.

Let's try one more:

```
>>> print 5 * 3
15
>>>
```

In pretty much all computer programs and languages, the * symbol is used for multiplication. That character is called an *asterisk* or *star*.

If you're used to writing "5 times 3" as "5 x 3" in math class, you'll have to get used to using * for multiplication in Python instead. (It's the symbol above the number 8 on most keyboards.)

Okay, how about this one:

```
>>> print 2345 * 6789
15920205
>>>
```

Okay, how about this one:

```
>>> print 12345678987654321234567789 * 9876543212345678987654321
121932632007315960006096522024081660722245112635269
>>>
```

That's right. With the computer, you can do math on really, really big numbers.

Here's something else you can do:

```
>>> print "cat" + "dog"
catdog
>>>
```

Or try this:

```
>>> print "Hello " * 20
Hello Hello Hello Hello Hello Hello Hello Hello Hello Hello
Hello Hello Hello Hello Hello Hello Hello Hello Hello Hello
```

Besides math, another thing computers are good at is doing things over and over again. Here we told Python to print "Hello" 20 times.

We'll do more in interactive mode later, but right now it's …

Time to program

The examples we've looked at so far are single Python instructions (in interactive mode). Although that's great for checking out some of the things Python can do, those examples aren't really programs. As I mentioned before, a program is a number of instructions collected together. So let's make our first Python program.

First, you need a way to type in the program. If you just type it in the interactive window, Python won't "remember" it. You need to use a text editor (like Notepad for Windows, or TextEdit for Mac OS X, or vi for Linux) that can save the program to the hard drive. IDLE comes with a text editor that is much better for what you need than Notepad. To find it, select **File > New Window** from IDLE's menus.

When I am talking about menu selections, like **File > New,** the first part (**File** in this case) is the main menu. The > tells you that the next thing (**New** in this case) is an item in the File menu. I will use that notation throughout the book.

You'll see a window like the one in the next figure. The title bar says **Untitled** because you haven't given the file a name yet.

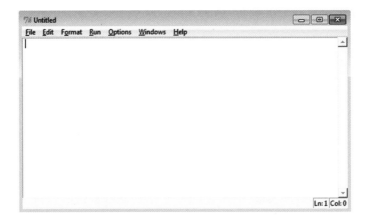

Now, type the program in the following listing into the editor.

Listing 1.1   Our first real program

```
print "I love pizza!"
print "pizza " * 20
print "yum " * 40
print "I'm full."
```

Notice the title that says "Listing 1.1"? When the example code makes a complete Python program, I will number it like this, so you can easily find it in the **\examples** folder or on the web site.

When you're done, save the program using the **File > Save** or **File > Save As** menu option. Call the file **pizza.py**. You can save it wherever you like (as long as you remember where it is, so you can find it later). You might want to create a new folder for saving your Python programs. The **.py** part at the end of the filename is important, because it tells your computer that this is a Python program and not just any old text file.

You might have noticed that the editor used some different colors in the program. Some words are in orange, and others are in green. This is because the IDLE editor assumed that you would be typing in a Python program. For Python programs, the IDLE editor shows Python keywords in orange and anything in quotation marks in green. This is meant to help you read your Python code more easily.

Running your first program

Once you've saved your program, go to the **Run** menu (still in the IDLE editor), and pick **Run Module** (as shown in the next figure). This will run your program.

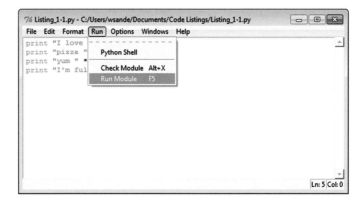

The Python shell window (the one that first came up when you started IDLE) becomes active again, and you'll see something like the following:

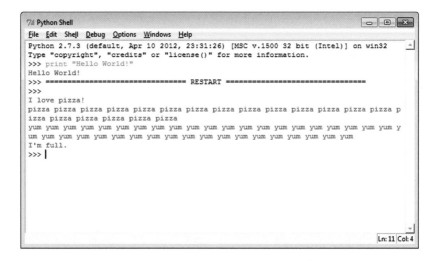

The **RESTART** part tells you that you started running a program. (This will be helpful when you're running your programs over and over again to test them.)

Then the program runs. Okay, so it doesn't do very much. But you got the computer to do what you told it to do. Our programs will get more interesting as we go along.

If something goes wrong

What happens if you have an error in your program, and it doesn't run? There are two different kinds of errors that can happen. Let's look at both kinds, so you'll know what to do if either one happens to you.

Syntax errors

IDLE does some checking of your program before it even tries to run it. If IDLE finds an error, it's usually a *syntax error*. Syntax is the spelling and grammar rules for a programming language, so a *syntax error* means you've typed something that isn't proper Python code.

Here is an example:

```
print "Hello, and welcome to Python!"
print "I hope you will enjoy learning to program."
print Bye for now!"
```

└── Missing quotation mark

We missed a quotation mark between **print** and **Bye for now!**"

If you tried to run this program, IDLE would pop up a message saying "There's an error in your program: invalid syntax." Then you would have to look at your code to see what's wrong. IDLE's editor will highlight (in red) the place where it found the error. It might not be exactly where the problem is, but it should be close.

Runtime errors

The second kind of error that can happen is one that Python (or IDLE) can't detect before it runs the program. This kind of error only happens when the program runs, so it's called a *runtime error*. Here's an example of a runtime error in a program:

```
print "Hello, and welcome to Python!"
print "I hope you will enjoy learning to program."
print "Bye for now!" + 5
```

If you save this and try to run it, the program actually starts to run. The first two lines are printed, but then you get an error message:

```
>>> =========================== RESTART ===========================
>>>
Hello, and welcome to Python!
I hope you will enjoy learning to program.

Traceback (most recent call last):          ◄──── Start of the        Where the
  File "C:/HelloWorld/examples/error1.py", line 3, in <module>  ◄──  error message   error was
    print "Bye for now!" + 5                ◄───── The "bad" line of code
TypeError: cannot concatenate 'str' and 'int' objects
>>>                                              What Python
                                                 thinks is wrong
```

The line starting with `Traceback` is the beginning of the error message. The next line tells you where the error happened—the filename and line number. Then it displays the bad line of code. This helps you find where the problem is in your code. The last part of the error message tells you what Python thinks is wrong. Once you know more about programming and Python, it will be easier to understand what the message means.

How come this works:
```
print "Bye for now!" * 5
```

But this *doesn't*:
```
print "Bye for now!" + 5
```

Well, Carter, it's kind of like that old saying about comparing apples to alligators. In Python, you can't add different kinds of things together, like a number and some text. That's why `print "Bye for now!"` + 5 gave us an error. It's like saying, "If I take 5 apples and add 3 alligators, how many do I have?" You have 8, but 8 of what? Adding these together doesn't really make sense. But you can multiply almost anything by a number to get more of that kind of thing. (If you have 2 alligators and you multiply by 5, you have 10 alligators!) That's why `print "Bye for now!"` * 5 works.

Thinking like a programmer
Don't worry if you get error messages. They are meant to help you figure out what went wrong so you can fix it. If there is something wrong with your program, you *want* to see an error message. The kinds of bugs that *don't* give you an error message are much harder to find!

Our second program

The first program didn't do much. It just printed some stuff on the screen. Let's try something a bit more interesting.

The code in listing 1.2 is for a simple number-guessing game. Start a new file in the IDLE editor using **File > New Window**, just like you did the first time. Type in the code from listing 1.2 and then save it. You can call it whatever you want, as long as it ends with **.py**. **NumGuess.py** might be a good name.

It's only 18 lines of Python instructions plus a few blank lines to make it easier to read. It shouldn't take too long to type in. Don't worry that we haven't talked about what this code all means yet. We'll get to that very soon.

Listing 1.2   Number-guessing game

```
import random
secret = random.randint(1, 99)          ◄─── Picks secret number
guess = 0
tries = 0
print "AHOY!  I'm the Dread Pirate Roberts, and I have a secret!"
print "It is a number from 1 to 99.  I'll give you 6 tries. "
while guess != secret and tries < 6:
    guess = input("What's yer guess? ")      ◄─── Gets player's guess
    if guess < secret:
        print "Too low, ye scurvy dog!"
    elif guess > secret:
        print "Too high, landlubber!"

    tries = tries + 1                    ◄─── Uses up one try

if guess == secret:
    print "Avast! Ye got it!  Found my secret, ye did!"
else:
    print "No more guesses!  Better luck next time, matey!"
    print "The secret number was", secret
```

Allows up to 6 guesses

Prints a message at the end of the game

When you're typing in the code, notice the indenting of the lines after the `while` instruction and the extra indenting of the lines after `if` and `elif`. Also notice the colons at the ends of some of the lines. If you type the colon in the correct place, the editor will help you by indenting the next line for you.

Once you've saved the code, run it using **Run > Run Module**, just like you did for the first program. Try playing the game and see what happens. Here is a sample of when I ran it:

```
>>> ====================== RESTART ========================
>>>
AHOY!  I'm the Dread Pirate Roberts, and I have a secret!
It is a number from 1 to 99.  I'll give you 6 tries.
What's yer guess? 40
Too high, landlubber!
What's yer guess? 20
Too high, landlubber!
What's yer guess? 10
Too low, ye scurvy dog!
What's yer guess? 11
Too low, ye scurvy dog!
What's yer guess? 12
Avast! Ye got it!  Found my secret, ye did!
>>>
```

It took me five guesses to get the secret number, which turned out to be 12.

You'll learn all about the `while`, `if`, `else`, `elif`, and `input` instructions in the next few chapters. But you can probably already get the basic idea of how this program works:

1. The secret number is randomly picked by the program.
2. The user inputs guesses.
3. The program checks each guess against the secret number: is it higher or lower?
4. The user keeps trying until he guesses the number or runs out of turns.

When the guess matches the secret number, the player wins.

What did you learn?

Whew! We covered quite a lot. In this chapter, you

- Installed Python
- Learned how to start IDLE
- Learned about interactive mode
- Gave Python some instructions, and it executed them
- Saw that Python knows how to do arithmetic (including really big numbers!)
- Started the IDLE text editor to type in your first program

- Ran your first Python program
- Learned about error messages
- Ran your second Python program: the number-guessing game

Test your knowledge

1 How do you start IDLE?

2 What does `print` do?

3 What is the symbol for multiplication in Python?

4 What does IDLE display when you start to run a program?

5 What is another word for running a program?

Try it out

1 In interactive mode, use Python to calculate the number of minutes in a week.

2 Write a short program to print three lines: your name, your birth date, and your favorite color. The output should look something like this:

```
My name is Warren Sande.
I was born January 1, 1970.
My favorite color is blue.
```

Save the program and run it. If the program doesn't do what you expect, or you get any error messages, try to fix it and make it work.

## CHAPTER 2

Remember This: Memory and Variables

What is a program? Hey, wait a minute, I thought we answered that in chapter 1! We said a program was a series of instructions to the computer.

Well, that's true. But almost all programs that do anything useful or fun have some other qualities:

- They get *input*.
- They *process* the input.
- They produce *output*.

Input, processing, output

Your first program (listing 1.1) didn't have any input or processing. That's one reason why it wasn't very interesting. The output was the messages the program printed on the screen.

Your second program, the number-guessing game (listing 1.2), had all three of the basic elements:

- The *input* was the guesses the player typed in.
- The *processing* was the program checking the guesses and counting the turns.
- The *output* was the messages the program printed.

Here's another example of a program that has all three elements: in a video game, the *input* is the signals from the joystick or game controller; the *processing* is the program figuring out whether you have shot the alien, dodged the ball of fire, completed the level, or whatever; and the *output* is the graphics on the screen and the sound from the speakers or headphones.

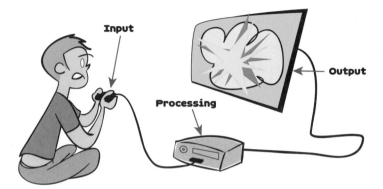

Input, processing, output. Remember that.

Okay, so the computer needs input. But what does it do with that input? In order to do something with the input, the computer has to remember it or keep it somewhere. The computer keeps things, including input (and the program itself), in its *memory*.

WHAT'S GOING ON IN THERE?

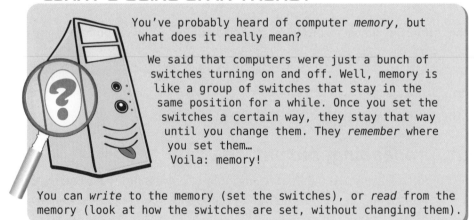

You've probably heard of computer *memory*, but what does it really mean?

We said that computers were just a bunch of switches turning on and off. Well, memory is like a group of switches that stay in the same position for a while. Once you set the switches a certain way, they stay that way until you change them. They *remember* where you set them...
Voila: memory!

You can *write* to the memory (set the switches), or *read* from the memory (look at how the switches are set, without changing them).

But how do we tell Python where in the memory to put something? And once it's there, how do we find it again?

In Python, if you want your program to remember something so you can use it later, all you have to do is give that "thing" a *name*. Python will make a place for the thing in the computer's memory, whether the thing is a number, some text, a picture, or a piece of music. When you want to refer to that thing again, you just use the same name.

Let's use Python in interactive mode and find out more about names.

Names

Go back to the Python Shell window. (If you closed IDLE since doing the example in chapter 1, open it again.) At the prompt, type

```
>>> Teacher = "Mr. Morton"
>>> print Teacher
```

(Remember, the >>> is the prompt that Python displays. You just type what is after it and press Enter.) You should see this:

```
Mr. Morton
>>>
```

You just created a thing that is made up of the letters "Mr. Morton", and you gave it the name **Teacher**.

The equal sign (=) tells Python to *assign* or "make equal to." You *assigned* the name **Teacher** to the series of letters "Mr. Morton".

Somewhere in a chunk of your computer's memory, the letters "Mr. Morton" exist. You don't need to know exactly where. You told Python that the name for that series of letters is **Teacher**, and that's how you will refer to it from now on. A name is like a label or tag or sticky note that you attach to something to identify what it is.

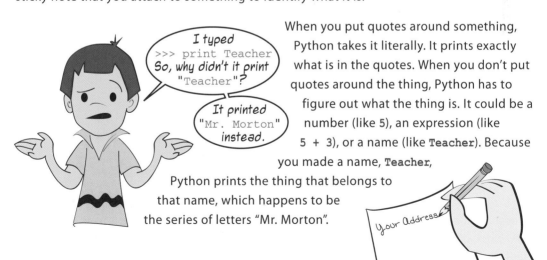

I typed
```
>>> print Teacher
```
So, why didn't it print
```
"Teacher"?
```

It printed
```
"Mr. Morton"
```
instead.

When you put quotes around something, Python takes it literally. It prints exactly what is in the quotes. When you don't put quotes around the thing, Python has to figure out what the thing is. It could be a number (like 5), an expression (like 5 + 3), or a name (like **Teacher**). Because you made a name, **Teacher**, Python prints the thing that belongs to that name, which happens to be the series of letters "Mr. Morton".

It's just like if someone said, "Write down your address." You wouldn't write this:

(Well, maybe Carter would, because he likes to kid around …)

You would write
something like this:

If you wrote "Your Address", you would be taking the statement literally. Python doesn't take things literally unless you use quote marks. Here's another example:

```
>>> print "53 + 28"
53 + 28
>>> print 53 + 28
81
```

With quote marks, Python printed exactly what you told it: 53 + 28.

Without quote marks, Python treated the 53 + 28 as an *arithmetic expression*, and it *evaluated* that expression. In this case, it was an expression for adding two numbers together, so Python gave you the sum.

WORD BOX

An *arithmetic expression* is a combination of numbers and symbols that Python can figure out the value of.

Evaluate just means "figure out the value of."

Python takes care of figuring out how much memory it needs to store the letters and what part of the memory it will use. To retrieve your information (get it back), you just need to use the same name again. You used the *name* along with the `print` keyword, which displays things (like numbers or text) on the screen.

Thinking like a programmer

When you assign a value to a name (like assigning the value "Mr. Morton" to `Teacher`), it is stored in memory and is called a *variable*. In most programming languages, we say you *store* a value in a variable.

But Python does things a little differently from most other computer languages. Instead of *storing values in variables,* it's more like *putting names on values.*

Some Python programmers say that Python doesn't have "variables"— it has "names" instead. But they behave pretty much the same way. This is a book about programming (that just happens to use Python), not a book only about Python. So we will use the terms *variable, name,* or *variable name* when talking about a Python *name*. It really doesn't matter what you call them, as long as you understand how variables behave and how to use them in your programs.

By the way, Guido van Rossum, the person who created Python, says in his Python tutorial: "The '=' sign is used to assign a value to a variable." So I guess he thinks Python has variables!

A clean way to store things

Using names in Python is like going to a dry cleaner… Your clothes are placed on a hanger, your name is attached, and they are put on a big revolving hanger-trolley. When you go back to pick up your clothes, you don't need to know exactly where they are stored on the big hanger-trolley. You just give the person your name, and they return your clothes. In fact, your clothes might be in a different spot than when you brought them in. But the dry cleaner keeps track of that for you. All you need is your name to retrieve your clothes.

Variables are the same. You don't need to know exactly where in memory the information is stored. You just need to use the same name as when you stored it.

You can create variables for other things besides letters. You can name numeric values. Remember our example from before?

```
>>> 5 + 3
8
```

Let's try that one with variables:

```
>>> First = 5
>>> Second = 3
>>> print First + Second
8
```

Here, we created two names, `First` and `Second`. The number 5 was assigned to `First`, and the number 3 was assigned to `Second`. Then we `print`ed the sum of the two.
There's another way to do this. Try this:

```
>>> Third = First + Second
>>> Third
8
```

Notice what we did here. In interactive mode, we can display the value of a variable just by typing its name, without using `print`. (This doesn't work in a program.)

In this example, instead of doing the sum in the `print` instruction, we took the thing named `First` and the thing named `Second` and added them together, creating a new thing, called `Third`. `Third` is the sum of `First` and `Second`.

You can have more than one name for the same thing. Try this in interactive mode:

```
>>> MyTeacher = "Mrs. Goodyear"
>>> YourTeacher = MyTeacher
>>> MyTeacher
"Mrs. Goodyear"
>>> YourTeacher
"Mrs. Goodyear"
```

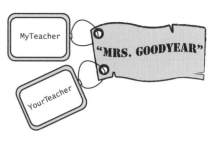

This is like sticking two tags on the same thing. One tag says **YourTeacher** and one tag says **MyTeacher**, but they are both stuck on "Mrs. Goodyear".

If we changed MyTeacher *to* "Mrs. Tysick", *would* YourTeacher *also be changed to* "Mrs. Tysick"?

That's a very good question, Carter. The answer is, no. What would happen is that a new thing, "Mrs. Tysick", would be created. The tag **MyTeacher** would get pulled off "Mrs. Goodyear" and stuck on "Mrs. Tysick". You still have two different names (two tags), but now they are stuck on two different things instead of being stuck on the same thing.

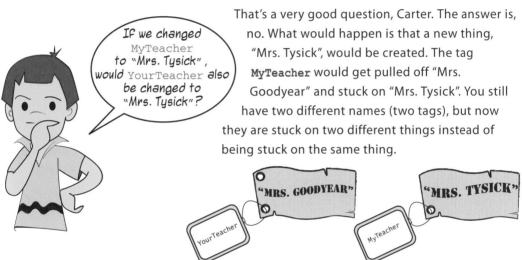

What's in a name?

You can call a variable anything you want (well, almost). The name can be as long as you want, and it can have letters and numbers in it, as well as the underscore character (_).

But there are a few rules about variable names. The most important one is that they are case-sensitive, which means that uppercase and lowercase matter. So, `teacher` and `TEACHER` are two different names. So are `first` and `First`.

Another rule is that a variable name has to start with a letter or the underscore character. It can't start with a number. So `4fun` is not allowed.

One more rule is that a variable name can't have any spaces in it.

If you want to know all the rules for variable names in Python, you can look in appendix A, at the back of the book.

Numbers and strings

So far, we have made variables for both letters (text) and numbers. But in the addition example, how did Python know that we meant the numbers 5 and 3, and not the characters "5" and "3"? Well, just like in the last sentence, the quote marks make all the difference.

A character, or series of characters (letters, numbers, or punctuation), is called a *string*. The way you tell Python that you are making a string is to put quotes around the characters. Python is not too fussy about whether you use single or double quotes. Either of these will work:

```
>>> teacher = "Mr. Morton"    ◁——— Double quotes

>>> teacher = 'Mr. Morton'    ◁——— Single quotes
```

But you do have to use the same kind of quotes at the start and the end of the string.

If you type in a number without quotes, Python knows you mean the numerical value, not the character. Try this to see the difference:

```
>>> first = 5
>>> second = 3
>>> first + second
8
>>> first = '5'
>>> second = '3'
>>> first + second
'53'
```

Without the quotes, the 5 and 3 were treated as numbers, so we got the sum. With quotes, the '5' and '3' were treated as strings, so we got the two characters "added" together, or '53'. You can also add strings of letters together, as you saw in chapter 1:

```
>>> print "cat" + "dog"
catdog
```

Notice that, when you add two strings together like this, there is no space between them. They get jammed right together.

BIG FANCY WORD ALERT!

Concatenate

It's not really correct to say "added" when talking about strings (like we just did). When you put characters or strings together to make a longer string, there is a special name for it. Instead of "adding" (which is only for numbers), it is called *concatenation*. This sounds like kon-kat-en-ay-shun.

We say that you *concatenate* two strings.

Long strings

If you want to have a string that spans more than one line, you have to use a special kind of string called a *triple-quoted string*. Here is what it looks like:

```
long_string = """Sing a song of sixpence, a pocket full of rye,
Four and twenty blackbirds baked in a pie.
When the pie was opened the birds began to sing.
Wasn't that a dainty dish to set before the king?"""
```

This kind of string starts and ends with three quote marks. The quote marks can be double or single quotes, so you could also do it this way:

```
long_string = '''Sing a song of sixpence, a pocket full of rye,
Four and twenty blackbirds baked in a pie.
When the pie was opened the birds began to sing.
Wasn't that a dainty dish to set before the king?'''
```

Triple-quoted strings can be very useful when you have several lines of text that you want to display together, and you don't want to use a separate string for each line.

How "variable" are they?

Variables are called "variables" for a reason. It's because they are … well … variable! That means you can *vary*, or change, the value that is assigned to them. In Python, you do this by creating a new thing that is different from the old thing, and sticking the old label (the name) on the new thing. We did that with `MyTeacher` in the last section. We took the tag `MyTeacher` off "Mrs. Goodyear" and attached it to a new thing, "Mrs. Tysick". We assigned a new value to `MyTeacher`.

Let's try another one. Remember the variable `Teacher` that you created before? Well, if you haven't closed IDLE, it's still there. Check and see:

```
>>> Teacher
'Mr. Morton'
```

Yup, still there. But we can change it to something else instead:

```
>>> Teacher = 'Mr. Smith'
>>> Teacher
'Mr. Smith'
```

We created a new thing, "Mr. Smith," and named it `Teacher`. The tag got moved from the old thing to the new thing. But what happened to the old thing, "Mr. Morton"?

Remember that things can have more than one name (more than one tag stuck on them). If "Mr. Morton" still has another tag on it, then it stays in the computer's memory. But if it no longer has any tags, Python figures that no one needs it anymore, so it gets deleted from memory.

That way, the memory doesn't fill up with things that nobody is using. Python does all this cleanup automatically, and you don't have to worry about it.

An important thing to know is that we didn't actually change "Mr. Morton" into "Mr. Smith". We just moved the tag (reassigned the name) from one thing to the other. Some kinds of things in Python (like numbers and strings) cannot be changed. You can reassign their names to something else (like you just did), but you can't change the original thing.

There are other kinds of things in Python that *can* be changed. You will learn more about this in chapter 12, when we talk about *lists*.

The new me

You can also make a variable equal to itself:

```
>>> Score = 7
>>> Score = Score
```

I bet you're thinking, "Well, that's pretty useless!" And you'd be right. It's kind of like saying "I am me." But with a small change, you can become a whole *new you*! Try this:

```
>>> Score = Score + 1
>>> print Score
8
```
Changes Score from 7 to 8

What happened here? In the first line, the **Score** tag was stuck on the value 7. We made a new thing, which was **Score + 1**, or 7 + 1. That new thing is 8. Then we took the **Score** tag off the old thing (7) and stuck it on the new thing (8). So **Score** has been reassigned from 7 to 8.

Whenever you make a variable equal something, the variable always appears on the left side of the equal sign (=). The trick is that the variable can also appear on the right. This turns out to be quite useful, and you'll see it in a lot of programs. The most common use is to *increment* a variable (increase it by a certain amount), like we just did, or the opposite, to *decrement* a variable (decrease it by a certain amount):

1 Start with **Score** = 7.

2 Make a new thing by adding 1 to it (which makes 8).

3 Give the name **Score** to the new thing.

So, **Score** changed from 7 to 8.

Here are a couple of important things to remember about variables:

- A variable can be reassigned (the tag can be stuck on a new thing) at any time by a program. This is very important to remember, because one of the most common "bugs" in programming is changing the wrong variable, or changing the right variable at the wrong time.

One way to help prevent this is to use variable names that are easy to remember. We could have used either of these:

```
t = 'Mr. Morton'
```

or

```
x1796vc47blahblah = 'Mr. Morton'
```

But that would make them harder to remember in a program. We would be more likely to make a mistake if we used those names. Try to use names that tell you what the variable is for.

- Variable names are case-sensitive. That means uppercase and lowercase matter. So, `teacher` and `Teacher` are two different names.

Remember, if you want to know all the variable naming rules for Python, you can look in appendix A.

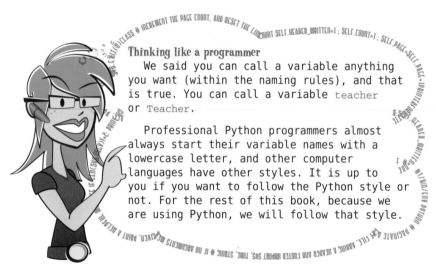

Thinking like a programmer

We said you can call a variable anything you want (within the naming rules), and that is true. You can call a variable `teacher` or `Teacher`.

Professional Python programmers almost always start their variable names with a lowercase letter, and other computer languages have other styles. It is up to you if you want to follow the Python style or not. For the rest of this book, because we are using Python, we will follow that style.

What did you learn?

In this chapter, you learned

- How to "remember" or keep things in the computer's memory using variables
- That variables are also called "names" or "variable names"
- That variables can be different kinds of things, such as numbers and strings

Test your knowledge

1 How do you tell Python that a variable is a string (characters) instead of a number?

2 Once you have created a variable, can you change the value that is assigned to it?

3 With variable names, is `TEACHER` the same as `TEACHEr`?

4 Is `'Blah'` the same as `"Blah"` to Python?

5 Is `'4'` the same as `4` to Python?

6 Which of the following is not a correct variable name? Why?

   a) `Teacher2`

   b) `2Teacher`

   c) `teacher_25`

   d) `TeaCher`

7 Is `"10"` a number or a string?

Try it out

1 Make a variable, and assign a number to it (any number you like). Then display your variable using `print`.

2 Modify your variable, either by replacing the old value with a new value, or by adding something to the old value. Display the new value using `print`.

3 Make another variable, and assign a string (some text) to it. Then display it using `print`.

4 Just like in the last chapter, in interactive mode, get Python to calculate the number of minutes in a week. But this time, use variables. Make variables for `DaysPerWeek`, `HoursPerDay`, and `MinutesPerHour` (or make up your own names), and then multiply them together.

5 People are always saying there's not enough time to get everything done. How many minutes would there be in a week if there were 26 hours in a day? (Hint: Change the `HoursPerDay` variable.)

## CHAPTER 3

Basic Math

When we first tried using Python in interactive mode, we saw that it can do simple arithmetic. Now we're going to see what else Python can do with numbers and math. You might not realize it, but math is everywhere! Especially in programming, math is used all the time. That doesn't mean you have to be a math whiz to learn programming, but think about it. Every game has a score of some kind that has to be added up. Graphics are drawn on the screen using numbers to figure out the positions and colors. Moving objects have a direction and speed, which are described with numbers. Almost any interesting program is going to use numbers and math in some way. So let's learn some basics about math and numbers in Python.

By the way, a lot of what we will learn here applies to other programming languages, and to other programs like spreadsheets. It's not only Python that does math this way.

The four basic operations

We already saw Python do a little math in chapter 1: addition, using the plus (+) sign, and multiplication, using the asterisk (*) sign.

Python uses the hyphen (-) (which is also called the minus sign) for subtraction, as you would expect:

```
>>> print 8 - 5
3
```

Because computer keyboards don't have a division (÷) symbol, all programs use the forward slash (/) for division:

```
>>> print 6/2
3
```

That worked. But sometimes Python does something you might not expect with division:

```
>>> print 3/2
1
```

Huh? I thought computers were good at math! Everyone knows that

3 / 2 = 1.5

What happened?

Well, although it seems to be acting dopey, Python is really *trying* to be smart. To explain this one, you need to know about integers and decimal numbers. If you don't know the difference, check out the word box for a quick explanation.

WORD BOX

Integers are the numbers you can easily count, like 1, 2, 3, as well as 0 and the negative numbers, like −1, −2, −3.

Decimal numbers (also called *real numbers*) are the numbers with a decimal point and some digits after it, like 1.25, 0.3752, and −101.2.

In computer programming, decimal numbers are also called *floating-point* numbers, or sometimes *floats* for short (or *float* for just one of them). This is because the decimal point "floats" around. You can have the number 0.00123456 or 12345.6 in a float.

Because we entered both the 3 and the 2 as integers, Python thinks we want an integer for the answer, too. So it rounded the answer 1.5 down to the nearest integer, which is 1. To put it another way, Python is doing division without the remainder.

To fix it, try this:

```
>>> print 3.0 / 2
1.5
```

That's better! If you enter either of the two numbers as a decimal number, Python knows you want the answer as a decimal number.

Floor division

The way Python 2 does division is called "floor division". But Python 3 works differently. In Python 3, if you use the regular division operator (forward slash), you'll get regular division, not floor division

```
>>> print 3/2
1.5
```

To get floor division in Python 3, you can use the double-forward-slash:

```
>>> print 3//2
1
```

This is one of the most noticeable differences between Python 2 and Python 3, and it is one that will break a lot of Python 2 programs if you try to run them in Python 3 and vice versa.

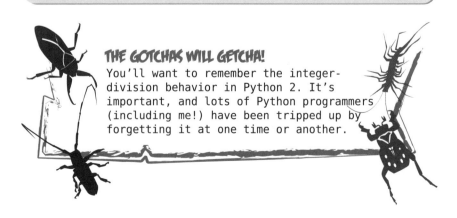

THE GOTCHAS WILL GETCHA!
You'll want to remember the integer-division behavior in Python 2. It's important, and lots of Python programmers (including me!) have been tripped up by forgetting it at one time or another.

Operators

The +, -, *, and / symbols are called *operators*. That's because they "operate on," or work with, the numbers you put around them. The = sign is also an operator, and it's called the *assignment operator*, because you use it to assign a value to a variable.

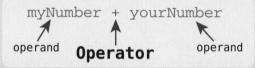

An *operator* is something that has an effect on, or "operates on," the things around it. The effect can be to assign a value to, test, or change one or more of those things.

The +, -, *, and / symbols we use for doing arithmetic are *operators*.

The things being operated on are called *operands*.

I learned in school that the so-called operands in addition are also called addends.

Order of operations

Which one of these is correct?

2 + 3 * 4 = 20

or

2 + 3 * 4 = 14

That depends on what order we do things in. If we do the addition first, we get

2 + 3 = 5, so then 5 * 4 = 20

If we do the multiplication first, we get

3 * 4 = 12, so then 2 + 12 = 14

The correct order is the second one, so the correct answer is 14. In math, there is something called the *order of operations* that tells you which operators should be done before others, even if they are written down after them.

In our example, even though the + sign comes before the * sign, the multiplication is done first. Python follows proper math rules, so it does multiplication before addition. We can try this in interactive mode to make sure:

```
>>> print 2 + 3 * 4
14
```

The order that Python uses is the same one you learned (or *will* learn) in math class. Exponents come first, then multiplication and division, and then addition and subtraction.

If you want to change the order of operations and *make* something go first, you just put *parentheses* (round brackets) around it, like this:

```
>>> print (2 + 3) * 4
20
```

This time, Python did the 2 + 3 first (because of the parentheses) to get 5, and then it multiplied 5 * 4 to get 20.

Again, this is exactly the same as in math class. Python (and all other programming languages) follow proper math rules and the order of operations.

Two more operators

There are two more math operators I want to show you. These two plus the four basic ones you just saw are all you will need for 99 percent of your programs.

Exponentiation—raising to a power

If you wanted to multiply 3 by itself 5 times, you could write

```
>>> print 3 * 3 * 3 * 3 * 3
243
```

But this is the same as 3^5, or "three exponent five," or "three to the power of five." Python uses a double star (asterisk) for exponents or raising a number to a power:

```
>>> print 3 ** 5
243
```

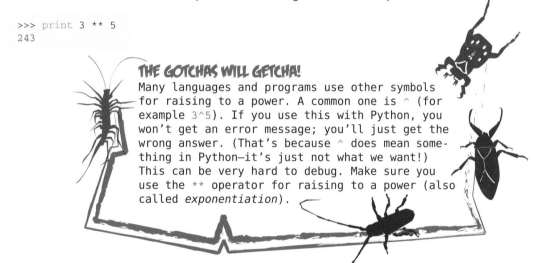

THE GOTCHAS WILL GETCHA!
Many languages and programs use other symbols for raising to a power. A common one is ^ (for example 3^5). If you use this with Python, you won't get an error message; you'll just get the wrong answer. (That's because ^ does mean something in Python—it's just not what we want!) This can be very hard to debug. Make sure you use the ** operator for raising to a power (also called *exponentiation*).

One reason for using an exponent instead of multiplying several times is that it's easier to type. But a more important reason is that with ** you can have exponents that are not integers, like this:

```
>>> print 3 ** 5.5
420.888346239
```

There is no easy way to do that using just multiplication.

Modulus—getting the remainder

When you first tried division in Python, you saw that, if you divide two integers, Python 2 gives you the answer as an integer. (And Python 3 does the same thing with the // operator.) It's doing integer division. But in integer division, the answer really has two parts.

Do you remember when you first learned about division? If the numbers didn't divide evenly, you ended up with a *remainder*:

7 / 2 = 3, with a remainder of 1

The answer for 7 / 2 has a *quotient* (3, in this case) and a *remainder* (1, in this case). If you divide two integers in Python, it gives you the quotient. But what about the remainder?

Python has a special operator for calculating the remainder for integer division. It's called the *modulus* operator, and the symbol is the percent symbol (%). You use it like this:

```
>>> print 7 % 2
1
```

So if you use / and % together, you can get the full answer for integer division problems:

```
>>> print 7 / 2
3
>>> print 7 % 2
1
```

The answer to 7 divided by 2 is 3, remainder 1. If you do floating-point division, you will get the decimal answer:

```
>>> print 7.0 / 2
3.5
```

I know of one more operator - a telephone operator!

Actually, now that you mention it, they are similar …. An arithmetic operator connects numbers together the way an old-fashioned telephone operator used to connect phones together.

There are *another* two operators I'd like to tell you about. I know, I said just two more, but these are really easy!

Increment and decrement

Remember the example from the last chapter: `score = score + 1`? We said that was called *incrementing*. A similar thing is `score = score - 1`, which is called *decrementing*. These operations are done so often in programming that they have their own operators: += (increment) and -= (decrement).

You use them like this

```
>>> number = 7          Number increased by 1
>>> number += 1    ◁──────╯
>>> print number
8
```

or

```
>>> number = 7          Number decreased by 1
>>> number -= 1    ◁──────╯
>>> print number
6
```

The first example adds one to the number. (It changes from 7 to 8.) The second one subtracts one from the number. (It changes from 7 to 6.)

Really big and really small

Remember, in chapter 1, when we multiplied those two really big numbers together? We got a very big number for the answer. Sometimes, Python shows you big numbers a bit differently. Try this in interactive mode:

```
>>> print 9938712345656.34 * 4823459023067.456
4.79389717413e+025
```

(It doesn't matter exactly what numbers you type in—any big numbers with decimals will do.)

What's that letter 'e' doing in the middle of the number?

The *e* is one way of displaying really big or really small numbers on a computer. It's called *E-notation*. When you're working with really big (or really small) numbers, showing all the digits and decimal places can be kind of a pain. These sorts of numbers show up a lot in math and science.

For example, if an astronomy program was displaying the number of kilometers from Earth to the star Alpha Centauri, it could show 38000000000000000 or 38,000,000,000,000,000 or 38 000 000 000 000 000. (That's 38 quadrillion kilometers!) But either way, you would get tired of counting all those zeros.

Another way to display this number is to use *scientific notation*, which uses powers of 10 along with decimal numbers. In scientific notation, the distance to Alpha Centauri would be written like this: 3.8×10^{16}. (See how the 16 is raised above the line, and is smaller?) This reads as "three point eight times ten to the power of sixteen" or "three point eight times ten to the sixteenth." What it means is, you take 3.8 and move the decimal point 16 places to the right, adding zeros as needed.

$$3.80000000000000000000000$$

Move the decimal right 16 places.

$$38000000000000000000.0 = 3.8 \times 10^{16}$$

Scientific notation is great if you can write the 16 as an exponent, raised above the line and smaller, like we did here. If you're working with pencil and paper, or a program that supports superscripts, then you can use scientific notation.

WORD BOX

Superscript means a character or characters that are raised above the rest of the text, like this: 10^{13}. The 13 here is the *superscript*. Usually, superscripts are also smaller than the main text.

Subscripts are similar, but they're characters that are below the rest of the text and smaller, like this: $\log_2$. The 2 here is a *subscript*.

But you can't always use superscripts, so another way to show the same thing is E-notation. E-notation is just another way of writing scientific notation.

E-notation

In E-notation, our number would be 3.8E16 or 3.8e16. This reads as "three point eight exponent sixteen" or "three point eight e sixteen" for short. It is assumed that the exponent is a power of 10. That's the same as writing 3.8×10^{16}.

Most programs and computer languages, including Python, let you use either an uppercase or a lowercase *E*.

For very small numbers, like 0.0000000000001752, a negative exponent is used. The scientific notation would be 1.752×10^{-13}, and the E-notation would be 1.752e-13. A negative exponent means to move the decimal place to the left instead of the right.

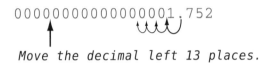

Move the decimal left 13 places.

$$0.0000000000011752 = 1.752e-13$$

You can use E-notation to enter very big and very small numbers (or any number, for that matter) into Python. Later you'll see how to make Python print numbers using E-notation.

Try entering some numbers in E-notation:

```
>>> a = 2.5e6
>>> b = 1.2e7
>>> print a + b
14500000.0
```

Although we entered the numbers in E-notation, the answer came out as a regular decimal number. That's because Python won't display numbers in E-notation unless you specifically tell it to, or the numbers are really big or really small (lots of zeros).

Try this:

```
>>> c = 2.6e75
>>> d = 1.2e74
>>> print c + d
2.72e+75
```

This time, Python displayed the answer in E-notation automatically because it wouldn't make sense to display a number with 73 zeros!

If you want numbers like 14,500,000 to display in E-notation, you need to give Python special instructions. You'll learn more about that later in the book (in chapter 21).

If you don't quite understand how E-notation works, don't worry. It's not used for the programs in the rest of this book. I just wanted to show you how it works in case you ever need it.

At least now, if you use Python to do some math and you get a number like 5.673745e16 for an answer, you will know that it is a really big number, and not some kind of error.

Exponents vs. E-notation

Don't get confused between raising a number to a power (also called *exponentiation*) and E-notation:

- 3**5 means 3^5, or "three to the fifth power" or 3 * 3 * 3 * 3 * 3, which is equal to 243.
- 3e5 means $3 * 10^5$ or "three times ten to the fifth power," or 3 * 10 * 10 * 10 * 10 *10, which is equal to 300,000.
- Raising to a power means you are raising the number itself to that power. E-notation means you are multiplying by a power of 10.

Some people would read both 3e5 and 3**5 as "three exponent five," but they are two different things. It doesn't matter so much how you say it, as long as you understand what each one means.

What did you learn?

In this chapter, you learned

- How to do basic math operations in Python
- About integers and floats
- About exponentiation (raising numbers to a power)
- How to calculate the modulus (the remainder)
- All about E-notation

Test your knowledge

1. What symbol does Python use for multiplication?
2. What answer would Python 2 give for 8 / 3?
3. How would you get the remainder for 8 / 3?
4. How would you get the decimal answer for 8 / 3 in Python 2?
5. What's another way of calculating 6 * 6 * 6 * 6 in Python?
6. How would you write 17,000,000 in E-notation?
7. What would 4.56e-5 look like in regular notation (not E-notation)?

Try it out

1. Solve the following problems either using interactive mode or by writing a small program:

    a) Three people ate dinner at a restaurant and want to split the bill. The total is $35.27, and they want to leave a 15% tip. How much should each person pay?

    b) Calculate the area and perimeter of a rectangular room, 12.5 meters by 16.7 meters.

2. Write a program to convert temperatures from Fahrenheit to Celsius. The formula for that is: C = 5 / 9 * (F - 32). (Hint: Watch out for the integer-division gotcha!)

3. Do you know how to figure out how long it will take to get somewhere in a car? The formula (in words) is "travel time equals distance divided by speed." Make a program to calculate the time it will take to drive 200 km at 80 km per hour and display the answer.

Types of Data

We have seen that there are at least three different types of things we can assign to a variable (to keep in the computer's memory): integers, floating-point numbers, and strings. There are other types of data in Python, which you'll learn about later, but for now these three will do. In this chapter, you're going to learn how you can tell what type something is. You'll also see how to make one type from another.

Changing types

Quite often, we need to convert data from one type to another. For instance, when we want to print a number, it needs to be converted to text in order for the text to appear on the screen. Python's `print` command can do that for us, but sometimes we need to convert without printing, or to convert from strings to numbers (which `print` can't do). This is called *type conversion*. So how does it work?

Python doesn't actually "convert" things from one type to another. It creates a new thing, of the type you want, from the original thing. Here are some functions that convert data from one type to another:

- `float()` will create a new float (decimal number) from a string or integer.
- `int()` will create a new integer from a string or float.
- `str()` will create a new string from a number (or any other type).

The parentheses at the end of `float()`, `int()`, and `str()` are there because they are not Python *keywords* (like `print`)—they are some of Python's built-in *functions*.

You'll learn a lot more about functions later in the book. For now, you just need to know that you put the value you want to convert *inside* the parentheses. The best way to show this is with some examples. Follow along in interactive mode in the IDLE shell.

Changing an int to a float

Let's start with an integer and create a new floating-point number (decimal number) from it, using `float()`:

```
>>> a = 24
>>> b = float(a)
>>> a
24
>>> b
24.0
```

Notice that `b` gets a decimal point and a 0 at the end. That tells us it is a float and not an integer. The variable `a` stays the same, because `float()` doesn't change the original value—it creates a new one.

Remember that, in interactive mode, you can just type a variable name (without using `print`), and Python will display the value of the variable. (You saw that in chapter 2.) That only works in interactive mode, not in a program.

Changing a float to an int

Now let's try the reverse—start with a decimal number and create an integer, using `int()`:

```
>>> c = 38.0
>>> d = int(c)
>>> c
38.0
>>> d
38
```

We created a new integer, `d`, which is the *whole number* part of `c`.

I tried to get Python to add 0.1 and 0.2, and the answer came out as 0.30000000000000004. And then I used `print` and it looked fine.

What's up with that?

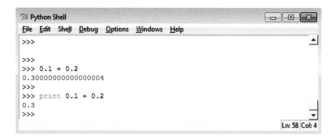

Yikes! How did that happen? Carter, I think your computer is going crazy!

Just kidding. Actually, there is an explanation for that, which you can see in the "WHAT'S GOING ON IN THERE?" box.

WHAT'S GOING ON IN THERE?

Remember how we said that computers use binary inside? Well, all the numbers that Python stores are stored as binary. For the sum of 0.1 and 0.2, Python creates a float (decimal number) with enough binary digits (bits) to give you 15 decimal places. But that binary number isn't exactly equal to 0.3, it's just very, very close. (In this case, it is wrong by 0.000000000000004.) The difference is called *roundoff error*.

When you typed the expression 0.1 + 0.2 in interactive mode, Python showed you the raw number it stored, with all the decimal places. When you used print, you got what you were expecting, because print is a little smarter, and it knows enough to round off and display 0.3.

It's like asking someone the time. They could say "twelve forty-four and fifty-three seconds." But most people would just say, "quarter to one," because they know you don't need to be so precise. Roundoff errors happen with floating point numbers in any computer language. The number of correct digits you get may vary from one computer to another or one language to another, but they all use the same basic method of storing floats.

Usually, roundoff errors are small enough that you don't need to worry about them.

Let's try another one:

```
>>> e = 54.99
>>> f = int(e)
>>> print e
54.99
>>> print f
54
```

Even though 54.99 is very close to 55, we still get 54 for the integer. The `int()` function always rounds down. It doesn't give the *nearest* integer, it gives the *next lowest* integer. The `int()` function basically chops off the decimal part.

If you want to get the nearest integer, there is a way. You'll learn about that in chapter 21.

Changing a string to a float

You can also create a number from a string, like this:

```
>>> a = '76.3'
>>> b = float(a)
>>> a
'76.3'
>>> b
76.3
```

Notice that, when we display **a**, the result has quotes around it. That's Python's way of telling us that **a** is a string. When we display **b**, we get the floating-point value.

Getting more information: type()

In the last section, we relied on seeing the quote marks to know that a value was a number or a string. There is a more direct way to find out.

Python has another function, type(), which explicitly tells us the type of a variable. Let's try it:

```
>>> a = '44.2'
>>> b = 44.2
>>> type(a)
<type 'str'>
>>> type(b)
<type 'float'>
```

The type() function tells us that a is of type 'str', which stands for *string*, and b is of type 'float'. No more guessing!

Type-conversion errors

Of course, if we give int() or float() something that is not a number, it won't work. Try it and see:

```
>>> print float('fred')
Traceback (most recent call last):
  File "<pyshell#1>", line 1, in <module>
    print float('fred')
ValueError: could not convert string to float: fred
```

We got an error message. The error message means that Python doesn't know how to create a number from "fred". Do you?

Using type conversions

Going back to your Fahrenheit to Celsius temperature-conversion program from the "Try it out" section in chapter 3, remember that you needed to fix the integer-division behavior to get the right answer, by changing the 5 to 5.0 or the 9 to 9.0:

```
cel = 5.0 / 9 * (fahr - 32)
```

The float() function gives you another way of doing this:

```
cel = float(5) / 9 * (fahr - 32)
```

or

```
cel = 5 / float(9) * (fahr - 32)
```

Try it and see.

What did you learn?

In this chapter, you learned about

- Converting between types (or, more correctly, *creating* types from other types): `str()`, `int()`, and `float()`
- Displaying values directly without using `print`
- Checking the type of a variable using `type()`
- Roundoff errors and why they happen

Test your knowledge

1 When you use `int()` to convert a decimal number to an integer, does the result get rounded up or down?

2 In your temperature-conversion program, would this have worked?

```
cel = float(5 / 9 * (fahr - 32))
```

What about this:

```
cel = 5 / 9 * float(fahr - 32)
```

If not, why not?

3 (Extra challenging question) Without using any other functions besides `int()`, how could you get a number to round off instead of round down? (For example, 13.2 would round down to 13, but 13.7 would round up to 14.)

Try it out

1 Use `float()` to create a number from a string like `'12.34'`. Make sure the result is really a number!

2 Try using `int()` to create an integer from a decimal number like `56.78`. Did the answer get rounded up or down?

3 Try using `int()` to create an integer from a string. Make sure the result is really an integer!

## CHAPTER 5

Input

Until now, if you wanted your program to "crunch some numbers," you had to put those numbers right in the code. For example, if you wrote the temperature-conversion program in the "Try it out" section of chapter 3, you probably put the temperature to convert right in the code. If you wanted to convert a different temperature, you would have to change the code.

What if you want to have the user enter any temperature she wants when the program runs? We said before that a program has three components: input, processing, and output. Our first program had only output. The temperature-conversion program had some processing (converting the temperature) and some output, but no input. It's time to add the third ingredient to our programs: *input*. Input means getting something, some kind of information, into a program while it is running.

That way we can write programs that interact with the user, which will make things a lot more interesting.

Python has a built-in function, called `raw_input()`, that is used to get input from the user. In the rest of this chapter, you'll learn how to use `raw_input()` in your programs.

raw_input()

The `raw_input()` function gets a string from the user. The normal way it gets this is from the keyboard—the user types in the input.

`raw_input()` is another one of Python's built-in functions, like `str()`, `int()`, `float()`, and `type()`. (You saw those in chapter 4.) You'll learn a lot more about functions later. But for now, you just need to remember to include the parentheses (round brackets) when you use `raw_input()`.

Raw input
In Python 3, the `raw_input()` function is called `input()`. It works exactly the same way as `raw_input()` in Python 2.

Here is how you use it:

```
someName = raw_input()
```

This will let the user type in a string and assign it the name `someName`.

Now let's put this into a program. Create a new file in IDLE, and type in the code in the following listing.

Listing 5.1   Getting a string using `raw_input`

```
print "Enter your name: "
somebody = raw_input()
print "Hi", somebody, "how are you today?"
```

Save and run this program in IDLE to see how it works. You should see something like this:

```
Enter your name:
Warren
Hi Warren how are you today?
```

I typed in my name, and the program assigned it the name `somebody`.

The `print` command and the comma

Usually, when you want input from the user, you have to tell him what you are looking for, with a short message like this:

```
print "Enter your name: "
```

Then you can get his response with the **`raw_input()`** function:

```
someName = raw_input()
```

When you run those code lines and type in your name, it looks like this:

```
Enter your name:
Warren
```

If you want the user to type his answer on the same line as the message, just put a comma at the end of the **print** statement, like this:

```
print "Enter your name: ",
someName = raw_input()
```

Notice that the comma goes outside the end quotes.

If you run this code, it will look like this:

```
Enter your name: Warren
```

The comma can be used to combine a number of **print** statements on one line. The comma really means "don't jump down to the next line after you print this." We did that in the last line of listing 5.1.

Try typing the following code into an IDLE editor window and running it.

Listing 5.2   What does the comma do?

```
print "My",
print "name",
print "is",
print "Dave."
```

You should get this when you run it:

```
My name is Dave.
```

Did you notice that there are no spaces at the ends of the individual words in the quotes, yet we got spaces between each word when we ran the program? Python adds a space when you use the comma to combine `print` statements on one line.

End comma
In Python3, the trick of putting a comma at the end to keep printing on the same line doesn't work. Also, in Python 3, when you use `print()`, the thing you're printing has to be in parentheses. So if you're using Python 3, listing 5.2 would look like this:

```
print("My", end=" ")
print("name", end=" ")
print("is", end=" ")
print("Dave.", end=" ")
```

Is there some shorter way to have a prompt in front of `raw_input()`?

I'm glad you asked! I was just going to talk about that.

A shortcut for `raw_input()` prompts

There is a shortcut for printing prompt messages. The `raw_input()` function can print the message for you, so you don't have to use a `print` statement:

```
someName = raw_input ("Enter your name: ")
```

It's like the `raw_input()` function has `print` built in. We'll use
that shortcut from now on.

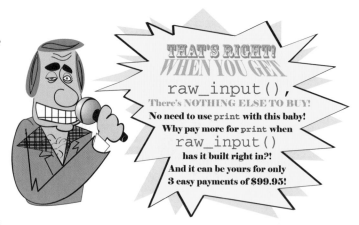

Inputting numbers

You have seen how to use `raw_input()` to get strings. But what if you want to get a number
instead? After all, the reason we started talking about input was to let the user enter
temperatures for the temperature-conversion program.

You already know the answer if you read chapter 4. We can use the `int()` or `float()` function to create a number from the string that `raw_input()` gives you. It would look like this:

```
temp_string = raw_input()
fahrenheit = float(temp_string)
```

We get the user's input as a string, using `raw_input()`. Then we make a number from that,
using `float()`. Once we have the temperature as a float, we give it the name `fahrenheit`.

But there is a little shortcut. We can do it all in one step, like this:

```
fahrenheit = float(raw_input())
```

This does exactly the same thing. It gets the string from the user and then creates a number
from it. It just does it with a bit less code.

Now let's use this in our temperature-conversion program. Try the following program, and
see what you get.

Listing 5.3   *Converting temperatures using* `raw_input()`

```
print "This program converts Fahrenheit to Celsius"
print "Type in a temperature in Fahrenheit: ",
fahrenheit = float(raw_input())                          ⟵——— Use float(raw_input())
celsius = (fahrenheit - 32) * 5.0 / 9                          to get Fahrenheit
print "That is",                                              temperature from user
print celsius,              | Notice the commas at
print "degrees Celsius"     | the ends of these lines
```

We can also combine the last three lines of listing 5.3 into one, like this:

```
print "That is", celsius, "degrees Celsius"
```

This is really just shorthand for the three `print` statements we had before.

Using `int()` with `raw_input()`

If the number you want the user to enter will always be an integer (no decimals), you can convert it with `int()`, like this:

```
response = raw_input("How many students are in your class: ")
numberOfStudents = int(response)
```

Thinking like a (Python) programmer
There is another way to get numbers as input. Python 2 has a function called `input()` that gives you a number directly, so you don't have to use `int()` or `float()` to convert it. We used it in the number-guessing program in chapter 1, because it is the simplest way to get a number from the user. But to keep things consistent, we will always use `raw_input()` for the rest of this book. Also, the `input()` function (the one that gets numbers directly without having to convert them) is removed in Python 3. There is only `raw_input()`. To make things just a little more confusing, the Python 2 `raw_input()` function is called `input()` in Python 3, but it is the same function that you saw in this chapter, the one that only gets strings. Because you know how to create a number from a string, I recommend you use `raw_input()` instead of `input()` in Python 2.

Input from the Web

Usually, you get input for a program from the user. But there are other ways to get input, too. You can get it from a file on your computer's hard drive (you'll learn about that in chapter 22), or you can get it from the Internet.

If you have an Internet connection, you can try the program in listing 5.4. It opens a file from the book's website and shows you the message that is in that file.

Listing 5.4   Getting input from a file on the Web

```
import urllib2
file = urllib2.urlopen('http://helloworldbook2.com/data/message.txt')
message = file.read()
print message
```

That's it. With just four lines of code, your computer reaches across the Web to get a file from the book's website and display it. If you try this program (assuming you have a working Internet connection), you will see the message.

If you are trying this program from an office or school computer, there's a chance it won't work. That's because some offices and schools use something called a proxy to connect to the Internet. A proxy is another computer that acts like a bridge or gateway between the Internet and the school or office. Depending on how the proxy is set up, this program might not know how to connect to the Internet through the proxy. If you get a chance to try it from home (or somewhere else that has a direct Internet connection with no proxy), it should work.

Thinking like a programmer

Depending on what operating system you are using (Windows, Linux, or Mac OS X), you might see little squares or something like \r at the end of each line when you try running the program in listing 5.4. The reason is that different operating systems use different ways to indicate the end of a line of text. Windows (and MS-DOS before it) use two characters: CR (Carriage Return) and LF (Line Feed). Linux uses just LF. Mac OS X uses just CR.

Some programs can handle any of these, but some, like IDLE, get confused if they don't see exactly the line-ending characters they are expecting. When that happens, they display a little square, which means, "I don't understand this character." You might or might not see the little squares, depending on what operating system you are using and how you run the program (using IDLE or some other method).

What did you learn?

In this chapter, you learned about

- Inputting text with `raw_input()`
- Adding a prompt message to `raw_input()`
- Inputting numbers using `int()` and `float()` with `raw_input()`
- Printing several things on one line, using a comma

Test your knowledge

1 With this code

```
answer = raw_input()
```

if the user types in 12, what type of data is `answer`? Is it a string or a number?

2 How do you get `raw_input()` to print a prompt message?

3 How do you get an integer using `raw_input()`?

4 How do you get a float (decimal number) using `raw_input()`?

Try it out

1 In interactive mode, make two variables, one for your first name and one for your last name. Then, using a single **print** statement, print your first and last names together.

2 Write a program that asks for your first name, then asks for your last name, and then prints a message with your first and last names in it.

3 Write a program that asks for the dimensions (in feet) of a rectangular room, and then calculates and displays the total amount of carpet needed to cover the room.

4 Write a program that does the same as in #3, but that also asks for the cost per square yard of carpet. Then have the program display these three things:

- The total amount of carpet, in square feet
- The total amount of carpet, in square yards (1 square yard = 9 square feet)
- The total cost of the carpet

5 Write a program that helps the user add up her change. The program should ask

- "How many quarters?"
- "How many dimes?"
- "How many nickels?"
- "How many pennies?"

Then it should give the total value of the change.

## CHAPTER 6

GUIs—Graphical User Interfaces

Up until now, all our input and output has been simple text in the IDLE window. But modern computers and programs use lots of graphics. It would be nice if we could have some graphics in our programs. In this chapter, we'll start making some simple GUIs. That means our programs will start to look more like the ones you're used to—with windows, buttons, and so on.

What's a GUI?

GUI is an abbreviation for *graphical user interface*. In a GUI, instead of just typing text and getting text back, the user sees graphical things like windows, buttons, text boxes, and so on, and she can use the mouse to click things as well as type on the keyboard. The types of programs we have done so far are *command-line* or *text-mode* programs. A GUI is just a different way of interacting with a program. Programs that have a GUI still have the three basic elements: input, processing, and output. But their input and output are a bit fancier.

By the way, the acronym GUI is usually pronounced "gooey," instead of saying the letters, like "Gee You Eye." It's okay to have a GUI on your computer, but you should avoid getting anything gooey on your computer. It gets stuck in the keys and makes it hard to type!

Our first GUI

You have already been using a GUI—in fact, several of them. A web browser is a GUI. IDLE is a GUI. Now you're going to make your own GUI. To do this, you're going to get some help from something called EasyGui.

EasyGui is a Python module that makes it very easy to make simple GUIs. We haven't really talked about modules yet (we will in chapter 15), but a module is a way of adding something to Python that isn't already built in.

If you installed Python using the book's installer, you already have EasyGui installed. If not, you can download it from **easygui.sourceforge.net/**.

Installing EasyGui

You can download **easygui.py** or a zip file that contains **easygui.py**. To install it, you just have to put the file **easygui.py** in a place where Python can find it. Where is that?

The Python path

Python has a list of places on the hard drive where it looks for modules it can use. This can be a bit complicated, because it's different for Windows, Mac OS X, and Linux. But if you put **easygui.py** in the same place where Python itself is installed, Python will find it. So, on your hard drive, look for a folder called **Python27**, and put **easygui.py** in that folder.

Let's get GUI-ing

Start IDLE, and type the following in interactive mode:

```
>>> import easygui
```

This tells Python that you're going to use the EasyGui module. If you don't get an error message, then Python found the EasyGui module. If you do get an error message, or EasyGui doesn't seem to be working, go to the book's web site (**www.helloworldbook2.com**) and you'll find some additional help.

Now, let's make a simple message box with an **OK** button:

```
>>> easygui.msgbox("Hello There!")
```

The EasyGui `msgbox()` function is used to create a message box. In most cases, the names of EasyGui functions are just shortened versions of the English words.

When you use `msgbox()`, you should see something that looks like this:

And if you click the **OK** button, the message box will close.

GUI input

You just saw a kind of GUI output—a message box. But what about input? You can get input with EasyGui too.

When you ran the previous example in interactive mode, did you click the **OK** button? If you did, you should have seen something like this in the shell or terminal or command window:

```
>>> import easygui
>>> easygui.msgbox("Hello there!")
'OK'
```

The `'OK'` part was Python and EasyGui telling you that the user clicked the **OK** button. EasyGui gives you back information to tell you what the user did in the GUI—what button she clicked, what she typed, and so on. You can give this response a name (assign it to a variable). Try this:

```
>>> user_response = easygui.msgbox("Hello there!")
```

Click **OK** in the message box to close it. Then type this:

```
>>> print user_response
OK
```

Now the user's response, `OK`, has the variable name **user_response**. Let's look at a few other ways to get input with EasyGui.

The message box that you just saw is really just one example of something called a *dialog box*. Dialog boxes are GUI elements that are used to tell the user something or get some input from the user. The input might be a button click (like **OK**), or a filename, or some text (a string).

The EasyGui `msgbox` is a dialog box with a message and a single button, **OK**. But you can have different kinds of dialog boxes with more buttons and other things.

Pick your flavor

We're going to use the example of choosing your favorite flavor of ice cream to look at some different ways to get input (the ice cream flavor) from the user with EasyGui.

Dialog box with multiple buttons

Let's make a dialog box (like a message box) with more than one button. The way to do this is with a *button box* (`buttonbox`). Let's make a program, rather than do it in interactive mode.

Start a new file in IDLE. Type in the program in the following listing.

Listing 6.1   Getting input using buttons

```
import easygui
flavor = easygui.buttonbox("What is your favorite ice cream flavor?",
                 choices = ['Vanilla', 'Chocolate', 'Strawberry'] )    ⟵— List of
easygui.msgbox ("You picked " + flavor)                                    choices
```

The part of the code in square brackets is called a *list*. We haven't talked about lists yet, but you'll learn all about them in chapter 12. For now, just type in the code so you can make the EasyGui program work. (Or, if you're really curious, you could skip ahead....)

Save the file (I called mine **ice_cream1.py**), and run it. You should see this:

And then, depending on which flavor you click, you'll see something like this:

How did this work? The label from whatever button the user clicked was the *input*. We assigned that input a variable name—in this case `flavor`. This is just like using `raw_input()`, except that the user doesn't type in the input, she just clicks a button. That's what GUIs are all about.

Choice box

Let's try another way for the user to select a flavor. EasyGui has something called a *choice box* (`choicebox`), which presents a list of choices. The user picks one and then clicks the **OK** button.

To try this, we only need to make one small change to our program from listing 6.1: change `buttonbox` to `choicebox`. The new version is shown next.

Listing 6.2   Getting input using a choice box

```python
import easygui
flavor = easygui.choicebox("What is your favorite ice cream flavor?",
                choices = ['Vanilla', 'Chocolate', 'Strawberry'] )
easygui.msgbox ("You picked " + flavor)
```

Save the program in listing 6.2, and run it. You should see something like this:

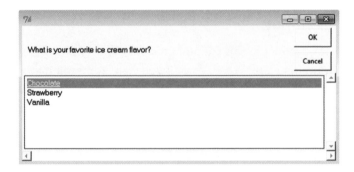

After you click a flavor and then click **OK**, you'll see the same kind of message box as before. Notice that, in addition to clicking choices with the mouse, you can select a flavor with the up and down arrow keys on the keyboard.

If you click **Cancel**, the program will end, and you'll also see an error. That's because the last line of the program is expecting some text (like `Vanilla`), but if you click **Cancel**, it doesn't get any.

The same thing happened to me. But that big choice box didn't fit very well in this book. So I cheated a bit! I modified **easygui.py** to let me make the choice box smaller so it would look nice in this book. It's not something you need to do, but if you really want to, here are the steps. I warn you, it's a bit complicated!

1   Find the section in the **easygui.py** file that starts with `def __choicebox` (around line 934 in my version of **easygui.py**). Remember that most editors show you the code line numbers somewhere near the bottom of the window.

2   About 30 lines down from that (around line 970), you'll see some lines that look like this:

```
root_width = int((screen_width * 0.8))
root_height = int((screen_height * 0.5))
```

Change the 0.8 to 0.4 and the 0.5 to 0.25. Save the changes to **easygui.py**. The next time you run the program, the choice box window will be smaller.

Text input

The examples in this chapter have let the user pick from a set of choices that you, as the programmer, provided. What if you want something more like `raw_input()`, where the user can type in text? That way, she can enter any flavor she wants. EasyGui has something called an *enter box* (`enterbox`) to do just that. Try the program in the following listing.

Listing 6.3   Getting input using an enter box

```
import easygui
flavor = easygui.enterbox("What is your favorite ice cream flavor?")
easygui.msgbox ("You entered " + flavor)
```

When you run it, you should see something like this:

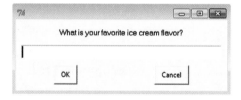

And then, when you type in your favorite flavor and click **OK**, it'll be displayed in the message box, just like before.

This is just like `raw_input()`. It gets text (a string) from the user.

Default input

Sometimes when a user is entering information, a certain answer is expected, common, or most likely to be entered. That is called a *default*. You might be able to save the user some typing by automatically entering the most common answer for him. Then he'd only have to type an answer if he had a different input.

To put a default in an enter box, change your program to look like this one.

Listing 6.4   How to make default choices

```
import easygui
flavor = easygui.enterbox("What is your favorite ice cream flavor?",
                          default = 'Vanilla')                            ←——— Here's the
easygui.msgbox ("You entered " + flavor)                                        default
```

Now, when you run it, "Vanilla" is already entered in the enter box. You can delete it and enter anything you want, but if your favorite flavor is vanilla, you don't have to type anything: just click **OK**.

What about numbers?

If you want to enter a number in EasyGui, you can always use an enter box to get a string, and then create a number from it using `int()` or `float()` (as we did in chapter 4).

EasyGui also has something called an *integer box* (`integerbox`), which you can use for entering integers. You can set a lower and upper limit to the number that can be entered.

It doesn't let you enter floats (decimal numbers), though. To enter decimal numbers, you'd have to use an enter box, get the string, and then use `float()` to convert the string.

The number-guessing game ... again

In chapter 1, we made a simple number-guessing program. Now let's try the same thing, but using EasyGui for the input and output. Here's the code.

Listing 6.5   Number-guessing game using EasyGui

```
import random, easygui
secret = random.randint(1, 99)          ← Picks a secret
guess = 0                                  number
tries = 0
easygui.msgbox("""AHOY!  I'm the Dread Pirate Roberts, and I have a secret!
It is a number from 1 to 99.  I'll give you 6 tries.""")
                                                   Gets the player's guess
while guess != secret and tries < 6:
    guess = easygui.integerbox("What's yer guess, matey?")  ←
    if not guess: break
    if guess < secret:
        easygui.msgbox(str(guess) + " is too low, ye scurvy dog!")   Allows up to
    elif guess > secret:                                             6 guesses
        easygui.msgbox(str(guess) + " is too high, landlubber!")
    tries = tries + 1          ← Uses up one try
if guess == secret:
    easygui.msgbox("Avast! Ye got it!  Found my secret, ye did!")    Prints
else:                                                                message at
    easygui.msgbox("No more guesses!  The number was " + str(secret))  end of game
```

You still haven't learned how all the parts of this program work, but type it in and give it a try. You should see something like this when you run it:

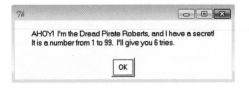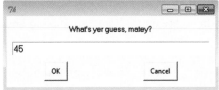

We'll be learning about `if`, `else`, and `elif` in chapter 7, and `while` in chapter 8. We'll learn about `random` in chapter 15, and we'll use it a lot more in chapter 23.

Other GUI pieces

EasyGui has a few other GUI pieces available, including a choice box that lets you pick multiple choices (instead of just one), and some special dialog boxes for getting filenames and so on. But the ones we have looked at are enough for now.

EasyGui makes generating some simple GUIs very easy, and it hides a lot of the complexity that is involved in GUIs so you don't have to worry about it. Later on, we'll look at another way to make GUIs that gives you a lot more flexibility and control.

If you want to find out more about EasyGui, you can go to the EasyGui home page at **easygui.sourceforge.net**.

Thinking like a (Python) programmer

If you want to find out more about something to do with Python, like EasyGui (or anything else), there is a built-in help system that you might want to try.

If you're in interactive mode, you can type

```
>>>help()
```

at the interactive prompt to get into the help system. The prompt will change to look like this:

```
help >
```

Once you're there, just type the name of the thing you want help with, like this:

```
help> time.sleep
```
or
```
help> easygui.msgbox
```

and you'll get some information.

To get out of the help system and back to the regular interactive prompt, just type the word quit:

```
help> quit
>>>
```

Some of the help is hard to read and understand, and you won't always find what you are looking for. But if you are looking for more information on something in Python, it's worth a try.

What did you learn?

In this chapter, you learned

- How to make simple GUIs with EasyGui
- How to display messages using a message box: `msgbox`
- How to get input using buttons, choice boxes, and text-entry boxes: `buttonbox`, `choicebox`, `enterbox`, `integerbox`
- How to set the default input for a text box
- How to use Python's built-in help system

Test your knowledge

1   How do you bring up a message box with EasyGui?
2   How do you get a string (some text) as input using EasyGui?
3   How can you get an integer as input using EasyGui?
4   How can you get a float (decimal number) as input using EasyGui?
5   What's a default value? Give an example of something you might use it for.

Try it out

1   Try changing the temperature-conversion program from chapter 5 to use GUI input and output instead of `raw_input()` and `print`.
2   Write a program that asks for your name, then house number, then street, then city, then province/territory/state, and then postal/zip code (all in EasyGui dialog boxes). The program should then display a mailing-style full address that looks something like this:

```
John Snead
28 Main Street
Akron, Ohio
12345
```

C H A P T E R   7

Decisions, Decisions

In the first few chapters, we saw some of the basic building blocks of a program. We can now make a program with *input*, *processing*, and *output*. We can even make our input and output a little fancier by using a GUI. We can assign the input to a variable, so we can use it later, and we can use some math to process it. Now we're going to start looking at ways to control what the program does.

If a program did the same thing every time, it would be a little boring and not very useful. Programs need to be able to make *decisions* on what to do. We're going to add some different decision-making techniques to our *processing* repertoire.

Testing, testing

Programs need to be able to do different things based on their input. Here are a few examples:

- *If* Tim got the right answer, add 1 point to his score.
- *If* Jane hit the alien, make an explosion sound.
- *If* the file isn't there, display an error message.

To make decisions, programs check (do a *test*) to see if a certain *condition* is true or not. In the first example above, the condition is "got the right answer."

Python has only a few ways to test something, and there are only two possible answers for each test: *true* or *false*.

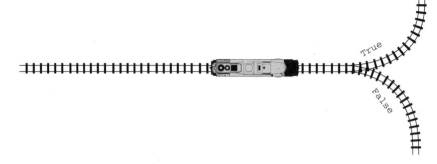

Here are some questions Python can ask to test something:

- Are two things equal?
- Is one thing less than another?
- Is one thing greater than another?

But wait a minute, "got the right answer" isn't one of the tests you can do, at least not directly. That means you need to describe the test in a way Python can understand.

When we want to know if Tim got the right answer, we'd probably know the correct answer, as well as Tim's answer. We could write something like this:

If Tim's Answer is equal to Correct Answer

If Tim had the correct answer, then the two variables would be equal, and the *condition* would be *true*. If he had the wrong answer, the two variables would not be equal, and the *condition* would be *false*.

WORD BOX

Doing tests and making decisions based on the results is called *branching*. The program decides which way to go, or which branch to follow, based on the result of the test.

Python uses the keyword `if` to test conditions, like this:

```
if timsAnswer == correctAnswer:
    print "You got it right!"
    score = score + 1
print "Thanks for playing."
```

These lines form a "block" of code because they're indented from the lines above and below

WORD BOX

A *block* of code is one or more lines of code that
are grouped together. They're all related to a
particular part of the program (like an `if` statement).
In Python, blocks of code are formed by indenting the
lines of code in the block.

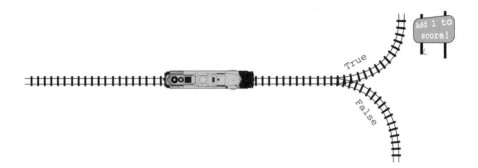

The colon (`:`) at the end of the `if` line tells Python that a *block* of instructions is coming next. The block includes every line that is *indented* from the `if` line, up until the next line that is *not* indented.

WORD BOX

Indenting means that a line of code is pushed over to
the right a bit. Instead of starting at the far left,
it has some spaces at the beginning, so it starts
a few characters away from the left side.

If the condition is *true*, everything in the following *block* will be done. In the previous short example, the second and third lines make up the *block* of statements for the `if` in the first line.

Now might be a good time to talk about *indenting* and *blocks* of code.

Indenting

In some languages, indenting is just a matter of style—you can indent however you like (or not at all). But in Python, indenting is a necessary part of how you write the code. Indenting tells Python where blocks of code start and where they end.

Some statements in Python, like the `if` statement, need a block of code to tell them what to do. In the case of the `if` statement, the block tells Python what to do *if* the condition is true.

It doesn't matter how far you indent the block, as long as the whole block is indented the same amount. A *convention* in Python is to use four spaces to indent blocks of code. It would be a good idea to follow this style in your programs.

WORD BOX

A *convention* just means lots of people do it that way.

Am I seeing double?

Are there actually *two* equal signs in that `if` statement (if `timsAnswer == correctAnswer`)? Yes, there are, and here's why.

Am I seeing double?

People say, "Five plus four is equal to nine," and they ask, "Is five plus four equal to nine?" One is a statement; the other is a question.

In Python we have the same kinds of things—*statements* and *questions*. A *statement* might assign a value to a variable. A *question* might check whether a variable is equal to a certain value. One means you're *setting* something (assigning it or making it equal). The other means you're *checking* or *testing* something (is it equal, yes or no?). So Python uses two different symbols.

You already saw the equal sign (=) used for setting or assigning values to variables. Here are a few more examples:

```
correctAnswer = 5 + 3
temperature = 35
name = "Bill"
```

For testing whether two things are equal, Python uses a double equal sign (==), like this:

```
if myAnswer == correctAnswer:
if temperature == 40:
if name == "Fred":
```

Testing or checking is also called *comparing*. The double equal sign is called a *comparison operator*. Remember, we talked about *operators* in chapter 3. An operator is a special symbol that operates on the values around it. In this case, the operation is to test whether the values are equal.

Other kinds of tests

Lucky for us, the other comparison operators are easier to remember: less than (<), greater than (>), and not equal to (!=). (You can also use <> for not equal to, but most people use !=.) You can also combine > or < with = to make greater than or equal to (>=) and less than or equal to (<=). You might have seen some of these in math class.

Not equal
In Python 3, the <> syntax for *not equal to* is no longer supported. In Python 3, you have to use != for *not equal to*.

You can also chain two greater-than or less-than operators together to make an in-between test, like this:

```
if 8 < age < 12:
```

This will check if the variable `age` has a value between, but not including, 8 and 12. This would be *true* if `age` was equal to 9, 10, or 11 (or 8.1 or 11.6, and so on). If we wanted to include the ages 8 and 12, we'd do this instead:

```
if 8 <= age <= 12:
```

WORD BOX

Comparison operators are also called *relational operators* (because they test the *relation* between the two sides: equal or not equal, greater than or less than). A comparison is also called a *conditional test* or *logical test*. In programming, *logical* refers to something where the answer is either true or false.

Listing 7.1 shows an example program using comparisons. Start a new file in the IDLE editor, type this program in, and save it—call it **compare.py**. Then **Run** it. Try running it several times, using different numbers. Try numbers where the first one is bigger, where the first one is smaller, and where the two numbers are equal, and see what you get.

Listing 7.1   Using the comparison operators

```
num1 = float(raw_input("Enter the first number: "))
num2 = float(raw_input("Enter the second number: "))
if num1 < num2:
    print num1, "is less than", num2
if num1 > num2:
    print num1, "is greater than", num2
if num1 == num2:                              Remember that
    print num1, "is equal to", num2           this is a double
if num1 != num2:                              equal sign
    print num1, "is not equal to", num2
```

What happens if the test is false?

You've seen how to make Python do something if the result of a test is *true*. But what does it do if the test is *false*? In Python, there are three possibilities:

- *Do another test.* If the first test comes out *false*, you can get Python to test something else with the keyword `elif` (which is short for "else if"), like this:

```
if answer >= 10:
    print "You got at least 10!"
elif answer >= 5:
    print "You got at least 5!"
elif answer >= 3:
    print "You got at least 3!"
```

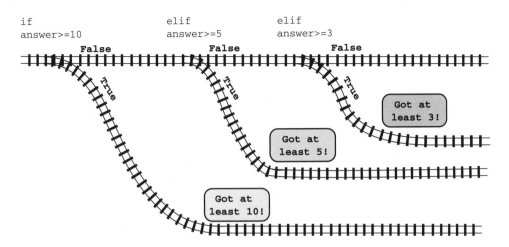

You can have as many `elif` statements as you want after the `if`.

■ *Do something else* if all the other tests come out *false*. You do this with the `else` keyword. This always goes at the end, after you've done the `if` and any `elif` statements:

```
if answer >= 10:
    print "You got at least 10!"
elif answer >= 5:
    print "You got at least 5!"
elif answer >= 3:
    print "You got at least 3!"
else:
    print "You got less than 3."
```

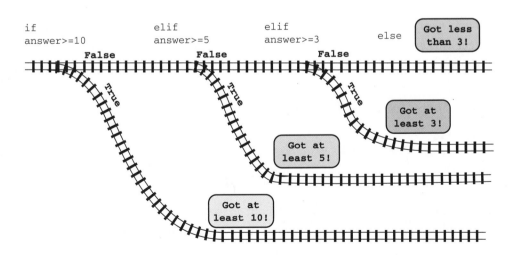

- *Move on.* If you don't put anything else after the `if` block, the program will continue on to the next line of code (if there is one) or will end (if there is no more code).

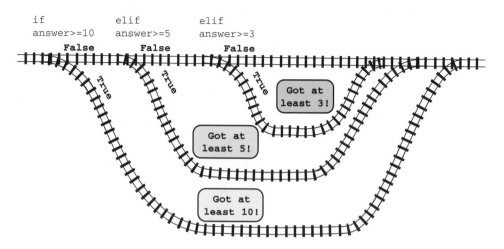

Try making a program with the code above by adding a line at the beginning to input a number:

```
answer = float(raw_input ("Enter a number from 1 to 15"))
```

Remember to save the file (you pick the name this time), and then run it. Try it a few times with different inputs to see what you get.

Testing for more than one condition

What if you want to test for more than one thing? Let's say we made a game that was for eight-year-olds and up, and we want to make sure the player is in at least third grade. There are two conditions to meet. Here is one way we could test for both conditions:

```
age = float(raw_input("Enter your age: "))
grade = int(raw_input("Enter your grade: "))
if age >= 8:
    if grade >= 3:
        print "You can play this game."
else:
    print "Sorry, you can't play the game."
```

Notice that the first **print** line is indented eight spaces, not just four spaces. That's because each **if** needs its own block, so each one has its own indenting.

> **Reminder**
> Remember, if you're using Python 3, you need to replace `raw_input()`
> with `input()`, and you need to use parentheses with `print`, like this:
>
> ```
> print("You can play this game.")
> ```

Using and

That last example will work fine. But there is a shorter way to do the same thing. You can combine conditions like this:

```
age = float(raw_input("Enter your age: "))
grade = int(raw_input("Enter your grade: "))
if age >= 8 and grade >= 3:
    print "You can play this game."
else:
    print "Sorry, you can't play the game."
```

Combine conditions with "and"

We combined the two conditions using the **and** keyword. The **and** means both of the conditions have to be true for the following block to execute.

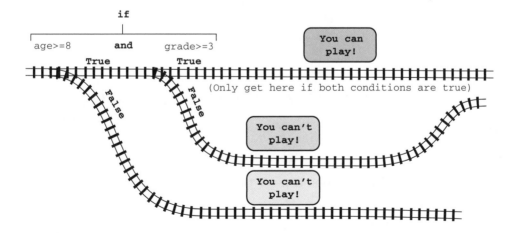

You can put more than two conditions together with **and**:

```
age = float(raw_input("Enter your age: "))
grade = int(raw_input("Enter your grade: "))
color = raw_input("Enter your favorite color: ")
if age >= 8 and grade >= 3 and color == "green":
    print "You are allowed to play this game."
else:
    print "Sorry, you can't play the game."
```

If there are more than two conditions, *all* the conditions have to be true for the **if** statement to be true.

There are other ways of combining conditions too.

Using or

The **or** keyword is also used to put conditions together. If you use **or**, the block is executed if *any* of the conditions are true:

```
color = raw_input("Enter your favorite color: ")
if color == "red" or color == "blue" or color == "green":
    print "You are allowed to play this game."
else:
    print "Sorry, you can't play the game."
```

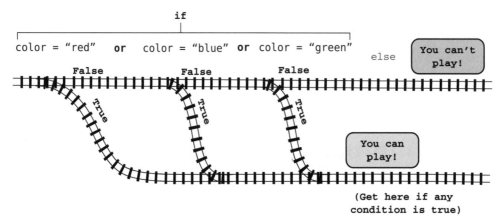

Using not

You can also flip around a comparison to mean the opposite, using **not**:

```
age = float(raw_input("Enter your age: "))
if not (age < 8):
    print "You are allowed to play this game."
else:
    print "Sorry, you can't play the game."
```

This line

```
if not (age < 8):
```

means the same as this one:

```
if age >= 8:
```

In both cases, the block executes if the age is 8 or higher, and it doesn't if the age is lower than 8.

In chapter 4, you saw *math operators* like +, -, *, and /. In this chapter, you saw the *comparison operators* <, >, ==, and so on. The **and**, **or**, and **not** keywords are also operators. They're called *logical operators*. They're used to modify comparisons by combining two or more of them (**and**, **or**) or reversing them (**not**).

Table 7.1 lists all the operators we've talked about so far.

Table 7.1   List of math and comparison operators

Operator	Name	What it does
		Math operators
=	Assignment	Assigns a value to a name (variable).
+	Addition	Adds two numbers together. This can also be used to concatenate strings.
-	Subtraction	Subtracts two numbers.
+=	Increment	Adds one to a number.
-=	Decrement	Subtracts one from a number.
*	Multiplication	Multiplies two numbers together.
/	Division	Divides two numbers. If both numbers are integers, the result will be just the integer quotient, with no remainder.
%	Modulus	Gets the remainder (or *modulus*) for integer division of two numbers.
**	Exponentiation	Raises a number to a power. Both the number and the power can be integers or floats.
		Comparison operators
==	Equality	Checks whether two things are equal.
<	Less than	Checks whether the first number is less than the second number.
>	Greater than	Checks whether the first number is greater than the second number.
<=	Less than or equal to	Checks whether the first number is less than or equal to the second number.
>=	Greater than or equal to	Checks whether the first number is greater than or equal to the second number.
!= <>	Not equal to	Checks whether two things are not equal. (Either operator can be used.)

You might want to bookmark this page so you can refer back to this table easily.

What did you learn?

In this chapter, you learned about

- Comparison tests and the relational operators
- Indenting and blocks of code
- Combining tests using `and` and `or`
- Reversing a test using `not`

Test your knowledge

1 What will the output be when this program is run?

```
my_number = 7
if my_number < 20:
    print 'Under 20'
else:
    print '20 or over'
```

2 From the program in the first question, what will the output be if you change `my_number` to 25?

3 What kind of `if` statement would you use to check if a number was greater than 30 but less than or equal to 40?

4 What kind of `if` statement would you use to check if the user entered the letter "Q" in either uppercase or lowercase?

Try it out

1 A store is having a sale. It's giving 10% off purchases of $10 or lower, and 20% off purchases of greater than $10. Write a program that asks the purchase price and displays the discount (10% or 20%) and the final price.

2 A soccer team is looking for girls from ages 10 to 12 to play on their team. Write a program to ask the user's age and whether the user is male or female (using "m" or "f"). Display a message indicating whether the person is eligible to play on the team.

Bonus: Make the program so that it doesn't ask for the age unless the user is a girl.

3 You're on a long car trip and arrive at a gas station. It's 200 km to the next station. Write a program to figure out if you need to buy gas here, or if you can wait for the next station.

The program should ask these questions:

- How big is your gas tank, in liters?
- How full is your tank (in percent—for example, half full = 50)?
- How many km per liter does your car get?

The output should look something like this

```
Size of tank:   60
percent full:   40
km per liter:   10
You can go another 240 km
The next gas station is 200 km away
You can wait for the next station.
```

or

```
Size of tank:   60
percent full:   30
km per liter:   8
You can go another 144 km
The next gas station is 200 km away
Get gas now!
```

Bonus: Include a 5 liter buffer in your program, in case the fuel gauge isn't accurate.

4   Make a program where the user has to enter a secret password to use the program. You'll know the password, of course (because it'll be in your code). But your friends will have to either ask you, guess the password, or learn enough Python to look at the code and figure it out!

The program can be anything you want, including one you have already written, or just a simple one that displays a message like "You're in!" when he enters the right password.

## CHAPTER 8

Loop the Loop

For most people, doing the same thing over and over again is very boring, so why not let the computer do that for us? Computers never get bored, so they're great at doing repetitive tasks. In this chapter, we'll see how to make the computer repeat things.

Computer programs often repeat the same steps over and over again. This is called *looping*. There are two main kinds of loops:

- *Those that repeat a certain number of times*—These are called *counting loops*.
- *Those that repeat until a certain thing happens*—These are called *conditional loops* because they keep going as long as some *condition* is true.

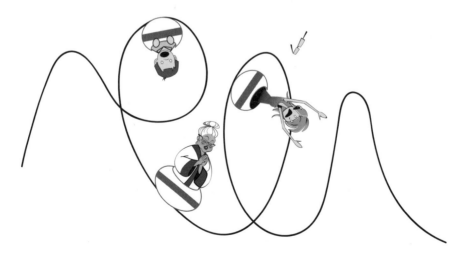

Counting loops

The first kind of loop is called a counting loop. You'll also hear it called a *for loop*, because many languages, including Python, use the `for` keyword to create this kind of loop in a program.

Let's try a program that uses a counting loop. Start a new text editor window in IDLE, using the **File > New** command (like we did for our first program). Then type in the following program.

Listing 8.1   A very simple `for` loop

```
for looper in [1, 2, 3, 4, 5]:
    print "hello"
```

Save it as **Loop1.py**, and run it. (You can use the **Run > Run Module** menu option or the shortcut of pressing the **F5** key.)

You should see something like this:

```
>>> ================ RESTART ================
>>>
hello
hello
hello
hello
hello
```

Hey, is there an echo in here? The program printed "hello" five times, even though there was only one `print` statement. How? The first line (`for looper in [1, 2, 3, 4, 5]:`) translated into plain English means this:

1   The variable `looper` starts with the value 1 (so `looper = 1`).
2   The loop does whatever is in the next *block* of instructions one time for each value in the list. (The list is those numbers in square brackets.)
3   Each time through the loop, `looper` is assigned the next value in the list.

The second line (`print "hello"`) is the block of code that Python executes each time around the loop. A `for` loop needs a block of code to tell the program what to do in each loop. That *block* (the indented part of the code) is called the *body of the loop*. (Remember, we talked about indenting and blocks in the last chapter.)

WORD BOX

Each time through the loop is called an *iteration*.

Let's try something else. Instead of printing the same thing every time, let's make the program print something different every time through the loop.

Listing 8.2   Doing something different each time through the `for` loop

```
for looper in [1, 2, 3, 4, 5]:
    print looper
```

Save this as **Loop2.py**, and run it. The results should look like this:

```
>>> ================ RESTART ================
>>>
1
2
3
4
5
```

This time, instead of printing "hello" five times, it printed the value of the variable `looper`. Each time through the loop, `looper` takes the next value in the list.

Runaway loops

Once I made a mistake in a program, and it kept looping forever!

How can I stop a runaway loop?

The same thing has happened to me, Carter! Runaway loops (also called endless loops or infinite loops) happen to every programmer once in a while. To stop a Python program at any time (even in a runaway loop), press **CTRL-C**. That means we press and hold down the **CTRL** key and, while holding it down, press the **C** key. This will come in very handy later! Games and graphics programs are constantly running in a loop. They need to keep getting input from the mouse, keyboard, or game controller, process that input, and update the screen. When we start writing these kinds of programs, we'll be using lots of loops. There's a good chance one of our programs will get stuck in a loop at some point, so we need to know how to get it unstuck!

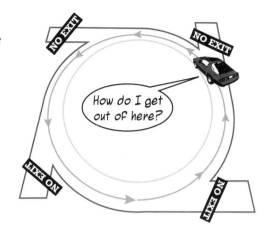

What are the square brackets for?

You might have noticed that the list of loop values is enclosed in square brackets. The square brackets and the commas between the numbers are the way you make a *list* in Python. You'll learn more about lists soon (in chapter 12, to be exact). But for now, just know that a list is a kind of "container" for storing a bunch of things together. In this case, the things are numbers—the values that `looper` takes as it goes through different iterations of the loop.

Using a counting loop

Now let's do something a bit more useful with loops. Let's print a multiplication table. It only takes a small change to our program. Here's the new version.

> **Listing 8.3   Printing the 8 times table**
>
> ```
> for looper in [1, 2, 3, 4, 5]:
>     print looper, "times 8 =", looper * 8
> ```

Save it as **Loop3.py**, and run it. You should see something like this:

```
>>> =================== RESTART ===================
>>>
1 times 8 = 8
2 times 8 = 16
3 times 8 = 24
4 times 8 = 32
5 times 8 = 40
```

Now we're starting to see the power of loops. Without loops, we'd have had to write a program like this one to get the same result:

```
print "1 times 8 =", 1 * 8
print "2 times 8 =", 2 * 8
print "3 times 8 =", 3 * 8
print "4 times 8 =", 4 * 8
print "5 times 8 =", 5 * 8
```

To make a longer multiplication table (say, up to 10 or 20), this program would be a lot longer, but our loop program would be almost the same (just with more numbers in the list). Loops make this much easier!

A shortcut—`range()`

In the previous example, we only looped 5 times:

```
for looper  in [1, 2, 3, 4, 5]:
```

But what if we wanted the loop to run 100 times, or 1,000 times? That would be a lot of typing!

Luckily, there's a shortcut. The `range()` function lets you enter just the starting and ending values, and it creates all the values in between for you. `range()` creates a list containing a range of numbers.

The next listing uses the `range()` function in the multiplication table example.

Listing 8.4   A loop using `range()`

```
for looper in range (1, 5):
    print looper, "times 8 =", looper * 8
```

Save this as **Loop4.py**, and run it. (You can use the **Run > Run Module** menu option or the shortcut of pressing the **F5** key.) You should see something like this:

```
>>> ================= RESTART =================
>>>
1 times 8 = 8
2 times 8 = 16
3 times 8 = 24
4 times 8 = 32
```

It's almost the same as the first result … except that it missed the last loop! Why?

The answer is that `range (1, 5)` gives us the list `[1, 2, 3, 4]`. You can try this in interactive mode:

```
>>> print range(1, 5)
[1, 2, 3, 4]
```

Why not 5?

Well, that's just the way the `range()` function works. It gives you a list of numbers starting at the first number and ending just *before* the last number. You need to take that into account and adjust the range to get the number of loops you want.

Range
If you do this in Python 3, you'll get something a little different:

```
>>> print(range(1, 5))

range(1,5)
```

This is because, in Python 3, the `range()` function doesn't give you a list of numbers, it gives you something called an *iterable*. This is something over which your loops can iterate. (Remember the Word Box above.)

As far as using `range()` in a `for` loop, it works exactly the same. It's just a little different under the hood.

The following listing shows our program modified to give us the 8 times table up to 10.

> **Listing 8.5   Printing the 8 times table up to 10 using `range()`**
>
> ```
> for looper in range(1, 11):
>     print looper, "times 8 =", looper * 8
> ```

And here's what we get when we run it:

```
>>> ================= RESTART ===================
>>>
1 times 8 = 8
2 times 8 = 16
3 times 8 = 24
4 times 8 = 32
5 times 8 = 40
6 times 8 = 48
7 times 8 = 56
8 times 8 = 64
9 times 8 = 72
10 times 8 = 80
```

In the program in listing 8.5, `range(1, 11)` gave us a list of numbers from 1 to 10, and the loop did one *iteration* for each number in the list. Each time through the loop, the variable `looper` took the next value in the list.

By the way, we called our loop variable `looper`, but you can call it anything you want.

A matter of style—loop variable names

A loop variable is no different from any other variable. There's nothing special about it—it's just a name for a value. It doesn't matter that you're using the variable as a loop counter.

We said before that you should use variable names that describe what the variables do. That's why I picked the name `looper` for the previous example. But loop variables are one place where you can sometimes make an exception. That's because there's a convention (remember, that means a common practice) in programming to use the letters `i`, `j`, `k`, and so on, for loop variables.

Because lots of people use `i`, `j`, and `k` for loop variables, programmers get used to seeing this in programs. It's perfectly fine to use other names for loop variables, like we did. But you shouldn't use `i`, `j`, and `k` for anything other than loop variables.

IN THE GOOD OLD DAYS

Why i, j, and *k* for loops?

That's because the early programmers were using programs to figure out math stuff, and math already uses *a*, *b*, *c*, and *x*, *y*, *z* for other things. Also, in one popular programming language, the variables *i*, *j*, and *k* were always integers—you couldn't make them any other type. Because loop counters are always integers, the programmers usually picked *i*, *j*, and *k* for their loop counters, and it became common practice.

If we used this convention, our program would look like this:

```
for i in range(1, 5):
    print i, "times 8 =", i * 8
```

And it would work exactly the same. (Try it and see!)

Which names you use for your loop variables is a matter of *style*. Style is about how your programs look, not about whether they work. But if you use the same style as other programmers, your programs will be easier to read, understand, and debug. You'll also be more used to this style, and it'll be easier for you to read other people's programs.

A `range()` shortcut

You don't always have to give `range()` two numbers as we did in listing 8.5. You can give it just one number:

```
for i in range(5):
```

This is the same as writing

```
for i in range(0, 5):
```

which gives you this list of numbers: `[0, 1, 2, 3, 4]`.

In fact, most programmers start their loops at 0 instead of 1. If you use `range(5)`, you'll get 5 iterations of the loop, which is easy to remember. You just have to know that the first time through, `i` will be equal to 0, not 1, and the last time through it'll equal 4, not 5.

IN THE GOOD OLD DAYS

So why do most programmers start loops from 0 instead of 1?

Well, back in the good old days, some people started from 1 and some people started from 0. They had these really geeky arguments about which one was better. In the end, the 0 people won.

So there you have it. Most people start at 0 today, but you can use whichever you like. Just remember to adjust the upper limit so you get the right number of iterations.

Well, Carter, you have discovered something about strings. A string is like a *list of characters*. You learned that counting loops use *lists* for their *iterations*. That means you can loop through a string. Each character in the string is one iteration through the loop. So if we print the loop variable, which Carter called `letter` in his example, we're printing the letters in the string, one at a time. Because each `print` statement starts a new line, each of the letters prints on its own line.

Experimenting and trying different things, like Carter did here, is a great way to learn!

Counting by steps

So far, your counting loops have been counting up by 1 each iteration. What if you want the loop to count in steps of 2? Or 5, or 10? What about counting backward?

The `range()` function can have an extra *argument* that allows you to change the size of the steps from the default of 1 to a different size.

WORD BOX

Arguments are the values that you put inside the parentheses when you use a function like `range()`. We say that you pass the argument to the function. The term *parameter* is also used, as in, "pass the parameter." We'll learn more about functions, arguments, and parameters in chapter 13.

Let's try some loops in interactive mode. When you type in the first line, with the colon at the end, IDLE will automatically indent the next line for you, because it knows that a `for` loop needs a block of code following it. When you complete the block of code, press the **Enter** (or **Return**) key twice. Try it:

```
>>> for i in range(1, 10, 2):
        print i

1
3
5
7
9
```

We added a third parameter, 2, to the `range()` function. Now the loop is counting in steps of 2. Let's try another one:

```
>>> for i in range(5, 26, 5):
        print i

5
10
15
20
25
```

Now we're stepping by 5. How about counting backward?

```
>>> for i in range(10, 1, -1):
        print i

10
9
8
7
6
5
4
3
2
```

When the third parameter in the **range**() function is negative, the loop counts *down* instead of up. Remember that the loop starts at the first number and goes up to (or down to) but not including the second number, so in our last example we only got down to 2, not 1.

We can use this to make a countdown timer program. We only need to add a couple more lines. Open a new editor window in IDLE, and type in the following program. Then try running it.

Listing 8.6   Ready for lift-off?

```
import time
for i in range(10, 0, -1):        ←——— Counts backward
    print i
    time.sleep(1)        ←——— Waits one second
print "BLAST OFF!"
```

Don't worry about the stuff in the program that I haven't told you about yet, like `import`, `time`, and `sleep`. You're going to find out all about that in the following chapters. Just try the program in listing 8.6 and see how it works. The important thing here is the `range` `(10, 0, -1)` part, which makes a loop that counts backward from 10 to 1.

Counting without numbers

In all the previous examples, the loop variable has been a number. In programming terms, we say that the loop *iterates over* a list of numbers. But the list doesn't have to be a list of numbers. As you already saw from Carter's experiment, it can be a list of characters (a string). It can also be a list of strings, or anything else.

The best way to see how this works is with an example. Try the next program and see what happens.

Listing 8.7 Who's the coolest of them all?

```
for cool_guy in ["Spongebob", "Spiderman", "Justin Timberlake", "My Dad"]:
    print cool_guy, "is the coolest guy ever!"
```

Now we're not looping over a list of numbers, we're looping over a list of strings. And instead of `i` for the loop variable, I used `cool_guy`. The loop variable `cool_guy` takes a different value in the list each time through. This is still a kind of *counting loop*, because even though the list isn't a list of numbers, Python *counts* how many items are in the list to know how many times to loop. (I won't show what the output looks like this time—you'll see it when you run the program.)

But what if you don't know ahead of time how many iterations you'll need? What if there's no list of values you can use? Don't touch that dial, because that's coming up next!

While we're on the subject ...

You just learned about the first kind of loop, a `for` *loop* or *counting loop*. The second kind of loop is called a `while` *loop* or *conditional loop*.

The `for` loop is great if you know in advance how many times you want the loop to run. But sometimes you want a loop to run until something happens, and you don't know how many iterations it'll be until that thing happens. A `while` loop lets you do that.

In the last chapter, you learned about *conditions* and *testing* and the `if` statement. Instead of counting how many times to run a loop, `while` loops use a *test* to decide when to stop a loop. `While` loops are also called *conditional loops*. A conditional loop keeps looping while some condition is met.

Basically, a `while` loop keeps asking, "Am I done yet? … Am I done yet? … Am I done yet? …" until it's done. It's done when the condition is no longer true.

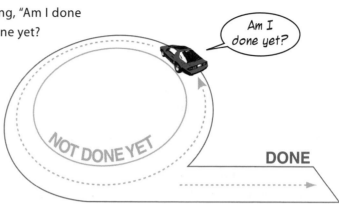

`While` loops use the Python keyword `while`. Listing 8.8 shows an example. Type the program in, try it, and see how it works. (Remember, you have to **Save** it and then **Run** it.)

Listing 8.8   A conditional or `while` loop

```
print "Type 3 to continue, anything else to quit."
someInput = raw_input()
while someInput == '3':
    print "Thank you for the 3.  Very kind of you."
    print "Type 3 to continue, anything else to quit."
    someInput = raw_input()
print "That's not 3, so I'm quitting now."
```

Keep looping as long as someInput ='3'

Body of the loop

This program keeps asking for input from the user. *While* the input is equal to 3, the condition is `true`, and the loop keeps running. That's why this kind of conditional loop is also called a `while` loop, and it uses the Python `while` keyword. When the input is *not* equal to 3, the condition is `false`, and the loop stops.

Bailing out of a loop—**break** and **continue**

Sometimes you want to get out of a loop in the middle, before a `for` loop is finished counting, or before a `while` loop has found its end condition. There are two ways to do this: you can jump ahead to the next iteration of the loop with `continue`, or you can stop looping altogether with `break`. Let's look at these more closely.

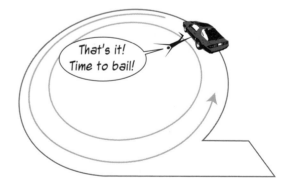

Jumping ahead—`continue`

If you want to stop executing the current iteration of the loop and skip ahead to the next iteration, the `continue` statement is what you need. The best way to show this is with an example.

```
Listing 8.9   Using continue in a loop

for i in range(1, 6):
    print
    print 'i =', i,
    print 'Hello, how',
    if i == 3:
        continue
    print 'are you today?'
```

If we run this program, the output looks like this:

```
>>> ================== RESTART ==================
>>>

i = 1 Hello how are you today?

i = 2 Hello how are you today?

i = 3 Hello how
i = 4 Hello how are you today?

i = 5 Hello how are you today?
```

Notice that, the third time through the loop (when `i == 3`), the body of the loop didn't finish—it jumped ahead to the next iteration (`i == 4`). That was the `continue` statement at work. It works the same way in `while` loops.

Bailing out—`break`

What if you want to jump out of the loop completely—never finish counting, or give up waiting for the end condition? The `break` statement does that.

Let's change only line 6 of listing 8.9, replacing `continue` with `break`, and rerun the program to see what happens:

```
>>> ================== RESTART ==================
>>>

i = 1 Hello how are you today?

i = 2 Hello how are you today?

i = 3 Hello how
```

This time, the loop didn't just skip the rest of iteration 3; it stopped altogether. That's what `break` does. It works the same way in `while` loops.

I should tell you that some people think using `break` and `continue` is a bad idea. Personally, I don't think they're *bad*, but I rarely use them. I thought I'd tell you about `break` and `continue` just in case you ever need them.

What did you learn?

In this chapter, you learned about

- `for` loops (also called counting loops)
- The `range()` function—a shortcut for counting loops
- Different step sizes for `range()`
- `while` loops (also called conditional loops)
- Skipping to the next iteration with `continue`
- Jumping out of a loop with `break`

Test your knowledge

1 How many times would the following loop run?

```
for i in range(1, 6):
    print 'Hi, Warren'
```

2 How many times would the following loop run? And what would the values of `i` be for each loop?

```
for i in range(1, 6, 2):
    print 'Hi, Warren'
```

3 What list of numbers would `range (1, 8)` give you?
4 What list of numbers would `range (8)` give you?
5 What list of numbers would `range (2, 9, 2)` give you?
6 What list of numbers would `range (10, 0, -2)` give you?
7 What keyword do you use to stop the current iteration of a loop and jump ahead to the next iteration?
8 When does a `while` loop end?

Try it out

1   Write a program to print a multiplication table (a times table). At the start, it should ask the user which table to print. The output should look something like this:

```
Which multiplication table would you like?
5
Here's your table:
5 x 1 = 5
5 x 2 = 10
5 x 3 = 15
5 x 4 = 20
5 x 5 = 25
5 x 6 = 30
5 x 7 = 35
5 x 8 = 40
5 x 9 = 45
5 x 10 = 50
```

2   You probably used a `for` loop in your program for question #1. That's how most people would do it. But just for practice, try doing the same thing with a `while` loop. Or if you used a `while` loop in question #1, try it with a `for` loop.

3   Add something else to the multiplication table program. After asking which table the user wants, ask her how high the table should go. The output should look like this:

```
Which multiplication table would you like?
7
How high do you want to go?
12
Here's your table:
7 x 1 = 7
7 x 2 = 14
7 x 3 = 21
7 x 4 = 28
7 x 5 = 35
7 x 6 = 42
7 x 7 = 49
7 x 8 = 56
7 x 9 = 63
7 x 10 = 70
7 x 11 = 77
7 x 12 = 84
```

You can do this with the `for` loop version of the program, the `while` loop version, or both.

## CHAPTER 9

Just for You—Comments

Up until now, everything we have typed into our programs (and in interactive mode) has been instructions to the computer. But it's a very good idea to include some notes to your-self in your programs, describing what the program does and how it works. This will help you (or someone else) look at your program later and figure out what you did.

In a computer program, these notes are called *comments*.

Adding comments

Comments are only for you to read, not for the computer to execute. Comments are part of the program's *documentation*, and the computer ignores them when it runs your program.

Python has a couple of ways to add comments to your program.

WORD BOX

Documentation
Documentation is information about a program that describes the program and how it works. Comments are one part of a program's documentation, but there may be other parts, outside the code itself, that describe things like

- why the program was written (its purpose)
- who wrote it
- who it's meant for (its audience)
- how it's organized

and much more. Larger, more complicated programs usually have more documentation.

The Python help that we mentioned in "Thinking like a (Python) programmer" in chapter 6 is a kind of documentation. It's meant to help users—like you—understand how Python works.

Single-line comments

You can make any line into a comment by starting it with the number sign character (#, sometimes called the *pound sign*):

```
# This is a comment in a Python program
print 'This is not a comment'
```

If we run these two lines, we get the following output:

```
This is not a comment
```

The first line is ignored when the program runs. The comment, which starts with the # character, is only for you and other people reading the code.

End-of-line comments

You can also put comments at the end of a line of code, like this:

```
area = length * width    # Calculate the area of the rectangle
```

The comment starts at the # character. Everything before the # is a normal line of code. Everything after that is a comment.

Multiline comments

Sometimes you want to use more than one line for comments. You can use several lines with the # character at the start of each, like this:

```
# ****************
# This is a program to illustrate how comments are used in Python
# The row of stars is used to visually separate the comments
# from the rest of the code
# ****************
```

Multiline comments are good for making sections of your code stand out visually when you're reading it. You can use them to describe what's going on in a section of code. A multiline comment at the start of a program could list the author's name, the name of the program, the date it was written or updated, and any other information you think might be useful.

Triple-quoted strings

There is another way to make something that acts like a multiline comment in Python. You can just make a triple-quoted string with no name. Remember from chapter 2 that a triple-quoted string is a string that can span multiple lines. So you can do this:

```
""" Here is a comment that is on multiple
lines, using a triple-quoted string.
It's not really a comment, but it
behaves like one.
"""
```

Because the string has no name and the program isn't "doing" anything with the string, it has no effect on the way the program runs. So it acts like a comment, even though it isn't a comment in strict Python terms.

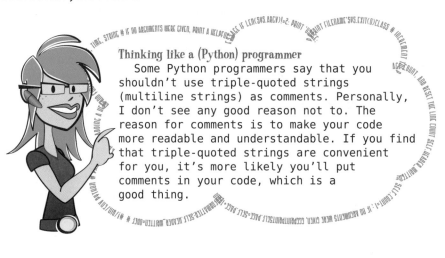

Thinking like a (Python) programmer

Some Python programmers say that you shouldn't use triple-quoted strings (multiline strings) as comments. Personally, I don't see any good reason not to. The reason for comments is to make your code more readable and understandable. If you find that triple-quoted strings are convenient for you, it's more likely you'll put comments in your code, which is a good thing.

If you type some comments into the IDLE editor, you'll see that the comments have their own color. This is meant to help you read your code more easily.

Most code editors let you change the color for comments (and for other parts of the code). The default color for comments in IDLE is red. Because triple-quoted strings are not true Python comments, they'll be a different color. In IDLE they'll be green, because green is IDLE's default color for strings.

Commenting style

So now you know how to add comments. But what kind of stuff should you put in them?

Because they don't affect how the program runs, we say that they're a matter of *style*. That means you can put anything you want in your comments (or not use any at all). But it doesn't mean comments are not important. Most programmers learn this the hard way, when they go back to a program they wrote several weeks, months, or years ago (or even one they wrote yesterday) and can't understand it! That's usually because they didn't put in enough comments to explain how the program worked. It might seem obvious when you're writing it, but it can be a complete mystery when you look at it later.

There are no hard-and-fast rules for what you should put in comments, but I encourage you to add as many comments as you like. For now, the more the better. It's better to err on the side of too many comments than too few. As you gain more experience with programming, you'll get a feel for how much and what kind of commenting works best for you.

Comments in this book

You won't see many comments in the printed code listings in this book. That's because this book uses *annotations*—those little notes alongside the code—instead. But if you look at the code listings in the **\examples** folder or on the website, you'll see comments in all the listings.

Commenting out

You can also use comments to temporarily exclude parts of the program from running. Anything that is a comment will be ignored:

```
#print "Hello"
print "World"

>>> =============== RESTART ================
>>>
World
```

Because `print "Hello"` was commented out, that line was not executed, so the word "Hello" didn't print.

This is useful when you're debugging a program and only want certain parts to run and other parts to be ignored. Just put a # in front of any line you want the computer to ignore, or put triple quotes around a section of code you want the computer to ignore.

Most code editors, including IDLE, have a feature that lets you comment (and uncomment) whole blocks of code quickly. In IDLE's editor, look in the **Format** menu.

What did you learn?

In this chapter, you learned that

- Comments are just for you (and other humans), not for the computer.
- Comments can also be used to block out parts of the code, to prevent them from running.
- You can use triple-quoted strings as a kind of comment that spans multiple lines.

Test your knowledge

Because comments are pretty simple, we'll take a break and not have any test questions for this chapter.

Try it out

Go back to the temperature-conversion program (from the "Try it out" section in chapter 3), and add some comments. Rerun the program to see that it still runs the same.

## CHAPTER 10

Game Time

One of the great traditions of learning to program is typing in code you don't understand. Really!

Sometimes just typing in code gives you a feel for how things work, even if you don't understand every line or keyword. We did that in chapter 1, with the number-guessing game. Now we're going to do the same thing, but with a longer, more interesting program.

Skier

Skier is a very simple skiing game, inspired by a game called SkiFree. (You can find out all about SkiFree here: **en.wikipedia.org/wiki/SkiFree**.)

You ski down a hill, trying to avoid trees and pick up flags. Picking up a flag earns 10 points. Crashing into a tree makes you lose 100 points.

When you run the program, it should look something like this:

Skier uses something called Pygame to help with the graphics. Pygame is a Python *module*. (You'll learn more about modules in chapter 15.) If you ran the book's installer, Pygame is installed. If not, you can download it from www.pygame.org. You'll learn all about Pygame in chapter 16.

You'll need some graphics files to go along with the program:

- **skier_down.png**   **skier_right1.png**
- **skier_crash.png**   **skier_right2.png**
- **skier_tree.png**   **skier_left1.png**
- **skier_flag.png**   **skier_left2.png**

You can find these in the **\examples\skier** folder (if you ran the installer) or on the book's website. Just put them in the same folder or directory where you save the program. That's pretty important. If they're not in the same directory as the program, Python won't find them, and the program won't work.

The code for Skier is in listing 10.1. The listing is a bit long, about 100 lines of code (plus some blank lines to make it easier to read), but I encourage you to take the time to type it in. The listing has some notes to give a bit of explanation of what the code does. Note that when you see __init__ in the code, there are two underscores on either side of init. That's two underscores before and two underscores after, not just one on either side.

Listing 10.1   Skier

```python
import pygame, sys, random

skier_images = ["skier_down.png", "skier_right1.png",
                "skier_right2.png", "skier_left2.png",
                "skier_left1.png"]

class SkierClass(pygame.sprite.Sprite):
    def __init__(self):
        pygame.sprite.Sprite.__init__(self)
        self.image = pygame.image.load("skier_down.png")     # Creates skier
        self.rect = self.image.get_rect()
        self.rect.center = [320, 100]
        self.angle = 0

    def turn(self, direction):
        self.angle = self.angle + direction
        if self.angle < -2:  self.angle = -2
        if self.angle > 2:  self.angle =  2
        center = self.rect.center
        self.image = pygame.image.load(skier_images[self.angle])     # Turns skier
        self.rect = self.image.get_rect()
        self.rect.center = center
        speed = [self.angle, 6 - abs(self.angle) * 2]
        return speed
```

```
    def move(self, speed):
        self.rect.centerx = self.rect.centerx + speed[0]
        if self.rect.centerx < 20:  self.rect.centerx = 20
        if self.rect.centerx > 620: self.rect.centerx = 620
```
Moves skier
left and right

```
class ObstacleClass(pygame.sprite.Sprite):
    def __init__(self, image_file, location, type):
        pygame.sprite.Sprite.__init__(self)
        self.image_file = image_file
        self.image = pygame.image.load(image_file)
        self.rect = self.image.get_rect()
        self.rect.center = location
        self.type = type
        self.passed = False
    def update(self):
        global speed
        self.rect.centery -= speed[1]
        if self.rect.centery < -32:
            self.kill()
```
Creates trees
and flags

Makes scenery
scroll up

Deletes obstacles that have
scrolled off the top of the screen

```
def create_map():
    global obstacles
    locations = []
    for i in range(10):
        row = random.randint(0, 9)
        col = random.randint(0, 9)
        location  = [col * 64 + 20, row * 64 + 20 + 640]
        if not (location in locations):
            locations.append(location)
            type = random.choice(["tree", "flag"])
            if type == "tree": img = "skier_tree.png"
            elif type == "flag":  img = "skier_flag.png"
            obstacle = ObstacleClass(img, location, type)
            obstacles.add(obstacle)
```
Creates one screen
full of random trees
and flags

```
def animate():
    screen.fill([255, 255, 255])
    obstacles.draw(screen)
    screen.blit(skier.image, skier.rect)
    screen.blit(score_text, [10, 10])
    pygame.display.flip()
```
Redraws screen

```
pygame.init()
screen = pygame.display.set_mode([640,640])
clock = pygame.time.Clock()
skier = SkierClass()
speed = [0, 6]
obstacles = pygame.sprite.Group()
map_position = 0
points = 0
create_map()
font = pygame.font.Font(None, 50)
```
Gets everything
ready

```
running = True
while running:
```
Starts main loop

```
clock.tick(30)                                        ← ———— Updates graphics
    for event in pygame.event.get():         30 times per second
        if event.type == pygame.QUIT:
            running = False                                         Checks for
        if event.type == pygame.KEYDOWN:                            keypresses or
            if event.key == pygame.K_LEFT:                          window close
                speed = skier.turn(-1)
            elif event.key == pygame.K_RIGHT:
                speed = skier.turn(1)
    skier.move(speed)                              ← ———— Moves skier

    map_position += speed[1]                       ← ———— Scrolls scenery

    if map_position >=640:
        create_map()                               Creates a new screen
        map_position = 0                           full of scenery

    hit =  pygame.sprite.spritecollide(skier, obstacles, False)
    if hit:
        if hit[0].type == "tree" and not hit[0].passed:
            points = points - 100
            skier.image = pygame.image.load("skier_crash.png")
            animate()
            pygame.time.delay(1000)
            skier.image = pygame.image.load("skier_down.png")       Checks for hitting
            skier.angle = 0                                         trees and
            speed = [0, 6]                                          getting flag
            hit[0].passed = True
        elif hit[0].type == "flag" and not hit[0].passed:
            points += 10
            hit[0].kill()

    obstacles.update()
    score_text = font.render("Score: " +str(points), 1, (0, 0, 0))   ← —— Displays
    animate()                                                            score
pygame.quit()
```

The code for listing 10.1 is in the **\examples\skier** folder, so if you get stuck or don't want to type it all in, you can use that file. But believe it or not, you'll learn more by typing it in than by just opening and looking at the listing.

In later chapters, you'll learn about all the keywords and techniques that are used in Skier. And at the end of the book, there's a whole chapter explaining in detail how the Skier program works. But for now, just type it in and give it a try.

Try it out

All you need to do in this chapter is type in the Skier program (listing 10.1) and try it out. If you get an error when you try to run it, look at the error message and try to figure out where the mistake is.

Good luck!

Nested and Variable Loops

We already saw that, within the body of a loop (which is a block of code), we can put other things that have their own blocks. If you look at the number-guessing program from chapter 1, you'll see this:

```
while guess != secret and tries < 6:
    guess = input("What's yer guess? ")          ———— while loop block
    if guess < secret:
        print "Too low, ye scurvy dog!"          ———— if block
    elif guess > secret:
        print "Too high, landlubber!"            ———— elif block
    tries = tries + 1
```

The outer, light gray block is a **while** loop block, and the dark gray blocks are **if** and **elif** blocks within that **while** loop block.

You can also put a loop within another loop. These loops are called *nested loops.*

Nested loops

Remember the multiplication table program you wrote for the "Try it out" section in chapter 8? Without the user-input part, it might look something like this:

```
multiplier = 5
for i in range (1, 11):
    print i, "x", multiplier, "=", i * multiplier
```

What if you wanted to print three multiplication tables at once? That's the kind of thing a *nested loop* is perfect for. A nested loop is one loop inside another loop. For *each* iteration of the outer loop, the inner loop goes through *all* of its iterations.

To print three multiplication tables, you'd just enclose the original loop (which prints a single multiplication table) in an outer loop (which runs three times). This makes the program print three tables instead of one. The following listing shows what the code looks like.

Listing 11.1   Printing three multiplication tables at once

```
for multiplier in range (5, 8):
    for i in range (1, 11):
        print i, "x", multiplier, "=", i * multiplier
    print
```

This inner loop prints a single table

This outer loop runs 3 iterations, with values 5, 6, 7

Notice that we had to indent the inner loop and the `print` statement an extra four spaces from the beginning of the outer `for` loop. This program will print the 5 times, 6 times, and 7 times tables, up to 10 for each table:

```
>>> =================== RESTART ===================
>>>
1 x 5 = 5
2 x 5 = 10
3 x 5 = 15
4 x 5 = 20
5 x 5 = 25
6 x 5 = 30
7 x 5 = 35
8 x 5 = 40
9 x 5 = 45
10 x 5 = 50

1 x 6 = 6
2 x 6 = 12
3 x 6 = 18
4 x 6 = 24
5 x 6 = 30
6 x 6 = 36
7 x 6 = 42
8 x 6 = 48
9 x 6 = 54
10 x 6 = 60

1 x 7 = 7
2 x 7 = 14
3 x 7 = 21
4 x 7 = 28
5 x 7 = 35
6 x 7 = 42
7 x 7 = 49
8 x 7 = 56
9 x 7 = 63
10 x 7 = 70
```

Although you might think it's pretty boring, a good way to see what's going on with nested loops is to just print some stars to the screen and count them. We'll do that in the next section.

Variable loops

Fixed numbers, like the ones you've used in the `range()` function, are also called *constants*. If you use constants in the `range()` function of a `for` loop, the loop will run the same number of times whenever the program is run. In that case, we say the number of loops is *hard-coded*, because it's defined in your code and never changes. That's not always what you want.

Sometimes you want the number of loops to be determined by the user or by another part of the program. For that, you need a variable.

For example, let's say you were making a space-shooter game. You'd have to keep redrawing the screen as aliens got wiped out. You'd have some sort of counter to keep track of how many aliens were left, and whenever the screen was updated, you'd need to loop through the remaining aliens and draw their images on the screen. The number of aliens would change every time the player wiped out another one.

Because you haven't learned how to draw aliens on the screen yet, here's a simple example program that uses a variable loop:

```
for i in range(1, numStars):
    print '*',
```

```
>>> ====================== RESTART ======================
>>>
How many stars do you want? 5
* * * *
```

The program asked the user how many stars he wanted, and then it used a variable loop to print that many. Well, almost! We asked for five stars and only got four! Oops, we forgot that the `for` loop stops one short of the second number in the `range`. So we need to add 1 to the user's input:

```
numStars = int(raw_input ("How many stars do you want? "))
for i in range(1, numStars + 1):          Adds 1, so if he asks for
    print '*',                            5 stars, he gets 5 stars
```

Another way to do the same thing is to start the loop counting at 0, instead of 1. (We mentioned that back in chapter 8.) This is very common in programming, and you'll see why in the next chapter. Here's how that would look:

```
numStars = int(raw_input ("How many stars do you want? "))
for i in range(0, numStars):
    print '*',
```

```
>>> ===================== RESTART =====================
>>>
How many stars do you want? 5
* * * * *
```

Variable nested loops

Now let's try a *variable nested loop*. That's just a nested loop where one or more of the loops uses a variable in the **range()** function. Here's an example.

Listing 11.2   A variable nested loop

```
numLines = int(raw_input ('How many lines of stars do you want? '))
numStars = int(raw_input ('How many stars per line? '))
for line in range(0, numLines):
    for star in range(0, numStars):
        print '*',
    print
```

Try running this program to see if it makes sense. You should see something like this:

```
>>> ============================= RESTART =============================
>>>
How many lines of stars do you want?   3
How many stars per line?   5
*****
*****
*****
```

The first two lines ask the user how many lines she wants and how many stars per line. It remembers the answers using the variables **numLines** and **numStars**. Then we have the two loops:

- The inner loop (**for star in range (0, numStars):**) prints each star and runs once for each star on a line.
- The outer loop (**for line in range (0, numLines):**) runs once for each line of stars.

The second **print** command is needed to start a new line of stars. If we didn't have that, all the stars would print on one line because of the comma in the first **print** statement.

You can even have nested-nested loops (or *double-nested loops*). They look like this.

Listing 11.3   Blocks of stars with double-nested loops

```
numBlocks = int(raw_input ('How many blocks of stars do you want? '))
numLines = int(raw_input ('How many lines in each block? '))
numStars = int(raw_input ('How many stars per line? '))
for block in range(0, numBlocks):
    for line in range(0, numLines):
        for star in range(0, numStars):
            print '*',
        print
  print
```

Here's the output:

```
>>> ======================= RESTART =======================
>>>
How many blocks of stars do you want? 3
How many lines of stars in each block? 4
How many stars per line? 8
* * * * * * * *
* * * * * * * *
* * * * * * * *
* * * * * * * *

* * * * * * * *
* * * * * * * *
* * * * * * * *
* * * * * * * *

* * * * * * * *
* * * * * * * *
* * * * * * * *
* * * * * * * *
```

We say the loop is nested "three deep."

Even more variable nested loops

The next listing shows a trickier version of the program from listing 11.3.

Listing 11.4   A trickier version of blocks of stars

```
numBlocks = int(raw_input('How many blocks of stars do you want? '))
for block in range(1, numBlocks + 1):
    for line in range(1, block * 2 ):            Formulas for number
        for star in range(1, (block + line) * 2):    of lines and stars
            print '*',
        print
    print
```

Here's the output:

```
>>> ======================= RESTART =======================
>>>
How many blocks of stars do you want? 3
* * * *

* * * * *
* * * * * * *
* * * * * * * * *

* * * * * *
* * * * * * * *
* * * * * * * * * *
* * * * * * * * * * * *
* * * * * * * * * * * * * *
```

In listing 11.4, the loop variables of the outer loops are used to set the ranges for the inner loops. So instead of each block having the same number of lines and each line having the same number of stars, they're different each time through the loop.

You can nest loops as deep as you want. It can get a bit hairy keeping track of what's going on, so it sometimes helps to print out the values of the loop variables, as shown next.

Listing 11.5   Printing the loop variables in nested loops

```
numBlocks = int(raw_input('How many blocks of stars do you want? '))
for block in range(1, numBlocks + 1):
    print 'block = ', block              ◁
    for line in range(1, block * 2 ):
        for star in range(1, (block + line) * 2):    ⟩ Displays variables
            print '*',                               ◁
        print ' line = ', line, 'star = ', star
    print
```

Here's the output of the program:

```
>>> ======================= RESTART =======================
>>>
How many blocks of stars do you want? 3
block =  1
* * *    line =  1  star = 3

block =  2
* * * * *    line =  1  star = 5
* * * * * * *    line =  2  star = 7
* * * * * * * * *    line =  3  star = 9

block =  3
* * * * * * *    line =  1  star = 7
* * * * * * * * *    line =  2  star = 9
* * * * * * * * * * *    line =  3  star = 11
* * * * * * * * * * * * *    line =  4  star = 13
* * * * * * * * * * * * * * *    line =  5  star = 15
```

Printing the values of variables can help you in lots of situations—not just with loops. It's one of the most common debugging methods.

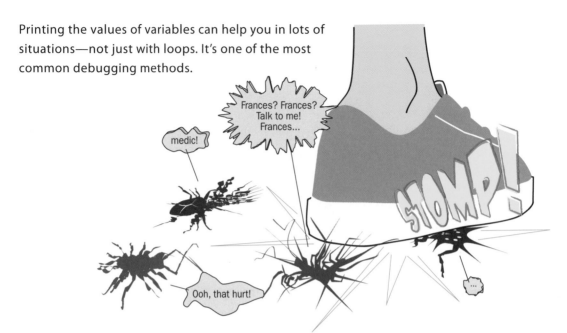

Using nested loops

So what can we do with all these nested loops? Well, one of the things they're good for is figuring out all the possible *permutations* and *combinations* of a series of decisions.

WORD BOX

Permutation is a mathematical term that means a unique way of combining a set of things. *Combination* means something very similar. The difference is that, with a combination, the order doesn't matter, but with a permutation, the order does matter.

If I asked you to pick three numbers from 1 to 20, you could pick
- 5, 8, 14
- 2, 12, 20

and so on. If we tried to make a list of all the permutations of three numbers from 1 to 20, these two would be separate entries:
- 5, 8, 14
- 8, 5, 14

That's because, with permutations, the order in which they appear matters. If we made a list of all the combinations, all these would count as a single entry:
- 5, 8, 14
- 8, 5, 14
- 8, 14, 5

That's because order doesn't matter for combinations.

The best way to explain this is with an example. Let's imagine we're running a hot dog stand at our school's spring fair, and we want to make a poster showing how to order all possible combinations of hot dog, bun, ketchup, mustard, and onions by number. So we need to figure out what all the possible combinations are.

One way to think about this problem is to use something called a *decision tree*. The next figure shows a decision tree for the hot dog problem.

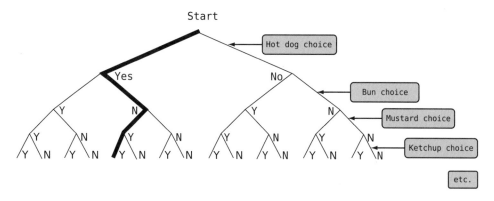

Each decision point has only two choices, Yes or No. Each different path down the tree describes a different combination of hot dog parts. The path I highlighted says "Yes" for hot dog, "No" for bun, "Yes" for mustard, and "Yes" for ketchup.

Now we're going to use nested loops to list all the combinations—all the paths through the decision tree. Because there are five decision points, there are five levels in our decision tree, so there will be five nested loops in our program. (The figure only shows the first four levels of the decision tree.)

Type the code in the following listing into an IDLE editor window, and save it as **hotdog1.py**.

Listing 11.6 *Hot dog combinations*

```
print "\tDog \tBun \tKetchup\tMustard\tOnions"
count = 1

for dog in [0, 1]:

    for bun in [0, 1]:

        for ketchup in [0, 1]:

            for mustard in [0, 1]:

                for onion in [0, 1]:
                    print "#", count, "\t",
                    print dog, "\t", bun, "\t", ketchup, "\t",
                    print mustard, "\t", onion
                    count = count + 1
```

dog
loop

bun
loop

ketchup
loop

mustard
loop

onion
loop

See how the loops are all one inside the other? That's what nested loops really are—loops inside other loops:

- The outer (`dog`) loop runs twice.
- The `bun` loop runs twice for each iteration of the `dog` loop. So it runs 2 x 2 = 4 times.
- The `ketchup` loop runs twice for each iteration of the `dog` loop. So it runs 2 x 2 x 2 = 8 times.

And so on.

The innermost loop (that's the one farthest in—the `onion` loop) runs 2 x 2 x 2 x 2 x 2 = 32 times. This covers all the possible combinations. So there are 32 possible combinations.

If you run the program in listing 11.6, you should get something like this:

```
>>> ============================= RESTART =============================
>>>
          Dog      Bun      Ketchup Mustard Onions
#  1      0        0        0        0        0
#  2      0        0        0        0        1
#  3      0        0        0        1        0
#  4      0        0        0        1        1
#  5      0        0        1        0        0
#  6      0        0        1        0        1
#  7      0        0        1        1        0
#  8      0        0        1        1        1
#  9      0        1        0        0        0
# 10      0        1        0        0        1
# 11      0        1        0        1        0
# 12      0        1        0        1        1
# 13      0        1        1        0        0
# 14      0        1        1        0        1
# 15      0        1        1        1        0
# 16      0        1        1        1        1
# 17      1        0        0        0        0
# 18      1        0        0        0        1
# 19      1        0        0        1        0
# 20      1        0        0        1        1
# 21      1        0        1        0        0
# 22      1        0        1        0        1
# 23      1        0        1        1        0
# 24      1        0        1        1        1
# 25      1        1        0        0        0
# 26      1        1        0        0        1
# 27      1        1        0        1        0
# 28      1        1        0        1        1
# 29      1        1        1        0        0
# 30      1        1        1        0        1
# 31      1        1        1        1        0
# 32      1        1        1        1        1
```

The five nested loops run through all possible combinations of dog, bun, ketchup, mustard, and onion.

In listing 11.6, we used the *tab* character to line everything up. That's the \t parts. We haven't talked about *print formatting* yet, but if you want to know more about it, you can have a peek at chapter 21.

We used a variable called count to number each combination. So, for example, a hot dog with a bun and
mustard would be #27. Of course, some of the 32
combinations don't make sense. (A hot dog with no
bun but with mustard and ketchup would be a little messy.) But you
know what they say: "The customer is always right!"

Mmmmm....
That's one good
dog!

Counting calories

Because everyone is concerned about nutrition these days, let's add a calorie count for each combination on the menu. (You might not care about
the calories, but I bet your parents do!) That will let us use some of Python's
math abilities, which we learned about back in chapter 3.

We already know which items are in each combination. All we need now are the calories for each item. Then we can add them all up in the innermost loop.

Here's some code that sets how many calories are in each item:

```
dog_cal = 140
bun_cal = 120
mus_cal = 20
ket_cal = 80
onion_cal = 40
```

Now we just need to add them up. We know there's either 0 or 1 of each item in each menu combination. So we can just multiply the quantity by the calories forevery item, like this:

```
tot_cal = (dog * dog_cal) + (bun * bun_cal) + \
          (mustard * mus_cal) + (ketchup * ket_cal) + \
          (onion * onion_cal)
```

Because the order of operations is multiplication first, then addition, I didn't
really need to put in the parentheses. I just put them in to make it easier to see
what's going on.

Long lines of code

Did you notice the backslash (\) characters at the end of the lines in the previous code? If you have a long expression that won't fit on a single line, you can use the backslash character to tell Python, "This line isn't done. Treat whatever is on the next line as if it's part of this line." Here we used two backslashes to split our long line into three short lines. The backslash is called a *line-continuation character*, and several programming languages have them.

You can also put an extra set of parentheses around the whole expression, and then you can split your expression over multiple lines without using the backslash, like this:

```
tot_cal = ((dog * dog_cal) + (bun * bun_cal) +
           (mustard * mus_cal) + (ketchup * ket_cal) +
           (onion * onion_cal))
```

Putting this all together, the new calorie-counter version of the hot dog program is shown next.

Listing 11.7 Hot dog program with calorie counter

```
dog_cal = 140
bun_cal = 120           Lists calories
ket_cal = 80            for each part
mus_cal  = 20           of the hot dog
onion_cal = 40
```

```
print "\tDog \tBun \tKetchup\tMustard\tOnions\tCalories"     ← Prints headings
count = 1
for dog in [0, 1]:        ← dog is the outer loop
    for bun in [0, 1]:
        for ketchup in [0, 1]:
            for mustard in [0, 1]:
                for onion in [0, 1]:
                    total_cal = (bun * bun_cal)+(dog * dog_cal) + \
                        (ketchup * ket_cal)+(mustard * mus_cal) + \
                            (onion * onion_cal)
                    print "#", count, "\t",
                    print dog, "\t", bun, "\t", ketchup, "\t",
                    print mustard, "\t", onion,
                    print "\t", total_cal
                    count = count + 1
```

Calculates calories in the inner loop

Nested loops

Try running the program in listing 11.7 in IDLE. The output should look like this:

```
>>> =========================== RESTART ===========================
>>>
          Dog     Bun     Ketchup  Mustard  Onions   Calories
# 1       0       0       0        0        0        0
# 2       0       0       0        0        1        40
# 3       0       0       0        1        0        20
# 4       0       0       0        1        1        60
# 5       0       0       1        0        0        80
# 6       0       0       1        0        1        120
# 7       0       0       1        1        0        100
# 8       0       0       1        1        1        140
# 9       0       1       0        0        0        120
# 10      0       1       0        0        1        160
# 11      0       1       0        1        0        140
# 12      0       1       0        1        1        180
# 13      0       1       1        0        0        200
# 14      0       1       1        0        1        240
# 15      0       1       1        1        0        220
# 16      0       1       1        1        1        260
# 17      1       0       0        0        0        140
# 18      1       0       0        0        1        180
# 19      1       0       0        1        0        160
# 20      1       0       0        1        1        200
# 21      1       0       1        0        0        220
# 22      1       0       1        0        1        260
# 23      1       0       1        1        0        240
# 24      1       0       1        1        1        280
# 25      1       1       0        0        0        260
# 26      1       1       0        0        1        300
# 27      1       1       0        1        0        280
# 28      1       1       0        1        1        320
# 29      1       1       1        0        0        340
# 30      1       1       1        0        1        380
# 31      1       1       1        1        0        360
# 32      1       1       1        1        1        400
```

Just imagine how tedious it would be to work out the calories for all these combinations by hand, even if you had a calculator to do the math. It's way more fun to write a program to figure it out for you. Looping and a bit of math in Python make it a snap!

What did you learn?

In this chapter, you learned about

- Nested loops
- Variable loops
- Permutations and combinations
- Decision trees

Test your knowledge

1 How do you make a variable loop in Python?

2 How do you make a nested loop in Python?

3 What's the total number of stars that will be printed by the following code?

```
for i in range(5):
    for j in range(3):
        print '*',
    print
```

4 What will the output from the code in question 3 look like?

5 If a decision tree has four levels and two choices per level, how many possible choices (paths through the decision tree) are there?

Try it out

1 Remember the countdown-timer program we created in chapter 8? Here it is, to refresh your memory:

```
import time
for i in range (10, 0, -1):
    print i
    time.sleep(1)
print "BLAST OFF!"
```

Modify the program to use a variable loop. The program should ask the user where the countdown should start, like this:

```
Countdown timer:  How many seconds?  4
4
3
2
1
BLAST OFF!
```

2 Take the program you wrote in question #1, and have it print a row of stars beside each number, like this:

```
Countdown timer:  How many seconds?  4
4 * * * *
3 * * *
2 * *
1 *
BLAST OFF!
```

(Hint: You probably need to use a nested loop.)

## CHAPTER 12

Collecting Things Together— Lists and Dictionaries

We've seen that Python can store things in its memory and retrieve them, using names. So far, we have stored *strings* and *numbers* (both *integers* and *floats*). Sometimes it's useful to store a bunch of things together in a kind of group or *collection*. Then you can do things to the whole collection at once and keep track of groups of things more easily. One of the kinds of collections is a *list*, and another is a *dictionary*. In this chapter, we're going to learn about lists and dictionaries—what they are and how to create, modify, and use them.

Lists are very useful, and they're used in many, many programs. We'll use a lot of them in the examples in upcoming chapters when we start doing graphics and game programming, because the many graphical objects in a game are often stored in a list.

What's a list?

If I asked you to make a list of the members of your family, you might write something like this:

In Python, you'd write this:

```
family = ['Mom', 'Dad', 'Junior', 'Baby']
```

If I asked you to write down your lucky numbers, you might write this:

2, 7, 14, 26, 30

In Python, you'd write this:

```
luckyNumbers = [2, 7, 14, 26, 30]
```

Both `family` and `luckyNumbers` are examples of Python lists, and the individual things inside lists are called *items*. As you can see, lists in Python aren't much different from lists you make in everyday life. Lists use square brackets to show where the list starts and ends, and they use commas to separate the items inside.

Creating a list

Both `family` and `luckyNumbers` are variables. We said before that you can assign different kinds of values to variables. We have already used them for numbers and strings, and they can also be assigned a list.

You create a list like you create any other variable—by assigning something to it, just like we did with `luckyNumbers`. You can also create an empty list, like this:

```
newList = []
```

There are no items inside the square brackets, so the list is empty. But what good is an empty list? Why would you want to create one?

Well, quite often, you don't know ahead of time what's going to be in a list. You don't know how many items will be in it, or what those items will be. You just know you'll be using a list to hold them. Once you have an empty list, the program can add things to it. So how do you do that?

Adding things to a list

To add things to a list, you use `append()`. Try this in interactive mode:

```
>>> friends = []          ⟵——— Makes a new, empty list
>>> friends.append('David')   ⟵——— Adds an item,
>>> print friends                     "David", to the list
```

You'll get this result:

```
['David']
```

Try adding another item:

```
>>> friends.append('Mary')
>>> print friends
['David', 'Mary']
```

Remember that you have to create the list (empty or not) before you start adding things to it. It's like if you're making a cake: you can't just start pouring ingredients together—you have to get a bowl out first to pour them into. Otherwise you'll end up with stuff all over the counter!

What's the dot?

Why did we use a dot between **friends** and **append()**? Well, that starts getting into a pretty big topic: objects. You'll learn more about objects in chapter 14, but for now, here's a simple explanation.

WORD BOX

Append means to add something to the end.

When you append something to a list, you add it to the end of the list.

Many things in Python are *objects*. To do something with an object, you need the object's name (the variable name), then a dot, and then whatever you want to do to the object. So to *append* something to the **friends** list, you'd write this:

```
friends.append(something)
```

Lists can hold anything

Lists can hold any kind of data that Python can store. That includes numbers, strings, objects, and even other lists. The items in a list don't have to be the same type or kind of thing. That means a single list can hold both numbers and strings, for example. A list could look like this:

```
my_list = [5, 10, 23.76, 'Hello', myTeacher, 7, another_list]
```

Let's make a new list with something simple, like the letters of the alphabet, so it's easier to see what's going on as we learn about lists. Type this in interactive mode:

```
>>> letters = ['a', 'b', 'c', 'd', 'e']
```

Getting items from a list

You can get single items from a list by their index number. The list index starts from 0, so the first item in our list is `letters[0]`:

```
>>> print letters[0]
a
```

Let's try another one:

```
>>> print letters[3]
d
```

Why does the index start from 0, not 1?

That's a question a lot of programmers, engineers, and computer scientists have argued about since computers were invented. I'm not going to get in the middle of that argument, so let's just say the answer is "because," and move on …

Hey, you're not getting off that easy!

Okay, okay! Have a look at "WHAT'S GOING ON IN THERE?" to see an explanation of why the index starts at 0 instead of 1.

WHAT'S GOING ON IN THERE?

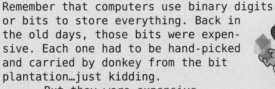

Remember that computers use binary digits or bits to store everything. Back in the old days, those bits were expensive. Each one had to be hand-picked and carried by donkey from the bit plantation…just kidding.
But they were expensive.

Binary counting starts at 0. So, to make the most efficient use of the bits and not waste any, things like memory locations and list indices started at 0 as well.

Hey, you crazy burro! Get back here!

You'll quickly get used to indices starting at 0. It's very common in programming.

BIG FANCY WORD ALERT!

Index means the position of something. The plural of *index* is *indices* (but some people also use *indexes* as the plural for index).

If you're the fourth person in line, your index in line is 4. But if you're the fourth person in a Python list, your index is 3, because Python list indices start at 0!

"Slicing" a list

You can also use indices to get more than one item from a list at a time. This is called *slicing* a list:

```
>>> print letters[1:4]
['b', 'c', 'd']
```

Similar to the **range()** in our **for** loops, slicing gets the items starting with the first index, but it stops *before* getting to the second index. That's why we got back three items, not four, in the previous example. One way to remember this is that the number of items you get back is always the difference between the two index numbers. (4 − 1 = 3, and we got three items back.)

Here's one other thing that is important to remember about slicing a list: What you get back when you slice a list is another (usually smaller) list. This smaller list is called a *slice* of the original list. The original list isn't changed. The slice is a partial *copy* of the original.

Look at the difference here:

```
>>> print letters[1]
b
>>> print letters[1:2]
['b']
```

In the first case, we got back an item. In the second case, we got back a list containing the item. It's a subtle difference, but you need to know about it. In the first case, we used a single index to get one *item* out of the list. In the second case, we used *slice notation* to get a one-item *slice* of the list.

To really see the difference, try this:

```
>>> print type(letters[1])
<type 'str'>
>>> print type(letters[1:2])
<type 'list'>
```

Displaying the `type` of each one tells you for certain that in one case you get a single item (a *string*, in this case), and in the other case you get a *list*.

The smaller list you get back when you slice a list is a copy of items from the original list. That means you can change it and the original list won't be affected.

Slice shorthand

There are some shortcuts you can take when using slices. They don't really save you much typing, but programmers are a lazy bunch, so they use shortcuts a lot. I want you to know what the shortcuts are, so you can recognize them when you see them in other people's code and understand what's going on. That's important, because looking at other people's code and trying to understand it is a good way to learn a new programming language, or programming in general.

If the slice you want includes the start of the list, the shortcut is to use a colon followed by the number of items you want, like this:

```
>>> print letters[:2]
['a', 'b']
```

Notice that there is no number before the colon. This will give you everything from the start of the list up to (but not including) the index you specify.

You can do something similar to get the end of a list:

```
>>> print letters[2:]
['c', 'd', 'e']
```

Using a number followed by a colon gives you everything from the index you specify to the end of the list.

If you don't put any numbers in, and just use a colon, you get the whole list:

```
>>> print letters[:]
['a', 'b', 'c', 'd', 'e']
```

Remember I said that slices make a copy of the original? So `letters[:]` makes a copy of the whole list. This is handy if you want to make some changes to a list but keep the original unchanged.

Modifying items

You can use the index to change one of the list items:

```
>>> print letters
['a', 'b', 'c', 'd', 'e']
>>> letters[2] = 'z'
>>> print letters
['a', 'b', 'z', 'd', 'e']
```

But you can't use the index to add new items to the list. Right now, there are five items in the list, with indices from 0 to 4. So you could *not* do something like this:

```
letters[5] = 'f'
```

It would not work. (Try it if you want.) It's like trying to change something that isn't there yet. To add items to a list, you have to do something else, and that's where we're going next. But before we do, let's change our list back to the way it was:

```
>>> letters[2] = 'c'
>>> print letters
['a', 'b', 'c', 'd', 'e']
```

Other ways of adding to a list

You already saw how to add things to a list using `append()`. But there are other ways. In fact, there are three methods for adding things to a list—`append()`, `extend()`, and `insert()`:

- `append()` adds one item to the end of the list.
- `extend()` adds multiple items to the end of the list.
- `insert()` adds one item somewhere in the list, not necessarily at the end. You tell it where to add the item.

Adding to the end: `append()`

You already saw how `append()` works. It adds one item to the end of a list:

```
>>> letters.append('n')
>>> print letters
['a', 'b', 'c', 'd', 'e', 'n']
```

Let's add one more:

```
>>> letters.append('g')
>>> print letters
['a', 'b', 'c', 'd', 'e', 'n', 'g']
```

Notice that the letters are not in order. That's because `append()` adds the item to the end of the list. If you want the items in order, you'll have to *sort* them. We'll get to sorting very soon.

Extending the list: `extend()`

`extend()` adds several items to the end of a list:

```
>>> letters.extend(['p', 'q', 'r'])
>>> print letters
['a', 'b', 'c', 'd', 'e', 'n', 'g', 'p', 'q', 'r']
```

Notice that what's inside the round brackets of the `extend()` method is a list. A list has square brackets, so for `extend()`, you could have both round and square brackets.

Everything in the list you give to `extend()` gets added to the end of the original list.

Inserting an item: `insert()`

`insert()` adds a single item somewhere in the list. You tell it at what position in the list you want the item added:

```
>>> letters.insert(2, 'z')
>>> print letters
['a', 'b', 'z', 'c', 'd', 'e', 'n', 'g', 'p', 'q', 'r']
```

Here, we added the letter *z* at index 2. Index 2 is the third position in the list (because indices start at 0). The letter that used to be in the third position, *c*, got bumped over by one place, to the fourth position. Every other item in the list also got bumped one position.

The difference between `append()` and `extend()`

Sometimes `append()` and `extend()` look very similar, but they do different things. Let's go back to our original list. First, try using `extend()` to add three items:

```
>>> letters = ['a','b','c','d','e']
>>> letters.extend(['f', 'g', 'h'])
>>> print letters
['a', 'b', 'c', 'd', 'e', 'f', 'g', 'h']
```

Now, we'll try to use `append()` to do the same thing:

```
>>> letters = ['a', 'b', 'c', 'd', 'e']
>>> letters.append(['f', 'g', 'h'])
>>> print letters
['a', 'b', 'c', 'd', 'e', ['f', 'g', 'h']]
```

What happened here? Well, we said before that `append()` adds *one* item to a list. How did it add three? It didn't. It added one item, which happens to be *another list containing three items*. That's why we got the extra set of square brackets inside our list. Remember that a list can hold anything, including other lists. That's what we've got.

`insert()` works the same way as `append()`, except that you tell it where to put the new item. `append()` always puts it at the end.

Deleting from a list

How do you delete or remove things from a list? There are three ways: `remove()`, `del`, and `pop()`.

Deleting with `remove()`

`remove()` deletes the item you choose from the list and throws it away:

```
>>> letters = ['a', 'b', 'c', 'd', 'e']
>>> letters.remove('c')
>>> print letters
['a', 'b', 'd', 'e']
```

You don't need to know where in the list the item is. You just need to know it's there somewhere. If you try to remove something that isn't in the list, you'll get an error:

```
>>> letters.remove('f')
Traceback (most recent call last):
  File "<pyshell#32>", line 1, in <module>
    letters.remove('f')
ValueError: list.remove(x): x not in list
```

So how can you find out if a list contains a certain item? That's coming right up. First, let's look at the other ways to delete something from a list.

Deleting with `del`

`del` lets you delete an item from the list using its index, like this:

```
>>> letters = ['a', 'b', 'c', 'd', 'e']
>>> del letters[3]
>>> print letters
['a', 'b', 'c', 'e']
```

Here, we deleted the fourth item (index 3), which was the letter *d*.

Deleting with `pop()`

`pop()` takes the *last* item off the list and gives it back to you. That means you can assign it a name, like this:

```
>>> letters = ['a', 'b', 'c', 'd', 'e']
>>> lastLetter = letters.pop()
>>> print letters
['a', 'b', 'c', 'd']
>>> print lastLetter
e
```

You can also use `pop()` with an index, like this:

```
>>> letters = ['a', 'b', 'c', 'd', 'e']
>>> second = letters.pop(1)
>>> print second
b
>>> print letters
['a', 'c', 'd', 'e']
```

Here, we popped the second letter (index 1), which was *b*. The item we popped was assigned to `second`, and it was also removed from `letters`.

With nothing inside the parentheses, `pop()` gives you the last item and removes it from the list. If you put a number in the parentheses, `pop(n)` gives you the item at that index and removes it from the list.

Searching a list

Once you have several items in a list, how do you find them? Two things you'll often need to do with a list are

- Find out whether an item is in a list or not
- Find out where an item is in the list (its index)

The `in` keyword

To find out whether something is in a list, you use the `in` keyword, like this:

```
if 'a' in letters:
    print "found 'a' in letters"
else:
    print "didn't find 'a' in letters"
```

The `'a' in letters` part is a *Boolean* or *logical* expression. It'll return the value `True` if *a* is in the list, and `False` otherwise.

WORD BOX

Boolean is a kind of arithmetic that only uses two values: 1 and 0, or true and false. It was invented by mathematician George Boole, and it is used when combining true and false conditions (represented by 1 and 0) together with `and`, `or`, and `not`, like we saw in Chapter 7.

You can try this in interactive mode:

```
>>> 'a' in letters
True
>>> 's' in letters
False
```

This is telling us that the list called `letters` does have an item *a*, but it does not have an item *s*. So *a* is in the list, and *s* isn't in the list. Now you can combine `in` and `remove()`, and write something that won't give you an error, even if the value isn't in the list:

```
if 'a' in letters:
    letters.remove('a')
```

This code only removes the value from the list if the value is in the list.

Finding the index

To find where in the list an item is located, you use the `index()` method, like this:

```
>>> letters = ['a', 'b', 'c', 'd', 'e']
>>> print letters.index('d')
3
```

So we know that *d* has index 3, which means it's the fourth item in the list.

Just like `remove()`, `index()` will give you an error if the value isn't found in the list, so it's a good idea to use it with `in`, like this:

```
if 'd' in letters:
    print letters.index('d')
```

Looping through a list

When we first talked about loops, you saw that loops iterate through a *list* of values. You also learned about the `range()` function and used it as a shortcut for generating lists of numbers for your loops. You saw that `range()` gives you a *list* of numbers.

But a loop can iterate through any list—it doesn't have to be a list of numbers. Let's say we wanted to print our list of letters with one item on each line. We could do something like this:

```
>>> letters = ['a', 'b', 'c', 'd', 'e']
>>> for letter in letters:
        print letter

a
b
c
d
e
```

This time, our loop variable is `letter`. (Before, we used loop variables like `looper` or `i`, `j`, and `k`.) The loop iterates over (loops through) all the values in the list, and each time through, the current item is stored in the loop variable, `letter`, and then is displayed.

Sorting lists

Lists are an *ordered* type of collection. This means the items in a list have a certain order, and each one has a place (its index). Once you have put items in a list in a certain order, they stay in that order unless you change the list with `insert()`, `append()`, `remove()`, or `pop()`. But that order might not be the order you want. You might want a list *sorted* before you use it.

To sort a list, you use the `sort()` method:

```
>>> letters = ['d', 'a', 'e', 'c', 'b']
>>> print letters
['d', 'a', 'e', 'c', 'b']
>>> letters.sort()
>>> print letters
['a', 'b', 'c', 'd', 'e']
```

`sort()` automatically sorts strings alphabetically and numbers numerically, from smallest to largest.

It's important to know that `sort()` modifies the list in place. That means it changes the original list you give it. It *does not* create a new, sorted list. That means you can't do this:

```
>>> print letters.sort()
```

If you do, you'll get "None." You have to do it in two steps, like this:

```
>>> letters.sort()
>>> print letters
```

Sorting in reverse order

There are two ways to get a list sorted in reverse order. One is to sort the list the normal way and then *reverse* the sorted list, like this:

```
>>> letters = ['d', 'a', 'e', 'c', 'b']
>>> letters.sort()
>>> print letters
['a', 'b', 'c', 'd', 'e']
>>> letters.reverse()
>>> print letters
['e', 'd', 'c', 'b', 'a']
```

Here you saw a new list method called **reverse()**, which reverses the order of items in a list.

The other way is to add a parameter to **sort()** to make it sort in descending order (from largest to smallest):

```
>>> letters = ['d', 'a', 'e', 'c', 'b']
>>> letters.sort (reverse = True)
>>> print letters
['e', 'd', 'c', 'b', 'a']
```

The parameter is called **reverse**, and it does exactly what you'd expect—it makes the list sort in reverse order.

Remember that all the sorting and reversing we just talked about modifies the original list. That means your original order is lost. If you want to preserve the original order and sort a *copy* of the list, you could use slice notation, which we talked about earlier in this chapter, to make a copy—another list equal to the original:

```
>>> original_list = ['Tom', 'James', 'Sarah', 'Fred']
>>> new_list = original_list[:]
>>> new_list.sort()
>>> print original_list
['Tom', 'James', 'Sarah', 'Fred']
>>> print new_list
['Fred', 'James', 'Sarah', 'Tom']
```

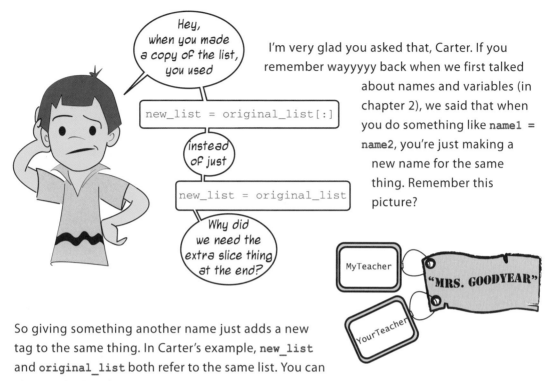

Hey, when you made a copy of the list, you used

```
new_list = original_list[:]
```

instead of just

```
new_list = original_list
```

Why did we need the extra slice thing at the end?

I'm very glad you asked that, Carter. If you remember wayyyyy back when we first talked about names and variables (in chapter 2), we said that when you do something like **name1 = name2**, you're just making a new name for the same thing. Remember this picture?

MyTeacher

"MRS. GOODYEAR"

YourTeacher

So giving something another name just adds a new tag to the same thing. In Carter's example, **new_list** and **original_list** both refer to the same list. You can change the list (for example, you can sort it) by using either name. But there is still only *one* list. It looks like this:

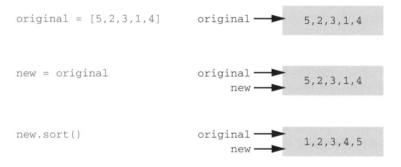

```
original = [5,2,3,1,4]      original ──▶   5,2,3,1,4


new = original             original ──▶
                                new ──▶    5,2,3,1,4


new.sort()                 original ──▶
                                new ──▶    1,2,3,4,5
```

We sorted **new**, but **original** also got sorted, because **new** and **original** are two different names for the same list. There are *not* two different lists.

You can, of course, move the `new` tag to a whole new list, like this:

That's the same thing we did with strings and numbers in chapter 2.

This means that, if you really want to make a *copy* of a list, you need to do something different from `new = original`. The easiest way to do this is to use slice notation, like I did above: `new = original[:]`. This means "copy everything in the list, from the first item to the last item." Then you get this:

```
original = [5,2,3,1,4]        original ──►   5,2,3,1,4

new = original[:]                  new ──►   5,2,3,1,4
```

There are now two separate lists. We made a copy of the original and called it `new`. Now if we sort one list, the other one won't be sorted.

Another way to sort—`sorted()`

There is another way to get a sorted copy of a list without changing the order of the original list. Python has a function called
`sorted()` for that purpose. It works like this:

```
>>> original = [5, 2, 3, 1, 4]
>>> newer = sorted(original)
>>> print original
[5, 2, 3, 1, 4]
>>> print newer
[1, 2, 3, 4, 5]
```

The `sorted()` function gives you a *sorted copy* of the original list.

Mutable and immutable

If you remember back to chapter 2, we said that you couldn't actually change a number or string, you could only change what number or string a *name* was assigned to (in other words, move the tag). But lists are one of the types in Python that *can be* changed. As you just saw, lists can have items appended or deleted, and the items can be sorted or reversed.

These two different kinds of variables are called *mutable* and *immutable*. *Mutable* just means "able to be changed" or "changeable." *Immutable* means "not able to be changed" or "unchangeable." In Python, numbers and strings are immutable (cannot be changed), and lists are mutable (can be changed).

Tuple—an immutable list

There are times when you don't want a list to be changeable. So, is there an immutable kind of list in Python? The answer is yes. There is a type called a *tuple*, which is exactly that, an immutable (unchangeable) list. You make one like this:

```
my_tuple = ("red", "green", "blue")
```

You use round brackets, instead of the square ones that lists use.

Because tuples are immutable (unchangeable), you can't do things like sort them or append or delete items. Once you create a tuple with a set of items, it stays that way.

Lists of lists: tables of data

When thinking about how data is stored in a program, it's useful to visualize it.

A variable has a single value.   `myTeacher` ⟶ ┌──────────────┐ `Mr. Wilson` └──────────────┘

A list is like a row of values strung together.

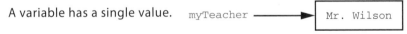

`myFriends` ⟶ | Curtis | Karla | Jenn | Kim | Shaun |

Sometimes you need a *table* with rows and columns.

`classMarks` ⟶

	Math	Science	Reading	Spelling
Joe	55	63	77	81
Tom	65	61	67	72
Beth	97	95	92	88

How can you save a table of data? You already know that you can make a list to hold several items. We could put each student's marks in a list, like this:

```
>>> joeMarks = [55, 63, 77, 81]
>>> tomMarks = [65, 61, 67, 72]
>>> bethMarks = [97, 95, 92, 88]
```

Or we could use a list for each subject, like this:

```
>>> mathMarks = [55, 65, 97]
>>> scienceMarks = [63, 61, 95]
>>> readingMarks = [77, 67, 92]
>>> spellingMarks = [81, 72, 88]
```

But you might want to collect all the data together in a single *data structure*.

WORD BOX

A *data structure* is a way of collecting, storing, or representing the data in a program. Data structures can include variables, lists, and some other things we haven't talked about yet. The term *data structure* really refers to the way the data is organized in a program.

To make a single data structure for our class marks, we could do something like this:

```
>>> classMarks = [joeMarks, tomMarks, bethMarks]
>>> print classMarks
[[55, 63, 77, 81], [65, 61, 67, 72], [97, 95, 92, 88]]
```

This gives us a list of items, where each item is itself a list. We have created a *list of lists*. Each of the items in the `classMarks` list is itself a list.

We could also have created `classMarks` directly, without first creating `joeMarks`, `tomMarks`, and `bethMarks`, like this:

```
>>> classMarks = [ [55,63,77,81], [65,61,67,72], [97,95,92,88] ]
>>> print classMarks
[[55, 63, 77, 81], [65, 61, 67, 72], [97, 95, 92, 88]]
```

Now let's try displaying our data structure. `classMarks` has three items, one for each student. So we can just loop through them using `in`:

```
>>> for studentMarks in classMarks:
        print studentMarks

[55, 63, 77, 81]
[65, 61, 67, 72]
[97, 95, 92, 88]
```

Here we looped through the list called `classMarks`. The loop variable is `studentMarks`. Each time through the loop, we print one item in the list. That one item is the marks for a single student, which is itself a list. (We created the student lists above.)

Notice that this looks very similar to the table on the previous page. So we have come up with a data structure to hold all our data in one place.

Getting a single value from the table

How do we get access to values in this table (our list of lists)? We already know that the first student's marks (`joeMarks`) are in a list that is the first item in `classMarks`. Let's check that:

```
>>> print classMarks[0]
[55, 63, 77, 81]
```

`classMarks[0]` is a list of Joe's marks in the four subjects. Now we want a single value from `classMarks[0]`. How do we do that? We use a second index.

If we want the third of his marks (his Reading mark), which has index 2, we'd do this:

```
>>> print classMarks[0][2]
77
```

This gave us the first item in `classMarks` (index 0), which was the list of Joe's marks, and the third item in that list (index 2), which was his Reading mark. When you see a name with two sets of square brackets, like `classMarks[0][2]`, that is usually referring to a list of lists.

classMarks ➤	Math	Science	Reading	Spelling
Joe	55	63	77	81
Tom	65	61	67	72
Beth	97	95	92	88

The `classMarks` list doesn't really know about the names Joe, Tom, and Beth, or the subjects Math, Science, Reading, and Spelling. We labeled them that way because we knew what we intended to store in the list. But to Python, they're just numbered places in a list. This is like the numbered mailboxes at a post office. They don't have names on them, just numbers. The postmaster keeps track of what belongs where, and you know which box is yours.

A more accurate way to label the **classMarks** table would be like this:

classMarks ⟶	[0]	[1]	[2]	[3]
classMarks[0]	55	63	77	81
classMarks[1]	65	61	67	72
classMarks[2]	97	95	92	88

Now it's easier to see that the mark 77 is stored in **classMarks[0][2]**.

If we were writing a program using **classMarks** to store our data, we'd have to keep track of which data was stored in which row and column. Just like the postmaster, we'd have the job of keeping track of which slot belongs to which piece of data.

Dictionaries

You just saw that a Python list is a way of collecting items together. Quite often in programming you want to collect things together in a way that lets you associate a value with some other value. This is like the way a phone book associates names and phone numbers, or the way a dictionary associates words and their definitions.

A Python *dictionary* is a way of associating two things to each other. These two things are called the *key* and the *value*. Each item or entry in a dictionary has a key and a value. You will hear these referred to as *key-value pairs*. A dictionary is a collection of key-value pairs.

A simple example is a list of phone numbers. Let's say you want to keep a list of your friends' phone numbers. You're going to use their first names to look up the numbers. (Hopefully none of your friends have the same first name.) The name would be the *key* (the thing you'll use to look up the information), and the phone number would be the *value* (the thing you'll look up).

Here's one way to create a Python dictionary to store names and phone numbers. First, let's create the empty dictionary:

```
>>> phoneNumbers = {}
```

This looks very similar to the way you create a list, except you use curly brackets (also called *curly braces* or sometimes just *braces*) instead of the square brackets you use for lists.

Then, let's add an entry:

```
>>> phoneNumbers["John"] = "555-1234"
```

If we then display our dictionary, it looks like this:

```
>>> print phoneNumbers
{'John': '555-1234'}
```

The key is listed first, followed by a colon, and then the value. The quotes are there because both the key and the value happen to be strings in this case (they don't have to be).

Another way to do the same thing is

```
>>> phoneNumbers = {"John": "555-1234"}
```

Let's add some more names. Unlike the `append()` method you use for lists, dictionaries don't have a method for adding new items. You just specify the new key and value:

```
>>> phoneNumbers["Mary"] = "555-6789"
>>> phoneNumbers["Bob"] = "444-4321"
>>> phoneNumbers["Jenny"] = "867-5309"
```

Let's look at the whole dictionary:

```
>>> print phoneNumbers
{'Bob': '444-4321', 'John': '555-1234', 'Mary': '555-6789', 'Jenny': '867-5309'}
```

Now, the whole reason we created a dictionary was so we could look things up. In this case, we want to look something up by name. You do that like this:

```
>>> print phoneNumbers["Mary"]
'555-6789'
```

Notice that you use square brackets to specify which key you want within the dictionary. But the dictionary as a whole is enclosed in curly brackets.

A dictionary is somewhat like a list, but there are a couple of main differences. Both types are *collections*; that is, they are a way of collecting together other types.

Here are some similarities:

- Both lists and dictionaries can hold any type (even lists and dictionaries), so you can have collections of numbers, strings, objects, and even other collections.
- Both lists and dictionaries give you ways to find things in the collection.

And here are some differences:

- Lists are *ordered*. If you put things in a list in a certain order, they stay in that order. And you can sort a list. Dictionaries are *unordered*. If you add things to a dictionary and then display the contents, they may be in a different order than you put them in.
- Items in a list are accessed by their index. Items in a dictionary are accessed by their key:

  ```
  >>> print myList[3]
  'eggs'
  >>> print myDictionary["John"]
  '555-1234'
  ```

As we mentioned before, many things in Python are objects, including lists and dictionaries. Just like lists, dictionaries have some methods you can use to work with them, using the dot notation you saw before.

The `keys()` method gives you a list of all the dictionary keys:

```
>>> phoneNumbers.keys()
['Bob', 'John', 'Mary', 'Jenny']
```

The `values()` method gives you a list of all the values:

```
>>> phoneNumbers.values()
['444-4321', '555-1234', '555-6789', '867-5309']
```

Other languages have things similar to Python dictionaries. They're generally called *associative arrays* (because they *associate* keys and values to each other). Another term you'll hear for them is *hash tables.*

Just like lists, the items in a dictionary can be any type, including simple types (int, float, string) or collections (lists or dictionaries) or compound types (objects).

Yes, you can have dictionaries that contain other dictionaries, just like you can have lists of lists. Actually, that's not entirely true. It is true for the *values* in a dictionary, but the *keys* are more restricted. Earlier we talked about *mutable* versus *immutable* types. Well, dictionary keys can only be immutable types (booleans, integers, floats, strings, and tuples). You can't use a list or a dictionary as a key, because these are mutable types.

I mentioned above that one of the things about dictionaries that's different from lists is that dictionaries are *unordered*. Notice that even though Bob's number was the third one we added to the dictionary, it was the first item when we displayed the contents of the dictionary. Dictionaries have no concept of order, so sorting a dictionary makes no sense. But sometimes you want to display the contents of a dictionary in some kind of order. Remember that lists *can* be sorted, so once you get a list of the keys, you can sort that and then display the dictionary in order of its keys. You can sort the list of keys using the `sorted()` function, like this:

```
>>> for key in sorted(phoneNumbers.keys()):
        print key, phoneNumbers[key]

Bob 444-4321
Jenny 867-5309
John 555-1234
Mary 555-6789
```

That's the same `sorted()` function you saw before for lists. If you think about it, this makes sense, because the collection of a dictionary's keys *is* a list.

What if you want to display the items in order of the values instead of the keys? In our phone numbers example, that would mean sorting by the phone numbers, from lowest number to highest number. Well, a dictionary is really a one-way lookup. It is meant to look up values using the keys, not the other way around. So it's a little more difficult to sort by the values. It's possible—it just takes a bit more work:

```
>>> for value in sorted(phoneNumbers.values()):
        for key in phoneNumbers.keys():
            if phoneNumbers[key] == value:
                print key, phoneNumbers[key]


Bob 444-4321
John 555-1234
Mary 555-6789
Jenny 867-5309
```

Here, once we got the sorted list of values, we took each value and found its key by looping through all the keys until we found the one that was associated to that value.

Here are a few other things you can do with dictionaries:

- Delete an item using `del`:

```
>>> del phoneNumbers["John"]
>>> print phoneNumbers
{'Bob': '444-4321', 'Mary': '555-6789', 'Jenny': '867-5309'}
```

- Delete all items (clear the dictionary) using `clear()`:

```
>>> phoneNumbers.clear()
>>> print phoneNumbers
{}
```

- Find out if a key exists in the dictionary using `in`:

```
>>> phoneNumbers = {'Bob': '444-4321', 'Mary': '555-6789', 'Jenny': '867-5309'}
>>> "Bob" in phoneNumbers
True
>>> "Barb" in phoneNumbers
False
```

Dictionaries are used in lots of Python code.

This certainly isn't a comprehensive overview of Python dictionaries. But it should give you the general idea so you can start using them in your code and recognize them when you see them in other code.

What did you learn?

In this chapter, you learned

- What lists are
- How to add things to a list
- How to delete things from a list
- How to find out if a list contains a certain value
- How to sort a list
- How to make a copy of a list
- About tuples
- About lists of lists
- About Python dictionaries

Test your knowledge

1   What are two ways to add something to a list?

2   What are two ways to remove something from a list?

3   What are two ways to get a sorted copy of a list, without changing the original list?

4   How do you find out whether a certain value is in a list?

5   How do you find out the location of a certain value in a list?

6   What's a tuple?

7   How do you make a list of lists?

8   How do you get a single value from a list of lists?

9   What is a dictionary?

10   How do you add an item to a dictionary?

11   How do you look up an item from its key?

Try it out

1   Write a program to ask the user for five names. The program should store the names in a list and print them all out at the end. It should look something like this:

```
Enter 5 names:
Tony
Paul
Nick
Michel
Kevin
The names are Tony Paul Nick Michel Kevin
```

2   Modify the program from question #1 to print both the original list of names and a sorted list.

3 Modify the program from question #1 to display only the third name the user typed in, like this:

```
The third name you entered is:  Nick
```

4 Modify the program from question #1 to let the user replace one of the names. She should be able to choose which name to replace and then type in the new name. Finally, display the new list like this:

```
Enter 5 names:
Tony
Paul
Nick
Michel
Kevin
The names are Tony Paul Nick Michel Kevin
Replace one name.  Which one? (1-5): 4
New name: Peter
The names are Tony Paul Nick Peter Kevin
```

5 Write a dictionary program that lets users enter certain words and definitions and then look them up later. Make sure you let the user know if their word isn't in the dictionary yet. It should look something like this when it runs:

```
Add or look up a word (a/l)? a
Type the word: computer
Type the definition: A machine that does very fast math
Word added!
Add or look up a word (a/l)? l
Type the word: computer
A machine that does very fast math
Add or look up a word (a/l)? l
Type the word: qwerty
That word isn't in the dictionary yet.
```

## CHAPTER 13

Functions

Pretty soon, our programs are going to start getting bigger and more complicated. We need some ways to organize them in smaller pieces so they're easier to write and keep track of.

There are three main ways to break programs into smaller parts. *Functions* are like building blocks of code that you can use over and over again. *Objects* are a way of describing pieces of your program as self-contained units. *Modules* are just separate files that contain parts of your program. In this chapter, we'll learn about functions, and in the next two chapters, we'll learn about objects and modules. Then we'll have all the basic tools we need to start using graphics and sounds, and to create games.

Functions—the building blocks

In the simplest of terms, a *function* is a chunk of code that does something. It's a small piece that you can use to build a bigger program. You can put the piece together with other pieces, just like building something with toy blocks.

You create or *define* a function with Python's def keyword. You then use or *call* the function by using its name. Let's start with a simple example.

Creating a function

The code in the following listing defines a function and then uses it. This function prints a mailing address to the screen.

Listing 13.1   Creating and using a function

```
def printMyAddress():
    print "Warren Sande"
    print "123 Main Street"
    print "Ottawa, Ontario, Canada"
    print "K2M 2E9"
    print
printMyAddress()
```
Defines (creates) the function

Calls (uses) the function

In line 1, we define a function, using the **def** keyword. We give the name of the function followed by parentheses **()** and then a colon:

```
def printMyAddress():
```

I will explain what the parentheses are for soon. The colon tells Python that a block of code is coming next (just like **for** loops, **while** loops, and **if** statements).

Then, we have the code that makes up the function.

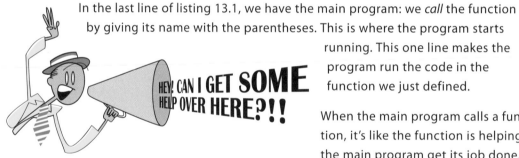

In the last line of listing 13.1, we have the main program: we *call* the function by giving its name with the parentheses. This is where the program starts running. This one line makes the program run the code in the function we just defined.

When the main program calls a function, it's like the function is helping the main program get its job done.

The code inside the **def** block isn't part of the main program, so when the program runs, it skips over that part and starts with the first line that isn't inside a **def** block. The next figure shows what happens when you call a function. I added one extra line at the end of the program that prints a message after the function is done.

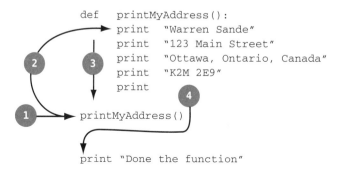

These are the steps in the previous figure:

1. Start here. This is the beginning of the main program.
2. When we call the function, we jump to the first line of code in the function.
3. Execute each line of the function.
4. When the function is finished, we continue where we left off in the main program.

Calling a function

Calling a function means running the code that is inside the function. If you define a function but never call it, that code will never run.

You call a function by using its name and a set of parentheses. Sometimes there's something in the parentheses and sometimes not.

Try running the program in listing 13.1 and see what happens. You should see something like this:

```
>>> =================== RESTART ====================
>>>
Warren Sande
123 Main Street
Ottawa, Ontario, Canada
K2M 2E9

>>>
```

Now, that's exactly the same output we'd have gotten from a simpler program that looks like this:

```
print "Warren Sande"
print "123 Main Street"
print "Ottawa, Ontario, Canada"
print "K2M 2E9"
print
```

So why did we go to the trouble of making things more complex and using a function in listing 13.1?

The main reason to use functions is that, once you have defined them, you can use them over and over again just by *calling* them. So if we wanted to print the address five times, we could do this:

```
printMyAddress()
printMyAddress()
printMyAddress()
printMyAddress()
printMyAddress()
```

And the output would be

```
Warren Sande
123 Main Street
Ottawa, Ontario, Canada
K2M 2E9

Warren Sande
123 Main Street
Ottawa, Ontario, Canada
K2M 2E9

Warren Sande
123 Main Street
Ottawa, Ontario, Canada
K2M 2E9

Warren Sande
123 Main Street
Ottawa, Ontario, Canada
K2M 2E9

Warren Sande
123 Main Street
Ottawa, Ontario, Canada
K2M 2E9
```

You might say that you could do the same thing with a loop instead of a function.

Well, I could do the same thing with a loop instead of using a function!

I knew that was coming…. In this case, you *could* do the same thing with a loop. But if you wanted to print the address at different places in a program instead of all at once, a loop wouldn't work.

Another reason to use a function is that you can make it behave differently each time it runs. You're going to see how to do that in the next section.

Passing arguments to a function

Now it's time to see what the parentheses are for: *arguments*!

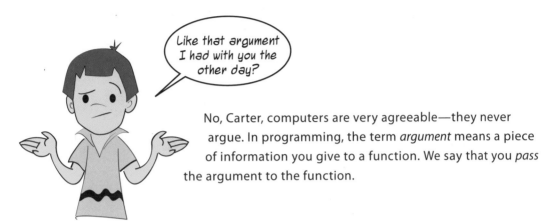

No, Carter, computers are very agreeable—they never argue. In programming, the term *argument* means a piece of information you give to a function. We say that you *pass* the argument to the function.

Imagine that you wanted to be able to use the address-printing function for any member of your family. The address would be the same for everybody, but the name would be different each time. Instead of having the name hard-coded as "Warren Sande" in the function, you can make it a variable. The variable is *passed* to the function when you call it.

An example is the easiest way to see how this works. In listing 13.2, I modified the address-printing function to use one argument for the name. Arguments are named, just like other variables. I called this variable `myName`.

When the function runs, the variable `myName` gets filled in with whatever argument we pass to the function when we call it. We pass the argument to the function by putting it inside the parentheses when we call the function.

So, in listing 13.2, the argument `myName` is assigned the value "Carter Sande".

Listing 13.2   Passing an argument to a function

```
def printMyAddress(myName):          ◄————   Passes myName argument
    print myName    ◄———— Prints the name     to the function
    print "123 Main Street"
    print "Ottawa, Ontario, Canada"
    print "K2M 2E9"                   Passes "Carter Sande" as the
    print                             argument to the function; the
                                      variable myName inside the
printMyAddress("Carter Sande")   ◄    function will have the value
                                      "Carter Sande"
```

If we run the code in listing 13.2, we get exactly what you'd expect:

```
>>> ===================== RESTART =====================
>>>
Carter Sande
123 Main Street
Ottawa, Ontario, Canada
K2M 2E9
```

This looks the same as the output we got from the first program, when we didn't use arguments. But now we can make the address print differently every time, like this:

```
printMyAddress("Carter Sande")
printMyAddress("Warren Sande")
printMyAddress("Kyra Sande")
printMyAddress("Patricia Sande")
```

And now, the output is different each time the function is called. The name changes, because we *pass* the function a different name each time:

```
>>> =========================== RESTART ===========================
>>>
Carter Sande
123 Main Street
Ottawa, Ontario, Canada
K2M 2E9

Warren Sande
123 Main Street
Ottawa, Ontario, Canada
K2M 2E9

Kyra Sande
123 Main Street
Ottawa, Ontario, Canada
K2M 2E9

Patricia Sande
123 Main Street
Ottawa, Ontario, Canada
K2M 2E9
```

Notice that whatever value we passed to the function was used inside the function and was printed as the name part of the address.

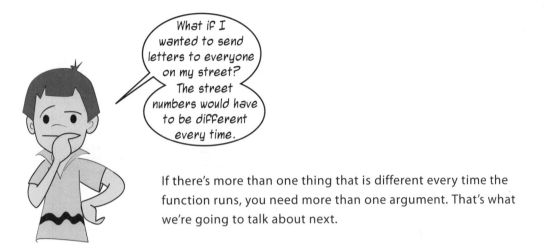

If there's more than one thing that is different every time the function runs, you need more than one argument. That's what we're going to talk about next.

Functions with more than one argument

In listing 13.2, our function had a single argument. But functions can have more than one argument. In fact, they can have as many as you need. Let's try an example with two arguments, and I think you'll get the idea. Then you can keep adding as many arguments as you need for the functions in your programs.

WORD BOX

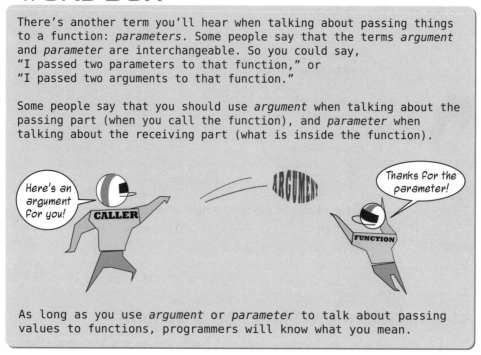

There's another term you'll hear when talking about passing things to a function: *parameters*. Some people say that the terms *argument* and *parameter* are interchangeable. So you could say, "I passed two parameters to that function," or "I passed two arguments to that function."

Some people say that you should use *argument* when talking about the passing part (when you call the function), and *parameter* when talking about the receiving part (what is inside the function).

As long as you use *argument* or *parameter* to talk about passing values to functions, programmers will know what you mean.

To send Carter's letters to everyone on the street, our address-printing function will need two arguments: one for the name, and one for the house number. The next listing shows what this would look like.

Listing 13.3   Function with two arguments

```
def printMyAddress(someName, houseNum):
    print someName
    print houseNum,
    print "Main Street"
    print "Ottawa, Ontario, Canada"
    print "K2M 2E9"
    print

printMyAddress("Carter Sande", "45")
printMyAddress("Jack Black", "64")
printMyAddress("Tom Green", "22")
printMyAddress("Todd White", "36")
```

Uses two variables, for two arguments

Both variables get printed

Comma makes house number and street print on the same line

Calls the function, passing it two parameters

When you use multiple arguments (or parameters), you separate them with a comma, just like items in a list, which brings us to our next topic....

How many is too many?

I said before that you can pass as many arguments as you want to a function. That is true, but if your function has more than five or six arguments, it might be time to think of doing things another way. One thing you can do is collect all the arguments in a *list* and then pass the list to the function. That way, you're passing a single variable (the list variable), which just happens to contain a bunch of values. It might make your code easier to read.

Functions that return a value

So far, our functions have just been doing stuff for us. But a very useful thing about functions is that they can also send you something back.

You have seen that you can send information (arguments) to functions, but functions can also send information back to the caller. The value that comes back from a function is called the *result* or *return value*.

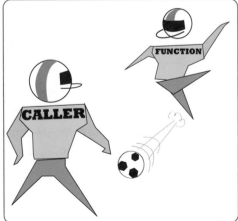

Returning a value

The way you make a function return a value is to use the Python `return` keyword inside the function. Here's an example:

```
def calculateTax(price, tax_rate):
    taxTotal = price + (price * tax_rate)
    return taxTotal
```

This will send the value `taxTotal` back out to the part of the program that called the function.

But when it's sent back, where does it go? Returned values go back to whatever code called the function. Here's an example:

```
totalPrice = calculateTax(7.99, 0.06)
```

The `calculateTax` function will return the value 8.4694, and that value will be assigned to `totalPrice`.

You can use a function to return values anywhere you'd use an expression. You can assign the return value to a variable (as we just did), use it in another expression, or print it, like this:

```
>>> print calculateTax(7.99, 0.06)
8.4694
>>> total = calculateTax(7.99, 0.06) + calculateTax(6.59,
   0.08)
```

You can also do nothing with the returned value, like this:

```
>>> calculateTax(7.49, 0.07)
```

In the last example, the function ran and calculated the total with tax, but we didn't use the result.

Let's make a program with a function that returns a value. In listing 13.4, the `calculateTax()` function returns a value. We give it the price before tax and the tax rate, and it returns the price after tax. We'll assign this value to a variable. So instead of just using the function's name like we did before, we need a variable, an equal sign (=), and then the function's name. The variable will be assigned the result that the `calculateTax()` function gives back.

Listing 13.4   Creating and using a function that returns a value

```
def calculateTax(price, tax_rate):
    total = price + (price * tax_rate)
    return total

my_price = float(raw_input ("Enter a price: "))

totalPrice = calculateTax(my_price, 0.06)
print "price = ", my_price, " Total price = ", totalPrice
```

Sends result back to the main program | Function calculates tax and returns total

Calls function and stores the result in totalPrice

Try typing in, saving, and running the program in listing 13.4. Notice that the tax rate is fixed as 0.06 (which equals 6 percent tax) in the code. If the program had to handle different tax rates, you could have the user enter the tax rate as well as the price.

Variable scope

You might have noticed that we have variables outside the function, like `totalPrice`, as well as variables inside the function, like `total`. These are just two names for the same thing. It's like back in chapter 2, when we had `YourTeacher = MyTeacher`.

In our `calculateTax` example, `totalPrice` and `total` are two tags attached to the same thing. With functions, the names inside the function are only created when the function runs. They don't even exist before the function runs or after it has finished running. Python has something called *memory management* that does this automatically. Python creates new names to use inside the function when it runs, *and then deletes them when the function is finished*. That last part is important: when the function is done running, any names inside it cease to exist.

While the function is running, the names *outside* the function are sort of on hold—they're not being used. Only the names inside the function are being used. The part of a program where a variable is used (or available to be used) is called its *scope*.

Local variables

In listing 13.4, the variables `price` and `total` were only used within the function. We say that `price`, `total`, and `tax_rate` are *in the scope* of the `calculateTax()` function. Another term that is used is *local*. The `price`, `total`, and `tax_rate` variables are *local variables* in the `calculateTax()` function.

One way to see what this means is to add a line to the program in listing 13.4 that tries to print the value of `price` somewhere outside the function. The following listing does this.

Listing 13.5   Trying to print a local variable

```
def calculateTax(price, tax_rate):          Defines a function to
    total = price + (price * tax_rate)      calculate tax and
    return total                            return the total

my_price = float(raw_input ("Enter a price: "))
                                            Calls the function and
totalPrice = calculateTax(my_price, 0.06)  ◁——— stores and prints the result
print "price = ", my_price, " Total price = ", totalPrice
print price                                  ◁——— Tries to print price
```

If you run this, you'll get an error that looks like this:

```
Traceback (most recent call last):
  File "C:/.../Listing_13-5.py", line 9, in <module>
    print price                          This line explains
NameError: name 'price' is not defined  ◁—  the error
```

The last line of the error message tells the story: when we're not inside the `calculateTax()` function, the variable `price` is *not defined*. It only exists while the function is running. When we tried to print the value of `price` from outside the function (when the function was not running), we got an error.

Global variables

In contrast to the *local* variable `price`, the variables `my_price` and `totalPrice` in listing 13.5 are defined *outside* the function, in the main part of the program. We use the term *global* for a variable that has a wider scope. In this case, *wider* means the main part of the program, not what's inside the function. If we expanded the program in listing 13.5, we could use the variables `my_price` and `totalPrice` in another place in the program, and they would still have the values we gave them earlier. They would still be *in scope*. Because we can use them anywhere in the program, we say they're *global variables*.

In listing 13.5, when we were outside the function and tried to print a variable that was inside the function, we got an error. The variable didn't exist; it was *out of scope*. What do you think will happen if we do the opposite: try to print a global variable from inside the function?

The next listing tries to print the variable `my_price` from inside the `calculateTax()` function. Try it and see what happens.

Listing 13.6 Using a global variable inside a function

```
def calculateTax(price, tax_rate):
    total = price + (price * tax_rate)
    print my_price                          ←——— Tries to print
    return total                                  my_price

my_price = float(raw_input ("Enter a price: "))

totalPrice = calculateTax(my_price, 0.06)
print "price = ", my_price, " Total price = ", totalPrice
```

Did it work? Yes! But why?

When we started talking about variable scope, I told you that Python uses memory management to automatically create local variables when a function runs. The memory manager does some other things, too. In a function, if you use a variable name that has been defined in the main program, Python will let you use the global variable as long as you don't try to change it.

So you can do this

```
print my_price
```

or this

```
your_price = my_price
```

because neither of these changes **my_price**.

If any part of the function tries to change the variable, Python creates a new local variable instead. So if you do this

```
my_price = my_price + 10
```

then **my_price** is a new local variable that Python creates when the function runs.

In the example in listing 13.6, the value that was printed was the *global* variable **my_price**, because the function didn't change it. The program in listing 13.7 shows you that, if you do try to change the global variable inside the function, you get a new, local variable instead. Try running it and see.

Listing 13.7   Trying to modify a global variable inside a function

```
def calculateTax(price, tax_rate):
    total = price + (price * tax_rate)        Modifies my_price
                                              inside the function        Prints the local
                                                                         version of my_price
    my_price = 10000
    print "my_price (inside function) = ", my_price
    return total

my_price = float(raw_input ("Enter a price: "))    Prints the global
                                                   version of my_price
totalPrice = calculateTax(my_price, 0.06)
print "price = ", my_price, " Total price = ", totalPrice
print "my_price (outside function) = ", my_price
```

Modifies my_price inside the function

Prints the local version of my_price

The variable my_price here is a different chunk of memory than the my_price here

Prints the global version of my_price

If you run the code in listing 13.7, the output will look like this:

```
>>> ========================= RESTART =========================
>>>
Enter a price: 7.99
my_price (inside function) =  10000
price =  7.99  Total price =  8.4694
my_price (outside function) =  7.99
```

Prints my_price from inside the function

Prints my_price from outside the function

As you can see, there are now two different variables called **my_price**, with different values. One is the *local variable* inside the **calculateTax()** function that we set to 10,000. The other is the *global variable* we defined in the main program to capture the user's input, which was 7.99.

Forcing a global

In the last section, you saw that, if you try to change the value of a *global variable* from inside a function, Python creates a new *local variable* instead. This is meant to prevent functions from accidentally changing global variables.

However, there are times when you *want* to change a global variable from inside a function. So how do you do it?

Python has a keyword, **global**, that lets you do that. You use it like this:

```
def calculateTax(price, tax_rate):      Tells Python you want to use
    global my_price                     the global version of my_price
```

If you use the `global` keyword, Python *won't* make a new local variable called `my_price`. It will use the global variable `my_price`. If there's no global variable called `my_price`, it will create one.

A bit of advice on naming variables

You saw in the previous sections that you can use the same names for global variables and local variables. Python will automatically create new local variables when it needs to, or you can prevent that with the `global` keyword. However, I strongly recommend that you don't reuse names.

As you might have noticed from some of the examples, it can be difficult to know whether the variable is the local version or the global version. It makes the code more confusing, because you have different variables with the same name. And wherever there's confusion, bugs love to creep in.

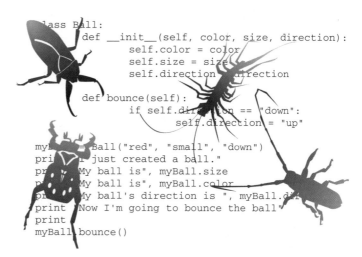

```
class Ball:
    def __init__(self, color, size, direction):
        self.color = color
        self.size = size
        self.direction = direction

    def bounce(self):
        if self.direction == "down":
            self.direction = "up"

myBall = Ball("red", "small", "down")
print "I just created a ball."
print "My ball is", myBall.size
print "My ball is", myBall.color
print "My ball's direction is ", myBall.direction
print "Now I'm going to bounce the ball"
print
myBall.bounce()
```

So for now, I recommend you use different names for local variables and global variables. That way, there's no confusion, and you'll keep the bugs at bay.

What did you learn?

In this chapter, you learned

- What a function is
- What arguments (or parameters) are
- How to pass an argument to a function
- How to pass multiple arguments to a function
- How to make a function return a value to the caller

- What variable scope is, and what local and global variables are
- How to use global variables in a function

Test your knowledge

1 What keyword do you use to create a function?
2 How do you call a function?
3 How do you pass information (arguments) to a function?
4 What's the maximum number of arguments a function can have?
5 How do you get information back from a function?
6 What happens to local variables in a function after the function is finished running?

Try it out

1 Write a function to print your name in big letters, like this:

```
  CCCC        A        RRRRR  TTTTTTT  EEEEE  RRRRR
 C    C     A A        R    R    T     E      R    R
 C         A   A       R    R    T     EEEE   R    R
 C        AAAAAAA      RRRRR     T     E      RRRRR
 C    C  A       A     R    R    T     E      R    R
  CCCC  A         A    R    R    T     EEEEE  R    R
```

Write a program that calls the function a number of times.

2 Make a function that will allow you to print any name, address, street, city, state or province, zip or postal code, and country in the world. (Hint: It needs seven arguments. You can pass them as individual arguments or as a list.)

3 Try using the example from listing 13.7, but making `my_price` global so you can see the difference in the resulting output.

4 Write a function to calculate the total value of some change—quarters, dimes, nickels, and pennies (just like in the last "Try it out" question from chapter 5). The function should return the total value of the coins. Then write a program that calls the function. The output should look like this when it runs:

```
quarters: 3
dimes: 6
nickels: 7
pennies: 2
total is $1.72
```

## CHAPTER 14

Objects

In the last few chapters, we've been looking at different ways of organizing data and programs and collecting things together. We have seen that *lists* are a way to collect variables (data) together, and *functions* are a way to collect some code together into a unit that you can use over and over again.

Objects take the idea of collecting things together one step further. Objects are a way to *collect functions and data together*. This is a very useful idea in programming, and it's used in many, many programs. In fact, if you look under the hood in Python, almost everything is an object. In programming terms, we say Python is *object oriented*. That means it's possible (in fact, quite easy) to use objects in Python. It isn't *necessary* to create your own objects, but it makes many things easier.

In this chapter, you'll learn what objects are and how to create and use them. In later chapters, when you start doing graphics, you'll be using objects a lot.

Objects in the real world

What's an object? If we were not talking about programming, and I asked you that question, we might have a conversation like this:

That's a good start at defining what an object is in Python, too. Take a ball, for example. You can do things to a ball, like pick it up, throw it, kick it, or inflate it (for some balls). We call these *actions*. You can also describe a ball by telling me its color, size, and weight. These are *attributes* of a ball.

WORD BOX

You can describe an object by describing its characteristics or *attributes*. One of the attributes of a ball is its shape. Most balls have a round shape. Other examples of attributes are color, size, weight, and cost. Another word for attributes is *properties*.

Real objects in the real world have

- Things that you can *do to* them (actions)
- Things that *describe* them (attributes or properties)

In programming, we have the same kind of thing.

Objects in Python

In Python, the characteristics, or "things you know" about an object, are also called *attributes*, so that should be easy to remember. In Python, the actions, or "things you can do" to an object, are called *methods*.

If you were to make a Python version or *model* of a ball, the ball would be an object and it would have *attributes* and *methods*.

The ball's *attributes* would look like this:

```
ball.color
ball.size
ball.weight
```

Those are all things you can *describe* about the ball.

The ball's *methods* would look like this:

```
ball.kick()
ball.throw()
ball.inflate()
```

Those are all things you can *do* to the ball.

What are attributes?

Attributes are all things you know (or can find out) about the ball. The ball's attributes are chunks of information—numbers, strings, and so on. Sound familiar? Yes, they're variables. They're just variables that are included inside the object.

You can display them:

```
print ball.size
```

You can assign values to them:

```
ball.color = 'green'
```

You can assign them to regular, non-object variables:

```
myColor = ball.color
```

You can also assign them to attributes in other objects:

```
myBall.color = yourBall.color
```

What are methods?

Methods are things you can *do* with an object. They're chunks of code that you can *call* to do something. Sound familiar? Yes, *methods* are just *functions* that are included inside the object.

You can do all the things with methods that you can do with any other function, including *passing arguments* and *returning values*.

Object = attributes + methods

So objects are a way of collecting together *attributes* and *methods* (things you know, and things you can do) for a thing. Attributes are information, and methods are actions.

What's the dot?

In our previous ball examples, you probably noticed the dot between the name of the object and the name of the attribute or method. That's just the Python notation for using the attributes and methods of an object: `object.attribute` or `object.method()`. Simple as that. It's called *dot notation*, and it's used in many programming languages.

Now you have the big picture about objects. Let's start making some!

Creating objects

There are two steps to creating an object in Python.

The first step is to define what the object will look like and act like—its attributes and methods. But creating this description doesn't actually create an object. It's kind of like the blueprints for a house. The blueprints tell you exactly what the house will look like, but a blueprint isn't a house. You can't live in a blueprint. You can just use it to build an actual house. In fact, you can use the blueprint to make many houses.

In Python the description or blueprint of an object is called a *class*.

The second step is to use the class to make an actual object. The object is called an *instance* of that class.

Let's look at an example of making a *class* and an *instance*. The following listing shows a class definition for a simple `Ball` class.

Listing 14.1 Creating a simple `Ball` class

```
class Ball:              ◁──────  This tells Python we're
                                  making a class
    def bounce(self):
        if self.direction == "down":         This is a method
            self.direction = "up"
```

In listing 14.1, we have a class definition for a ball with one method: `bounce()`. But what about attributes? Well, attributes don't really belong to the class, they belong to each instance. That's because each instance can have different attributes.

There are a couple of ways you can set the instance attributes. You'll see both ways in the following sections.

Creating an instance of an object

As we mentioned before, a class definition isn't an object. It's just the blueprints. Now let's build a house.

If we want to create an *instance* of a `Ball`, we do it like this:

```
myBall = Ball()
```

Our ball does not have any attributes yet, so let's give it some:

```
myBall.direction = "down"
myBall.color = "green"
myBall.size = "small"
```

This is one of the ways to define attributes for the object. You'll see the other way in the next section.

Now, let's try out one of the methods. Here's how we'd use the `bounce()` method:

```
myBall.bounce()
```

Let's put this all together into a program, with some `print` statements to see what's going on.

Listing 14.2   Using the Ball class

```
class Ball:

    def bounce(self):
        if self.direction == "down":
            self.direction = "up"

myBall = Ball()
myBall.direction = "down"
myBall.color = "red"
myBall.size = "small"

print "I just created a ball."
print "My ball is", myBall.size
print "My ball is", myBall.color
print "My ball's direction is", myBall.direction
print "Now I'm going to bounce the ball"
print
myBall.bounce()
print "Now the ball's direction is", myBall.direction
```

Here's our class, same as before

Makes an instance of our class

Sets some attributes

Prints the object's attributes

Uses a method

If you run the program in listing 14.2, you should see this:

```
>>> ========================= RESTART =========================
>>>
I just created a ball.
My ball is small
My ball is red
My ball's direction is down
Now I'm going to bounce the ball

Now the ball's direction is up
```

The attributes as we set them

Now we bounce() the ball

It changed direction, from down to up

Notice that after we called the `bounce()` method, the ball's `direction` changed from `down` to `up`, which is exactly what the code in the `bounce()` method is supposed to do.

Initializing an object

When we created our ball object, it didn't have anything filled in for the `size`, `color`, or `direction`. We had to fill those in *after* we created the object. But there's a way to set the properties of an object when it's being created. This is called *initializing* the object.

WORD BOX

Initializing means "getting something ready at the start." When we *initialize* something in software, we make it ready to use by getting it into the state or condition that we want.

When you create the class definition, you can define a special method called __init__()
that will run whenever a new instance of the class is created. You can pass arguments to the
__init__() method to create the instance with its properties set however you want. Here's
how this works.

Listing 14.3   Adding an __init__() method

```
class Ball:
    def __init__(self, color, size, direction):
        self.color = color
        self.size = size
        self.direction = direction

    def bounce(self):
        if self.direction == "down":
            self.direction = "up"

myBall = Ball("red", "small", "down")
print "I just created a ball."

print "My ball is", myBall.size
print "My ball is", myBall.color
print "My ball's direction is ", myBall.direction
print "Now I'm going to bounce the ball"
print
myBall.bounce()
print "Now the ball's direction is", myBall.direction
```

Here's the __init__() method.
2 underscores on either side
of init. Total of 4 underscores,
2 on either side.

← Attributes are passed in as
arguments to __init__()

If you run the program in listing 14.3, you should get the same output you got from
listing 14.2. The difference is, listing 14.3 uses the __init__() method to set the attributes.

If you say
print myBall,

you get something weird like this:
<__main__.Ball instance at 0x00BB83A0>

To change that,
put in a method called
__str__().

Make it return
what you want printed.
Then, every time you use
print myBall,
it'll say what you want.

It's one of the
"magic" __xxxx__() class
methods in Python!

Thanks for the tip, Carter. In the
next section, we'll see what these
"magic" methods are all about.

A "magic" method: __str__()

Objects in Python have some "magic" methods, as Carter calls them. They're not really magic, of course! They're just some methods that Python includes automatically when you create any class. Python programmers usually call them *special methods*.

You already saw the __init__() method that initializes an object when it's created. Every object has an __init__() method built in. If you don't put one in your class definition, the built-in one takes over, and all it does is create the object.

Another special method is __str__(), which tells Python what to display when you `print` an object. By default, Python tells you

- Where the instance is defined (in Carter's case __main__, which is the main part of the program)
- The class name (`Ball`)
- The memory location where the instance is being stored (that's the `0x00BB83A0` part)

But if you want `print` to display something different for your object, you can define your own __str__(), which will override the built-in one. The next listing shows an example.

Listing 14.4   Using __str__() to change how the object prints

```
class Ball:
    def __init__(self, color, size, direction):
        self.color = color
        self.size = size
        self.direction = direction

    def __str__(self):                                      Here's the
        msg = "Hi, I'm a " + self.size + " " + self.color + " ball!"   __str__()
        return msg                                          method
myBall = Ball("red", "small", "down")
print myBall
```

Now, if we run the program in listing 14.4, here's what we get:

```
>>> ================= RESTART =================
>>>
Hi, I'm a small red ball!
```

That looks a lot more friendly than `<__main__.Ball instance at 0x00BB83A0>`, don't you think? All the "magic" methods use two underscores before and two underscores after the name of the method.

What's `self`?

You might have noticed that the term "self" shows up in a few places in the class attributes and method definitions, like this:

```
def bounce(self):
```

What does `self` mean? Well, remember that we said you could use blueprints to build more than one house? You can also use a class to create more than one instance of an object, like this:

```
cartersBall = Ball("red", "small", "down")      Creating two instances
warrensBall = Ball("green", "medium", "up")     of the Ball class
```

When we call a method for one of these instances, like this,

```
warrensBall.bounce()
```

the method has to know which instance called it. Is it `cartersBall` that needs to bounce, or `warrensBall`? The `self` argument is what tells the method which object called it. It's called the *instance reference*.

But wait a minute! When we called the method, there was no argument in the parentheses of `warrensBall.bounce()`, but there's a `self` argument in the method. Where did the `self` argument come from, if we didn't pass anything? That's another little bit of "magic" that Python does with objects. When you call a class method, the information about which instance called—the *instance reference*—is automatically passed to the method.

It's like writing this:

```
Ball.bounce(warrensBall)
```

In this case, we told the `bounce()` method which ball to bounce. In fact, this code will work too, because that is exactly what Python does behind the scenes when you write `warrensBall.bounce()`.

By the way, the name **self** has no special meaning in Python. That's just the name everybody uses for the instance reference. It's another one of those conventions that make your code easier to read. You could name the instance variable whatever you want, but I strongly suggest you follow the convention and use **self**—it'll make things much less confusing.

In chapter 11, we made a program about hot dogs. Now, as an example of how to use objects, we're going to make a class for a hot dog.

An example class—HotDog

For this example, we'll assume that hot dogs always have a bun. (It's too messy otherwise.) We'll give our hot dog some attributes and some methods.

These are the attributes:

- **cooked_level**—A number that lets us know how long the hot dog has been cooked. We'll use 0–3 for raw, over 3 for medium, and over 5 for well-done, and anything over 8 will be charcoal! Our hot dogs will start out raw.
- **cooked_string**—A string describing how well-done the hot dog is.
- **condiments**—A list of what's on the hot dog, like ketchup, mustard, and so on.

These are the methods:

- **cook()**—Cooks the hot dog for some period of time. This will make the hot dog more well-done.
- **add_condiment()**—Adds condiments to the hot dog.
- **__init__()**—Creates our instance and sets the default properties.
- **__str__()**—Makes the **print** look nicer.

First, we need to define the class. Let's start with the **__init__()** method, which will set the default attributes for a hot dog:

```
class HotDog:
    def __init__(self):
        self.cooked_level = 0
        self.cooked_string = "Raw"
        self.condiments = []
```

We start with a raw hot dog and no condiments.

Now, let's make a method to cook our hot dog:

```
def cook(self, time):
    self.cooked_level = self.cooked_level + time   ←—— Increases the
    if self.cooked_level > 8:                           cooked level by the
        self.cooked_string = "Charcoal"                 amount of time
    elif self.cooked_level > 5:
        self.cooked_string = "Well-done"       Sets the strings for the
    elif self.cooked_level > 3:                different cooked levels
        self.cooked_string = "Medium"
    else:
        self.cooked_string = "Raw"
```

Before we go any further, let's test this part. First, we need to create an instance of a hot dog, and we'll check the attributes, too:

```
myDog = HotDog()
print myDog.cooked_level
print myDog.cooked_string
print myDog.condiments
```

Let's put this together into a program and run it. Here's the complete program (so far).

Listing 14.5   *Start of our hot dog program*

```
class HotDog:
    def __init__(self):
        self.cooked_level = 0
        self.cooked_string = "Raw"
        self.condiments = []
    def cook(self, time):
        self.cooked_level = self.cooked_level + time
        if self.cooked_level > 8:
            self.cooked_string = "Charcoal"
        elif self.cooked_level > 5:
            self.cooked_string = "Well-done"
        elif self.cooked_level > 3:
            self.cooked_string = "Medium"
        else:
            self.cooked_string = "Raw"
myDog = HotDog()
print myDog.cooked_level
print myDog.cooked_string
print myDog.condiments
```

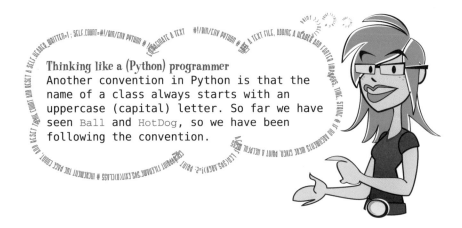

Thinking like a (Python) programmer
Another convention in Python is that the name of a class always starts with an uppercase (capital) letter. So far we have seen `Ball` and `HotDog`, so we have been following the convention.

Now, run the code in listing 14.5 and see what you get. It should look like this:

```
>>>
0          ◁——————— The cooked_level
Raw        ◁——————— The cooked_string
[]         ◁——————— The condiments
```

We see that the attributes are `cooked_level = 0`, `cooked_string = "Raw"`, and `condiments` is empty.

Now, let's test the `cook()` method. Add the lines below to the code in listing 14.5:

```
print "Now I'm going to cook the hot dog"          Cooks the hot dog
myDog.cook(4)                              ◁——————— for 4 minutes
print myDog.cooked_level        Checks the new
print myDog.cooked_string       cooked attributes
```

Run the program again. Now, the output should look like this:

```
>>>
0
Raw        Before cooking
[]
Now I'm going to cook the hot dog
4
Medium     After cooking
```

So our `cook()` method seems to work. The `cooked_level` went from 0 to 4, and the string updated too (from `Raw` to `Medium`).

Let's try adding some condiments. We need a new method for that. We could also add our __str__() function so it'll be easier to print the object. Edit the program so it looks like this.

Listing 14.6   HotDog class with cook(), add_condiments(), and __str__()

```
class HotDog:
    def __init__(self):
        self.cooked_level = 0
        self.cooked_string = "Raw"
        self.condiments = []
    def __str__(self):
        msg = "hot dog"
        if len(self.condiments) > 0:
            msg = msg + " with "
        for i in self.condiments:
            msg = msg+i+", "
        msg = msg.strip(", ")
        msg = self.cooked_string + " " + msg + "."
        return msg
    def cook(self, time):
        self.cooked_level=self.cooked_level+time
        if self.cooked_level > 8:
            self.cooked_string = "Charcoal"
        elif self.cooked_level > 5:
            self.cooked_string = "Well-done"
        elif self.cooked_level > 3:
            self.cooked_string = "Medium"
        else:
            self.cooked_string = "Raw"
    def addCondiment(self, condiment):
        self.condiments.append(condiment)

myDog = HotDog()
print myDog
print "Cooking hot dog for 4 minutes..."
myDog.cook(4)
print myDog
print "Cooking hot dog for 3 more minutes..."
myDog.cook(3)
print myDog
print "What happens if I cook it for 10 more minutes?"
myDog.cook(10)
print myDog
print "Now, I'm going to add some stuff on my hot dog"
myDog.addCondiment("ketchup")
myDog.addCondiment("mustard")
print myDog
```

Defines the new __str__() method

Defines the class

Defines the new add_condiments() method

Creates the instance

Tests to see if everything is working

This code listing is a bit long, but I still encourage you to type it all in. You already have part of it from listing 14.5. But if your fingers are tired or you don't have time, you can find it in the **\examples** folder or on the book's website.

Run the program, and see what you get. It should look like this:

```
>>> =============================== RESTART ===============================
>>>
Raw hot dog.
Cooking hot dog for 4 minutes...
Medium hot dog.
Cooking hot dog for 3 more minutes...
Well-done hot dog.
What happens if I cook it for 10 more minutes?
Charcoal hot dog.
Now, I'm going to add some stuff on my hot dog
Charcoal hot dog with ketchup, mustard.
```

The first part of the program creates the class. The second part tests the methods to cook our virtual hot dog and add some condiments. But judging by that last couple of lines, I think we cooked it too much. What a waste of ketchup and mustard!

Hiding the data

You might have realized that there are two ways you can view or change the data (attributes) inside an object. You can either access an attribute directly, like this

```
myDog.cooked_level = 5
```

or you can use a method that modifies the attribute, like this:

```
myDog.cook(5)
```

If the hot dog started out raw (`cooked_level = 0`), these would both do the same thing. They'd set the `cooked_level` to 5. So why did we bother making a method to do this? Why not just do it directly?

I can think of at least two reasons:

- If we were accessing the attributes directly, then cooking the hot dog would require at least two parts: changing the `cooked_level` and changing the `cooked_string`. With a method, we just make one method call, and it does everything we need.
- If we were accessing the attributes directly, we could do something like this:

```
cooked_level = cooked_level - 2
```

That would make the hot dog *less* cooked than it was before. But you can't *uncook* a hot dog! So that doesn't make sense. Using a method, we can make sure that the `cooked_level` only increases and never decreases.

WORD BOX

In programming terms, restricting the access to an object's data so you can only get it or change it by using methods is called *data hiding*. Python doesn't have any way to enforce data hiding, but you can write code that follows this rule if you want to.

So far, you have seen that objects have attributes and methods. You have seen how to create objects and how to initialize them with a special method called `__init__()`. You have also seen another special method called `__str__()` that makes objects print more nicely.

Polymorphism and inheritance

Next, we're going to look at the two aspects of objects that are probably the most important: *polymorphism* and *inheritance*. Those are two big long words, but they make objects very useful. I'll clearly explain what they mean in the next sections.

Polymorphism—same method, different behavior

Very simply, *polymorphism* means you can have two (or more) methods with the same name for different classes. These methods can behave differently, depending on which class they're applied to.

For example, let's say you were making a program to practice geometry, and you needed to calculate the area of different shapes, like triangles and squares. You might create two classes, like this:

```
class Triangle:
    def __init__(self, width, height):
        self.width = width
        self.height = height

    def getArea(self):
        area = self.width * self.height / 2.0
        return area

class Square:
    def __init__(self, size):
        self.size = size

    def getArea(self):
        area = self.size * self.size
        return area
```

Here is the Triangle class

Both have a method called getArea()

Here is the Square class

Both the `Triangle` class and the `Square` class have a method called `getArea()`. So if we had an instance of each class, like this,

```
>>> myTriangle = Triangle(4, 5)
>>> mySquare = Square(7)
```

then we could calculate the area of either one using `getArea()`:

```
>>> myTriangle.getArea()
10.0
>>> mySquare.getArea()
49
```

We used the method name `getArea()` for both shapes, but the method did something different for each shape. This is an example of polymorphism.

Inheritance—learning from your parents

In the real (non-programming) world, people can *inherit* things from their parents or other relatives. You can inherit traits like red hair, or you can inherit stuff like money or property.

In object-oriented programming, classes can inherit attributes and methods from other classes. This allows you to have whole "families" of classes that share common attributes and methods. That way, you don't have to start from scratch every time you want to add a member to the family.

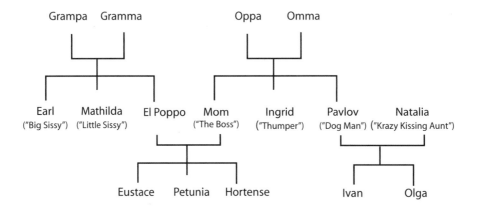

A class that inherits attributes or methods from another class is called a *derived class* or *subclass*. An example will help explain this.

Imagine we're making a game where the player can pick up various things along the way, like food, money, or clothing. We could make a class called `GameObject`. The `GameObject` class would have attributes like `name` (for example, "coin", "apple", or "hat") and methods like `pickUp()` (which would add the object to the player's collection of objects). All game objects would have these common methods and attributes.

Then, we could make a *subclass* for coins. The `Coin` class would be *derived* from `GameObject`. It would *inherit* the attributes and methods of `GameObject`, so the `Coin` class would automatically have a `name` attribute and a `pickUp()` method. The `Coin` class would also need a `value` attribute (how much the coin is worth) and a `spend()` method (so you could use the coin to buy something).

Let's see what the code might look like for these classes:

```
class GameObject:
    def __init__(self, name):
        self.name = name
                                              Defines GameObject class
    def pickUp(self, player):
        # put code here to add the object
        # to the player's collection
                            Coin is a subclass
class Coin(GameObject):  ←        of GameObject
    def __init__(self, value):
        GameObject.__init__(self, "coin")  ←— In __init__(), inherit GameObject's
        self.value = value                     init and add stuff to it

    def spend(self, buyer, seller):
        # put code here to remove the coin   A new spend() method
        # from the buyer's money and          for the Coin class
        # add it to the seller's money
```

Thinking ahead

In the last example, we didn't put any real code in the methods, just some comments explaining what the methods would do. It's a way of planning or thinking ahead for what you'll add later. The actual code would depend on how the game worked. Programmers often do this as a way to organize their thoughts when they're writing more complex code. The "empty" functions or methods are called *code stubs*.

If you tried to run the previous example, you'd get an error, because a function definition can't be empty.

They aren't empty. They have comments in them!

That's true, Carter, but comments don't count, because they're only for you, not for the computer.

The Python **pass** keyword is used as a placeholder when you want to make a code stub. So the code should really look like this:

```
class Game_object:
    def __init__(self, name):
        self.name = name

    def pickUp(self):
        pass
        # put code here to add the object
        # to the player's collection

class Coin(Game_object):
    def __init__(self, value):
        GameObject.__init__(self, "coin")
        self.value = value

    def spend(self, buyer, seller):
        pass
        # put code here to remove the coin
        # from the buyer's money and
        # add it to the seller's money
```

Add the pass keyword in these two places

I'm not going to give more detailed examples using objects, polymorphism, and inheritance in this chapter. You'll see many examples of objects and how they're used as you go through the rest of this book. You'll get a much better understanding of how to use objects when you use them in real programs, like games.

What did you learn?

In this chapter, you learned about

- What objects are
- Attributes and methods
- What a class is
- Creating an instance of a class
- Special methods: `__init__()` and `__str__()`
- Polymorphism
- Inheritance
- Code stubs

Test your knowledge

1. What keywords do you use to define a new object type?
2. What are attributes?
3. What are methods?
4. What's the difference between a class and an instance?
5. What name is usually used for the *instance reference* in a method?
6. What's polymorphism?
7. What's inheritance?

Try it out

1. Make a class definition for a `BankAccount`. It should have attributes for its name (a string), account number (a string or integer), and balance (a float). It should have methods to display the balance, make deposits, and make withdrawals.
2. Make a class called `InterestAccount` that earns interest. It should be a subclass of `BankAccount` (so it inherits the attributes and methods). It should also have an attribute for interest rate and a method to add interest. To keep things simple, assume that the `addInterest()` method will be called once each year to calculate the interest and update the balance.

Modules

This is the last chapter that talks about ways of collecting things together. We have already learned about *lists*, *functions*, and *objects*. In this chapter, we'll learn about *modules*. In the next chapter, we'll use a module called Pygame to start drawing some graphics.

What's a module?

A *module* is a piece or part of something. We say something is *modular* if it comes in pieces or you can easily separate it into pieces. LEGO blocks might be the perfect example of something modular. You can take a bunch of different pieces and build many different things with them.

In Python, modules are smaller pieces of a bigger program. Each module, or piece, is a separate file on your hard drive. You can take a big program and split it up into more than one module, or file. Or you can go the other way—start with one small module and keep adding pieces to make a big program.

Why use modules?

So why go to all the trouble of splitting a program up into smaller pieces, when you're going to need them all to make the program work? Why not just leave everything in one big file?

There are a few reasons:

- It makes the files smaller, which makes it easier to find things in your code.
- Once you create a module, you can use it in lots of programs. That saves you from starting all over again next time you need the same functions.
- You don't always need to use all the modules together. Being modular means that you can use different combinations of the parts to do different jobs, just as you can make many different things out of the same set of LEGO blocks.

Buckets of blocks

In the chapter about functions (chapter 13), we said that functions are like building blocks. You can think of a module as a bucket of building blocks. You can have as few or as many blocks in a bucket as you want, and you can have many different buckets. Maybe you have one bucket for all the square blocks, one for the flat pieces, and one for all the odd-shaped blocks. That's usually how programmers use modules—they collect similar kinds of functions together in a module. Or they might collect all the functions they need for a project together in a module, just as you would gather all the blocks you need for a castle together in one bucket.

How do we create modules?

Let's create a module. A module is just a Python file, like the one in listing 15.1. Type the code from the listing in an IDLE editor window, and save it as **my_module.py**.

Listing 15.1   Creating a module

```
# this is the file "my_module.py"
# we're going to use it in another program
def c_to_f(celsius):
    fahrenheit = celsius * 9.0 / 5 + 32
    return fahrenheit
```

That's it! You have just created a module! Your module has one function in it, the `c_to_f()` function, which converts a temperature from Celsius to Fahrenheit.

Next, we'll use **my_module.py** in another program.

How do we use modules?

In order to use something that is in a module, you first have to tell Python which modules you want to use. The Python keyword that lets you include other modules in your program is `import`. You use it like this:

```
import my_module
```

Let's write a program that uses the module we just wrote. We're going to use the `c_to_f()` function to do a temperature conversion.

You already saw how to use a function and pass parameters (or arguments) to it. The only difference here is that the function will be in a separate file from our main program, so we'll have to use `import`. The program in the next listing uses the module we just wrote, **my_module.py**.

Listing 15.2   Using a module

```
import my_module                        ◁─────  my_module contains
                                                the c_to_f() function
celsius = float(raw_input ("Enter a temperature in Celsius: "))
fahrenheit = c_to_f(celsius)
print "That's ", fahrenheit, " degrees Fahrenheit"
```

Create a new IDLE editor window, and type in this program. Save it as **modular.py**, and then run it to see what happens. You will need to save it in the same folder (or directory) as **my_module.py**.

Did it work? You should have seen something like this:

```
>>> ========================= RESTART =========================
>>>
Enter a temperature in Celsius: 34

Traceback (most recent call last):
  File "C:/MyPythonPrograms/modular.py", line 4, in <module>
    fahrenheit = c_to_f(celsius)
NameError: name 'c_to_f' is not defined
```

It didn't work! What happened? The error message says that the function `c_to_f()` isn't defined. But we know it's defined in **my_module**, and we *did* import that module.

The answer is that we have to be more specific in telling Python about functions that are defined in other modules. One way to fix the problem is to change the line

```
fahrenheit = c_to_f(celsius)
```

to

```
fahrenheit = my_module.c_to_f(celsius)
```

Now we're specifically telling Python that the `c_to_f()` function is in the **my_module** module. Try the program with this change and see if it works.

Namespaces

You can also import certain features from a module like

```
>>> from time import sleep
```
or
```
>>> from pygame import display
```

You see? You can use `from` to import certain parts of a module.

What Carter mentioned is related to something called *namespaces*. This is a bit of a complicated topic, but it's something you need to know about, so now is a good time to talk about it.

What's a namespace?

Imagine that you're in Mr. Morton's class at school, and there's someone named Shawn in your class. Now imagine that, in another class in your school taught by Mrs. Wheeler, there's another Shawn. If you're in your own class and you say, "Shawn has a new backpack," everyone in your class will know (or at least they'll assume) that you mean the Shawn in your class. If you meant the other one, you'd say, "Shawn in Mrs. Wheeler's class," or "the other Shawn," or something like that.

In your class, there's only one Shawn, so when you say "Shawn," your classmates know which person you're talking about. To put this another way, in the space of your class, there's only one name "Shawn." Your class is your *namespace*, and in that namespace, there's only one Shawn, so there's no confusion.

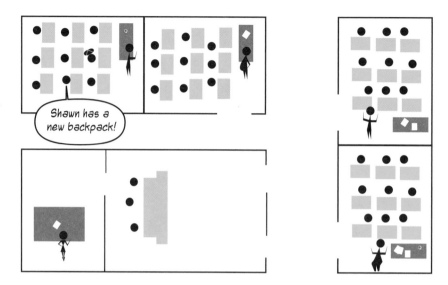

Now, if the principal has to call Shawn to the office over the public address system, she can't just say, "Would Shawn please come to the office." If she did that, both Shawns would show up at the office. For the principal using the public address system, the namespace is the whole school. That means everyone in the school is listening for the name, not just one class. So she has to be more specific about which Shawn she means. She would have to say something like, "Would Shawn from Mr. Morton's class please come to the office."

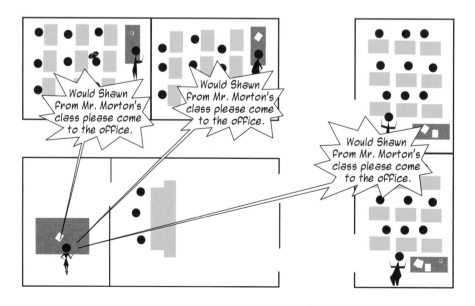

The other way the principal could get the correct Shawn is to go to the doorway of your class and say, "Shawn, would you please come with me." There would be only one Shawn listening, and she would get the right one. In that case, the namespace would be just one classroom, not the whole school.

In general terms, programmers refer to smaller namespaces (like your classroom) as *local* namespaces and larger ones (like the whole school) as *global* namespaces.

Importing namespaces

Let's assume that there's nobody named Fred in your school, John Young School. If the principal goes on the public address system and asks for Fred, she won't get anyone. Now imagine that another school down the road, Stephen Leacock School, is having some repairs done, so one of their classes moves into a portable at your school. In that class, there's a student named Fred. But that portable isn't connected to the public address system yet. If the principal calls for Fred, she won't get anybody. But if she connects the new portable to the public address system and then calls for Fred, she will get the Fred from Stephen Leacock School.

Connecting the portable from the other school is like importing a module in Python. When you import a module, you have access to all the names in that module: all the variables, all the functions, and all the objects.

Importing a module means the same thing as importing a namespace. When you import the module, you import the namespace.

There are two ways to import a namespace (or module). You can do it like this:

```
import StephenLeacock
```

If you do it that way, **StephenLeacock** is still a separate namespace. You have access to the namespace, but you have to specify which namespace you want before you use it. So the principal would have to do something like this:

```
call_to_office(StephenLeacock.Fred)
```

She would still have to give the namespace (**StephenLeacock**) as well as the name (**Fred**) if she wanted to reach Fred. That's what we did a few pages ago with our temperature-conversion program. To make it work, we wrote this:

```
fahrenheit = my_module.c_to_f(celsius)
```

We specified the namespace (**my_module**) as well as the name of the function (**c_to_f**).

Importing using `from`

The other way to import a namespace is like this:

```
from StephenLeacock import Fred
```

If the principal does it that way, the name **Fred** from **StephenLeacock** gets included in her namespace, and she can reach Fred like this:

```
call_to_office(Fred)
```

Because **Fred** is now in her namespace, she doesn't have to go to the **StephenLeacock** namespace to get **Fred**.

In this example, the principal only imported one name, **Fred**, from **StephenLeacock** into her local namespace. If she wanted to import everyone, she could do this:

```
from StephenLeacock import *
```

Here, the star (*) means *all*. But she has to be careful. If there are any students with the same names from Stephen Leacock School as there are from John Young School, there will be confusion.

Whew!

At this point, the whole namespace thing might still be a little fuzzy. Don't worry! It'll become clearer as you do examples in later chapters. Whenever you need to import modules, I'll explain exactly what you're doing.

Standard modules

Now that you know how to create and use modules, do you always have to write your own modules? No! That's one of the great things about Python.

Python comes with a bunch of standard modules to let you do things like find files, tell the time (or count time), or generate random numbers, among other things. Sometimes, people say Python has "batteries included," and that's what they're talking about—all of Python's standard modules. This is known as the *Python Standard Library*.

Why do these things have to be in separate modules? Well, they don't have to be, but the people who designed Python decided that it would be more efficient. Otherwise, every Python program would have to include every possible function. This way, you just include the ones you need.

Of course, some things (like `print`, `for`, and `if-else`) are basic commands in Python, so you don't need a separate module for them—they're in the main part of Python.

If Python doesn't have a module for something you want to do (like make a graphical game), there are other add-on modules that you can download, usually for free! We have included several of these with this book, and they were installed if you used the install program on the book's website. If not, you can always install them separately.

Let's look at a couple of the standard modules.

Time

The `time` module lets you get information from your computer's clock, like the date and the time. It also lets you add delays to your programs. (Sometimes the computer does things too quickly, and you have to slow it down.)

The `sleep()` function in the `time` module is used to add a delay— that is, to make the program wait and do nothing for a while. It's like putting your program to sleep, which is why the function is called `sleep()`. You tell it how many seconds you want it to sleep.

The program in the following listing demonstrates how the `sleep()` function works. Try typing, saving, and running it, and see what happens.

Listing 15.3   Putting your program to sleep

```
import time
print "How",
time.sleep(2)
print "are",
time.sleep(2)
print "you",
time.sleep(2)
print "today?"
```

Notice that, when we called the `sleep()` function, we had to put `time.` in front of it. That's because, even though we `imported` `time`, we didn't make it part of the main program's namespace. So every time we want to use the `sleep()` function, we have to call `time.sleep()`.

If we tried something like this,

```
import time
sleep(5)
```

it wouldn't work, because `sleep()` isn't in our namespace. We'd get an error message like this:

```
NameError: name 'sleep' is not defined
```

But if you import it like this,

```
from time import sleep
```

that tells Python, "Look for the variable (or function or object) named `sleep` in the `time` module, and include it in my namespace." Now we could use the `sleep()` function without putting `time.` in front of it:

```
from time import sleep
print 'Hello, talk to you again in 5 seconds...'
sleep(5)
print 'Hi again'
```

If you want the convenience of importing names into the local namespace (so you don't have to specify the module name every time), but you don't know which names in the module you'll need, you can use the star (*) to import all names into your namespace:

```
from time import *
```

The * means *all*, so this imports all the available names from the module. You have to be careful with this one. If you create a name in your program that is the same as one in the `time` module, there will be a conflict. Importing with * isn't the best way to do it. It's better to only import the parts that you need.

Remember the countdown program we made in chapter 8 (listing 8.6)? Now you know what the line `time.sleep(1)` in that program was doing.

Random numbers

The `random` module is used for generating random numbers. This is very useful in games and simulations.

Let's try using the `random` module in interactive mode:

```
>>> import random
>>> print random.randint(0, 100)
4
>>> print random.randint(0, 100)
72
```

Each time you use `random.randint()`, you get a new, random integer. Because we passed the arguments 0 and 100 to it, the integer will be between 0 and 100. We used `random.randint()` in the number-guessing program in chapter 1 to create the secret number.

If you want a random decimal number, use `random.random()`. You don't have to put anything between the brackets, because `random.random()` always gives you a number between 0 and 1:

```
>>> print random.random()
0.270985467261
>>> print random.random()
0.569236541309
```

If you want a random number between, say, 0 and 10, you can just multiply the result by 10:

```
>>> print random.random() * 10
3.61204895736
>>> print random.random() * 10
8.10985427783
```

What did you learn?

In this chapter, you learned

- What a module is
- How to create a module
- How to use a module in another program
- What namespaces are
- What's meant by *local* and *global* namespaces and variables
- How to bring names from other modules into your namespace

And you also saw a couple of examples of Python's standard modules.

Test your knowledge

1. What are some of the advantages of using modules?
2. How do you create a module?
3. What Python keyword do you use when you want to use a module?
4. Importing a module is the same as importing a _____.
5. What are two ways to import the `time` module so that you have access to all the names (that is, all the variables, functions, and objects) in that module?

Try it out

1. Write a module that has the "print your name in big letters" function from the "Try it out" section in chapter 13. Then write a program that imports the module and calls the function.
2. Modify the code in listing 15.2 so that you bring `c_to_f()` into the main program's namespace. That is, change it so you can write

   ```
   fahrenheit = c_to_f(celsius)
   ```

   instead of

   ```
   fahrenheit = my_module.c_to_f(celsius)
   ```

3. Write a short program to generate a list of five random integer numbers from 1 to 20, and print them out.
4. Write a short program that prints out a random decimal number every 3 seconds for 30 seconds.

## CHAPTER 16

Graphics

You have been learning about a lot of the basic elements of computer programming: input and output, variables, decisions, loops, lists, functions, objects, and modules. I hope you have enjoyed filling up your brain with all this stuff! Now it's time to start having a bit more fun with programming and Python.

In this chapter, you'll learn how to draw things on the screen, like lines, shapes, colors, and even a bit of animation. This will help us make some games and other programs in the next few chapters.

Getting some help—Pygame

Getting graphics (and sound) to work on your computer can be a little complicated. It involves the operating system, your graphics  card, and a lot of low-level code that we don't really want to worry about for now. So we're going to use a Python module called Pygame to help make things a bit simpler.

Pygame lets you create graphics and the other things you need to make games work on different computers and operating systems, without having to know all the messy details of each system. Pygame is free, and a version of Pygame comes with this book. It should be installed if you used the book's installer to install Python. If not, you'll have to install it separately. You can get it from the Pygame website, **www.pygame.org**.

A Pygame window

The first thing we need to do is make a window where we'll start drawing our graphics. Here's a very simple program that just makes a Pygame window.

Listing 16.1   Making a Pygame window

```
import pygame
pygame.init()
screen = pygame.display.set_mode([640, 480])
```

Try running this program. What do you see? Depending on what operating system you have, you might see a window (filled with black) pop up on the screen very briefly. Or you might get a window that doesn't close when you try to close it. What's up with that?

Well, Pygame is meant for making games. Games don't just do things on their own—they have to interact with the player. So Pygame programs have something called an *event loop* that constantly checks for the user doing something, like pressing keys, moving the mouse, or closing the window. Pygame programs need to have an event loop running all the time. In our first Pygame program, we didn't start the event loop, so the program didn't work properly.

The way we keep the Pygame event loop running is by using a `while` loop. We want the loop to keep running as long as the user is running our game. Because Pygame programs don't usually have a menu, the user will close the program by using the X in the top-right corner of the window (in Windows) or the close button in the top-left corner (for MacOS). For Linux systems, the window-closing icon varies depending on the window manager and GUI framework that is used—but if you're using Linux, I'm assuming you know how to close a window!

The code in the next listing opens a Pygame window and keeps it open until the user closes the window

Listing 16.2   Making the Pygame window work properly

```
import pygame
pygame.init()
screen = pygame.display.set_mode([640, 480])
running  = True
while running:
    for event in pygame.event.get():
        if event.type == pygame.QUIT:
            running = False
pygame.quit()
```

Run the listing, and you should see a Pygame window that works properly and closes when you try to close it.

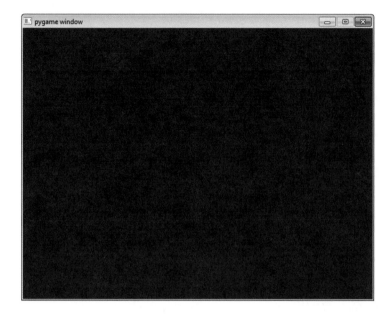

How exactly does the code in that `while` loop work? It uses the Pygame *event loop*. But we're going to save that topic for chapter 18, where we talk all about events in Pygame.

Drawing in the window

Now we have a Pygame window that stays open until we close it—and closes gracefully when we do. The [640, 480] in the third line of listing 16.2 is the size of our window: 640 pixels wide by 480 pixels high. Let's start drawing some graphics in there. Change your program so it looks like this.

Listing 16.3   Drawing a circle

```
import pygame, sys
pygame.init()
screen = pygame.display.set_mode([640,480])
screen.fill([255,255,255])
pygame.draw.circle(screen, [255,0,0],[100,100], 30, 0)
pygame.display.flip()
running = True
while running:
    for event in pygame.event.get():
        if event.type == pygame.QUIT:
            running = False
pygame.quit()
```

Fills the window with a white background

Add these three lines

Draws a circle

Flips your monitor over... Just kidding!

What's the "flip"?

The display object in Pygame (ours is called `screen`, which we created in line 3 of listing 16.3) has two copies of whatever is displayed in the Pygame window. The reason is that, when we start doing animation, we want to make it as smooth and fast as possible. So instead of updating the display every time we make a small change to our graphics, we can make a number of changes and then "flip" to the new version of the graphics. This makes the changes appear all at once, instead of one by one. This way we don't get half-drawn circles (or aliens, or whatever) on our display.

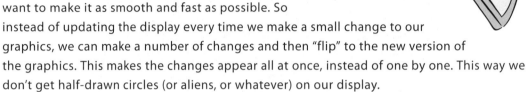

Think of the two copies as being a current screen and a "next" screen. The current screen is what you see right now. The "next" screen is what you'll see when you do a flip. You make all your changes on the "next" screen and then flip to it so you can see them.

How to make a circle

When you run the program in listing 16.3, you should see a red circle near the upper-left corner of the window, like this:

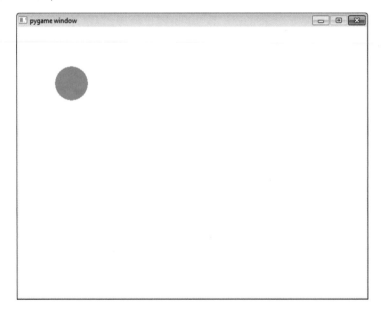

Not surprisingly, the `pygame.draw.circle()` function draws a circle. You have to tell it five things:

- On what *surface* to draw the circle. (In this case, it's on the surface we defined in line 3, called `screen`, which is the display surface.)

- What *color* to draw it. (In this case, it's red, which is represented by the `[255, 0, 0]`).
- At what *location* to draw it. (In this case, it's at `[100, 100]`, which is 100 pixels down and 100 pixels over from the top-left corner.)
- What *size* to draw it. (In this case, it's 30, which is the radius in pixels—the distance from the center of the circle to its outer edge.)
- The *width of the line*. (If `width = 0`, the circle is filled in completely, as it is here.)

Now we're going to look at these five things in more detail.

WORD BOX

The word *pixel* is short for "picture element." This means one dot on your screen or in an image. If you look at any picture with an image viewer and zoom in (make the image really big), you can see the individual pixels. Here's a regular view of a photo and a zoomed-in version where you can see the pixels.

Pixels

When I look closely at a computer screen, I see these little lines. Do they separate the pixels?

Wow, you have good eyes! The little lines are actually the rows of pixels. A typical computer screen might have 768 rows of pixels, with each row having 1,024 pixels in it. We'd say that screen has "1024 x 768 resolution." Some screens have more pixels, and some have fewer.

Pygame surfaces

If I asked you to draw a picture in real life, one of your first questions would be, "What should I draw it on?" In Pygame, a *surface* is what you draw on. The *display surface* is the one you see on the screen. That's the one we called `screen` in listing 16.3. But a Pygame program can have many surfaces, and you can copy images from one surface to another. You can also do things to surfaces, like rotate them and resize them (make them bigger or smaller).

As I mentioned before, there are two copies of the display surface. In software lingo, we say the display surface is *double-buffered*. This is so you don't get half-completed shapes and images drawn on the screen. You draw your circles, aliens, or whatever in the buffer and then "flip" the display surface to show you the completely drawn images.

Colors in Pygame

The color system used in Pygame is a common one used in many computer languages and programs. It's called *RGB*. The R, G, and B stand for red, green, and blue.

You might have learned in science class that you can make any color by combining or mixing the three *primary colors* of light: red, green, and blue. That's the same way it works on computers. Each color—red, green, and blue—gets a number from 0 to 255. Colors are given as a list of three integers, each one ranging from 0 to 255. If all the numbers are 0, there is none of any color, which is completely dark, so you get the color black. If they're all 255, you get the brightest of all three colors mixed together, which is white. If you have something like [255, 0, 0], that would be pure red with no green or blue. Pure green would be [0, 255, 0]. Pure blue would be [0, 0, 255]. If all three numbers are the same, like [150, 150, 150], you get some shade of grey. The lower the numbers, the darker the shade; the higher the numbers, the brighter the shade.

Color names

Pygame has a list of named colors you can use if you don't want to use the [R, G, B] notation. Over 600 color names are defined. I won't list them all here, but if you want to see what they are, search your hard drive for a file called **colordict.py**, and open it in a text editor.

If you want to use the color names, you have to add this line at the start of your program:

```
from pygame.color import THECOLORS
```

Then, when you want to use one of the named colors, you'll do it like this (in our circle example):

```
pygame.draw.circle(screen, THECOLORS["red"],[100,100], 30, 0)
```

If you want to play around and experiment with how the red, green, and blue combine to make different colors, you can try out the **colormixer.py** program that was put in the **\examples** folder when you ran this book's installer. This will let you try any combination of red, green, and blue to see what color you get.

WHAT'S GOING ON IN THERE?

Why 255? The range from 0 to 255 gives us 256 different values for each primary color (red, green, and blue). So, what's special about that number? Why not 200 or 300 or 500?

Two hundred and fifty-six is the number of different values you can make with 8 bits. That's all the possible combinations of eight 1s and 0s. Eight bits is also called a byte, and a byte is the smallest chunk of memory that has its own address. An address is the computer's way of finding particular pieces of memory.

It's like on your street. Your house or apartment has an address, but your room doesn't have its own address. A house is the smallest "addressable unit" on the street. A byte is the smallest "addressable unit" in your computer's memory.

They could have used more than 8 bits for each color, but the next amount that makes sense would be 16 bits (2 bytes), because it's not very convenient to use only part of a byte. And it turns out that, because of the way the human eye sees color, 8 bits is enough to make realistic-looking colors.

Because there are three values (red, green, blue), each with 8 bits, that's 24 bits in total, so this way of representing color is also known as "24-bit color." It uses 24 bits for each pixel, 8 for each primary color.

Locations—screen coordinates

If you want to draw or place something on the screen, you need to specify where on the screen it should go. There are two numbers: one for the *x*-axis (horizontal direction) and one for the *y*-axis (vertical direction). In Pygame, the numbers start at [0, 0] in the upper-left corner of the window.

When you see a pair of numbers like [320, 240], the first number is horizontal, or the distance from the left side. The second number is vertical, or the distance down from the top. In math and programming, the letter *x* is often used for horizontal distance, and *y* is often used for vertical distance.

We made our window 640 pixels wide by 480 pixels high. If we wanted to put the circle in the middle of the window, we'd need to draw it at [320, 240]. That's 320 pixels over from the left-hand edge and 240 pixels down from the top edge.

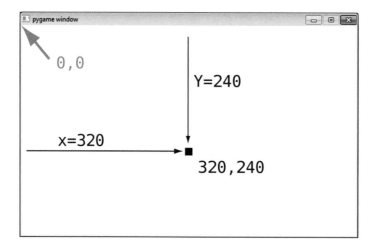

Let's try drawing the circle in the middle of the window. Here's the program.

Listing 16.4   Putting the circle in the middle of the window

```
import pygame, sys
pygame.init()
screen = pygame.display.set_mode([640,480])
screen.fill([255, 255, 255])
pygame.draw.circle(screen, [255,0,0],[320,240], 30, 0)
pygame.display.flip()
running = True
while running:
    for event in pygame.event.get():
        if event.type == pygame.QUIT:
            running = False
pygame.quit()
```

Change this from
[100, 100] to
[320, 240]

The location [320, 240] is used as the center of the circle. Compare the results of running listing 16.3 to the results you saw when you ran listing 16.4 to see the difference.

Size of shapes

When you use Pygame's **draw** functions to draw shapes, you have to specify what size to make the shape. For a circle, there is only one size: the radius. For something like a rectangle, you'd have to specify the length and width.

Pygame has a special kind of object called a **rect** (short for *rectangle*) that is used for defining rectangular areas. You define a **rect** using the coordinates of its top-left corner and its width and height:

```
Rect(left, top, width, height)
```

This defines both the location and the size. Here's an example:

```
my_rect = Rect(250, 150, 300, 200)
```

This creates a rectangle where the top-left corner is 250 pixels from the left side of the window and 150 pixels down from the top of the window. The rectangle is 300 pixels wide and 200 pixels high. Let's try it and see.

Substitute this line for line 5 in listing 16.4, and see what it looks like:

```
pygame.draw.rect(screen, [255,0,0], [250, 150, 300, 200], 0)
```

Color of the   Location and size of   Line width
rectangle   the rectangle   (or filled)

The location and size of the rectangle can be a simple list (or tuple) of numbers or a Pygame **Rect** object. So we could also substitute the preceding line with two lines like this

```
my_list = [250, 150, 300, 200]
pygame.draw.rect(screen, [255,0,0], my_list, 0)
```

or

```
my_rect = pygame.Rect(250, 150, 300, 200)
pygame.draw.rect(screen, [255,0,0], my_rect, 0)
```

Here's what the rectangle should look like. I added some dimensions to show you which numbers mean what:

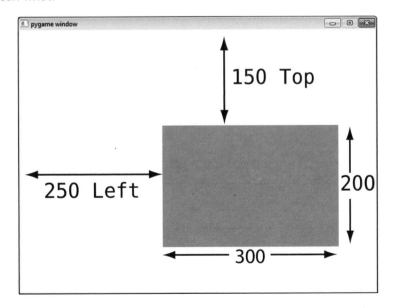

Notice that we only pass four arguments to `pygame.draw.rect`. That's because the `rect` has both location and size in a single argument. In `pygame.draw.circle`, the location and size are two different arguments, so we pass it five arguments.

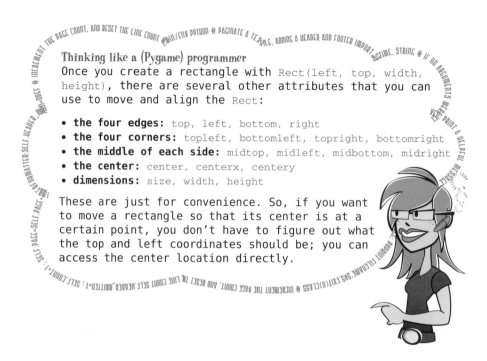

Thinking like a (Pygame) programmer
Once you create a rectangle with `Rect(left, top, width, height)`, there are several other attributes that you can use to move and align the `Rect`:

- **the four edges:** top, left, bottom, right
- **the four corners:** topleft, bottomleft, topright, bottomright
- **the middle of each side:** midtop, midleft, midbottom, midright
- **the center:** center, centerx, centery
- **dimensions:** size, width, height

These are just for convenience. So, if you want to move a rectangle so that its center is at a certain point, you don't have to figure out what the top and left coordinates should be; you can access the center location directly.

Line width

The last thing you need to specify when drawing shapes is how thick to make the line. In the examples so far, we used a line width of 0, which fills in the whole shape. If we used a different line width, we'd see an outline of the shape.

Try changing the line width to 2:

```
pygame.draw.rect(screen, [255,0,0], [250, 150, 300, 200], 2)
                                                    Make this 2
```

Try it and see how it looks. Try other line widths too.

Modern art?

Want to try making some computer-generated modern art? Just for fun, try the code in listing 16.5. You can start with what you had from listing 16.4 and modify it, or start from scratch.

Listing 16.5   Using `draw.rect` to make art

```python
import pygame, sys, random
pygame.init()
screen = pygame.display.set_mode([640,480])
screen.fill([255, 255, 255])
for i in range (100):
    width = random.randint(0, 250)
    height = random.randint(0, 100)
    top = random.randint(0, 400)
    left = random.randint(0, 500)
    pygame.draw.rect(screen, [0,0,0], [left, top, width, height], 1)
pygame.display.flip()
running = True
while running:
    for event in pygame.event.get():
        if event.type == pygame.QUIT:
            running = False
pygame.quit()
```

Run this and see what you get. It should look something like this:

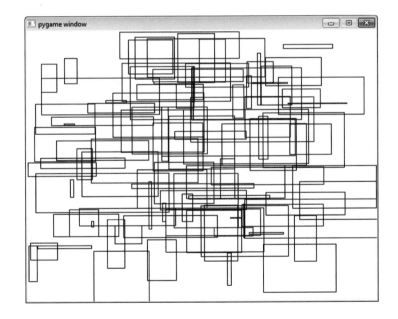

Do you understand how the program works? It draws 100 rectangles with random sizes and positions. To make it even more "artsy," add some color and make the line width random too, as in the following listing.

Listing 16.6   *Modern art with color*

```
import pygame, sys, random
from pygame.color import THECOLORS
pygame.init()
screen = pygame.display.set_mode([640,480])
screen.fill([255, 255, 255])
for i in range (100):
    width = random.randint(0, 250); height = random.randint(0, 100)
    top = random.randint(0, 400); left = random.randint(0, 500)
    color_name = random.choice(THECOLORS.keys())          Don't worry about
    color = THECOLORS[color_name]                         how this line works
    line_width = random.randint(1, 3)                     for now
    pygame.draw.rect(screen, color, [left, top, width, height], line_width)
pygame.display.flip()
running = True
while running:
    for event in pygame.event.get():
        if event.type == pygame.QUIT:
            running = False
pygame.quit()
```

When you run this, you'll get something that looks different every time. If you get a result that looks really nice, give it a fancy title like "Voice of the Machine" and see if you can sell it to your local art gallery!

Individual pixels

Sometimes you don't want to draw a circle or rectangle, but you want to draw individual dots or pixels. Maybe you're creating a math program and want to draw a sine wave, for example.

Hey, mon! Them there sine waves usually be **used for sound**. Like in music.

Me? I prefer makin' music on de waves of de ocean.

Don't Worry, Be Happy!

Don't worry if you don't know what a sine wave is. For the purposes of this chapter, it is just a wavy shape.

Also don't worry about the math formulas in the next few example programs. Just type them in as they appear in the listings. They are just a way to get a wavy shape that is a nice size to fill our Pygame window.

Because there is no `pygame.draw.sinewave()` method, we have to draw it ourselves from individual points. One way to do this is to draw tiny circles or rectangles, with a size of just one or two pixels. The following listing shows how that would look using rectangles.

Listing 16.7 Drawing curves using a lot of small rectangles

```
import pygame, sys
import math                          ←——— Imports the math functions,
                                           including sin()
pygame.init()
screen = pygame.display.set_mode([640,480])
screen.fill([255, 255, 255])        ←——— Loops from
                                           left to right,
for x in range(0, 640):                    x = 0 to 639
    y = int(math.sin(x/640.0 * 4 * math.pi) * 200 + 240)    ←——— Calculates the y-
    pygame.draw.rect(screen, [0,0,0],[x, y, 1, 1], 1)             position (vertical)
pygame.display.flip()                                             of each point
running = True
while running:                      Draws the point using a
    for event in pygame.event.get():   small rectangle
        if event.type == pygame.QUIT:
            running = False
pygame.quit()
```

And here's what it looks like when it runs:

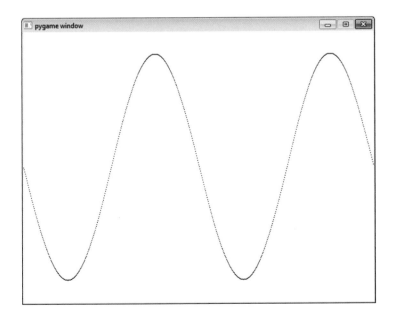

To draw each point, we used a rectangle 1 pixel wide by 1 pixel high. Note that we also used a line width of 1, not 0. If we used a line width of 0, nothing would show up, because there's no "middle" to fill in.

Connect the dots

If you look really closely, you might notice that the sine wave isn't continuous—there are spaces between the points in the middle. That's because, at the steep part of the sine wave, we have to move up (or down) by 3 pixels when we move one pixel to the right. And because we're drawing individual points, not lines, there's nothing to fill the space in between.

Let's try the same thing using a short line to join each plot point. Pygame has a method to draw a single line, but it also has a method that will draw lines between a series of points (like "connect the dots"). That method is `pygame.draw.lines()`, and it needs five parameters:

- The `surface` to draw on.
- A `color`.
- Whether the shape will be `closed` by drawing a line joining the last point back to the first one. We don't want to enclose our sine wave, so this will be `False` for us.
- A `list` of points to connect.
- The `width` of the line.

So in our sine wave example, the `pygame.draw.lines()` method would look like this:

```
pygame.draw.lines(screen, [0,0,0],False, plotPoints, 1)
```

In the `for` loop, instead of drawing each point, we'll just create the list of points that `draw.lines()` will connect. Then we have a single call to `draw.lines()`, which is outside the `for` loop. The whole program is shown next.

Listing 16.8   A well-connected sine wave

```
import pygame, sys
import math
pygame.init()
screen = pygame.display.set_mode([640,480])
screen.fill([255, 255, 255])
plotPoints = []
for x in range(0, 640):
    y = int(math.sin(x/640.0 * 4 * math.pi) * 200 + 240)
    plotPoints.append([x, y])
pygame.draw.lines(screen, [0,0,0],False, plotPoints, 1)
pygame.display.flip()
running = True
while running:
    for event in pygame.event.get():
        if event.type == pygame.QUIT:
            running = False
pygame.quit()
```

Calculates y-position for each point

Adds each point to the list

Draws the whole curve with the draw.lines() function

Now when we run it, it looks like this:

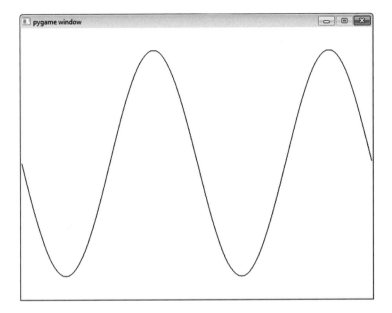

That's better—no gaps between the points. If we increase the line width to 2, it looks even better:

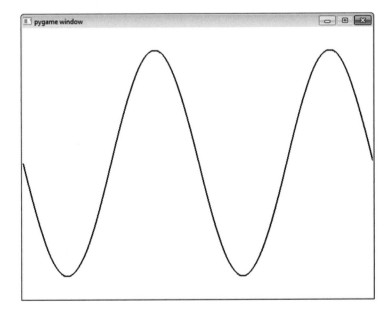

Connect the dots, again

Remember those connect-the-dots puzzles you did when you were young? Here's a Pygame version.

The program in listing 16.9 creates a shape using the `draw.lines()` function and a list of points. To reveal the secret picture, type in the program. There's no cheating this time! This one isn't in the **\examples** folder—you have to type it in if you want to see the mystery picture. But typing in all the numbers can be a bit tedious, so you can find the `dots` list in a text file in the **\examples** folder or on the website.

Listing 16.9 Connect-the-dots mystery picture

```
import pygame, sys
pygame.init()

dots = [[221, 432], [225, 331], [133, 342], [141, 310],
        [51, 230],  [74, 217],  [58, 153],  [114, 164],
        [123, 135], [176, 190], [159, 77],  [193, 93],
        [230, 28],  [267, 93],  [301, 77],  [284, 190],
        [327, 135], [336, 164], [402, 153], [386, 217],
        [409, 230], [319, 310], [327, 342], [233, 331],
        [237, 432]]

screen = pygame.display.set_mode([640,480])
screen.fill([255, 255, 255])
pygame.draw.lines(screen, [255,0,0],True, dots, 2)       ←——— This time
pygame.display.flip()                                          closed=True
running = True
while running:
    for event in pygame.event.get():
        if event.type == pygame.QUIT:
            running = False
pygame.quit()
```

Drawing point-by-point

Let's go back to drawing point-by-point for a moment. It seems kind of silly to draw a tiny circle or rectangle when all we want to do is change the color of one pixel. Instead of using the `draw` functions, you can access each individual pixel on a surface with the `Surface.set_at()` method. You tell it what pixel you want to set, and what color to set it:

```
screen.set_at([x, y], [0, 0, 0])
```

If we use this line of code in our sine wave example (in place of line 8 in listing 16.7), it looks the same as when we used one-pixel-wide rectangles.

You can also check what color a pixel is already set to with the `Surface.get_at()` method. You just pass it the coordinates of the pixel you want to check, like this: `pixel_color = screen.get_at([320, 240])`. In this example, `screen` was the name of the surface.

Images

Drawing shapes, lines, and individual pixels on the screen is one way to do graphics. But sometimes we want to use pictures that we get from somewhere else—maybe from a digital photo, something we downloaded from the Web, or something created in an image-editing program. In Pygame, the simplest way to use images is with the `image` functions.

Let's look at an example. We're going to display an image that is already on your hard drive if you installed Python from the book's installer. The installer created an **images** subfolder in the **\examples** folder, and the file we're going to use for this example is **beach_ball.png**. So, for example, in Windows, you'd find it at **c:\Program Files\helloworld\examples\images\beach_ball.png**.

You should copy the **beach_ball.png** file to wherever you're saving your Python programs as you work through these examples. That way, Python can easily find it when the program runs. Once you have the **beach_ball.png** file in the correct location, type in the program in listing 16.10 and try it.

If you didn't use the book's installer, you can download **beach_ball.png** from the book's web site, at **www.helloworldbook2.com**.

Listing 16.10   Displaying a beach ball image in a Pygame window

```
import pygame, sys
pygame.init()
screen = pygame.display.set_mode([640,480])
screen.fill([255, 255, 255])
my_ball = pygame.image.load("beach_ball.png")      These are the only
screen.blit(my_ball, [50, 50])                     lines that are new
pygame.display.flip()
running = True
while running:
    for event in pygame.event.get():
        if event.type == pygame.QUIT:
            running = False
pygame.quit()
```

When you run this program, you should see the image of a beach ball displayed near the top-left corner of the Pygame window, like this:

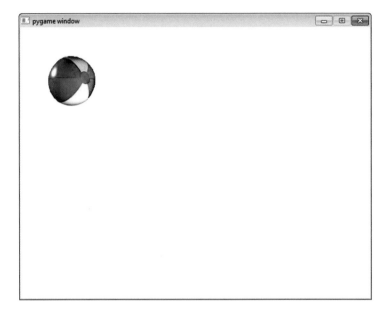

In listing 16.10, the only lines that are new are lines 5 and 6. Everything else you have seen before in listings 16.3 to 16.9. We replaced the `draw` code from our previous examples with code that loads an image from disk and displays it.

In line 5, the `pygame.image.load()` function loads the image from disk and creates an object called `my_ball`. The `my_ball` object is a surface. (We talked about surfaces a few pages ago.) But we can't see this surface. It's only in memory. The only surface we can see is the *display* surface, which is called `screen`. (We created it in line 3.) Line 6 copies the `my_ball` surface onto the `screen` surface. Then `display.flip()` makes it visible, just like we did before.

I can't play volleyball with the ball just standing there!

That's okay, Carter. Pretty soon we'll start moving the ball around!

You might have noticed a funny-looking thing in line 6 of listing 16.10: `screen.blit()`. What does `blit` mean? See the "WORD BOX" to find out.

WORD BOX

When doing graphics programming, copying pixels from one place to another is something we do quite a lot (like copying from a variable to the screen, or from one surface to another). Pixel-copying has a special name in programming. It's called *blitting*. We say that we *blit* an image (or part of an image, or just a bunch of pixels) from one place to another. It's just a fancy way of saying "copy," but when you see "blit," you know it refers to copying pixels, not copying some other kind of thing.

In Pygame, you copy or *blit* pixels from one *surface* to another. Here we copied the pixels from the `my_ball` surface to the `screen` surface.

In line 6 of listing 16.10, we *blitted* the beach ball image to the location 50, 50. That means 50 pixels from the left edge and 50 pixels from the top of the window. When you're working with a `surface` or `rect`, this sets the location of the top-left corner of the image. So the left edge of the beach ball is 50 pixels from the left edge of the window, and the top edge of the beach ball is 50 pixels from the top of the window.

Let's get moving!

Now that we can get graphics onto our Pygame window, let's start moving them around. That's right, we're going to do some animation! Computer animation is really just about moving images (groups of pixels) from one place to another. Let's try moving our beach ball.

To move it, we need to change its location. First, let's try moving it sideways. To make sure we can see the motion, let's move it 100 pixels to the right. The left-right direction (horizontal) is the first number in the pair of numbers that specify location. So to move something to the right by 100 pixels, we need to increase the first number by 100. We'll also put in a delay so we can see the animation happen.

Change the program from listing 16.10 to look like the one in listing 16.11. (You'll need to add lines 8, 9, and 10 before the `while` loop.)

Listing 16.11 Trying to move a beach ball

```
import pygame, sys
pygame.init()
screen = pygame.display.set_mode([640,480])
screen.fill([255, 255, 255])
my_ball = pygame.image.load('beach_ball.png')
screen.blit(my_ball,[50, 50])
pygame.display.flip()
pygame.time.delay(2000)
screen.blit(my_ball,[150, 50])          These are the
pygame.display.flip()                    three new lines
running = True
while running:
    for event in pygame.event.get():
        if event.type == pygame.QUIT:
            running = False
pygame.quit()
```

Run the program, and see what happens. Did the ball move? Well, sort of. You should have seen two beach balls:

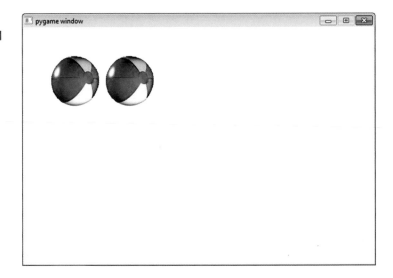

The first one showed up in the original position, and then the second one appeared to the right of it a couple of seconds later. So we *did* move the beach ball to the right, but we forgot one thing. We need to erase the first ball!

Animation

When you're doing animation with computer graphics, there are two steps to moving something:

1 You draw the thing in its new position.
2 You erase the thing from its old position.

You already saw the first part. We drew the ball in a new position. Now we have to erase the ball from where it was before. But what does "erasing" really mean?

Erasing images

When you draw something on paper or on a blackboard, it's easy to erase it. You just use an eraser, right? But what if you made a painting? Let's say you made a painting of blue sky, and then you painted a bird in the sky. How would you "erase" the bird? You can't erase paint. You'd have to paint some new blue sky over where the bird was.

Computer graphics are like paint, not like pencil or chalk. In order to "erase" something, what you really have to do is "paint over" it. But what do you paint over it with? In the case of your sky painting, the sky is blue, so you'd paint over the bird with blue. Our background is white, so we have to paint over the beach ball's original image with white.

Let's try that. Modify your program from listing 16.11 to match the following listing. There's only one new line to add.

Listing 16.12   Trying to move a beach ball again

```
import pygame, sys
pygame.init()
screen = pygame.display.set_mode([640,480])
screen.fill([255, 255, 255])
my_ball = pygame.image.load('beach_ball.png')
screen.blit(my_ball,[50, 50])
pygame.display.flip()
pygame.time.delay(2000)
screen.blit(my_ball, [150, 50])
pygame.draw.rect(screen, [255,255,255], [50, 50, 90, 90], 0)
pygame.display.flip()
running = True
while running:
    for event in pygame.event.get():
        if event.type == pygame.QUIT:
            running = False
pygame.quit()
```

This line "erases" the first ball

We added line 10 to draw a white rectangle over the first beach ball. The beach ball image is about 90 pixels wide by 90 pixels high, so that's how big we made the white rectangle. If you run the program in listing 16.12, it should look like the beach ball moves from its original location to the new location.

What's under there?

Painting over our white background (or the blue sky in your painting) is fairly easy. But what if you painted the bird on a cloudy sky? Or on a background of trees? Then you'd have to paint over the bird with clouds or trees to erase it. The important idea here is that you have to keep track of what's in the background, "underneath" your images, because when you move them, you have to put back or repaint what was there before.

This is pretty easy for our beach ball example, because the background is just white. But if the background was a scene of a beach, it would be trickier. Instead of painting just white, we'd have to paint the correct portion of the background image. Another option would be to repaint the whole scene and then place the beach ball in its new location.

Smoother animation

So far, we have made our ball move once! Let's see if we can get it moving in a more realistic way. When animating things on the screen, it's usually good to move them in small steps, so the motion appears smooth. Let's try moving our ball in smaller steps.

We're not just going to make the steps smaller—we're going to add a loop to move the ball (because we want to make many small steps). Starting with listing 16.12, edit the code so it looks like this.

Listing 16.13   Moving a beach ball image smoothly

```
import pygame, sys
pygame.init()
screen = pygame.display.set_mode([640,480])
screen.fill([255, 255, 255])
my_ball = pygame.image.load('beach_ball.png')
x = 50                                              Add these lines          Uses x and y (instead
y = 50                                                                       of numbers)
screen.blit(my_ball, [x, y])
pygame.display.flip()                   Starts a for loop
for looper in range (1, 100):                           time.delay value changed
    pygame.time.delay(20)                               from 2000 to 20
    pygame.draw.rect(screen, [255,255,255], [x, y, 90, 90], 0)
    x = x + 5
    screen.blit(my_ball, [x, y])
    pygame.display.flip()

running = True
while running:
    for event in pygame.event.get():
        if event.type == pygame.QUIT:
            running = False
pygame.quit()
```

If you run this program, you should see the ball moving from its original position over to the right side of the window.

Keeping the ball moving

In the previous program, the ball moved over to the right side of the window and then stopped. Now we'll try to keep the ball moving.

If we just keep increasing **x**, what will happen? The ball will keep moving to the right as its x-value increases. But our window (the display surface) stops at **x = 640**. So the ball will disappear. Try changing the **for** loop in line 10 of listing 16.13 to this:

```
for looper in range (1, 200):
```

Now that the loop runs twice as long, the ball disappears off the edge! If we want to continue seeing the ball, we have two choices:

- We make the ball *bounce* off the side of the window.
- We make the ball *wrap around* to the other side of the window.

Let's try both ways to see how to do them.

Bouncing the ball

If we want to make the ball appear to *bounce* off the side of the window, we need to know when it "hits" the edge of the window, and then we need to reverse its direction. If we want to keep the ball moving back and forth, we need to do this at both the left and right edges of the window.

At the left edge, it's easy, because we just check for the ball's position to be 0 (or some small number).

At the right side, we need to check to see if the right side of the ball is at the right side of the window. But the ball's position is set from its left side (the top-left corner), not its right side. So we have to subtract the width of the ball:

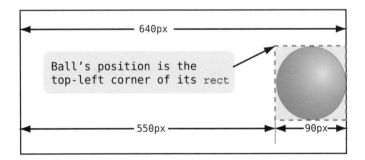

When the ball is moving toward the right edge of the window, we need to bounce it (reverse its direction) when its position is 550.

To make things easier, we're going to make some changes to our code:

- We're going to have the ball bouncing around forever (or until we close the Pygame window). Because we already have a `while` loop that runs as long as the window is open, we'll move our ball-display code inside that loop. (That's the `while` loop that is in the last part of the program.)
- Instead of always adding 5 to the ball's position, we'll make a new variable, `speed`, to determine how fast to move the ball on each iteration. We're also going to speed the ball up a bit by setting this value at 10.

The new code is in the following listing.

Listing 16.14   Bouncing a beach ball

```
import pygame, sys
pygame.init()
screen = pygame.display.set_mode([640,480])
screen.fill([255, 255, 255])
my_ball = pygame.image.load('beach_ball.png')
x = 50
y = 50
x_speed = 10          Here's the
                      speed variable          Put the ball-display
                                              code here, inside
running = True                                the while loop
while running:
    for event in pygame.event.get():
        if event.type == pygame.QUIT:
            running = False

    pygame.time.delay(20)
    pygame.draw.rect(screen, [255,255,255], [x, y, 90, 90], 0)
    x = x + x_speed
    if x > screen.get_width() - 90  or  x < 0:    When ball hits either
        x_speed = - x_speed                       edge of the window ...
    screen.blit(my_ball, [x, y])
    pygame.display.flip()              ... reverse direction by making
pygame.quit()                         speed the opposite sign
```

The key to bouncing the ball off the sides of the window is lines 19 and 20. In line 19 (`if x > screen.get_width() - 90 or x < 0:`), we detect whether the ball is at the edge of the window, and if it is, we reverse its direction in line 20 (`x_speed = - x_speed`).

Try this and see how it works.

Bouncing in 2-D

So far, we only have the ball moving back and forth, or one-dimensional motion. Now, let's get it moving up and down at the same time. To do this, we only need a few changes, as shown here.

Listing 16.15 Bouncing a beach ball in 2-D

```
import pygame, sys
pygame.init()
screen = pygame.display.set_mode([640,480])
screen.fill([255, 255, 255])
my_ball = pygame.image.load('beach_ball.png')
x = 50
y = 50
x_speed = 10                    Add code for y-speed
y_speed = 10          ◄─────    (vertical motion)
running = True
while running:
    for event in pygame.event.get():
        if event.type == pygame.QUIT:
            running = False
    pygame.time.delay(20)
    pygame.draw.rect(screen, [255,255,255], [x, y, 90, 90], 0)  ◄─┐
    x = x + x_speed
    y = y + y_speed      ◄──────────────────────     Add code for y-speed
    if x > screen.get_width() - 90  or  x < 0:        (vertical motion)
        x_speed = - x_speed
    if y > screen.get_height() - 90 or y < 0:    │ Bounces ball off top
        y_speed = -y_speed                       │ or bottom of window
    screen.blit(my_ball, [x, y])
    pygame.display.flip()
pygame.quit()
```

We added lines 9 (`y_speed = 10`), 18 (`y = y + y_speed`), 21 (`if y > screen.get_height()`
`- 90 or y < 0:`), and 22 (`y_speed = -y_speed`) to the previous program. Try it now and see
how it works!

If we want to slow down the ball, there are a couple of ways to do it:

- We can reduce the speed variables (**x_speed** and **y_speed**). This reduces how far the
  ball moves on each animation step, so the motion will also be smoother.
- We could also increase the delay setting. In listing 16.15, it's 20. That is measured in
  milliseconds, which is thousandths of a second. So each time through the loop, the
  program waits for 0.02 seconds. If we increase this number, the motion will slow
  down. If we decrease it, the motion will speed up.

Try playing around with the speed and delay to see the effects.

Wrapping the ball

Now let's look at the second option for keeping the ball moving. Instead of bouncing it off
the side of the screen, we're going to *wrap* it around. That means when the ball disappears
off the right side of the screen, it'll reappear on the left side.

To make things simpler, we'll go back to just moving the ball horizontally. The program is in the next listing.

Listing 16.16   Moving a beach ball image with wrapping

```
import pygame, sys
pygame.init()
screen = pygame.display.set_mode([640,480])
screen.fill([255, 255, 255])
my_ball = pygame.image.load('beach_ball.png')
x = 50
y = 50
x_speed = 5
running = True
while running:
    for event in pygame.event.get():
        if event.type == pygame.QUIT:
            running = False
    pygame.time.delay(20)
    pygame.draw.rect(screen, [255,255,255], [x, y, 90, 90], 0)
    x = x + x_speed
    if x > screen.get_width():        If the ball is at the far right ...
        x = 0                         ... start over at the left side
    screen.blit(my_ball, [x, y])
    pygame.display.flip()
pygame.quit()
```

In lines 17 (`if x > screen.get_width():`) and 18 (`x = 0`), we detected when the ball reached the right edge of the window, and we moved it back, or wrapped it back, to the left side.

You might have noticed that, when the ball appears on the right, it "pops in" at [0, 50]. It would look more natural if it "slid in" from off screen. Change line 18 (`x = 0`) to `x = -90` and see if you notice the difference.

What did you learn?

Whew! That was a busy chapter! In it, you learned

- How to use Pygame
- How to create a graphics window and draw some shapes in it
- How to set colors in computer graphics
- How to copy images to a graphics window
- How to animate images, including "erasing" them when you move them to a new place
- How to make a beach ball "bounce" around the window
- How to make a beach ball "wrap" around the window

Test your knowledge

1. What color does the RGB value [255, 255, 255] make?
2. What color does the RGB value [0, 255, 0] make?
3. What Pygame method can you use to draw rectangles?
4. What Pygame method can you use to draw lines joining a number of points together?
5. What does the term *pixel* mean?
6. In a Pygame window, where is the location [0, 0]?
7. If a Pygame window is 600 pixels wide by 400 pixels high, what letter in the diagram below is at [50, 200]?

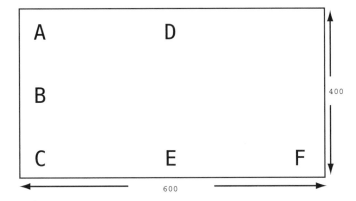

8. What letter in the diagram is at location [300, 50]?
9. What Pygame method is used to copy images to a surface (like the display surface)?
10. What are the two main steps when you're "moving" or animating an image?

Try it out

1. We talked about drawing circles and rectangles. Pygame also has methods to draw lines, arcs, ellipses, and polygons. Try using these to draw some other shapes in a program.

   You can find out more about these methods in the Pygame documentation at **www.pygame.org/docs/ref/draw.html**. If you don't have Internet access, you can also find it on your hard drive (it's installed with Pygame), but it can be hard to find. Search your hard drive for a file called **pygame_draw.html**.

   You can also use Python's help system (which we talked about at the end of chapter 6). One thing SPE doesn't have is an interactive shell that works, so start IDLE and type the following:

   ```
   >>> import pygame
   >>> help()
   help> pygame.draw
   ```

You'll get a list of the different draw methods and some explanation for each one.

2 Try changing one of the sample programs that uses the beach ball image to use a different image. You can find some sample images in the **\examples\images** folder, or you can download or draw one of your own. You could also use a piece of a digital photo.

3 Try changing the **x_speed** and **y_speed** values in listing 16.15 or 16.16 to make the ball move faster or slower and in different directions.

4 Try to change listing 16.15 to make the ball "bounce" off an invisible wall or floor that isn't the edge of the window.

5 In listings 16.5 to 16.9 (the modern art, sine wave, and mystery picture programs), try moving the line `pygame.display.flip` inside the `while` loop. To do that, just indent it four spaces. After that line, and also inside the `while` loop, add a delay with this line and see what happens:

```
pygame.time.delay(30)
```

Sprites and Collision Detection

In this chapter, we'll continue using Pygame to do animation. We'll look at things called *sprites,* which help us keep track of lots of images moving on the screen. We'll also see how to detect when two images overlap or hit each other, like when a ball hits a paddle or a spaceship hits an asteroid.

Sprites

In the last chapter, you saw that simple animation isn't quite so simple after all. If you have a lot of images and are moving them around, it can be a lot of work keeping track of what's "under" each image so you can repaint when you move the image. In our first example with the beach ball, the background was just white, so it was easier. But you can imagine that, with graphics in the background, it would get more complicated.

Fortunately, Pygame provides some extra help. The individual images or parts of an image that move around are called *sprites,* and Pygame has a special module for handling sprites. This lets you move graphical objects around more easily.

In the last chapter, we had a beach ball bouncing around the screen. What if we want a whole bunch of beach balls bouncing around? We could write the code to manage each ball individually, but instead we're going to use Pygame's `sprite` module to make things easier.

WORD BOX

Sprite means a group of pixels that are moved and displayed as a single unit, a kind of graphical object.

> The term 'sprite' is a holdover from older computer and game machines. These older boxes were unable to draw and erase normal graphics fast enough for them to work as games. These machines had special hardware to handle game-like objects that needed to animate very quickly. These objects were called 'sprites' and had special limitations, but could be drawn and updated very fast . . . These days computers have become generally fast enough to handle sprite-like objects without dedicated hardware. The term 'sprite' is still used to represent just about anything in a 2D game that is animated.

(excerpted from "Pygame Tutorials - Sprite Module Introduction" by Pete Shinners **www.pygame.org/docs/tut/SpriteIntro.html**)

What's a sprite?

Think of a sprite as a little piece of graphics—a kind of graphical object that will move around the screen and interact with other graphical objects. Most sprites have a couple of basic properties:

- An *image*—the graphics that are displayed for the sprite
- A *rect*—the rectangular area that contains the sprite

The image can be one that you draw using Pygame's draw functions (like you saw in the last chapter) or one that you get from an image file.

A sprite class

Pygame's `sprite` module provides a base sprite class called `Sprite`. (Remember when we talked about objects and classes a couple of chapters ago?) Normally you don't use the base class directly, but instead create your own subclass, based on `pygame.sprite.Sprite`. Let's do that in an example and call the class `MyBallClass`. The code to create it looks like this:

```
class MyBallClass(pygame.sprite.Sprite):
    def __init__(self, image_file, location):
        pygame.sprite.Sprite.__init__(self)
        self.image = pygame.image.load(image_file)
        self.rect = self.image.get_rect()
        self.rect.left, self.rect.top = location
```

Initializes the sprite

Loads an image file into it

Gets the rectangle that defines the boundaries of the image

Sets the initial location of the ball

The last line in this code is worth taking a closer look at. `location` is an [x, y] location, which is a list with two items. Because we have a list with two items on one side of the = sign (`x` and `y`), we can assign two things on the other side. Here, we assigned the `left` and `top` attributes of the sprite's rectangle.

Now that we've defined `MyBallClass`, we have to create some instances of it. (Remember, the class definition is just a blueprint; now we have to build some houses.) We still need the same code we used in the last chapter to create a Pygame window. We're also going to create some balls on the screen, arranged in rows and columns. We'll do that with a nested loop:

```
img_file = "beach_ball.png"
balls = []
for row in range (0, 3):                  Makes the location different
    for column in range (0, 3):           each time through the loop
        location = [column * 180 + 10, row * 180 + 10]
        ball = MyBallClass(img_file, location)        Creates a ball
        balls.append(ball)                            at that location
                                    Collect the balls in a list
```

We also need to *blit* the balls to the display surface. (Remember that funny word, *blit*? We talked about it in the last chapter.)

```
for ball in balls:
    screen.blit(ball.image, ball.rect)
pygame.display.flip()
```

Putting it all together, our program is shown in the following listing.

Listing 17.1 Using sprites to put multiple ball images on the screen

```
import sys, pygame

class MyBallClass(pygame.sprite.Sprite):
    def __init__(self, image_file, location):
        pygame.sprite.Sprite.__init__(self)              Defines ball
        self.image = pygame.image.load(image_file)       subclass
        self.rect = self.image.get_rect()
        self.rect.left, self.rect.top = location

size = width, height = 640, 480
screen = pygame.display.set_mode(size)      Sets window size
screen.fill([255, 255, 255])
img_file = "beach_ball.png"
balls = []
for row in range (0, 3):
    for column in range (0, 3):
        location = [column * 180 + 10, row * 180 + 10]
        ball = MyBallClass(img_file, location)
        balls.append(ball)                    Adds balls to a list
```

```
for ball in balls:
    screen.blit(ball.image, ball.rect)
pygame.display.flip()

running = True
while running:
    for event in pygame.event.get():
        if event.type == pygame.QUIT:
            running = False
pygame.quit()
```

If you run this, you should see nine beach balls appear in the Pygame window, like this:

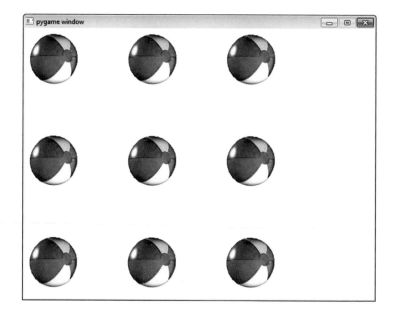

In a minute, we'll start moving them around.

Did you notice the small change in lines 10 and 11, which set the size of the Pygame window? We replaced

```
screen = pygame.display.set_mode([640,480])
```

with

```
size = width, height = 640, 480
screen = pygame.display.set_mode(size)
```

This code not only sets the size of the window—like before—but also defines two variables, **width** and **height,** which we can use later. The neat thing here is that we have defined a list, called **size**, with two items in it, and we have also defined two integer variables, **width** and `height`, all in one statement. We also didn't use square brackets around our list, and Python is fine with that.

I just wanted to show you that there are sometimes different ways to do things in Python. One isn't necessarily better than the other (as long as they both work). Even though you have to follow Python's syntax (rules of language), there's still some room for freedom of expression. If you asked 10 programmers to write the same program, you probably wouldn't get any two pieces of code that were identical.

A `move ()` method

Because we're creating the balls as instances of `MyBallClass`, it makes sense to move them using a class method. So let's create a new class method called `move ()`:

```
def move(self):
    self.rect = self.rect.move(self.speed)
    if self.rect.left < 0 or self.rect.right > width:
        self.speed[0] = -self.speed[0]

    if self.rect.top < 0 or self.rect.bottom > height:
        self.speed[1] = -self.speed[1]
```

Checks for hitting the sides of the window, and if so, reverses the x-speed

Checks for hitting the top or bottom of the window, and if so, reverses the y-speed

Sprites (actually the `rects` within them) have a built-in method called `move ()`. This method requires a parameter called `speed` to tell it how far (that is, how fast) to move the object. Because we're dealing with 2-D graphics, `speed` is a list of two numbers, one for x-speed and one for y-speed. We also check for the ball hitting the edges of the window so we can "bounce" the balls around the screen.

Let's change the `MyBallClass` definition to add the `speed` property and the `move ()` method:

```
class MyBallClass(pygame.sprite.Sprite):
    def __init__(self, image_file, location, speed):
        pygame.sprite.Sprite.__init__(self)
        self.image = pygame.image.load(image_file)
        self.rect = self.image.get_rect()
        self.rect.left, self.rect.top = location
        self.speed = speed

    def move(self):
        self.rect = self.rect.move(self.speed)
        if self.rect.left < 0 or self.rect.right > width:
            self.speed[0] = -self.speed[0]

        if self.rect.top < 0 or self.rect.bottom > height:
            self.speed[1] = -self.speed[1]
```

Adds the speed argument

Adds this line to create a speed attribute for the ball

Adds this method for moving the ball

Notice the change in line 2 (`def __init__(self, image_file, location, speed):`) and the addition of line 7 (`self.speed = speed`), as well as the new `move()` method in lines 9 to 15.

Now when we create each instance of a ball, we need to tell it the speed as well as the image file and location:

```
speed = [2, 2]
ball = MyBallClass(img_file, location, speed)
```

The preceding code will create all the balls with the same speed (same direction), but it would be fun to see the balls move around a bit randomly. Let's use the `random.choice()` function to set the speed, like this:

```
from random import *
speed = [choice([-2, 2]), choice([-2, 2])]
```

This will choose either -2 or 2 for both the x and y speed.

Here's the complete program.

Listing 17.2   A program for moving balls around using sprites

```
import sys, pygame
from random import *

class MyBallClass(pygame.sprite.Sprite):
    def __init__(self, image_file, location, speed):
        pygame.sprite.Sprite.__init__(self)
        self.image = pygame.image.load(image_file)
        self.rect = self.image.get_rect()
        self.rect.left, self.rect.top = location
        self.speed = speed

    def move(self):
        self.rect = self.rect.move(self.speed)
        if self.rect.left < 0 or self.rect.right > width:
            self.speed[0] = -self.speed[0]

        if self.rect.top < 0 or self.rect.bottom > height:
            self.speed[1] = -self.speed[1]

size = width, height = 640, 480
screen = pygame.display.set_mode(size)
screen.fill([255, 255, 255])
img_file = "beach_ball.png"
balls = []
```

Ball class definition

⟵ Creates a list to keep track of balls

```
for row in range (0, 3):
    for column in range (0, 3):
        location = [column * 180 + 10, row * 180 + 10]
        speed = [choice([-2, 2]), choice([-2, 2])]
        ball = MyBallClass(img_file, location, speed)
        balls.append(ball)                      Adds each ball to the
running = True                                  list as it's created
while running:
    for event in pygame.event.get():
        if event.type == pygame.QUIT:
            running = False
    pygame.time.delay(20)
    screen.fill([255, 255, 255])
    for ball in balls:
        ball.move()                             Redraws the screen
        screen.blit(ball.image, ball.rect)
    pygame.display.flip()
pygame.quit()
```

This program uses a list to keep track of all the balls. In line 32 (`balls.append(ball)`), each ball is added to the list as it's created.

The code in the last five lines redraws the screen. Here we cheat a bit, and instead of " erasing" (painting over) each ball separately, we just fill the window with white and then redraw all the balls.

You can experiment with this code by having more (or fewer) balls, changing their speed, changing how they move and "bounce," and so on. You'll notice that the balls move around and bounce off the sides of the window, but they don't bounce off each other—yet!

Bump! Collision detection

In most computer games, you need to know when one sprite hits another one. For example, you might need to know when a bowling ball hits the pins or when your missile hits the spaceship.

You might be thinking that, if you know the position and size of every sprite, you can write some code to check those against the position and size of every other sprite, to see where they overlap. But the folks who wrote Pygame have already done that for us. Pygame has what's called *collision detection* built in.

WORD BOX

Collision detection simply means knowing when two sprites are touching or overlapping. When two things that are moving run into each other, it's called a collision.

Pygame also has a way of *grouping* sprites together. For example, in a bowling game, all the pins might be in one group, and the ball would be in a group of its own.

Groups and collision detection go hand in hand. In the bowling example, you'd want to detect when the ball hits any of the pins, so you'd look for collisions between the ball sprite and any sprites in the pins group. You can also detect collisions within a group (like the pins hitting each other).

Let's work through an example. We'll start with our bouncing beach balls, but to make it easier to see what's going on, we'll start with just four balls instead of nine. And instead of making a list of the balls like we did in the last example, we'll use Pygame's **group** class.

We'll also clean up the code a bit by putting the part that animates the balls (the last few lines in listing 17.2) into a function, which we'll call **animate()**. The **animate()** function will also have the code for collision detection. When two balls collide, we'll make them reverse direction.

The next listing shows the code.

Listing 17.3   Collision detection, using a sprite group instead of a list

```python
import sys, pygame
from random import *

class MyBallClass(pygame.sprite.Sprite):                          ⎫
    def __init__(self, image_file, location, speed):              ⎪
        pygame.sprite.Sprite.__init__(self)                       ⎪
        self.image = pygame.image.load(image_file)                ⎪
        self.rect = self.image.get_rect()                         ⎪
        self.rect.left, self.rect.top = location                  ⎬ The ball
        self.speed = speed                                        ⎪  class
                                                                  ⎪  definition
    def move(self):                                               ⎪
        self.rect = self.rect.move(self.speed)                    ⎪
        if self.rect.left < 0 or self.rect.right > width:         ⎪
            self.speed[0] = -self.speed[0]                        ⎪
        if self.rect.top < 0 or self.rect.bottom > height:        ⎪
            self.speed[1] = -self.speed[1]                        ⎭

def animate(group):                                               ⎫
    screen.fill([255,255,255])                                    ⎪
    for ball in group:                          Removes sprite    ⎪
        group.remove(ball)        ←──────────   from the group    ⎪
        if pygame.sprite.spritecollide(ball, group, False): ←──   ⎬ The new
            ball.speed[0] = -ball.speed[0]                        ⎪  animate()
            ball.speed[1] = -ball.speed[1]   Checks for collisions⎪  function
                                             between the sprite   ⎪
        group.add(ball)      ←──  Adds ball back  and the group   ⎪
        ball.move()               into the group                 ⎪
        screen.blit(ball.image, ball.rect)                        ⎪
    pygame.display.flip()                                         ⎪
    pygame.time.delay(20)                                         ⎭
```

```
size = width, height = 640, 480
screen = pygame.display.set_mode(size)
screen.fill((255, 255, 255))
img_file = "beach_ball.png"
group = pygame.sprite.Group()
for row in range (0, 2):
    for column in range (0, 2):
        location = [column * 180 + 10, row * 180 + 10]
        speed = [choice([-2, 2]), choice([-2, 2])]
        ball = MyBallClass(img_file, location, speed)
        group.add(ball)
running = True
while running:
    for event in pygame.event.get():
        if event.type == pygame.QUIT:
            running = False
    animate(group)
pygame.quit()
```

The main program starts here →

Creates the sprite group

Creates only four balls this time

Adds each ball to the group

Calls animate()

function, passing the group to it

The most interesting new thing here is how the collision detection works. The Pygame **sprite** module has a function called **spritecollide()**, which looks for collisions between a single sprite and any sprite in a group. If you're checking for collisions between sprites in the *same group*, you have to do it in three steps:

1   Remove the sprite from the group.

2   Check for collisions between the sprite and the rest of the group.

3   Add the sprite back to the group.

This happens in the **for** loop in lines 21 to 29 (in the middle part of the **animate()** function). If we don't remove the sprite from the group first, **spritecollide()** will detect a collision between the sprite and itself, because it's in the group. This might seem kind of odd at first, but it makes sense if you think about it for a while.

Run the program and see how it looks. Did you notice any strange behavior? I noticed two things:

- When the balls collide, they do a "stutter," or a double bump.

- Sometimes a ball gets stuck along the edge of the window and stutters along for a while.

Why does this happen? Well, it has to do with the way we wrote the animate() function. Notice that we move one ball, then we check its collisions, then we move another ball, then we check its collisions, and so on. We should probably do all the moving first and then do all the collision checking after that.

So we want to take line 28, ball.move(), and put it in its own loop, like this:

```
def animate(group):
    screen.fill([255,255,255])
    for ball in group:
        ball.move()
    for ball in group:
        group.remove(ball)
        if pygame.sprite.spritecollide(ball, group, False):
            ball.speed[0] = -ball.speed[0]
            ball.speed[1] = -ball.speed[1]
        group.add(ball)
    screen.blit(ball.image, ball.rect)
    pygame.display.flip()
    pygame.time.delay(20)
```

Moves all the balls first

Then does collision detection and bounces them

Try this and see if it works a little better.

You can play with the code, changing things like the speed (the time.delay() number), number of balls, original location of the balls, randomness, and so on to see what happens to the balls.

Rect collision vs. pixel-perfect collision

One thing you'll notice is that the balls aren't always completely touching when they " collide." That's because spritecollide() doesn't use the round shape of the ball to detect collisions. It uses the ball's rect, the rectangle around the ball.

If you want to see this, draw a rectangle around the ball image, and use that new image instead of the regular beach ball image. I've made one for you, so you can try it:

```
img_file = "b_ball_rect.png"
```

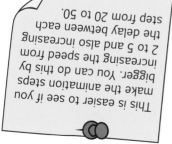

This is easier to see if you make the animation steps bigger. You can do this by increasing the speed from 2 to 5 and also increasing the delay between each step from 20 to 50.

It should look something like this:

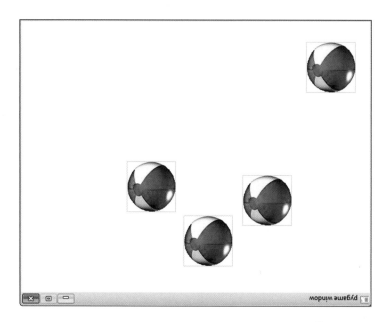

If you wanted the balls to bounce off each other only when the round parts of the balls (not the edges of the rectangles) actually touched, you'd have to use something called *pixel-perfect collision detection*. The `spritecollide()` function doesn't do this, but instead uses the simpler *rect collision detection*.

Here's the difference. With rect collision detection, two balls will collide when any part of their rectangles touch each other. With pixel-perfect collision detection, two balls will only collide when the balls themselves touch, like this:

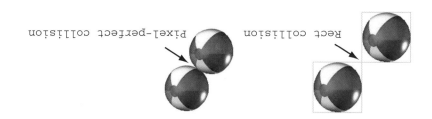

Pixel-perfect collision detection is more realistic. (You haven't felt any invisible rectangles around any *real* beach balls, have you?) But it's more complicated to do in a program. For most things you'll do in Pygame, rect collision detection is good enough. Pixel-perfect collision detection takes more code, and it'll make your games run slower, so only use it if you really, really need it. Several pixel-perfect modules are available (at least two on the

Pygame website the last time I checked). Some web searching will find them if you want to try out pixel-perfect collision detection.

Counting time

Up until now, we have been using `time.delay()` to control how fast our animation runs. But that isn't the best way because, when you use `time.delay()`, you don't really know how long each loop will be. The code in the loop takes some time to run (an unknown time), and then the delay takes some more time (a known time). So part of the timing is known, but part is unknown.

If you want to know how often your loop runs, you need to know the total time of each loop, which is code time + delay time. To calculate time for animation, it's convenient to use milli-seconds, or thousandths of a second. The abbreviation is *ms*, so 25 milliseconds is 25 ms.

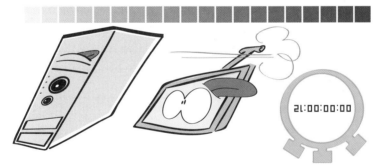

In our example, let's assume that the code time is 15 ms. That means it takes 15 ms for the code in the `while` loop to run, not including the delay time. We know the delay time because we set it to 20 ms using `time.delay(20)`. The total time for the loop is 20 ms + 15 ms = 35 ms, and there are 1,000 ms in one second. If each loop takes 35 ms, we get 1,000 ms / 35 ms = 28.57. This means we'll get about 29 loops per second. In computer graphics, each animation step is called a *frame*, and game programmers talk about *frame rate* and *frames per second* when they discuss how fast their graphics are updating. In our example, the frame rate would be about 29 frames per second, or 29 fps.

The problem is, you can't really control the "code time" part of the equation. If you add or remove code, the time will change. Even with the same code, if there is a different number of sprites (for example, as game objects appear and disappear), the time it takes to draw them all will change. Also, the same code will run faster or slower on different machines. Instead of 15 ms, the code time might be 10 ms or 20 ms. It would be good if there were a more predictable way to control the frame rate. Fortunately, Pygame's `time` module gives us the tools to do this, with a class called `Clock`.

Controlling the frame rate with **pygame.time.Clock()**

Rather than adding a delay to each loop, **pygame.time.Clock()** controls how often each loop runs. It's like a timer that keeps going off, saying "Start the next loop now! Start the next loop now! Start the next loop now! ...."

Before you start using a Pygame clock, you have to create an instance of a Clock object. That works just the same as creating an instance of any other class:

```
clock = pygame.time.Clock()
```

Then, in the body of the main loop, you tell the clock how often it should "tick"—that is, how often the loop should run:

```
clock.tick(60)
```

The number you pass clock.tick() isn't a number of milliseconds. Instead, it's the number of times per second the loop should run. So this loop should run 60 times per second. I say "should run," because your computer can only run it as fast as your computer can make it run. At 60 loops (or frames) per second, that's 1,000 / 60 = 16.66 ms (about 17 ms) per loop. If the code in the loop takes longer than 17 ms to run, it won't be done by the time clock tells it to start the next loop.

Basically, this means there's a limit to how many frames per second your graphics can run. That limit depends on how complex the graphics are, the size of the window, and the speed of the computer the program is running on. For a certain program, one computer might be able to run at 90 fps, while an older, slower computer chugs along at 10 fps.

For reasonably complex graphics, most modern computers won't have any problem running Pygame programs at 20 to 30 fps. So if you want your games to run at the same speed on most computers, pick a frame rate of 20 to 30 fps or less. This is fast enough to produce smooth-looking motion. We'll use clock.tick(30) for the examples in this book from now on.

Checking the frame rate

If you want to know how fast your program can run, you can check the frame rate with a function called clock.get_fps(). Of course, if you set the fame rate to 30, it'll always go at 30 fps (assuming your computer can run that fast). To see the fastest a particular program can run on a particular machine, set the clock.tick very fast (like 200 fps) and then run the program and check the actual frame rate with clock.get_fps(). (An example is coming up soon.)

Scaling the frame rate

If you want to be really sure your animation runs at the same speed on every machine, there's a trick you can do with clock.tick() and clock.get_fps(). Because you know the speed you want to run at and the speed you're actually running at, you can adjust, or *scale*, the speed of your animation according to the speed of the machine.

For example, let's say you have clock.tick(30), which means you're trying to run at 30 fps. If you use clock.get_fps() and find you're only getting 20 fps, you know that objects on the screen are moving slower than you'd like. Because you're getting fewer frames per second, you have to move your objects farther in each frame to make them *appear* to move at the correct speed. You'll probably have a variable (or attribute) called **speed** for your moving objects, which tells them how far to move in each frame. You just need to increase **speed to make up for a slower machine.**

How much to increase it? You increase it by the ratio of desired fps / actual fps. If your object's current speed is 10 for the desired 30 fps, and the program is actually running at 20 fps, you'd have

```
object_speed = current_speed * (desired_fps / actual_fps)
object_speed = 10 * (30 / 20)
object_speed = 15
```

So instead of moving 10 pixels per frame, you'd move the object 15 pixels per frame to make up for the slower frame rate.

Here's a listing of the beach ball program using the things we have discussed in the last couple of sections: Clock and get_fps().

Listing 17.4   Using Clock and get_fps() in the beach ball program

```
import sys, pygame
from random import *

class MyBallClass(pygame.sprite.Sprite):
    def __init__(self, image_file, location, speed):
        pygame.sprite.Sprite.__init__(self)
        self.image = pygame.image.load(image_file)
        self.rect = self.image.get_rect()
        self.rect.left, self.rect.top = location
        self.speed = speed

    def move(self):
        self.rect = self.rect.move(self.speed)
        if self.rect.left < 0 or self.rect.right > width:
            self.speed[0] = -self.speed[0]
        if self.rect.top < 0 or self.rect.bottom > height:
            self.speed[1] = -self.speed[1]
```

The ball class
definition

```
def animate(group):
    screen.fill([255,255,255])
    for ball in group:
        ball.move()
    for ball in group:
        group.remove(ball)
        if pygame.sprite.spritecollide(ball, group, False):
            ball.speed[0] = -ball.speed[0]
            ball.speed[1] = -ball.speed[1]
        group.add(ball)
        screen.blit(ball.image, ball.rect)
    pygame.display.flip()

size = width, height = 640, 480
screen = pygame.display.set_mode(size)
screen.fill([255, 255, 255])
img_file = "beach_ball.png"
clock = pygame.time.Clock()
group = pygame.sprite.Group()
for row in range (0, 2):
    for column in range (0, 2):
        location = [column * 180 + 10, row * 180 + 10]
        speed = [choice([-4, 4]), choice([-4, 4])]
        ball = MyBallClass(img_file, location, speed)
        group.add(ball)   #add the ball to the group

running = True
while running:
    for event in pygame.event.get():
        if event.type == pygame.QUIT:
            running = False
            frame_rate = clock.get_fps()
            print "frame rate = ", frame_rate
    animate(group)
    clock.tick(30)
pygame.quit()
```

The animate function

time.delay() has been removed

Creates instance of Clock

Initializes everything and draws beach balls

The main while loop starts here

Checks the frame rate

clock.tick now controls the frame rate (limited by the speed of the computer)

That covers the basics of Pygame and sprites. In the next chapter, we'll make a real game using Pygame, and you'll see some other things you can do, like adding text (for game scores) and mouse and keyboard input.

What did you learn?

In this chapter, you learned about

- Sprites in Pygame and how to use them to handle multiple moving images
- Groups of sprites

- Collision detection
- pygame.clock and frame rate

Test your knowledge

1 What is rect collision detection?
2 What is pixel-perfect collision detection, and how is it different from rect collision detection?
3 What are two ways to keep track of a number of sprite objects together?
4 What are two ways to control the speed of animation in your code?
5 Why is using pygame.clock more accurate than using pygame.time.delay()?
6 How can you tell what frame rate your program is running at?

Try it out

If you typed in all the code examples in this chapter, you've tried enough out. If you didn't, go back and do that. I promise you'll learn something from it!

A New Kind of Input—Events

Up until now, we have had very simple kinds of inputs for our programs. Either the user typed in strings using raw_input(), or we got numbers and strings from EasyGui (in chapter 6). I also showed you how you could use the mouse to close a Pygame window, but I didn't really explain how that worked.

In this chapter, you'll learn about a different kind of input called *events*. Along the way, we'll look at exactly what the exit code for the Pygame window is doing and how it works. We'll also get input from the mouse and make our programs react immediately to a key being pressed, without having to wait for the user to press **Enter**.

Events

If I asked you, "What's an event?" in real life, you might say that it's "something that happens." That's a pretty good definition, and that same definition is true in programming. Many programs need to react to "things that happen," like

- The mouse being moved or clicked
- Keys being pressed
- A certain amount of time passing

Most of the programs we have written so far have followed a fairly predictable path from beginning to end, maybe with some loops or conditions in the middle. But there's another whole class of programs, called *event-driven* programs, that don't work that way. Event-driven programs basically sit there and do nothing, waiting until something—an

event—happens. When an event does happen, they spring into action, doing whatever is necessary to handle the event.

A good example of this is the Windows operating system (or any other GUI). If you turn on your Windows computer, it will just sit there once it's done booting up. No programs will start, and you won't see the mouse cursor zipping around the screen. But if you start moving or clicking the mouse, things begin to happen. The mouse cursor moves on the screen, the Start menu pops up, or whatever.

The event loop

In order for an event-driven program to "see" events happening, it has to be "looking" for them. The program must constantly scan the part of the computer's memory that's used to signal when an event has happened. It does this over and over again, as long as the program is running. Back in chapter 8, you learned how programs do things over and over again—they use a loop. The special loop that keeps looking for events is called an *event loop*.

In the Pygame programs we have been making in the last two chapters, there was always a `while` loop at the end. We said that this loop ran the whole time the program was running. That `while` loop is Pygame's *event loop*. (There's the first piece of the puzzle about how the exit code works.)

The event queue

All these events happen whenever somebody moves or clicks the mouse or presses a key. Where do they go? In the last section, I said that the event loop constantly scans part of the memory. The part of memory where events are stored is called the *event queue*.

WORD BOX

The word *queue* is pronounced "cue." In everyday use, it means a waiting line.

In programming, queue usually means a list of things that have arrived in a particular order or that will be used in a particular order.

The event queue is a list of all the events that have happened, in the order they happened.

Event handlers

If you're writing a GUI program or a game, the program has to know whenever the user presses a key or moves the mouse. Those clicks, and mouse moves are all *events*, and the program needs to know what to do with them. It has to *handle* them. A part of a program that handles a certain kind of event is called an *event handler*.

Not every event will be handled. As you move the mouse across the desk, hundreds of events are created, because the event loop runs very fast. Every fraction of a second, if the mouse has moved even a tiny bit, a new event is generated. But your program may not care about every tiny movement of the mouse. It may only care when the user clicks a certain thing. So your program might ignore mouseMove events and only pay attention to mouseClick events.

Event-driven programs have event *handlers* for the kinds of events they care about. If you have a game that uses the arrow keys on the keyboard to control the movement of a ship, you might write a handler for the keyDown event. If instead you're using the mouse to control the ship, you might write a handler for the mouseMove event.

We'll start looking now at some specific events that you can use in your programs. We're going to use Pygame again, so all the events we'll talk about in the rest of this chapter will come from Pygame's event queue. Other Python modules have different sets of events that you can use. For example, we'll look at another module called PyQt in chapter 20. PyQt has its own set of events, some of which are different from Pygame's. But the way events are handled is generally the same from one set of events to another (and even from one programming language to another). It's not exactly the same for each event system, but there are more similarities than differences.

Keyboard events

Let's start with an example of a keyboard event. Let's say we want something to happen as soon as a key is pressed on the keyboard. In Pygame, the event for that is KEYDOWN. To illustrate how this is used, let's use our bouncing ball example from listing 16.15, which just moves the ball sideways, bouncing off the sides of the window. But before we start adding events, let's update that program with the new stuff we have learned:

- Using sprites
- Using Clock.tick() instead of time.delay()

First we need a class for the ball. That class will have an __init__() method and a move() method. We'll create an instance of the class, and in the main while loop, we'll use clock.tick(30). The following listing shows the code with those changes.

Listing 18.1 Bouncing ball program, with sprites and Clock.tick()

```
import pygame, sys
pygame.init()
screen = pygame.display.set_mode([640,480])
background = pygame.Surface(screen.get_size())
background.fill([255, 255, 255])
clock = pygame.time.Clock()
```

```
class Ball(pygame.sprite.Sprite):
    def __init__(self, image_file, speed, location):
        pygame.sprite.Sprite.__init__(self)
        self.image = pygame.image.load(image_file)
        self.rect = self.image.get_rect()
        self.rect.left, self.rect.top = location
        self.speed = speed
    def move(self):
        if self.rect.left <= screen.get_rect().left or \
            self.rect.right >= screen.get_rect().right:
            self.speed[0] = - self.speed[0]
        newpos = self.rect.move(self.speed)
        self.rect = newpos
```

The Ball class, including the move() method

```
my_ball = Ball('beach_ball.png', [10,0], [20, 20])
```

Makes an instance → of the ball   Speed, location

```
running = True
while running:
    for event in pygame.event.get():
        if event.type == pygame.QUIT:
            running = False
    clock.tick(30)                    ← This is the clock
    screen.blit(background, (0, 0))
    my_ball.move()
    screen.blit(my_ball.image, my_ball.rect)
    pygame.display.flip()
pygame.quit()
```

Redraws everything

One thing to notice here is that we did something different to "erase" the ball when we moved it. You have seen two ways to erase sprites before repainting them in their new positions: one is to paint the background color over each sprite's old position, and the other is to repaint the whole background for each frame—basically starting over with a blank screen each time. In this case, we did the second one. But instead of using screen.fill() every time through the loop, we made a surface called background and filled it with white. Then, each time through the loop, we *blit* that background onto the display surface, screen. It accomplishes the same thing; it's just a slightly different way of doing it.

Key events

Now we'll add an event handler that makes the ball move up when the *up* arrow is pressed and move down when the *down* arrow is pressed. Pygame is made up of a number of different modules. The module we'll use in this chapter is **pygame.event**.

We already have the Pygame event loop running (the `while` loop). That loop is looking for a special event called QUIT:

```
while running:
    for event in pygame.event.get():
        if event.type == pygame.QUIT:
            running = False
```

The `pygame.event.get()` method gets a list of all the events from the event queue. The `for` loop iterates through each event in the list, and if it sees the QUIT event, it sets `running` to `False`, which causes the `while` loop to exit, and the program ends. So now you have the whole story on how the "click the X to end the program" code works.

For this example, though, we also want to detect a different type of event. We want to know when a key is pressed, so we need to look for the KEYDOWN event. We need something like this:

```
if event.type == pygame.KEYDOWN
```

Because we already have an `if` statement, we can just add another condition with `elif`, like you learned in chapter 7:

```
while running:
    for event in pygame.event.get():
        if event.type == pygame.QUIT:
            running = False
        elif event.type == pygame.KEYDOWN:    | This is the new part where
            # do something                    | we detect the key press
```

What "something" do we want to do when a key is pressed? We said that, if the up arrow was pressed, we'd make the ball move up, and if the down arrow was pressed, we'd move it down. So we could do something like this:

```
while True:
    for event in pygame.event.get():
        if event.type == pygame.QUIT:
            running = False
        elif event.type == pygame.KEYDOWN:
            if event.key == pygame.K_UP:              ↗ Makes the ball move
                my_ball.rect.top = my_ball.rect.top - 10    up by 10 pixels
            elif event.key == pygame.K_DOWN:
                my_ball.rect.top = my_ball.rect.top + 10  ↗ Makes the ball move
                                                            down by 10 pixels
```

K_UP and K_DOWN are Pygame's names for the up and down arrow keys. Make the change to listing 18.1, and the program should now look like this.

Listing 18.2   Bouncing ball with up and down arrow keys

```python
import pygame, sys
pygame.init()
screen = pygame.display.set_mode([640,480])               Initializes everything
background = pygame.Surface(screen.get_size())
background.fill([255, 255, 255])
clock = pygame.time.Clock()
class Ball(pygame.sprite.Sprite):
    def __init__(self, image_file, speed, location):
        pygame.sprite.Sprite.__init__(self)
        self.image = pygame.image.load(image_file)
        self.rect = self.image.get_rect()                  The Ball class definition,
        self.rect.left, self.rect.top = location           including move() method
        self.speed = speed
    def move(self):
        if self.rect.left <= screen.get_rect().left or \
           self.rect.right >= screen.get_rect().right:
            self.speed[0] = - self.speed[0]
        newpos = self.rect.move(self.speed)
        self.rect = newpos
my_ball = Ball('beach_ball.png', [10,0], [20, 20])         Makes an instance
running = True                                             of the ball
while running:
    for event in pygame.event.get():
        if event.type == pygame.QUIT:
            running = False
        elif event.type == pygame.KEYDOWN:
            if event.key == pygame.K_UP:
                my_ball.rect.top = my_ball.rect.top - 10    Checks for key presses
            elif event.key == pygame.K_DOWN:                and moves ball up or down
                my_ball.rect.top = my_ball.rect.top + 10
    clock.tick(30)
    screen.blit(background, (0, 0))
    my_ball.move()
    screen.blit(my_ball.image, my_ball.rect)                Redraws everything
    pygame.display.flip()
pygame.quit()
```

Run the program in listing 18.2, and try the up and down arrow keys. Does it work?

Repeating keys

You might have noticed that, if you hold down the up or down arrow key, the ball only moves one step up or down. That's because we didn't tell our program what to do if a key was held *down*. When the user pressed the key, it generated a single KEYDOWN event, but there's a setting

in Pygame to make it generate multiple **KEYDOWN** events if a key is held down. This is known as *key repeat*. You tell it how long to wait before it starts repeating, and how often to repeat. The values are in milliseconds (thousandths of a second). It looks like this:

```
delay = 100
interval = 50
pygame.key.set_repeat(delay, interval)
```

The **delay** value tells Pygame how long to wait before starting to repeat, and the **interval** value tells Pygame how fast the key should repeat—in other words, how long between each **KEYDOWN** event.

Try adding this to listing 18.2 (somewhere after pygame.init, but before the while loop) to see how it changes the behavior of the program.

Event names and key names

When we were looking for the up and down arrow keys being pressed, we looked for the **KEYDOWN** event type and the **K_UP** and the **K_DOWN** key names. What other events are available? What are the names of the other keys?

There are quite a lot of them, so I won't list them all here. But they're on the Pygame web site. You can find the list of events in the event section of the Pygame documentation:

www.pygame.org/docs/ref/event.html

The list of key names is in the key section:

www.pygame.org/docs/ref/key.html

Here are a few of the common events you'll use:

- QUIT
- KEYDOWN
- KEYUP
- MOUSEMOTION
- MOUSEBUTTONUP
- MOUSEBUTTONDOWN

Pygame also has names for each key that can be pressed. You saw the up arrow and down arrow, K_UP and K_DOWN. You'll see some of the other key names as we go along, but they all start with K_ followed by the name of the key, like this:

- K_a, K_b, and so on (for letter keys)
- K_SPACE
- K_ESCAPE

and so on.

Mouse events

You just saw how to get key events from the keyboard and use them to control something in your program. We made the beach ball move up and down using the arrow keys. Now we're going to use the mouse to control the ball. This will show you how to handle mouse events and how to use the mouse position information.

The three types of mouse events that are most commonly used are

- **MOUSEBUTTONUP**
- **MOUSEBUTTONDOWN**
- **MOUSEMOTION**

The simplest thing to do is have the beach ball follow the mouse position any time the mouse is moved within the Pygame window. To move the beach ball, we'll use the ball's `rect.center` attribute. That way, the center of the ball will follow the mouse.

We'll replace the code that detected key events in the **while** loop with code to detect the mouse events:

```
while running:
    for event in pygame.event.get():
        if event.type == pygame.QUIT:
            running = False
        elif event.type == pygame.MOUSEMOTION:          Detects mouse movement
            my_ball.rect.center = event.pos              and moves the ball
```

This is even simpler than the keyboard example. Make this change to listing 18.2, and try it. The **event.pos** part is the position (x and y coordinates) of the mouse. We move the center of the ball to that location. Notice that the ball follows the mouse as long as the mouse is moving—that is, as long as **MOUSEMOVE** events are happening. Changing the ball's **rect.center** changed both the x and y positions. We're no longer just moving the ball up or down, but also sideways. When there are no mouse events—either because the mouse isn't moving or because the mouse cursor is outside the Pygame window—the ball continues its side-to-side bouncing.

Now let's try making our mouse control work *only* when the mouse button is held down. Moving the mouse while a mouse button is held down is called *dragging*. There's no **MOUSEDRAG** event type, so we'll use the ones we have to get the effect we want.

How can you tell if the mouse is being dragged? Dragging means the mouse is being moved while a mouse button is being held down. You can tell when the button goes down with the **MOUSEBUTTONDOWN** event, and you can tell when it's released (goes back up) with the

`MOUSEBUTTONUP` event. Then you just have to keep track of the status of the button. You can do that by making a variable; call it something like `held_down`. Here's how that would look:

```
held_down = False
while running:
    for event in pygame.event.get():
        if event.type == pygame.QUIT:
            running = False
        elif event.type == pygame.MOUSEBUTTONDOWN:
            held_down = True
        elif event.type == pygame.MOUSEBUTTONUP:
            held_down = False
        elif event.type == pygame.MOUSEMOTION:
            if held_down:
                my_ball.rect.center = event.pos
```

Determines whether the mouse button is being held down or not

Executes when the mouse is being dragged

The dragging condition (the mouse moving while a button is held down) is detected in the last `elif` block in the preceding code. Try making this change to the `while` loop in your previously modified version of listing 18.2. Run it, and see how it works.

> Now we're getting into some programming!

Hey, we've been programming since chapter 1! But now that we're doing things with graphics, sprites, and the mouse, it's getting more interesting. I told you we'd get there. You just had to stick with me and learn some of the basics first.

Timer events

So far in this chapter, you've seen keyboard events and mouse events. Another kind of event that's very useful, especially in games and simulations, is a *timer* event. A timer generates an event at regular intervals, like your alarm clock. If you set it and leave the alarm on, it will ring at the same time every day.

Pygame timers can be set for any interval. When the timer goes off, it creates an event that the event loop can detect. And what kind of event does it generate? It generates something called a *user event*.

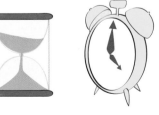

Pygame has a number of predefined event types. These events are numbered, starting from 0, and they also have names to make them easier to remember. You've already seen some of them, like MOUSEBUTTONDOWN and KEYDOWN. There's also room in Pygame for *user-defined* events. These are events that Pygame has not set aside for anything specific, and you can use them for whatever you want. One of the things they can be used for is timers.

To set a timer in Pygame, you use the set_timer() function, like this:

```
pygame.time.set_timer(EVENT_NUMBER, interval)
```

EVENT_NUMBER is the number of the event, and interval is how often (in milliseconds) the timer will go off and generate an event.

What EVENT_NUMBER should you use? You should use one that Pygame isn't already using for something else. You can ask Pygame what numbers are already used. Try this in interactive mode:

```
>>> import pygame
>>> pygame.USEREVENT
24
```

This tells us that Pygame is using event numbers from 0 to 23, and the first one available for user events is 24. So we need to pick a number of 24 or higher. How high can we go? Let's ask Pygame again:

```
>>> pygame.NUMEVENTS
32
```

NUMEVENTS tells us that the maximum number of event types we can have in Pygame is 32 (from 0 to 31). So we have to pick a number of 24 or greater, but less than 32. We could set up our timer like this:

```
pygame.time.set_timer(24, 1000)
```

But if for some reason the value of USEREVENT changes, the code might not work. It would be better to do it this way:

```
pygame.time.set_timer(pygame.USEREVENT, 1000)
```

If we had to set up another user event, we could use USEREVENT + 1, and so on. The 1000 in this example means 1,000 milliseconds, which is one second, so this timer will go off once every second. Let's put this into our bouncing ball program.

Like before, we'll use the event to move the ball up or down. But because the ball won't be controlled by a user this time, we should make it bounce off the top and bottom as well as the sides. The complete program, based on modifying listing 18.2, is shown next.

Listing 18.3   Using a timer event to move the ball up and down

```
import pygame, sys
pygame.init()
screen = pygame.display.set_mode([640,480])          Initializes everything
background = pygame.Surface(screen.get_size())
background.fill([255, 255, 255])

clock = pygame.time.Clock()
class Ball(pygame.sprite.Sprite):
    def __init__(self, image_file, speed, location):
        pygame.sprite.Sprite.__init__(self)
        self.image = pygame.image.load(image_file)
        self.rect = self.image.get_rect()
        self.rect.left, self.rect.top = location          The Ball class definition
        self.speed = speed
    def move(self):
        if self.rect.left <= screen.get_rect().left or \
                self.rect.right >= screen.get_rect().right:
            self.speed[0] = - self.speed[0]                   This line
        newpos = self.rect.move(self.speed)               ❶ continues
        self.rect = newpos

my_ball = Ball('beach_ball.png', [10,0], [20, 20])          Makes an instance of Ball
pygame.time.set_timer(pygame.USEREVENT, 1000)
direction = 1                                               Creates a timer: 1000
running = True                                              ms = 1 second
while running:

    for event in pygame.event.get():
        if event.type == pygame.QUIT:
            running = False
        elif event.type == pygame.USEREVENT:
            my_ball.rect.centery = my_ball.rect.centery + (30*direction)    The event
            if my_ball.rect.top <= 0 or \                                   handler for
                my_ball.rect.bottom >= screen.get_rect().bottom:            the timer
                    direction = -direction              This line
    clock.tick(30)                                    ❶ continues
    screen.blit(background, (0, 0))
    my_ball.move()
    screen.blit(my_ball.image, my_ball.rect)          Redraws everything
    pygame.display.flip()
pygame.quit()
```

Remember, the \ is the line-continuation character ❶. You can use it to write something on two lines that would normally go on a single line. (Just don't type any spaces after the \ or the line continuation won't work.)

If you save and run the program in listing 18.3, you should see the ball moving back and forth (side to side), as well as moving 30 pixels up or down (once per second). That up or down movement is coming from the timer event.

Time for another game—PyPong

In this section, we'll put together some of the things we have learned—including sprites, collision detection, and events—to make a simple paddle-and-ball game, similar to Pong.

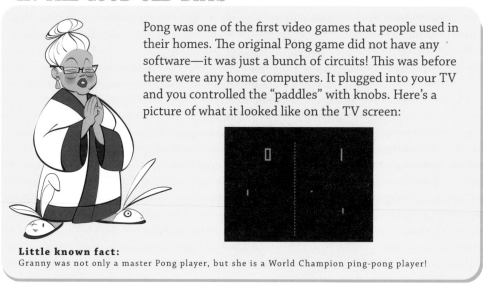

IN THE GOOD OLD DAYS

Pong was one of the first video games that people used in their homes. The original Pong game did not have any software—it was just a bunch of circuits! This was before there were any home computers. It plugged into your TV and you controlled the "paddles" with knobs. Here's a picture of what it looked like on the TV screen:

Little known fact:
Granny was not only a master Pong player, but she is a World Champion ping-pong player!

We'll start with a simple one-player version. Our game will need

- A ball to bounce around
- A paddle to hit the ball with
- A way to control the paddle
- A way to keep score and display the score in the window
- A way to keep track of "lives"—how many turns you get

We'll cover each of these requirements one by one as we build our program.

The ball

The beach ball we have been using so far is a bit big for a Pong game. We need something smaller. Carter and I came up with this wacky tennis-ball guy for our game:

He looks a little scared.

Hey, you'd be scared too if you were about to get whacked around by a paddle!

We're going to use sprites for this game, so we need to make a sprite for our ball and then create an instance of it. We'll use the `Ball` class with `__init__()` and `move()` methods:

```
class MyBallClass(pygame.sprite.Sprite):
    def __init__(self, image_file, speed, location):
        pygame.sprite.Sprite.__init__(self)
        self.image = pygame.image.load(image_file)
        self.rect = self.image.get_rect()
        self.rect.left, self.rect.top = location
        self.speed = speed

    def move(self):
        self.rect = self.rect.move(self.speed)
        if self.rect.left < 0 or self.rect.right > width:
            self.speed[0] = -self.speed[0]

        if self.rect.top <= 0 :
            self.speed[1] = -self.speed[1]
```

Bounces off the sides of the window

Bounces off the top of the window

When we create the instance of the ball, we'll tell it which image to use, the speed of the ball, and its starting location:

```
myBall = MyBallClass('wackyball.bmp', ball_speed, [50, 50])
```

We'll also need to add the ball to a group, so we can do collision detection between the ball and the paddle. We can create the group and add the ball to it at the same time:

```
ballGroup = pygame.sprite.Group(myBall)
```

The paddle

For the paddle, we'll stick with the Pong tradition and use a simple rectangle. We'll use a white background, so we'll make the paddle a black rectangle. We'll make a sprite class and instance for the paddle too:

```
class MyPaddleClass(pygame.sprite.Sprite):
    def __init__(self, location):                    Creates a surface for the paddle
        pygame.sprite.Sprite.__init__(self)
        image_surface = pygame.surface.Surface([100, 20])
        image_surface.fill([0,0,0])          ◁────── Fills the surface with black
        self.image = image_surface.convert()
        self.rect = self.image.get_rect()              Converts the
        self.rect.left, self.rect.top = location       surface to an image

paddle = MyPaddleClass([270, 400])
```

Notice that, for the paddle, we didn't load an image from an image file; we created one by filling a rectangular surface with black. But every sprite needs an `image` attribute, so we used the `Surface.convert()` method to convert the surface into an image.

The paddle can only move left or right, not up or down. We'll make the paddle's x-position (its left-right position) follow the mouse, so the user will control the paddle with the mouse. Because we'll do this right in the event loop, we don't need a separate `move()` method for the paddle.

Controlling the paddle

As I mentioned in the last section, we're going to control the paddle with the mouse. We'll use the MOUSEMOTION event, which means the paddle will move whenever the mouse moves inside the Pygame window. Because Pygame only "sees" the mouse when it's inside the Pygame window, the paddle will automatically be limited to the edges of the window. We'll make the center of the paddle follow the mouse.

The code should look like this:

```
elif event.type == pygame.MOUSEMOTION:
    paddle.rect.centerx = event.pos[0]
```

`event.pos` is a list with the [x, y] values of the mouse's position. So `event.pos[0]` gives us the x-location of the mouse whenever it's moved. Of course, if the mouse is at the left or right edge, the paddle will be halfway out of the window, but that's okay.

The last thing we need is *collision detection* between the ball and the paddle. This is how we "hit" the ball with the paddle. When there is a collision, we'll simply reverse the y-speed of the ball (so when it's going down and hits the paddle, it will bounce and start going up). The code looks like this:

```
if pygame.sprite.spritecollide(paddle, ballGroup, False):
    myBall.speed[1] = -myBall.speed[1]
```

We also have to remember to redraw things every time through the loop. If we put this all together, we get a very basic Pong-like program. Here's the complete code (so far).

Listing 18.4   The first version of PyPong

```
import pygame, sys
from pygame.locals import *

class MyBallClass(pygame.sprite.Sprite):
    def __init__(self, image_file, speed, location):
        pygame.sprite.Sprite.__init__(self)
        self.image = pygame.image.load(image_file)
        self.rect = self.image.get_rect()
        self.rect.left, self.rect.top = location         The ball class definition
        self.speed = speed

    def move(self):
        self.rect = self.rect.move(self.speed)
        if self.rect.left < 0 or self.rect.right > screen.get_width():
            self.speed[0] = -self.speed[0]
                                                         Moves the ball (bounces
                                                          it off top and sides)
        if self.rect.top <= 0 :
            self.speed[1] = -self.speed[1]

class MyPaddleClass(pygame.sprite.Sprite):
    def __init__(self, location = [0,0]):
        pygame.sprite.Sprite.__init__(self)
        image_surface = pygame.surface.Surface([100, 20])
        image_surface.fill([0,0,0])                      The paddle
        self.image = image_surface.convert()             class definition
        self.rect = self.image.get_rect()
        self.rect.left, self.rect.top = location

pygame.init()
screen = pygame.display.set_mode([640,480])
clock = pygame.time.Clock()
ball_speed = [10, 5]                                     Initializes Pygame,
myBall = MyBallClass('wackyball.bmp', ball_speed, [50, 50])   clock, ball, paddle
ballGroup = pygame.sprite.Group(myBall)
paddle = MyPaddleClass([270, 400])

running = True                        The start of the
while running:                        main while loop
    clock.tick(30)
    screen.fill([255, 255, 255])
```

```
    for event in pygame.event.get():
        if event.type == QUIT:
            running = False
        elif event.type == pygame.MOUSEMOTION:          Moves paddle if
            paddle.rect.centerx = event.pos[0]           mouse moves

    if pygame.sprite.spritecollide(paddle, ballGroup, False):    Checks for ball
        myBall.speed[1] = -myBall.speed[1]                        hitting paddle
    myBall.move()                              Moves the ball
    screen.blit(myBall.image, myBall.rect)
    screen.blit(paddle.image, paddle.rect)               Redraws everything
    pygame.display.flip()
pygame.quit()
```

Here's what the program should look like when it runs:

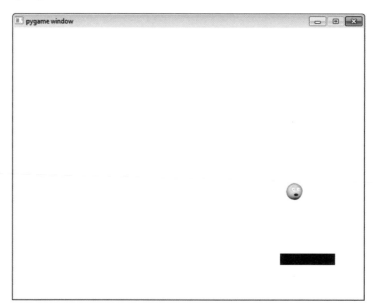

I tried this out, and it's a little boring.

Okay, so it's not the most exciting game, but we're just getting started with making games in Pygame. Let's add a few more things to our PyPong game.

Keeping score and displaying it with `pygame.font`

We need to keep track of two things: the number of lives and the number of points. To make things simple, we'll give one point each time the ball hits the top of the window. We'll give the player three lives.

We also need a way to display the score. Pygame uses a module called **font** to display text. Here's how you use it:

- Make a **font** object, telling Pygame the font style and size you want.
- *Render* the text, passing a string to the font object, which returns a new *surface* with the text drawn on it.
- Blit this surface onto the display surface.

WORD BOX

In computer graphics, *render* means to draw something or make it visible.

The string, in our case, will be the player's score (but we'll have to convert it from an **int** to a **string** first).

We need some code like this, just before the event loop (after the
`paddle = MyPaddleClass([270, 400])` line) in listing 18.4:

```
score_font = pygame.font.Font(None, 50)      ⟵── Creates the font object
score_surf = score_font.render(str(score), 1, (0, 0, 0))   ⟵──  Renders the
score_pos = [10, 10]           ⟵── Sets the text location              text onto the
                                                                       surface
                                                                       score_surf
```

The **None** in the first line is where we could tell Pygame what font (type style) we want to use. By putting **None**, we tell Pygame to use a default font.

Then, inside the event loop, we need something like this:

```
screen.blit(score_surf, score_pos)   ⟵── Blits the surface containing
                                         score text at that location
```

This will redraw the score text each time through the loop.

I tried that and it gave me a `NameError`!

Of course, Carter, we haven't made a **score** variable yet. (I was just getting to that.) Add this line just before the code that creates the **font** object:

```
score = 0
```

Now to keep track of the points …. We already detect when the ball hits the top of the window, in the ball's **move()** method (in order to bounce it). We just need to add a couple of lines there:

```
if self.rect.top <= 0 :
    self.speed[1] = -self.speed[1]
    score = score + 1
    score_surf = score_font.render(str(score), 1, (0, 0, 0))
```

The two new lines

```
Traceback (most recent call last):
    File "C:...", line 59, in <module>
myBall.move()
    File "C:\...", line 24, in move
score = score + 1
UnboundLocalError: local variable 'score'
referenced before assignment
```

Oops! We forgot something about *namespaces*. Remember that big, long explanation in chapter 15? Now you can see a real example of it. Although we do have a variable called **score**, we're trying to use it from within the **move()** method of the **Ball** class. The class is looking for a *local* variable called **score**, which doesn't exist. Instead, we want to use the *global* variable we already created, so we need to tell the **move()** method to use the global **score**, like this:

```
def move(self):
    global score
```

We also need to make **score_font** (the font object for the score) and **score_surf** (the surface that contains the rendered text) global as well, because they are updated in the **move()** method. So the code should actually look like this:

```
def move(self):
    global score, score_font, score_surf
```

Now it should work! Try it: you should see the score in the upper-left corner of the window, and the score should increase as you bounce the ball off the top of the window.

Keeping track of lives

Now let's keep track of the lives. Currently, if you miss the ball, it just drops off the bottom of the window, never to be seen again. We want to give the player three lives, or chances, so let's make a variable called `lives` and set it equal to 3:

```
lives = 3
```

After the player misses the ball and it drops to the bottom of the window, we'll subtract 1 from `lives`, wait a couple of seconds, and then start over with a new ball:

```
if myBall.rect.top >= screen.get_rect().bottom:
    lives = lives - 1
    pygame.time.delay(2000)
    myBall.rect.topleft = [50, 50]
```

This code goes inside the `while` loop. By the way, the reason we write `myBall.rect` for the ball and `get_rect()` for `screen` is this:

- `myBall` is a sprite, and sprites have a `rect` included.
- `screen` is a surface, and a surface does not have a `rect` included. You can find the `rect` that encloses a surface with the `get_rect()` function.

If you make these changes and run the program, you'll see that the player now has three lives.

Adding a life counter

Most games that give the player a number of lives have a way of showing how many lives are left. We can do the same thing with our game.

One easy way is to show a number of balls equal to the number of lives remaining. We can put these in the upper-right corner. Here's a little formula in a `for` loop that will draw the life counter:

```
for i in range (lives):
    width = screen.get_rect().width
    screen.blit(myBall.image, [width - 40 * i, 20])
```

This code also needs to go inside the main `while` loop, just before the event loop (after the `screen.blit(score_text, textpos)` line).

Game over

The last thing we need to add is a "Game Over" message when the player uses up the last life. We'll make a couple of font objects that include our message and the player's final score, render them (create surfaces with the text on them), and blit the surfaces to `screen`.

We also need to stop the ball from reappearing after the last turn. To help with that, we'll make a **done** variable to tell us when we're at the end of the game. The following code will do that—it goes inside the main **while** loop:

```python
if myBall.rect.top >= screen.get_rect().bottom:
    lives = lives - 1                                ←————— Subtracts a life if the ball
    if lives == 0:                                           hits the bottom
        final_text1 = "Game Over"
        final_text2 = "Your final score is:  " + str(score)
        ft1_font = pygame.font.Font(None, 70)
        ft1_surf = ft1_font.render(final_text1, 1, (0, 0, 0))    Centers the text
        ft2_font = pygame.font.Font(None, 50)                    in the window
        ft2_surf = ft2_font.render(final_text2, 1, (0, 0, 0))
        screen.blit(ft1_surf, [screen.get_width()/2 - \    ←—— Line-continuation
                    ft1_surf.get_width()/2, 100])              characters
        screen.blit(ft2_surf, [screen.get_width()/2 - \    ←—
                    ft2_surf.get_width()/2, 200])
        pygame.display.flip()
        done = True
    else:    #wait 2 seconds, then start the next ball
        pygame.time.delay(2000)
        myBall.rect.topleft = [(screen.get_rect().width) - 40*lives, 20]
```

If we put this all together, the final PyPong program looks like the following listing.

Listing 18.5   Final PyPong code

```python
import pygame, sys

class MyBallClass(pygame.sprite.Sprite):
    def __init__(self, image_file, speed, location):
        pygame.sprite.Sprite.__init__(self)
        self.image = pygame.image.load(image_file)
        self.rect = self.image.get_rect()
        self.rect.left, self.rect.top = location
        self.speed = speed

    def move(self):                                          Defines ball class
        global score, score_surf, score_font
        self.rect = self.rect.move(self.speed)
        if self.rect.left < 0 or self.rect.right > screen.get_width():
            self.speed[0] = -self.speed[0]

        if self.rect.top <= 0 :
            self.speed[1] = -self.speed[1]
            score = score + 1
            score_surf = score_font.render(str(score), 1, (0, 0, 0))

class MyPaddleClass(pygame.sprite.Sprite):
    def __init__(self, location = [0,0]):
        pygame.sprite.Sprite.__init__(self)                  Defines paddle class
        image_surface = pygame.surface.Surface([100, 20])
        image_surface.fill([0,0,0])
```

```
        self.image = image_surface.convert()
        self.rect = self.image.get_rect()
        self.rect.left, self.rect.top = location

pygame.init()
screen = pygame.display.set_mode([640,480])
clock = pygame.time.Clock()
myBall = MyBallClass('wackyball.bmp', [10,5], [50, 50])
ballGroup = pygame.sprite.Group(myBall)
paddle = MyPaddleClass([270, 400])
lives = 3
score = 0
score_font = pygame.font.Font(None, 50)
score_surf = score_font.render(str(score), 1, (0, 0, 0))
score_pos = [10, 10]
done = False
running = True
while running:
    clock.tick(30)
    screen.fill([255, 255, 255])
    for event in pygame.event.get():
        if event.type == pygame.QUIT:
            running = False
        elif event.type == pygame.MOUSEMOTION:
            paddle.rect.centerx = event.pos[0]
    if pygame.sprite.spritecollide(paddle, ballGroup, False):
        myBall.speed[1] = -myBall.speed[1]
    myBall.move()
    if not done:
        screen.blit(myBall.image, myBall.rect)
        screen.blit(paddle.image, paddle.rect)
        screen.blit(score_surf, score_pos)
        for i in range (lives):
            width = screen.get_width()
            screen.blit(myBall.image, [width - 40 * i, 20])
        pygame.display.flip()
    if myBall.rect.top >= screen.get_rect().bottom:
        lives = lives - 1
        if lives == 0:
            final_text1 = "Game Over"
            final_text2 = "Your final score is:  " + str(score)
            ft1_font = pygame.font.Font(None, 70)
            ft1_surf = ft1_font.render(final_text1, 1, (0, 0, 0))
            ft2_font = pygame.font.Font(None, 50)
            ft2_surf = ft2_font.render(final_text2, 1, (0, 0, 0))
            screen.blit(ft1_surf, [screen.get_width()/2 - \
                    ft1_surf.get_width()/2, 100])
            screen.blit(ft2_surf, [screen.get_width()/2 - \
                    ft2_surf.get_width()/2, 200])
            pygame.display.flip()
            done = True
        else:
            pygame.time.delay(2000)
            myBall.rect.topleft = [50, 50]
pygame.quit()
```

Defines paddle class

Initializes everything

Creates the font object

The start of the main program (while loop)

Detects mouse motion to move the paddle

Detects collisions between the ball and paddle

Moves the ball

Redraws everything

Decreases life counter if ball hits bottom

Creates and draws the final score text

Starts a new life, after 2-second delay

If you run the code in
listing 18.5, you should
see something like this:

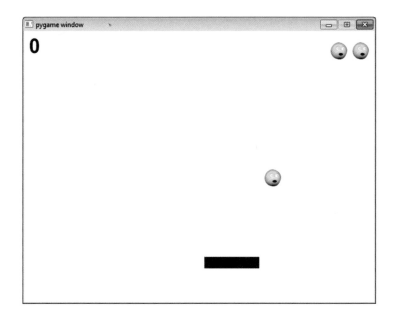

If you were paying attention in the editor, this is about 75 lines of code (plus some blank lines). That's the biggest program we have created so far, but it also has a lot of stuff going on, even though it looks pretty simple when you run it.

In the next chapter, you'll learn about sounds in Pygame, and we'll add some sound to our PyPong game.

What did you learn?

In this chapter, you learned about

- Events
- The Pygame event loop
- Event handling
- Keyboard events
- Mouse events
- Timer events (and user event types)
- `pygame.font` (for adding text to Pygame programs)
- Putting all these things together to make a game!

Test your knowledge

1   What are two kinds of events that a program can respond to?

2   What do you call the piece of code that deals with an event?

3   What is the name of the event type that Pygame uses to detect keys being pressed?

4   What attribute of a `MOUSEMOVE` event tells you where in the window the mouse is located?

5   How do you find out what the next available event number is in Pygame (for example, if you want to add a user event)?

6   How do you create a timer to generate timer events in Pygame?

7   What kind of object is used to display text in a Pygame window?

8   What are the three steps to make text appear in a Pygame window?

Try it out

1   Did you notice anything strange that happens when the ball hits the side of the paddle instead of the top? It kind of bounces along through the middle of the paddle for a while. Can you figure out why? Can you fix it? Give it a try before looking at my solution in the answer section.

2   Try rewriting the program (either listing 18.4 or 18.5) so that there's some randomness to the ball's bounces. You might change the way the ball bounces off the paddle or the walls, make the speed random, or something else you can think of. (You saw `random.randint()` and `random.random()` in chapter 15, so you know how to generate random numbers, both integers and floats.)

## CHAPTER 19

Sound

In the last chapter, we made our first graphical game, PyPong, using what we have learned about graphics, sprites, collisions, animation, and events. In this chapter, we'll add another piece of the puzzle: sound. Every video game and many other programs use sound to make them more interesting and enjoyable.

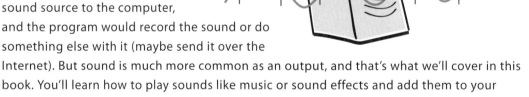

Sound can be both an input and an output. As an input, you'd connect a microphone or other sound source to the computer, and the program would record the sound or do something else with it (maybe send it over the Internet). But sound is much more common as an output, and that's what we'll cover in this book. You'll learn how to play sounds like music or sound effects and add them to your programs, like PyPong.

More help from Pygame—mixer

Sound is another one of those things, like graphics, that can get complicated, because different computers have different hardware and software for playing sounds. To make things simpler, we're going to get some help from Pygame again.

Pygame has a module for working with sound, called `pygame.mixer`. In the real, non-programming world, a device that takes in different sounds and merges them together is called a *mixer,* and that's where Pygame got the name.

Making sounds vs. playing sounds

There are two basic ways for a program to produce sounds. The program can generate or *synthesize* the sounds—that means create them from scratch by making sound waves of different pitch and volume. Or the program can *play back* a recorded sound. This could be a piece of music on a CD, an MP3 sound file, or some other type of sound file.

In this book, you're only going to learn about playing back sounds. Making your own sounds from scratch is a pretty big topic, and there's only so much room in this book. If you're interested in computer-generated sounds, there are many programs for generating music and sound from your computer.

Playing sounds

When you play back a sound, you're taking a sound file from your hard drive (or from a CD or sometimes the Internet) and turning it into sound that you can hear on the computer's speakers or headphones. There are many different types of sound files you can use on a computer. These are some of the more common ones:

- *Wave* files—The filenames end in **.wav**, like **hello.wav**.
- *MP3* files—The filenames end in **.mp3**, like **mySong.mp3**.
- *WMA* (Windows Media Audio) files—The filenames end in .**wma**, like **someSong.wma**.
- *Ogg Vorbis* files—The filenames end in **.ogg**, like **yourSong.ogg**.

In our examples, we're going to use **.wav** and **.mp3** files. All the sounds we'll use are in the **\sounds** folder, where HelloWorld was installed. For example, on Windows computers, it should be at **c:\Program Files\HelloWorld\examples\sounds**.

There are two ways to include a sound file in your program. You can copy the sound file into the same folder where the program is saved. This is where Python expects to find the file, so you can just use the name of the file in your program, like this:

```
sound_file = "my_sound.wav"
```

If you don't copy the sound file into the same folder as the program, you have to tell Python exactly where the sound file is located, like this:

```
sound_file = "c:\Program Files\HelloWorld\sounds\my_sound.wav"
```

For our examples, I'll assume you have copied the sound files to the folder where you save your programs. This means that, wherever a sound file is used in the examples, you'll just see the filename and not the full location of the file. If you don't copy the sound files to the program folder, you'll need to replace the filenames with the full file locations.

All the sound files for these examples are already on your hard drive if you used the book's installation program. Otherwise, you can find them on the book's web site: **www.helloworldbook2.com.**

Starting `pygame.mixer`

In order to play sounds, you have to *initialize* `pygame.mixer`. Remember what *initializing* means? It means to get something ready at the start.

Getting `pygame.mixer` ready is very easy. We just need to add the line

```
pygame.mixer.init()
```

after we initialize Pygame. So the code at the start of a program that uses Pygame for sound looks like this:

```
import pygame
pygame.init()
pygame.mixer.init()
```

Now we're ready to play some sounds. There are two main types of sounds you'll use in your programs. The first is sound effects or sound clips. These are usually short, and they're most commonly stored in **.wav** files. For these kinds of sounds, `pygame.mixer` uses a `Sound` object, like this:

```
splat = pygame.mixer.Sound("splat.wav")
splat.play()
```

The other kind of sound you'll use a lot is music. Music is most commonly stored in **.mp3**, **.wma**, or **.ogg** files. To play these, Pygame uses a module within `mixer` called `music`. You use it like this:

```
pygame.mixer.music.load("bg_music.mp3")
pygame.mixer.music.play()
```

This will play the song (or whatever is in the music file) once and then stop.

Let's try playing some sounds. First, let's try playing a "splat" sound.

We still need a `while` loop to keep the Pygame program running. Also, even though we won't be drawing any graphics right now, Pygame programs are not happy unless they have a window. And on some systems, `mixer` takes a little time to initialize. If you try to start playing a sound too quickly, you'll hear only part of it or none at all. So we will wait a bit for `mixer` to get ready. The code should look something like the following listing.

Listing 19.1   Trying out sounds in Pygame

```
import pygame, sys
pygame.init()                                    Initializes Pygame
pygame.mixer.init()                              and mixer
                                                                Creates a Pygame window
screen = pygame.display.set_mode([640,480])
pygame.time.delay(1000)                          Waits a second for mixer
                                                 to finish initializing
splat = pygame.mixer.Sound("splat.wav")          Creates the sound object
splat.play()          Plays the sound

running = True
while running:
    for event in pygame.event.get():             The usual Pygame
        if event.type == pygame.QUIT:            event loop
            running = False
pygame.quit()
```

Try this and see how it works.

Now let's try playing some music using the `mixer.music` module. We only need to change a couple of lines in listing 19.1. The new code is shown next.

Listing 19.2   Playing music

```
import pygame, sys
pygame.init()
pygame.mixer.init()

screen = pygame.display.set_mode([640,480])
pygame.time.delay(1000)

pygame.mixer.music.load("bg_music.mp3")          These are the two
pygame.mixer.music.play()                        changed lines

running = True
while running:
    for event in pygame.event.get():
        if event.type == pygame.QUIT:
            running = False
pygame.quit()
```

Give that a try, and make sure you can hear the music play.

I don't know about you, but it seemed a bit loud to me. I had to turn the volume way down on my computer. Let's find out how to control the sound volume in your programs.

Controlling volume

You can control the volume of sound on your computer by using the volume controls. In Windows, this is done with the little speaker icon in the system tray. That setting controls the volume of all the sounds on your computer. You might also have a volume knob on the speakers themselves.

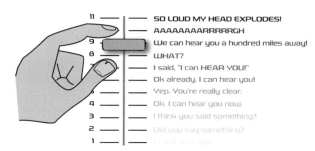

But you can also control the volume that Pygame sends to your computer's sound card.

Like some video games that have their own volume control.

And the good thing is, you can control the volume of each sound individually—like making the music quieter and the "splat" a bit louder, if you want.

For music, you use `pygame.mixer.music.set_volume()`. For sounds, there's a `set_volume()` method for each sound object. In our first example, `splat` was the name of our sound object, so we'd use `splat.set_volume()`. The volume is a floating-point number from 0 to 1; for example, 0.5 would be 50 percent or half volume.

Now let's try having music and sound in the same program. How about playing a song and then playing the "splat" sound at the end. We'll also turn down the volume of our sound a bit. We'll set the music to 30 percent and the "splat" sound to 50 percent. The code should look something like this.

Listing 19.3   Music and sound with volume adjustment

```
import pygame, sys
pygame.init()
pygame.mixer.init()
screen = pygame.display.set_mode([640,480])
pygame.time.delay(1000)
pygame.mixer.music.load("bg_music.mp3")
pygame.mixer.music.set_volume(0.30)          ◁——— Adjusts the volume
pygame.mixer.music.play()                              of the music
```

```
splat = pygame.mixer.Sound("splat.wav")
splat.set_volume(0.50)                    <------   Adjusts the volume
splat.play()                                        of the sound effect
running = True
while running:
    for event in pygame.event.get():
        if event.type == pygame.QUIT:
            running = False
pygame.quit()
```

Give this a try and see how it works.

> Hey, it "splatted" me right at the start! It didn't wait for the song to finish.
>
> Why not?

What Carter noticed is that, as soon as the program starts the music, it goes on to do the next thing, which happens to be playing the "splat" sound. The reason for this is that music is quite often used in the background, and you won't always want the program to sit there and play the entire song before doing something else. In the next section, we'll make this work the way we want.

Playing background music

Background music is meant to play in the background while the game is being played. So once you start the background song, Pygame has to get ready to do other things, like moving sprites around or checking the mouse and keyboard for input. It doesn't wait for the song to finish.

But what if you want to know when the song ends? Maybe you want to start a different song or play another sound (like we want to do). How do you know when the music is done? Pygame has a way to tell you: you can ask the `mixer.music` module if it's still busy playing a song. If it is, you know the song isn't done yet. If it is not busy, you know the song is done. Let's try that.

To find out if the music module is still busy playing a song, you use the `mixer.music` module's `get_busy()` function. This will return the value `True` if it's still busy or `False` if it isn't. This time, we'll make our program play the song, then play the sound effect, and then end the program automatically. The next listing shows you how.

Listing 19.4   Waiting for the end of the song

```
import pygame, sys
pygame.init()
pygame.mixer.init()

screen = pygame.display.set_mode([640,480])
pygame.time.delay(1000)

pygame.mixer.music.load("bg_music.mp3")
pygame.mixer.music.set_volume(0.3)
pygame.mixer.music.play()
splat = pygame.mixer.Sound("splat.wav")
splat.set_volume(0.5)
running = True
while running:
    for event in pygame.event.get():
        if event.type == pygame.QUIT:
            running = False

    if not pygame.mixer.music.get_busy():        ◁———   Checks if the music
        splat.play()                                     is done playing
        pygame.time.delay(1000)          ◁———   Waits a second for the
        running = False                          "splat" sound to finish
pygame.quit()
```

This code will play the song once and then play the sound effect, and then the program will end.

Repeating music

If you're going to use a song as background music for a game, you probably want to have the music continue as long as the program is running. The **music** module can do this for you. You can *repeat* the playback a certain number of times, like this

```
pygame.mixer.music.play(3)
```

This will play the song three times.

The documentation for Pygame says that the code
`pygame.mixer.music.play(3)`
will play the song four times: the first time plus three repeats. They goofed on that one. It will really play the song three times.

You can also make the song repeat forever by passing a special value, -1, like this:

```
pygame.mixer.music.play(-1)
```

This will keep repeating the song forever, or as long as the Pygame program is running. (Actually, it doesn't have to be -1. Any negative number will do the trick.)

Adding sounds to PyPong

Now that you know the basics of playing sounds, let's add some sound to our PyPong game.

First we'll add a sound every time the ball hits the paddle. We already know when that is, because we're using collision detection to reverse the direction of the ball when it hits the paddle. Remember this code from listing 18.5?

```
if pygame.sprite.spritecollide(paddle, ballGroup, False):
    myBall.speed[1] = -myBall.speed[1]
```

Now we need to add the code that plays a sound. We need to add `pygame.mixer.init()` near the start of the program, and we'll also create the sound object so it's ready to use:

```
hit = pygame.mixer.Sound("hit_paddle.wav")
```

We'll also set the volume so it's not too loud:

```
hit.set_volume(0.4)
```

Then, when the ball hits the paddle, we'll play the sound:

```
if pygame.sprite.spritecollide(paddle, ballGroup, False):
    myBall.speed[1] = -myBall.speed[1]
    hit.play()                          ⟵——— Plays the sound
```

Try adding this to the PyPong program from listing 18.5. Make sure you copy the **hit_paddle.wav** file to the same place you're saving your program. When you run it, you should hear a sound every time the ball hits the paddle.

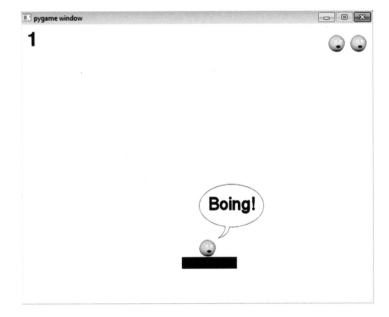

More wacky sounds

Now that we have the `hit` sound when the ball hits the paddle, let's add a few other sounds. We'll add sounds for these things:

- When the ball hits the side walls
- When the ball hits the top wall and the player scores a point
- When the player misses the ball and the ball hits the bottom
- When a new life starts
- When the game ends

First we need to create sound objects for all of these. You can put the code anywhere after `pygame.mixer.init()` but before the `while` loop:

```
hit_wall = pygame.mixer.Sound("hit_wall.wav")
hit_wall.set_volume(0.4)
get_point = pygame.mixer.Sound("get_point.wav")
get_point.set_volume(0.2)
splat = pygame.mixer.Sound("splat.wav")
splat.set_volume(0.6)
new_life = pygame.mixer.Sound("new_life.wav")
new_life.set_volume(0.5)
bye = pygame.mixer.Sound("game_over.wav")
bye.set_volume(0.6)
```

I picked the volume levels by just trying it out to see what sounded right. You can set them to whatever you like. And remember to copy all the sound files to wherever you're saving your code. All of these sounds can be found in the **\examples\sounds** folder or on the website.

Now we need to add the `play()` methods to the places where these events occur. The `hit_wall` sound should happen whenever we hit the sides of the window. We detect this in the ball's `move()` method, and we reverse the ball's *x*-speed (to make the ball "bounce" off the sides). In the original listing 18.5, this is in line 14:

```
if self.rect.left < 0 or self.rect.right > screen.get_width():
```

So when we reverse direction, we can also play our sound. The code looks like this:

```
if self.rect.left < 0 or self.rect.right > screen.get_width():
    self.speed[0] = -self.speed[0]
    hit_wall.play()                              ⟵——— Plays the sound for
                                                       hitting the side wall
```

We can do the same thing for the `get_point` sound. Just a little farther down in the ball's `move()` method, we detect the ball hitting the top of the window. That's where we bounce the ball and add a point to the player's score. Now we're going to play a sound as well. The new code looks like this:

```
if self.rect.top <= 0 :
    self.speed[1] = -self.speed[1]
    points = points + 1
    score_text = font.render(str(points), 1, (0, 0, 0))
    get_point.play()
```

Plays the sound for getting a point

Give these additions a try to see how they work.

Next we can add the code to play a sound when the player misses the ball and loses a life. We detect this in the main **while** loop, in line 63 of the original listing 18.5 (**if myBall.rect.top >= screen.get_rect().bottom:**). We just need to add a line like this:

```
if myBall.rect.top >= screen.get_rect().bottom:
    splat.play()
    # lose a life if the ball hits the bottom
    lives = lives - 1
```

Plays the sound for missing a ball and losing a life

We can also add a sound when a new life starts. This happens in the last three lines of listing 18.5, in the **else** block. This time we'll give our sound effect a little time to play before we start the new life:

```
else:
    pygame.time.delay(1000)
    new_life.play()
    myBall.rect.topleft = [50, 50]
    screen.blit(myBall.image, myBall.rect)
    pygame.display.flip()
    pygame.time.delay(1000)
```

Instead of waiting two seconds (like we did in the original program), we wait one second (1,000 milliseconds), play the sound, and then wait another second before starting the new turn. Give it a try and see how it sounds.

There's one more sound effect to add, and that's when the game is over. This happens in line 65 of listing 18.5 (**if lives == 0:**). Add the line to play the "bye" sound here:

```
if lives == 0:
    bye.play()
```

Try this and see how it works.

At the end of the game, the bye sound and the splat sound started playing over and over!

Oops! We forgot something. The code that plays the "bye" sound and the "splat" sound is in the main `while` loop, which doesn't stop until the Pygame window is closed, so it keeps playing over and over as long as the `while` loop runs! We need to add something to make sure it only plays once.

One thing we can use is the variable called `done`, which tells us when the game is over. We can change our code to look like this:

```
if myBall.rect.top >= screen.get_rect().bottom:
        if not done:
            splat.play()          Makes sure the sound
        lives = lives - 1         only plays once
        if lives == 0:
            if not done:
                bye.play()
```

Try that and make sure it works.

I noticed something else.

Even after the game is over, it sounds like the ball is still bouncing off the walls!?

Hmmm … We might need to think about this one a bit. We have our `done` variable to tell us when the game is over, and we're using that to know when to play our "bye" sound and also when to display the final message with the score. But what's the ball doing?

Even though the ball has reached the bottom of the window, it's still moving! There's nothing to stop the ball from going farther down, so its y-value just keeps getting bigger. It's "below" the bottom of the screen where we can't see it, but we can still *hear* it! The ball is still moving, so it's still bouncing off the "sides" whenever its x-value gets big enough or small enough. That happens in the `move()` method, and that method keeps running as long as the `while` loop is running.

How can we fix it? There are a few ways:

- Stop the ball from moving by setting its speed to [0,0] when the game is over.
- Check if the ball is below the bottom of the window, and don't play the `hit_wall` sound if it is.
- Check the `done` variable, and don't play the `hit_wall` sound if the game is done.

I picked the second option, but any of them would work. I'll leave it up to you to choose one and modify your code to fix this problem.

Adding music to PyPong

There's just one thing left to do—add the music. We need to load the music file, set the volume, and start it playing. We want it to keep repeating while the game is playing, so we'll use the special value of -1, like this:

```
pygame.mixer.music.load("bg_music.mp3")
pygame.mixer.music.set_volume(0.3)
pygame.mixer.music.play(-1)
```

This code can go anywhere before the main `while` loop. That will start the music playing. Now we need to stop the music at the end, and there's a nice way to do this. `pygame.mixer.music` has a method called `fadeout()` that will fade the music out gradually instead of stopping it abruptly. You just tell it how long the fadeout should be, like this:

```
pygame.mixer.music.fadeout(2000)
```

That's 2,000 milliseconds, which is 2 seconds. This line can go in the same place where we set `done = True`. (It doesn't matter if it comes before or after.)

The program is now complete with sound effects and music. Give it a try, and see how it sounds! In case you want to see how the whole thing goes together, I have included my final version as listing 19.5. You will need to make sure that **wackyball.bmp** and all the sound files are in the same folder as the program.

Listing 19.5   PyPong with sound and music

```python
import pygame, sys

class MyBallClass(pygame.sprite.Sprite):
    def __init__(self, image_file, speed, location = [0,0]):
        pygame.sprite.Sprite.__init__(self)
        self.image = pygame.image.load(image_file)
        self.rect = self.image.get_rect()
        self.rect.left, self.rect.top = location
        self.speed = speed

    def move(self):
        global points, score_text
        self.rect = self.rect.move(self.speed)
        if self.rect.left < 0 or self.rect.right > screen.get_width():
            self.speed[0] = -self.speed[0]
            if self.rect.top < screen.get_height():
                hit_wall.play()

        if self.rect.top <= 0 :
            self.speed[1] = -self.speed[1]
            points = points + 1
            score_text = font.render(str(points), 1, (0, 0, 0))
            get_point.play()

class MyPaddleClass(pygame.sprite.Sprite):
    def __init__(self, location = [0,0]):
        pygame.sprite.Sprite.__init__(self)
        image_surface = pygame.surface.Surface([100, 20])
        image_surface.fill([0,0,0])
        self.image     = image_surface.convert()
        self.rect = self.image.get_rect()
        self.rect.left, self.rect.top = location
pygame.init()
pygame.mixer.init()

pygame.mixer.music.load("bg_music.mp3")
pygame.mixer.music.set_volume(0.3)
pygame.mixer.music.play(-1)
hit = pygame.mixer.Sound("hit_paddle.wav")
hit.set_volume(0.4)
new_life = pygame.mixer.Sound("new_life.wav")
new_life.set_volume(0.5)
splat = pygame.mixer.Sound("splat.wav")
splat.set_volume(0.6)
hit_wall = pygame.mixer.Sound("hit_wall.wav")
hit_wall.set_volume(0.4)

get_point = pygame.mixer.Sound("get_point.wav")
get_point.set_volume(0.2)
bye = pygame.mixer.Sound("game_over.wav")
bye.set_volume(0.6)
screen = pygame.display.set_mode([640,480])
clock = pygame.time.Clock()
```

Plays sound when the ball hits the side wall

Plays sound when the ball hits the top (player gets a point)

Initializes Pygame's sound module

Loads music file

Sets volume of the music

Starts playing the music; repeats forever

Creates sound objects, loads sounds, and sets volume for each

```
myBall = MyBallClass('wackyball.bmp', [12,6], [50, 50])
ballGroup = pygame.sprite.Group(myBall)
paddle = MyPaddleClass([270, 400])
lives = 3
points = 0

font = pygame.font.Font(None, 50)
score_text = font.render(str(points), 1, (0, 0, 0))
textpos = [10, 10]
done = False

running = True
while running:
    clock.tick(30)
    screen.fill([255, 255, 255])
    for event in pygame.event.get():
        if event.type == pygame.QUIT:
            running = False
        elif event.type == pygame.MOUSEMOTION:
            paddle.rect.centerx = event.pos[0]

    if pygame.sprite.spritecollide(paddle, ballGroup, False):
        hit.play()
        myBall.speed[1] = -myBall.speed[1]

    myBall.move()

    if not done:
        screen.blit(myBall.image, myBall.rect)
        screen.blit(paddle.image, paddle.rect)
        screen.blit(score_text, textpos)
        for i in range(lives):
            width = screen.get_width()
            screen.blit(myBall.image, [width - 40 * i, 20])
        pygame.display.flip()

    if myBall.rect.top >= screen.get_rect().bottom:
        if not done:
            splat.play()
        lives = lives - 1
        if lives <= 0:
            if not done:
                pygame.time.delay(1000)
                bye.play()
            final_text1 = "Game Over"
            final_text2 = "Your final score is:  " + str(points)
            ft1_font = pygame.font.Font(None, 70)
            ft1_surf = font.render(final_text1, 1, (0, 0, 0))
            ft2_font = pygame.font.Font(None, 50)

            ft2_surf = font.render(final_text2, 1, (0, 0, 0))
            screen.blit(ft1_surf, [screen.get_width()/2 - \
                    ft1_surf.get_width()/2, 100])
            screen.blit(ft2_surf, [screen.get_width()/2 - \
                    ft2_surf.get_width()/2, 200])
```

Plays sound when the ball hits the paddle

Plays sound when the player loses a life

Waits one second and then plays the ending sound

```
            pygame.display.flip()
            done = True
            pygame.mixer.music.fadeout(2000)          ◁──── Fades out the music
        else:
            pygame.time.delay(1000)            │ Plays sound when
            new_life.play()                    │ a new life starts
            myBall.rect.topleft = [50, 50]
            screen.blit(myBall.image, myBall.rect)
            pygame.display.flip()
            pygame.time.delay(1000)
    pygame.quit()
```

That's getting long-ish! (It's around 100 lines, plus blank lines.) This could be made quite a bit shorter, but it might also be harder to read and understand. We've been building the program a little at a time in these chapters, so you didn't have to type it all at once.

If you followed along with the book, you should understand what each part of the program does and how the parts go together. And just in case you need it, the full listing is in the **\examples** folder on your computer (if you installed it) and on the website.

In the next chapter, we'll make a different kind of graphical program: one with buttons, menus, and so on—a GUI.

What did you learn?

In this chapter, you learned

- How to add sound to your programs
- How to play sound clips (usually **.wav** files)
- How to play music files (usually **.mp3** files)
- How to know when a sound is done playing
- How to control the volume of sound effects and music
- How to make music repeat so it plays over and over
- How to fade out music gradually

Test your knowledge

1 What are three types of files that are used for storing sound?
2 What Pygame module is used for playing music?
3 How do you set the volume for a Pygame sound object?
4 How do you set the volume for background music?
5 How do you make music fade out?

Try it out

1 Try adding sounds to the number-guessing game in chapter 1. Even though the game is text-mode, you'll need to add a Pygame window, like we did in the examples in this chapter. There are some sounds you can use in the **\examples\sounds** folder (and on the website):

- **Ahoy.wav**
- **TooLow.wav**
- **TooHigh.wav**
- **WhatsYerGuess.wav**
- **AvastGotIt.wav**
- **NoMore.wav**

Or it might be fun to record your own sounds. You would use something like Sound Recorder in Windows, or you could download the free program Audacity (which is available for multiple operating systems) at **audacity.sourceforge.net/**.

## CHAPTER 20

More GUIs

We made some simple GUIs back in chapter 6, when we used EasyGui to make some dialog boxes (or just *dialogs* for short). But GUIs need more than dialogs. In most modern programs, the whole program runs in a GUI. In this chapter, we're going to explore making GUIs with PyQt, which gives you more flexibility and control over how things look.

PyQt is a module that helps you create GUIs. We're first going to use it to make a version of our temperature-conversion program.

Working with PyQt

Before using PyQt, you have to make sure it's installed on your computer. If you installed Python using the book's installer, PyQt is already installed. If not, you'll have to download and install it separately. You can get PyQt from **www.riverbankcomputing.com/software/pyqt/download**. Make sure you get the correct version for your operating system and the version of Python you're using (version 2.7.3, if you ran our installer). We're using PyQt 4.1.

There is also a version 5 of PyQt, which is quite different from version 4. If you don't use our installer, make sure you install PyQt4.

There are basically two main parts to writing a GUI program. You need to create the user interface itself (the "UI"), and you need to create the code that makes the UI do what you want. Creating the UI involves placing things like buttons, text boxes, choice boxes, and so on in the window. Then you write code that makes stuff happen when you click a button, type in a text box, or select a choice from a choice box.

When using Qt, you create the UI using something called Qt Designer. Let's see how that works.

Qt Designer

When you installed PyQt, one of the things that was installed was a program called Qt Designer. Find the icon for it (for example, in the Start menu in Windows), and launch Qt Designer. When you do, you should see the Qt window open, and in the middle, you'll see the **New Form** dialog:

Form is the programming term for a GUI window. Because you're going to make a new GUI window, pick the **Main Window** option and then click the **Create** button. Now let's look at the rest of the Qt window.

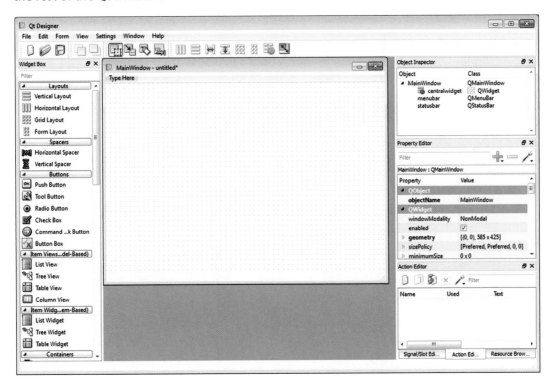

On the left is the Widget Box, where you see all the different graphical elements you can use in your GUI. They are grouped into a few different categories.

On the right are the Object Inspector and Property Editor. These are where you can examine and change the properties of the widgets. There is also a third box whose function is selected by the tabs at the bottom. It can be the Signal/Slot Inspector, Action Editor, or Resource Browser.

In the middle is the new, blank form you just created. It says **Main Window – untitled** at the top, because you haven't given it a name yet. This blank space is where you will put the widgets to make up your UI. (On a Mac, to get this view you'll need to go into **Qt Designer > Preferences** and change the user interface mode from Multiple Top-Level Windows to Docked Window. Otherwise all the panes will float in separate windows.)

Adding a button

Let's add a button to the GUI. On the left side of the Qt Designer window, find the **Buttons** section, and look for the **Push Button** widget.

Drag the **Push Button** over to the blank form, and drop it somewhere. Now you have a button on your form, and it has the label **PushButton**.

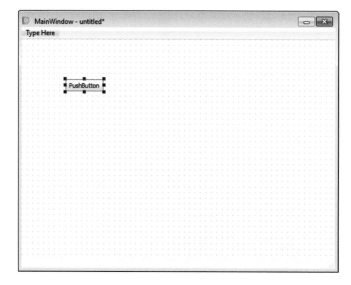

Now look over on the right side, at the Property Editor. If the button is still selected (if it has the little blue squares around it), then you will see its properties in the Property Editor. You can see that the name of the button is **PushButton**. If you scroll through some of the other properties in the Properties list, you can see things like the button's width and height, its x and y position, and so on.

Changing the button

There are two ways to change the button's size or position in the window: drag it with the mouse, or change the Size or Position properties. Try both ways of moving and resizing the button to see how they work. To move the button with the mouse, click anywhere on the button and drag it to a new position. To resize it with the mouse, click one of the blue squares around the edge of the button (they are called *handles*), and drag an edge or corner of the button to make it bigger or smaller. To resize it using the properties, click the little triangle next to the **geometry** property, and it will expand to show the **X**, **Y**, **Width**, and **Height** properties. Just type in different numbers to move or resize the button.

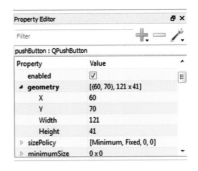

You can also change the text that appears on the button. Right now the text is the same as the name of the button, but it doesn't have to be. Let's change it so the text on the button says **I'm a Button!**. In the Property Editor, scroll down until you find the property called **text**. Change the text to **I'm a Button!**. You can also change the button text by double-clicking the button and editing the text directly on the button.

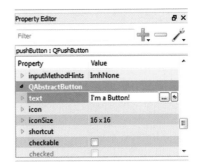

If you look over at the button on the form, it has now changed to say **I'm a Button!**. But the name of the widget (the **objectName** property) is still **PushButton**. That's how you would refer to it in the code if you wanted to do something with the button.

Saving the GUI

Let's save what we have so far. In PyQt, the description of the GUI is saved in a **.ui** file. This file has all the information about the window, menu, and widgets. This is the same information that was displayed in property windows on the right side of Qt Designer, and now you need to save it into a file for the PyQt program to use when it runs.

To save the UI, go to the **File** menu and choose **Save As**, and give the file a name. Let's call our GUI **MyFirstGui**. You'll notice that the file extension is automatically set to **.ui**. So the UI will be saved as **MyFirstGui.ui**. Make sure you save it to the folder you want. By default, Designer will save it in the folder where its own files are, which is probably not what you want. Browse to the folder where you save your Python programs before you click **Save**.

You can look at this file in any text editor, including the IDLE editor. If you open it, you'll see something like this:

```xml
<?xml version="1.0" encoding="UTF-8"?>
<ui version="4.0">
 <class>MainWindow</class>
 <widget class="QMainWindow" name="MainWindow">
  <property name="geometry">
   <rect>
    <x>0</x>
    <y>0</y>
    <width>576</width>
    <height>425</height>
   </rect>
  </property>
  <property name="windowTitle">
   <string>MainWindow</string>
  </property>
  <widget class="QWidget" name="centralwidget">
   <widget class="QPushButton" name="pushButton">
    <property name="geometry">
     <rect>
      <x>60</x>
      <y>70</y>
      <width>121</width>
      <height>41</height>
     </rect>
    </property>
    <property name="toolTip">
     <string/>
    </property>
    <property name="text">
     <string>I'm a Button!</string>
    </property>
   </widget>
  </widget>
  <widget class="QMenuBar" name="menubar">
   <property name="geometry">
    <rect>
     <x>0</x>
     <y>0</y>
     <width>576</width>
     <height>21</height>
    </rect>
   </property>
  </widget>
  <widget class="QStatusBar" name="statusbar"/>
 </widget>
 <resources/>
 <connections/>
</ui>
```

Defines the window (the background)

Defines the button

It looks a little confusing, but if you take a closer look, you'll see the part that describes the window and the part that describes the button, as well as some other parts we haven't talked about yet, like the menu and status bar.

Making our GUI do something

We now have a very basic GUI—a window with a button. But it doesn't do anything. We haven't written any code to tell the program what to do when someone clicks the button. It's like having a car with four wheels and a body, but no engine. It looks nice, but it won't go anywhere.

She's a real beauty, ain't she? She can do zero to zero in 1 second flat.

We need a little bit of code to make our program run. For a PyQt program, the minimum you need is something like this.

Listing 20.1   PyQt minimum code required

```
import sys
from PyQt4 import QtCore, QtGui, uic          ⟵  Imports needed
                                                  PyQt libraries

form_class = uic.loadUiType("MyFirstGui.ui")[0]     ⟵ ❶  Loads the UI
                                                            we created in
class MyWindowClass(QtGui.QMainWindow, form_class):      Designer
    def __init__(self, parent=None):          │ Defines
        QtGui.QMainWindow.__init__(self, parent)  │ a class for
        self.setupUi(self)                     │ the main
                                               │ window
app = QtGui.QApplication(sys.argv)    ⟵  PyQt object that runs the event loop
myWindow = MyWindowClass()            ⟵
myWindow.show()          │ Starts the program and        Makes an instance of
app.exec_()              │ displays the GUI window        the window class
```

If you're wondering what the `[0]` is at the end of line ❶, there's an explanation in the Note.

The reason for the [0] at the end of the line that loads the UI is that the `uic.loadUiType()` method returns a list with two things in it: something called a `form_class` and something called a `base_class`. For our purposes, we only need the first item, the `form_class`, which is `item[0]` in the list.

As you might expect with Python, everything in PyQt is an object. Each window is an object, defined with the `class` keyword. This program, and all the PyQt programs we will make, have a class that inherits from the PyQt class `QMainWindow`. In listing 20.1, we called the class `MyWindowClass` (in line 6), but we could have used any name. Remember that a class definition is just a blueprint. We still have to build a house—make an *instance* of the class—and we do that with the line `myWindow = MyWindowClass()` near the bottom. `myWindow` is an instance of the class `MyWindowClass`.

Type this into an IDLE or SPE editor window, and save it as **MyFirstGui.py**:

- *Main code*—**MyFirstGui.py**
- *UI file*—**MyFirstGui.ui**

The two files need to be saved in the same location, so the main program can find the UI file and load it at the start of the program.

You can now run this from IDLE. You'll see the window open, and you can click the button. But nothing happens yet. We have our program running, but we still haven't written any code for the button. Close the program by clicking the X in the title bar.

Let's do something simple. When we click the button, let's make it move to a new place in the window. Add the code in lines 10 to 17 of listing 20.2 to the code you typed in listing 20.1.

Listing 20.2   Adding an event handler for the button from listing 20.1

```
import sys
from PyQt4 import QtCore, QtGui, uic

form_class = uic.loadUiType("MyFirstGui.ui")[0]

class MyWindowClass(QtGui.QMainWindow, form_class):
    def __init__(self, parent=None):
        QtGui.QMainWindow.__init__(self, parent)
        self.setupUi(self)
        self.pushButton.clicked.connect(self.button_clicked)

    def button_clicked(self):
        x = self.pushButton.x()
        y = self.pushButton.y()
        x += 50
        y += 50
        self.pushButton.move(x, y)

app = QtGui.QApplication(sys.argv)
myWindow = MyWindowClass()
myWindow.show()
app.exec_()
```

Connects the event handler to the event

The event handler

Add these lines to make the button move on each mouse click

Moves the button when we click it

Make sure you indent the whole `def` block four spaces in from the `class` statement, as shown in the listing. You need to do that because all components are *inside*, or *are part of*, the window. So the code for the button's event handler goes inside the class definition.

Try running it to see what happens. We're going to look at this code in detail in the next section.

The return of event handlers

In our Pygame programs in the last few chapters, you learned about *event handlers* and how to use them to look for keyboard and mouse activity, or *events*. The same thing applies for PyQt.

In `MyWindowClass`, we define the event handlers for the window. Because the button is in our main window, the event handler for the button goes there.

First we have to tell the main window that we are making an event handler for a particular widget. In listing 20.2, that happens in line 10:

```
self.pushButton.clicked.connect(self.button_clicked)
```

Here we *connect* or *bind* the *event* (`self.pushButton.clicked`) to the *event handler* (`self.button_clicked`). The definition of the `button_clicked` event handler starts on line 12. `clicked` is just one of the events we can get for the button. Others include `pressed` and `released`.

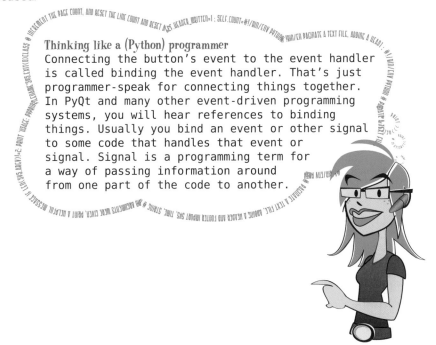

Thinking like a (Python) programmer
Connecting the button's event to the event handler is called binding the event handler. That's just programmer-speak for connecting things together. In PyQt and many other event-driven programming systems, you will hear references to binding things. Usually you bind an event or other signal to some code that handles that event or signal. Signal is a programming term for a way of passing information around from one part of the code to another.

What is `self`?

In the `button_clicked()` event handler, there is one parameter: `self`. Just like when we first talked about objects in chapter 14, `self` refers to the instance that's calling the method. In this case, all events come from the background or main window, so it's the window object that's calling the event handler. Here, `self` refers to the main window. You might think that `self` refers to the *component* that was clicked, but it doesn't; it refers to the *window containing the component*.

Moving the button

When you want to do something to the button, how do you refer to it? PyQt keeps track of all the widgets in a window. Because you know that `self` refers to the window and `pushButton` is the name of the widget, you can use `self.pushButton` to access that widget.

In our example in listing 20.2, we made the button move every time we clicked it. The button's position in the window is determined by its `geometry` property, which contains the `x`, `y`, `width`, and `height` properties. There are two ways to change these properties.

One way is to use a method called `setGeometry()` to change the geometry properties. The other way (which we used in listing 20.2) is to use the `move()` method, which changes only the `x` and `y` parts of the geometry and leaves the `width` and `height` alone. The *x*-position is the distance from the left side of the window, and the *y*-position is the distance from the top of the window. The upper-left corner of the window is [0, 0] (just like in Pygame).

When you run this program, you'll see that, after a few clicks, the button disappears off the bottom-right corner of the window. If you want, you can resize the window (drag the edge or corner) to make it bigger and find the button again. When you're done, you can close the window by clicking the X in the title bar (or whatever is used to close a window in your operating system).

Notice that, unlike in Pygame, you don't need to worry about "erasing" the button from its old position and redrawing it in the new position. You just move it. PyQt takes care of all the erasing and redrawing for you.

More useful GUIs

Our first PyQt GUI was good for looking at the basics of how to make a GUI in PyQt, but it's not useful, and not much fun either. So, in the rest of this chapter and in chapter 22, we're going to work on a couple more projects, one small and one a bit bigger, that will let us learn more about using PyQt.

The first project will be a PyQt version of our temperature-conversion program. In chapter 22, we'll use PyQt to make a GUI version of the game Hangman. Later in the book, we'll use PyQt again to make a Virtual Pet program.

TempGUI

In chapter 3 (in the "Try it out" section), you made your first temperature-conversion program. In chapter 5, we added user input to it, so the temperature to be converted didn't have to be hard-coded into the program. In chapter 6, we used EasyGui to get the input and display the output. Now we're going to use PyQt to make a graphical version of the temperature-conversion program.

TempGUI components

Our temperature-conversion GUI will be pretty simple. We only need a few things:

- Places to enter the temperatures (Celsius or Fahrenheit)
- Buttons to make the temperature conversion happen
- Some labels to show the user what's what

Just for fun, let's use two different kinds of entry widgets for Celsius and Fahrenheit. You'd never do that in a real program (it would only confuse people), but we're here to learn!

When we're done making the GUI layout, it should look something like this:

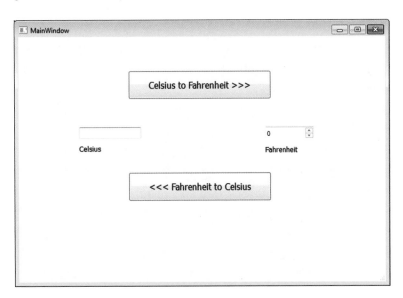

You can probably do this on your own, because Qt Designer is pretty user-friendly. But just in case you need any help, I'm going to explain the steps. This will also make sure we're using the same names for our components, which will make it easier to follow the code later on.

Don't worry about getting the components exactly lined up or exactly the same as shown here, as long as they're roughly the same.

Creating the new GUI

The first step is to make a new PyQt project. When you close the UI you have open (MyFirstGui), Designer will open the **New Form** window again, and you can make sure **Main Window** is selected as the type of form, and click **Create**.

Now you need to start adding widgets: the Celsius entry box is a **Line Edit** widget, the Fahrenheit entry box is a **Spin Box**, the labels under each temperature entry box are **Label** widgets, and there are two **Push Button** components. You'll have to scroll down in the Widget Box on the left side to find some of these. Here are the steps to make the GUI:

1   Find the **Push Button** widget in the Widget Box. Drag it over onto the form, and it will make a new button on the form. Then do the following:
- Make the button the size you want by dragging the handles or entering new numbers in the **geometry** properties (like you saw in MyFirstGui).
- Change the button's **objectName** property to **btnFtoC**.
- Change the button's **text** property to **<<< Fahrenheit to Celsius**.
- Change the button's **font size** to **12**. If you find the **font** property in the Property Editor and click the little button with three dots in it that looks like **this:** ⬚. You'll get a Font dialog just like one you've probably seen in your favorite word processor.

2   Drag another **Push Button** onto the form, place it above the first button, make it the size you want, and change these settings:
- Change the button's **objectName** property to **btnCtoF**.
- Change the button's **text** property to **Celsius to Fahrenheit >>>**.
- Change the button's **font size** to **12**.

3   Drag a **Line Edit** widget onto the form, and place it to the left of the two buttons:
- Change the Line Edit widget's **objectName** property to **editCel**.

4   Drag a **Spin Box** widget onto the form, and place it to the right of the two buttons:
- Change the **objectName** of the Spin Box to **spinFahr**.

5   Drag a **Label** widget onto the form, and place it below the Line Edit widget:
- Change the **text** property of the label to **Celsius**.
- Change the label's **font size** to **10**.

6 Drag a **Label** widget onto the form, and place it below the Spin Box widget:

■ Change the **text** property of the label to **Fahrenheit**.

■ Change the label's **font size** to **10**.

Now we have the GUI elements (widgets, or components, or controls) placed, and we have given them the names and labels we want. Save the UI file as **tempconv.ui** by selecting **File > Save As** in Qt Designer. Remember to change the location where the file is saved to the location where you normally save your Python programs.

Next, start a new file in IDLE, and type in the basic PyQt code (or copy it from our first program):

```
import sys
from PyQt4 import QtCore, QtGui, uic

form_class = uic.loadUiType("tempconv.ui")[0]

class MyWindowClass(QtGui.QMainWindow, form_class):
    def __init__(self, parent=None):
        QtGui.QMainWindow.__init__(self, parent)
        self.setupUi(self)

app = QtGui.QApplication(sys.argv)
myWindow = MyWindowClass()
myWindow.show()
app.exec_()
```

Converting Celsius to Fahrenheit

First, let's get the Celsius to Fahrenheit function working. The formula for converting Celsius to Fahrenheit is

```
fahr = cel * 9.0 / 5 + 32
```

We need to get the Celsius temperature from the `editCel` Line Edit widget, do the calculation, and put the result in the `spinFahr` Fahrenheit Spin Box widget. That should all happen when the user clicks the **Celsius to Fahrenheit** button, so the code to do it should go in that button's event handler.

First we need to connect the button's `clicked` event to the event handler:

```
self.btn_CtoF.clicked.connect(self.btn_CtoF_clicked)
```

This code goes in the `__init__()` method of the `MyWindow` class, just like it did in our first program.

Then we need to define the event handler. To get the value from the **Celsius** box (the Line Edit widget called `editCel`), we use `self.editCel.text()`. This value is a string, so we have to convert it to a float:

```
cel = float(self.editCel.text())
```

Then we need to do the conversion:

```
fahr = cel * 9.0 / 5 + 32
```

Next, we need to put that value in the **Fahrenheit** box, which is the Spin Box widget called `spinFahr`. There's one catch here: spin boxes can only have integer values in them, not floats. We have to make sure we convert the value to an `int` before putting it in the spin box. The number in the spin box is its `value` property, so the code looks like this:

```
self.spinFahr.setValue(int(fahr))
```

And we add 0.5 to the result so that when we use `int()` to convert the float to an integer, it gets *rounded off* to the nearest integer, instead of *rounded down* to the next lowest integer. Putting that all together gives us this:

```
def btn_CtoF_clicked(self):                          Gets Celsius value
        cel = float(self.editCel.text())      ◁
        fahr = cel * 9.0 / 5 + 32      ◁        Converts to Fahrenheit
        self.spinFahr.setValue(int(fahr + 0.5))   ◁
app = QtGui.QApplication(sys.argv)
myWindow = MyWindowClass()
myWindow.show()                               Rounds off and puts in
app.exec_()                                   Fahrenheit spin box
```

Converting Fahrenheit to Celsius

The code for converting the other way (from Fahrenheit to Celsius) is very similar. The formula for that conversion is

```
cel = (fahr - 32) * 5.0 / 9
```

It goes in the event handler for the **Fahrenheit to Celsius** button. We connect the event handler to the button (in the `__init__()` method of the window):

```
self.btn_FtoC.clicked.connect(self.btn_FtoC_clicked)
```

Then, in the event handler, we need to get the Fahrenheit temperature from the spin box:

```
fahr = self.spinFahr.value()
```

This value is already an integer, so we don't have to do any type conversion. Then we apply the formula:

```
cel = (fahr - 32) * 5.0 / 9
```

Finally, we convert this to a string and put it in the **Celsius** box:

```
self.editCel.setText(str(cel))
```

The whole thing should look like the following listing.

Listing 20.3   Temperature-conversion program

```
import sys
from PyQt4 import QtCore, QtGui, uic

form_class = uic.loadUiType("tempconv.ui")[0]      ← Loads the UI definition
class MyWindowClass(QtGui.QMainWindow, form_class):
    def __init__(self, parent=None):
        QtGui.QMainWindow.__init__(self, parent)
        self.setupUi(self)
        self.btn_CtoF.clicked.connect(self.btn_CtoF_clicked)    ⎱ Binds the event handlers
        self.btn_FtoC.clicked.connect(self.btn_FtoC_clicked)    ⎰ of the buttons

    def btn_CtoF_clicked(self):
        cel = float(self.editCel.text())              ⎫ Event handler for
        fahr = cel * 9 / 5.0 + 32                      ⎬ the CtoF button
        self.spinFahr.setValue(int(fahr + 0.5))        ⎭

    def btn_FtoC_clicked(self):
        fahr = self.spinFahr.value()                   ⎫ Event handler for
        cel = (fahr - 32) * 5 / 9.0                    ⎬ the FtoC button
        self.editCel.setText(str(cel))                 ⎭

app = QtGui.QApplication(sys.argv)
myWindow = MyWindowClass(None)
myWindow.show()
app.exec_()
```

Save this program as **TempGui.py**. You can run it and try out the GUI.

A small improvement

One thing you'll notice when you run the program is that, when you convert a Fahrenheit temperature to Celsius, the answer has a lot of decimal places, and some of them might get cut off in the text box. There's a way to fix this—it's called *print formatting*. We haven't covered it yet, so you can either skip ahead to chapter 21 to get the full explanation of how it works, or you can just type in the code I'll give you here. Replace the last line of the `btn_FtoC_clicked` event handler with these two lines:

```
cel_text = '%.2f' % cel
self.editCel.setText(cel_text)
```

This will display the number with two decimal places.

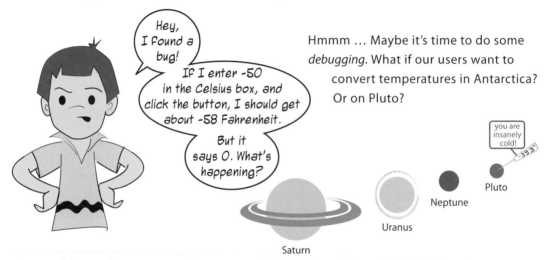

Squashing a bug

We said before that one good way to see what's going on in the program is to print out the value of some of the variables while the program is running. So let's try that.

Because it's the Fahrenheit value in the Celsius to Fahrenheit conversion that seems not to be working, we'll start there. Add this line after the last line in the `btn_CtoF_clicked` event handler in listing 20.3:

```
print 'cel = ', cel, '  fahr = ', fahr
```

Now, whenever you click the **Celsius to Fahrenheit** button, you can see the `cel` and `fahr` variables printed out in the IDLE shell window. Try it with a few different values for `cel` and see what happens. I got something like this:

```
>>> =========================== RESTART ============================
>>>
cel =  50.0    fahr =  122.0
cel =  0.0   fahr =  32.0
cel =  -10.0   fahr =  14.0
cel =  -50.0   fahr =  -58.0
```

It looks like the `fahr` value is being computed correctly. So why won't the **Fahrenheit** box display anything less than 0 (or more than 99, for that matter!)?

Go back to Qt Designer, and click the `spinFahr` spin box widget that we used for showing and entering the Fahrenheit temperature. Now look at the Property Editor and scroll through the different properties. Do you see two properties called *minimum* and *maximum* (near the bottom of the list of properties for the spin box)? What are their values? Can you guess what the problem is now?

What's on the menu?

Our temperature-conversion GUI has buttons to make the conversions happen. Many programs also have a *menu* to perform some functions. Sometimes these are the same things you can do by clicking a button, so why would you want to have two different ways to do the same thing?

Well, some users are more comfortable using menus than clicking buttons. Complex programs have many functions that would require a lot of buttons, making a very cluttered GUI if they didn't use menus. Also, you can operate menus from the keyboard, and some people find it faster to use menus than to take their hands off the keyboard and use the mouse.

Let's add some menu items to give our users a different way to make the temperature conversions happen. We can also add a **File > Exit** menu option, which almost every program has.

PyQt includes a way to create and edit menus. If you look in the upper-left corner of the form in Designer, you'll see something that says **Type Here**. This is where we start creating menus. In many programs, the first menu is the **File** menu, so let's begin with that. Click in the area where it says **Type Here**, type **File**, then press **Enter**. You should see a **File** menu appear, and also space to type more menu items beside and below it, like this:

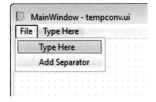

Adding a menu item

Under the **File** menu, we're going to add a menu item for **Exit**. Where it says **Type Here** below the **File** menu, type **Exit**, and then press **Enter**.

Now let's add a menu item for converting temperatures (if the user doesn't want to use the buttons). In the place where it says **Type Here** to the right of the **File** menu, type **Convert**. Then, below that, make two new menu items for **C to F** and **F to C**. When you're done, it should look like this:

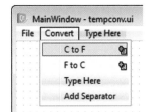

If you look at the Object Inspector in the upper-right corner of the Qt Designer window, you should see something like this:

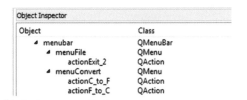

You can see the **File** and **Convert** menus, and the **Exit**, **C to F**, and **F to C** menu items. In PyQt's terminology, the menu items are instances of the `QAction` class. That makes sense, because you want some *action* to happen when you select the menu item.

Save your modified Designer file as **tempconv_menu.ui**.

Now that you have menu items (or actions), you need to bind (or connect) their events to event handlers. For the **C to F** and **F to C** menu items, we already have event handlers—the ones we made for the buttons. We want the same thing to happen from the menu as when we click the buttons. So we can just connect the menu items to the same event handlers.

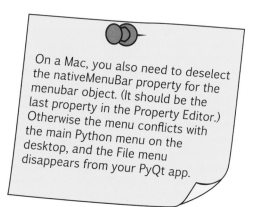

On a Mac, you also need to deselect the nativeMenuBar property for the menubar object. (It should be the last property in the Property Editor.) Otherwise the menu conflicts with the main Python menu on the desktop, and the File menu disappears from your PyQt app.

For a menu item (an *action*), it's not a *clicked* event we need to handle, it's a *triggered* event. The thing we're connecting to the event handler is a called `action_CtoF`. And the event handler we're connecting to is the button's event handler, `btn_CtoF_clicked`. The code to connect the event handler for the menu item looks like this:

```
self.action_CtoF.triggered.connect(self.btn_CtoF_clicked)
```

And there is another one for the **FtoC** menu item.

For the **Exit** menu item, we need to create a new event handler and bind it to the event. We'll call that event hander `menuExit_selected`, and the code to connect that event handler looks like this:

```
self.actionExit.triggered.connect(self.menuExit_selected)
```

The actual event handler for the **Exit** menu has just a single line in the body, which closes the window:

```
def menuExit_selected(self):
    self.close(
```

Finally, change the UI file that gets loaded (in the third line) to the one with menus that you saved above, **tempconv_menu.ui.**

Making all those changes, the code should look like the following listing.

Listing 20.4 Complete temperature-conversion program with menus

```
import sys
from PyQt4 import QtCore, QtGui, uic

form_class = uic.loadUiType("tempconv_menu.ui")[0]        ←——— Loads the UI file that
                                                               includes the menus
class MyWindowClass(QtGui.QMainWindow, form_class):
    def __init__(self, parent=None):
        QtGui.QMainWindow.__init__(self, parent)
        self.setupUi(self)
        self.btn_CtoF.clicked.connect(self.btn_CtoF_clicked)
        self.btn_FtoC.clicked.connect(self.btn_FtoC_clicked)
        self.action_CtoF.triggered.connect(self.btn_CtoF_clicked)    ←——— Connects Convert
        self.action_FtoC.triggered.connect(self.btn_FtoC_clicked)         menu item event
        self.actionExit.triggered.connect(self.menuExit_selected)         handlers

    def btn_CtoF_clicked(self):                                      ←——— Connects Exit menu
        cel = float(self.editCel.text())                                 item event handler
        fahr = cel * 9 / 5.0 + 32
        self.spinFahr.setValue(int(fahr + 0.5))

    def btn_FtoC_clicked(self):
        fahr = self.spinFahr.value()
        cel = (fahr - 32) * 5 / 9.0
        self.editCel.setText(str(cel))
```

```
        def menuExit_selected(self):
            self.close()
```
The new Exit menu item event handler

```
app = QtGui.QApplication(sys.argv)
myWindow = MyWindowClass(None)
myWindow.show()
app.exec_()
```

Hotkeys

We said before that one reason some people prefer using menus to using buttons is that they can use menus with the keyboard, without having to use the mouse. Right now, our menus work with the mouse, but we haven't made them work with the keyboard yet. The way we do that is by adding hotkeys.

Hotkeys (also called *shortcut keys*) let you select menu items by using only the keyboard. In Windows and Linux, you activate the menu system by using the **Alt** key. (We'll talk about Mac OS in a minute.) When you press the **Alt** key, you'll see a certain letter of each menu item highlighted, usually with an underline. The underlined letter is the one you use to activate that menu. So, for instance, to get into the **File** menu, you press **Alt-F**. That is, you hold down **Alt** and then press the **F** key. Once you have done that, you can see the items in the **File** menu, and you can see what the hotkeys are for each menu item. Try this with the IDLE shell window:

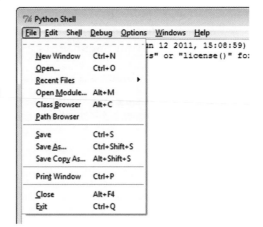

To open a new window, you use **Alt-F-N**. (Hold Down **Alt**, press **F**, and then press **N**.)

Now, we're going to define hotkeys in the menu for the temperature-conversion GUI. To define a hotkey, all you have to do is put the **&** character in front of the letter that you want to be the hotkey. You do this in the **Title** property for a menu (like **File**) or in the **Text** property for a menu item (like **Exit**). For the **File** menu, the convention is to make **F** the hotkey; and for **Exit**, make **X** the hot key. So **File** becomes **&File**, and **Exit** becomes **E&xit**.

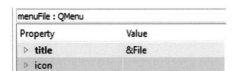

We need to decide what hotkeys to use for the **Convert** menu items. Let's use **C** for **Convert**, **C** for Celsius to Fahrenheit, and **F** for Fahrenheit to Celsius. So we have **&Convert**, **&C to F** and **&F to C**. The hotkey combinations are **Alt-C-C** (for Celsius to Fahrenheit) and **Alt-C-F** (for Fahrenheit to Celsius).

Once you define the hotkeys in Qt Designer, there's nothing else to do—no new code to write. PyQt and the operating system take care of underlining the hotkey and handling the keyboard input. Just save your UI file. You could save it under a different name, like **tempconv_menu_hotkeys.ui**. If you do, be sure you change the third line in listing 20.4 to load that UI file:

```
form_class = uic.loadUiType("tempconv_menu_hotkeys.ui")[0]
```

> I tried this on my Mac, and when I press the **Option** key, which also says **Alt** on it, I don't see any underlined or highlighted characters in the menu items.
>
> Are there menu hotkeys in Mac OS X?

The short answer is "no." Because all Macs have come with a mouse (or touchpad) since day one, the Mac OS assumes you'll use the mouse to operate the menus. There is no keyboard shortcut or hotkey system for menu items on the Mac OS. There are keyboard shortcuts for many functions, and some of them correspond to menu items. But you can't directly operate the menu system with hotkeys the way you can in Windows.

That's it for the temperature-conversion GUI. In chapter 22, we'll use PyQt to make a version of the Hangman game.

What did you learn?

In this chapter, you learned about

- PyQt
- Qt Designer
- Widgets—the buttons, text, and so on, that make up the GUI
- Event handlers—making your components do something
- Menu items and hotkeys

Test your knowledge

1 What are three names for the things like buttons, text fields, and so on, that make up a GUI?

2 What's the term for the letter that you press along with **ALT** to get into a menu?

3 What must you put at the end of the filename for Qt Designer files?

4 What are five types of widgets you can include in a GUI using PyQt?

5 To make a widget (like a button) do something, it needs to have an _____ _____.

6 What special character is used in menus to define a hotkey?

7 The content of spin box in PyQt is always an _____.

Try it out

1 You made a text-based number-guessing program in chapter 1, and you made a simple GUI version of the same game in chapter 6. Try making a GUI version of the number-guessing game using PyQt.

2 Did you find the problem with the spin box when it wouldn't display any values below 0? (Carter found this bug in listing 20.2.) Fix the spin box properties to solve this problem. Make sure you fix both ends of the scale so the spinner can display very high temperatures as well as very low ones. (Maybe your user is going to convert the temperatures on Mercury and Venus, as well as on Pluto!)

## CHAPTER 21

Print Formatting and Strings

Waaaayyyy back in chapter 1, you learned about the `print` statement. It was the first command you ever used in Python. You've also seen (in chapter 5) that you can put a comma at the end of a `print` statement to make Python keep printing the next thing on the same line. (At least, in Python 2. Not in Python 3.) You used that to make prompts for `raw_input()`, until you learned the shortcut of putting the prompt right in the `raw_input()` function.

In this chapter, we're going to look at *print formatting*—ways to make your program's output look the way you want it to. We'll look at things like

- Starting new lines (and when you should do that)
- Spacing things out horizontally (and lining things up in columns)
- Printing variables in the middle of a string
- Formatting numbers in integer, decimal, or E-notation format, and setting how many decimal places they should have

You'll also learn about some of Python's built-in methods for working with strings. These methods can do things like

- Splitting strings into smaller parts
- Joining strings together
- Searching for strings
- Searching within strings
- Removing parts of strings
- Changing case (uppercase and lowercase)

All of these things will be useful for text-mode (non-GUI) programs, and most of them will find their way into GUIs and game programs as well. There's a lot more Python can do with print formatting, but this should be all you will need for 99 percent of your programs.

New lines

You have already seen the `print` statement many times. What happens if you use it more than once? Try this short program:

```
print "Hi"
print "There"
```

When you run it, the output should look like this:

```
>>> =================== RESTART ===================
>>>
Hi
There
```

Why did these two things print on different lines? Why didn't the output look like this:

```
HiThere
```

Unless you tell it otherwise, Python will start each `print` on a new line. After the `Hi`, Python moves down one line and back to the first column to print `There`. Python inserts a *newline* character between the two words. A newline is like pressing **Enter** in your text editor.

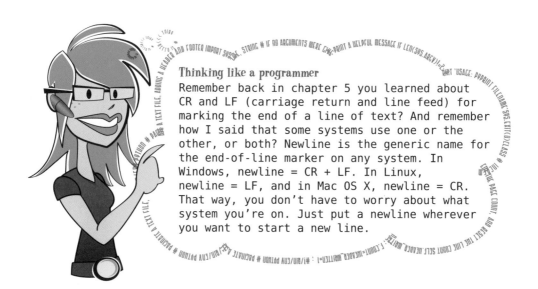

Thinking like a programmer
Remember back in chapter 5 you learned about CR and LF (carriage return and line feed) for marking the end of a line of text? And remember how I said that some systems use one or the other, or both? Newline is the generic name for the end-of-line marker on any system. In Windows, newline = CR + LF. In Linux, newline = LF, and in Mac OS X, newline = CR. That way, you don't have to worry about what system you're on. Just put a newline wherever you want to start a new line.

`print` and the comma

The `print` statement automatically puts a newline at the end of whatever it prints, unless you tell it not to. And how do you tell it not to? By adding a comma (like you saw in chapter 5):

```
print 'Hi',
print 'There'

>>> =================== RESTART ===================
>>>
Hi There
```

(Again, this won't work in Python 3.) Notice that there's a space between `Hi` and `There`. When you use a comma to prevent Python from printing the newline, it prints a space instead.

If you want to print two things right together without a space, you can use *concatenation*, which you saw before:

```
print 'Hi' + 'There'

>>> =================== RESTART ===================
>>>
HiThere
```

Remember that concatenation is *like* adding strings together, but it has a special name because "adding" is only for numbers.

Adding our own newlines

What if you want to add your own newlines? For example, what if you want an extra row of space between `Hi` and `There`? The easiest way is just to add an extra `print` statement:

```
print "Hi"
print
print "There"
```

When you run it, you'll get this:

```
>>> =================== RESTART ===================
>>>
Hi

There
```

Special printing codes

There's another way to add newlines. Python has some special codes you can add to strings to make them print differently. These special printing codes all start with a backlash (\) character.

The code for a newline is \n. Try this in interactive mode:

```
>>> print "Hello World"
Hello World
>>> print "Hello \nWorld"
Hello
World
```

The \n made the two words `Hello` and `World` print on different lines, because it added a newline in between.

Horizontal spacing—tabs

You just saw how to control vertical spacing (by adding newlines or using commas to prevent newlines). Now we'll look at how to control the spacing of things across the screen, horizontally, with *tabs*.

Tabs are useful for lining things up in columns. To understand how tabs work, think of each line on the screen as being divided into blocks, with each block being the same size. Let's say each block is eight characters wide. When you insert a tab, you move over to the start of the next block.

The best way to see how this works is to try it. The special code for tab is \t, so try this in interactive mode:

```
>>> print 'ABC\tXYZ'
ABC     XYZ
```

Notice that the **XYZ** is a few characters away from the **ABC**. In fact, the **XYZ** is exactly eight characters from the start of the line. That's because the size of the block is eight. Another way to say this is that there's a *tab stop* every eight characters.

Here's an example of some different **print** statements, with some shading added to show where the tab stops are:

```
>>> print 'ABC\tXYZ'
ABC     XYZ

>>> print 'ABCDE\tXYZ'
ABCDE   XYZ

>>> print 'ABCDEF\tXYZ'
ABCDEF  XYZ

>>> print 'ABCDEFG\tXYZ'
ABCDEFG XYZ

>>> print 'ABCDEFGHI\tXYZ'
ABCDEFGHI       XYZ
```

You can think of the screen (or each line) as being laid out in blocks of eight spaces. Notice that, as the **ABC** sequence gets longer, the **XYZ** stays in the same place. The \t tells Python to start the **XYZ** at the next tab stop, or at the next available block. But once the **ABC** sequence gets big enough to fill the first block, Python moves the **XYZ** over to the next tab stop.

Tabs are good for arranging things in columns so that everything lines up. Let's use this, as well as what you know about loops, to print a table of squares and cubes. Open a new window in IDLE, and type in the short program from the following listing. Save it, and run it. (I called mine **squbes.py**, short for "squares and cubes.")

Listing 21.1   A program to print squares and cubes

```
print "Number \tSquare \tCube"
for i in range (1, 11):
    print i, '\t', i**2, '\t', i**3
```

When you run it, you should see output that's nicely lined up, like this:

```
>>> ====================== RESTART ======================
>>>
Number  Square  Cube
1       1       1
2       4       8
3       9       27
4       16      64
5       25      125
6       36      216
7       49      343
8       64      512
9       81      729
10      100     1000
```

How do we print a backslash?

Because the backslash character (\) is used for special printing codes, how do you tell Python when you want to actually print a \ character instead of using it as part of a code? The trick is just to put two of them together:

```
>>> print 'hi\\there'
hi\there
```

The first \ tells Python that something special is coming, and the second one tells Python what the special thing is: a \ character.

WORD BOX

When you use two backslashes to print a backslash character, the first backslash is called an *escape character*. We say the first backslash is *escaping* the second one, so that the second backslash is treated like a normal character instead of a special character.

Inserting variables in strings

Up until now, when you wanted to put a variable in the middle of a string, you did something like this:

```
name = 'Warren Sande'
print 'My name is', name, 'and I wrote this book.'
```

If we ran that code, we'd get this:

```
My name is Warren Sande and I wrote this book.
```

But there's another way to insert variables into strings that gives you more control over how they'll look, especially numbers. You can use *format strings*, which use the percent sign (%). Let's say you want to insert a string variable in the middle of a `print` statement, like we just did. The way to do it with format strings is like this:

```
name   = 'Warren Sande'
print 'My name is %s and I wrote this book' % name
```

The % sign is used in two places. It's used in the middle of the string to say where the variable will go. Then it's used again after the string to tell Python that the variable you want to insert in the string is coming next.

The %s means it's a string variable you want to insert. For an integer, you'd use %i; for a float, you'd use %f.

Here are a couple more examples:

```
age = 13
print 'I am %i years old.' % age
```

When you run this, you'll get the following:

```
I am 13 years old.
```

Here's another one:

```
average = 75.6
print 'The average on our math test was %f percent.' % average
```

When you run this, you'll get the following:

```
The average on our math test was 75.600000 percent.
```

The %s, %f, and %i are called *format strings*, and they're a kind of code for how you want the variable to look.

There are some other things you can add to the format strings to make numbers print exactly how you want. There are also a few different format strings you can use to get things like E-notation. (Remember that from chapter 3?) We'll look at these in the next few sections.

Number formatting

When we print numbers, we'd like to have control over how they look:

- How many decimal places they display
- Whether to use regular or E-notation
- Whether to add leading or trailing zeros
- Whether to display + or – signs in front of the numbers

With format strings, Python gives us the flexibility we need to do all this and more!

For example, if you were using a program that told you the weather forecast, which would you rather see:

```
Today's High: 72.45672132, Low 45.4985756
```

or

```
Today's High: 72, Low: 45
```

Getting numbers to look right is important for many programs.

Let's start with an example. Suppose we want to print a decimal number with exactly two decimal places. Try this in interactive mode:

```
>>> dec_number = 12.3456
>>> print 'It is %.2f degrees today.' % dec_number
It is 12.35 degrees today
```

In the middle of the **print** statement, there's our format string. But instead of just using %f, this time we used %.2f. That tells Python to show two digits after the decimal place, with floating-point format. (Notice that Python was smart enough to *round* the number correctly to two decimal places, instead of just chopping off the extra digits.)

After the string, the second % sign tells Python that the number to be printed is coming next. The number is printed with the formatting that's described in the format string. A few more examples will make this clearer.

I thought the % sign was used for the modulus operator!

You have a good memory, Carter! The % sign is used for *modulus* (the remainder in integer division), as you learned in chapter 3, but it's also used to indicate format strings. Python can tell from the way it's used whether you mean modulus or a format string.

Integers: %d or %i

To print something as an integer, use the %d or %i format string (I don't know why there are two, but you can use either one):

```
>>> number = 12.67
>>> print '%i' % number
12
```

Notice that, this time, the number wasn't rounded. It was *truncated* (which means "chopped off"). If it were rounded, we would have seen 13 instead of 12. When you use integer formatting, the number is truncated, and when you use floating-point formatting, the number is rounded.

There are three things to notice here:

- You don't have to have any other text in the string—you can have the format string by itself.
- Even though our number was a float, we printed it as an integer. You can do that with format strings.
- Python truncated the value to the next lowest integer. But this is different from the int() function (which you saw in chapter 4), because format strings don't create a new value like int() does—they just change how the value is displayed.

Just now, we printed 12.67 in integer format, and Python printed 12. But the value of the variable **number** has not been changed. Check it and see:

```
>>> print number
12.67
```

The value of **number** hasn't changed. We just made it print differently using the format string.

Floating point numbers: %f or %F

For decimal numbers, you can use either the uppercase or lowercase *f* in the format string (%f or %F):

```
>>> number = 12.3456
>>> print '%f' % number
12.345600
```

If you use %f by itself, the number will display with six decimal places. If you add .n before the f, where n is any integer, it'll round the number off to that many decimal places:

```
>>> print '%.2F' % number
12.35
```

You can see how it rounded the number 12.3456 to two decimal places: 12.35.

If you specify more decimal places than are in the number, Python will *pad* (fill in) the number with zeros:

```
>>> print '%.8f' % number
12.34560000
```

Here the number had only four places after the decimal, but we asked for eight, so the other four were filled in with zeros.

If the number is negative, %f will always display the – sign. If you want the number to always display a sign, even if it's positive, use a + sign right after the % (this is good for lining up lists of positive and negative numbers):

```
>>> print '%+f' % number
+12.345600
```

If you want your list of positive and negative numbers to line up, but you don't want to see the + sign on positive numbers, use a space instead of the +, right after the %:

```
>>> number2 = -98.76
>>> print '% .2f' % number2
-98.76
>>> print '% .2f' % number
 12.35
```

Notice that there is a space before 12 in the output, so that the 12 and 98 line up one below the other, even though one has a sign and the other doesn't.

E-notation: `%e` and `%E`

When we talked about E-notation (in chapter 3), I promised I'd show you how to make numbers print using E-notation. Well, here it is:

```
>>> number = 12.3456
>>> print '%e' % number
1.234560e+01
```

The `%e` format string is used to print E-notation. It always prints six decimal places unless you tell it otherwise.

You can print more or fewer decimal places by using a `.n` after the `%`, just like you can with floats:

```
>>> number = 12.3456
>>> print '%.3e' % number
1.235e+01
>>> print '%.8e' % number
1.23456000e+01
```

The `%.3e` rounded off to three decimal places, and the `%.8e` added some zeroes to make up the extra digits.

You can use a lowercase or uppercase *e*, and the output will use the same case you used in the format string:

```
>>> print '%E' % number
1.234560E+01
```

Automatic float or E-notation: `%g` and `%G`

If you want Python to automatically choose float notation or E-notation for you, use the `%g` format string. Again, if you use uppercase, you'll get an uppercase *E* in the output:

```
>>> number1 = 12.3
>>> number2 = 456712345.6
>>> print '%g' % number1
12.3
>>> print '%g' % number2
4.56712e+08
```

Did you notice how Python automatically chose E-notation for the big number and regular floating-point notation for the smaller number?

How do we print a percent sign?

You might be wondering, because the percent sign (%) is a special character for format strings, how you make a % sign print?

Well, sometimes Python is smart enough to figure out when you're using a `%` sign to start a format string and when you just want to print one. Try this:

```
>>> print 'I got 90% on my math test!'
I got 90% on my math test!
```

In this case, there wasn't a second % outside the string, and there was no variable to format, so Python assumed that the % was just another character in your string.

But if you are printing with format strings and you want to print a percent sign, you use two percent signs, just like you used two backslashes to print a backslash. We say the first percent sign is *escaping* the second percent sign, just like in the Word Box earlier in this chapter:

```
>>> math = 75.4
>>> print 'I got %.1f%% on my math test' % math
I got 75.4% on my math test
```

The first `%` starts the format string. The two `%%` together tell Python that you actually want to print a % character. Then you have the `%` outside the quotes that tells Python the variable you want to print is coming next.

More than one format string

What if you want to put more than one format string in a single `print` statement? Here's how you do that:

```
>>> math = 75.4
>>> science = 82.1
>>> print 'I got %.1f in math and %.1f in science' % (math, science)
```

You can put as many format strings as you want in the `print` statement and then a tuple of variables you want to print. Remember that a tuple is like a list, except it uses round brackets instead of square ones, and a tuple is immutable. This is one instance where Python is picky—you have to use a tuple; you can't use a list. The only exception is when you have just a single variable to format; then it doesn't need to be in a tuple. (You saw that in most of our examples.) Make sure the number of format strings (inside the quotes) and the number of variables (outside the quotes) matches, or you'll get an error message.

Storing formatted numbers

Sometimes you don't want to print the formatted number right away, but rather store it in a string to use later. That's easy. Instead of printing it, just assign it to a variable, like this:

```
>>> my_string = '%.2f' % 12.3456
>>> print my_string
12.35
>>> print 'The answer is', my_string
The answer is 12.35
```

Instead of directly printing the formatted number, we assigned it to the variable `my_string`. Then we combined `my_string` with some other text and printed our sentence.

Storing the formatted number as a string is very useful for GUIs and other graphical programs like games. Once you have a variable name for the formatted string, you can display it however you want: in a text box, button, dialog, or game screen.

Formatting, the new way

The syntax for formatting strings that you just learned about works in all versions of Python. But there is a different way of doing the same thing in Python 2.6 and later. Because we're using Python 2.7 in this book, I thought we'd look at the new way, too. You might see it in Python code, so this way you'll at least know what it means. You can decide which syntax—the old or the new—you want to use for string formatting.

The `format()` method

Python strings (in versions 2.6 and later) have a method called `format()`. This works very similarly to the `%` format strings you saw above. In fact, the format specifiers—the **f**, **g**, **e**, and so on—are the same. You just use them a little differently. The best way to see it is with an example.

Here's the old way:

```
print 'I got %.1f in math, %.1f in science' % (math, science)
```

And here's the new way:

```
print 'I got {0:.1f} in math, {1:.1f} in science'.format(math, science)
```

In the new way, instead of starting the format specifier with `%`, you put it in curly brackets. The 0 or 1 tells Python which variable from the tuple of variables you're going to format.

Remember that Python counting starts at 0, so the first item in the tuple (the variable `math`) has index 0, and the second (the variable `science`) has index 1. Then you use the `.1f` just like you do with the old method.

That's all there is to it. You can store the formatted string to a variable, just like you can with the old, % formatting:

```
distance = 149597870700
myString = 'The sun is {0:.4e} meters from the earth'.format(distance)
```

And because you don't use the % sign to indicate format strings any more, you don't need to do anything special if you want to print a % sign:

```
>>> print 'I got {0:.1f}% in math'.format(math)
I got 87% in math
```

Python programmers will say that using the `format()` syntax is preferred, especially in Python 3. But you can use whichever syntax you want. The examples in this book all use the % syntax.

Strings 'n' things

When you first learned about strings (back in chapter 2), you saw that you could combine two of them with the + sign, like this:

```
>>> print 'cat' + 'dog'
catdog
```

Now you're going to find out more things you can do with strings.

Strings in Python are really *objects* (see, everything is an object …), and they have their own *methods* for doing things like searching, splitting, and combining. These are known as *string methods*. The `format()` method you just saw is one of the string methods.

Splitting strings

Sometimes you need to split up a long string into a number of smaller ones. Usually you want to do this at particular points in the string, like whenever a certain character appears. For example, a common way of storing data in a text file is to have items separated from each other by a comma. So you might have a list of names that looks like this:

```
>>> name_string = 'Sam,Brad,Alex,Cameron,Toby,Gwen,Jenn,Connor'
```

Suppose you want to put these names in a list, with each item being one name. You need to split this string wherever there's a comma. The Python method for doing this is called `split()`, and it works like this:

```
>>> names = name_string.split(',')
```

You tell it what character to use as the split marker, and it gives you back a list, which is the original string broken into parts. If we printed the output from this example, the one big string of names would be split into individual items in a list:

```
>>> print names
['Sam','Brad','Alex','Cameron','Toby','Gwen','Jenn','Connor']

>>> for name in names:
        print name

Sam
Brad
Alex
Cameron
Toby
Gwen
Jenn
Connor
```

You can have more than one character as the split marker. For instance, you could use `'Toby,'` as the split marker, and you'd get the following list:

```
>>> parts = name_string.split('Toby,')
>>> print parts
['Sam,Brad,Alex,Cameron', 'Gwen,Jenn,Connor']

>>> for part in parts:
        print part

Sam,Brad,Alex,Cameron
Gwen,Jenn,Connor
```

This time, the string got split into two parts: all the stuff on one side of `'Toby,'` and all the stuff on the other side of `'Toby,'`. Notice that `'Toby,'` doesn't appear in the list, because the split marker gets thrown away.

There's one other thing to know. If you don't give Python any split marker, it'll split the string at any *whitespace*:

```
>>> names = name_string.split()
```

Whitespace means any spaces, tab characters, or newlines.

Joining strings

You just saw how to split a string into smaller pieces. How about joining two or more strings to make one larger string? You already saw, way back in chapter 2, that you can join strings using the + operator. It's like adding two strings together, except that it's called *concatenating*.

There's another way to join strings. You can use the `join()` function. You tell it what strings you want to join and what characters (if any) you want inserted between the parts when they are joined. It's basically the opposite of `split()`. Here's an example in interactive mode:

```
>>> word_list = ['My', 'name', 'is', 'Warren']
>>> long_string = ' '.join(word_list)
>>> long_string
'My name is Warren'
```

I admit that this looks a little odd. The characters that will go between each piece of the joined string go *in front* of `join()`. In this case, we wanted a space between each word, so we used `' '.join()`. That's different from what most people expect, but that's just how Python's `join()` method works.

The following example makes me sound like a dog:

```
>>> long_string = ' WOOF WOOF '.join(word_list)
>>> long_string
'My WOOF WOOF name WOOF WOOF is WOOF WOOF Warren'
```

To put it another way, the string in front of `join()` is used as the *glue* to hold the other strings together.

Searching for strings

Suppose you want to make a program for your mom that takes recipes and displays them in a GUI. You want to put the ingredients in one place and the instructions in another. Let's imagine that the recipe looks something like this:

```
Chocolate Cake
Ingredients:
2 eggs
1/2 cup flour
1 tsp baking soda
1 lb chocolate

Instructions:
Preheat oven to 350F
Mix all ingredients together
Bake for 30 minutes
```

Assume that the lines of the recipe are in a *list*, and that each line is a separate item in the list. How would you find the "Instructions" section? Python has a couple of methods that would help you.

The `startswith()` method tells you whether a string starts with a certain character or characters. An example is the easiest way to show this. Try this in interactive mode:

```
>>> name = "Frankenstein"
>>> name.startswith('F')
True
>>> name.startswith("Frank")
True
>>> name.startswith("Flop")
False
```

The name Frankenstein starts with the letter *F*, so the first one was `True`. The name Frankenstein starts with the letters *Frank*, so the second one was `True`. The name Frankenstein does *not* start with *Flop*, so that one was `False`.

Because the `startswith()` method returns a `True` or `False` value, you can use it in comparisons or `if` statements, like this:

```
>>> if name.startswith("Frank"):
        print "Can I call you Frank?"
```

Can I call you Frank?

There's a similar method called `endswith()` that does just what you'd expect:

```
>>> name = "Frankenstein"
>>> name.endswith('n')
True
>>> name.endswith('stein')
True
>>> name.endswith('stone')
False
```

Now to get back to the problem at hand …. If we wanted to find the start of the "Instructions" section of the recipe, we could do something like this:

```
i = 0
while not lines[i].startswith("Instructions"):
    i = i + 1
```

This code will keep looping until it finds a line that starts with "Instructions." Remember that `lines[i]` means `i` is the *index* for `lines`. So you'd start with `lines[0]` (the first line), then `lines[1]` (the second line), and so on. When the `while` loop finishes, `i` will be equal to the index of the line that starts with "Instructions," which is the one we're looking for.

Searching anywhere in a string: `in` and `index()`

The `startswith()` and `endswith()` methods work really well for finding things at the start or end of a string. But what if you want to find something in the middle of a string?

Let's say we had a bunch of strings that had street addresses, like this:

```
657 Maple Lane
47 Birch Street
95 Maple Drive
```

Maybe we want to find all the addresses with "Maple" in them. None of them start or end with "Maple," but two of them contain the word *Maple*. How would you find them?

Actually, you already saw how to do this. When we were talking about *lists* (back in chapter 12), you saw that you could check whether an item is in a list by doing this:

```
if someItem in my_list:
    print "Found it!"
```

We used the keyword `in` to check whether a certain item was in the list. The `in` keyword also works for strings. A string is basically a list of characters, so you can do this:

```
>>> addr1 = '657 Maple Lane'
>>> if 'Maple' in addr1:
        print "That address has 'Maple' in it."
```

WORD BOX

> When you're looking for a smaller string, like "Maple", within a bigger string, like "657 Maple Lane", the smaller string is called a *substring*.

The `in` keyword just tells you whether the substring is *somewhere* in the string you're checking. It doesn't tell you where it is. For that, you need the `index()` method. Like with lists, `index()` tells you where in the bigger string the smaller string starts. Here's an example:

```
>>> addr1 = '657 Maple Lane'
>>> if 'Maple' in addr1:
        position = addr1.index('Maple')
        print "found 'Maple' at index", position
```

If you run this code, you'll get the following output:

```
found 'Maple' at index 4
```

The word *Maple* starts at position 4 of the string "657 Maple Lane". Just like with lists, the indexes (or positions) of letters within a string start at 0, so the *M* is at index 4.

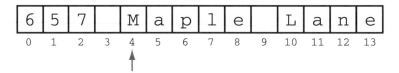

Notice that, before we tried using `index()`, we first checked to see if the substring "Maple" was `in` the bigger string. That's because, if you use `index()` and the thing you're looking for is *not* in the string, you'll get an error. Checking with `in` first ensures that you won't get an error. This is the same thing we did with lists in chapter 12.

Removing part of a string

Quite often you'll want to remove or *strip off* part of a string. Usually, you'll want to strip something off the end, like a newline character or some extra spaces. Python has a string method called `strip()` to do exactly this. You just tell it what you want stripped off, like this:

```
>>> name = 'Warren Sande'
>>> short_name = name.strip('de')
>>> short_name
'Warren San'
```

In this case, we stripped the "de" off the end of my name. If there were no "de" at the end, nothing would be stripped off:

```
>>> name = 'Bart Simpson'
>>> short_name = name.strip('de')
>>> short_name
'Bart Simpson'
```

If you don't tell **strip()** what to strip off, it'll strip off any whitespace. Like we said before, that includes spaces, tabs, and newlines. So if we had extra spaces to get rid of, we could do this:

```
>>> name = "Warren Sande      "
>>>> short_name = name.strip()
>>> short_name
'Warren Sande'
```

See the extra spaces
at the end of my name?

Notice that the extra spaces after my name were removed. The good thing is that you don't need to tell **strip()** how many spaces to remove. It'll remove all whitespace at the end of the string.

Changing case

I want to show you two more string methods. They are for changing the case of a string from uppercase to lowercase or vice versa. Sometimes you want to compare two strings like "Hello" and "hello", and you want to know if they have the same letters, even if the case is not the same. One way to do this is to make all the letters in both strings lowercase and then do the comparison.

Python has a string method for that. It's called **lower()**. Try this in interactive mode:

```
>>> string1 = "Hello"
>>> string2 = string1.lower()
>>> print string2
hello
```

There is a similar method called **upper()**:

```
>>> string3 = string1.upper()
>>> print string3
HELLO
```

You can make all-lowercase (or all-uppercase) copies of your original strings and then compare the copies to check if they are the same, ignoring case.

What did you learn?

In this chapter, you learned

- How to adjust vertical spacing (adding or deleting newlines)
- How to set horizontal spacing with tabs
- How to display different number formats using format strings
- Two ways of using format strings—the % sign, and the `format()` method
- How to split strings with `split()` and join them with `join()`
- How to search strings with `startswith()`, `endswith()`, `in`, and `index()`
- How to remove things from the end of strings with `strip()`
- How to make strings all uppercase or all lowercase with `upper()` and `lower()`

Test your knowledge

1 If you have two separate `print` statements, like this

```
print "What is"
print "your name?"
```

how would you make everything print on the same line?

2 How can you add extra blank lines when printing something?

3 What special printing code do you use to line things up in columns?

4 What format string do you use to force a number to print in E-notation?

Try it out

1 Write a program that asks for a person's name, age, and favorite color, and then prints them out in one sentence. A run of the program should look like this:

```
>>> ======================== RESTART ========================
>>>
What is your name? Sam
How old are you? 12
What is your favorite color? green
Your name is Sam you are 12 years old and you like green
```

2 Remember our times-table program from chapter 8 (listing 8.5)? Write an improved version that uses tabs to make sure everything lines up nicely in columns.

3 Write a program that calculates all the fractions of 8 (for example, 1/8, 2/8, 3/8, ... up to 8/8) and displays them with exactly three decimal places.

## CHAPTER 22

File Input and Output

Have you ever wondered how your favorite computer game remembers the high scores, even after the computer is turned off? How about your browser remembering your favorite web sites? In this chapter, you're going to learn how.

We have talked several times about how programs have three main aspects: input, processing, and output. Up until now, the input has mostly come directly from the user, from the keyboard and mouse. The output has been sent directly to the screen (or the speakers, in the case of sound). But sometimes you need to use input that comes from other sources. Quite often, programs need to use input that's stored somewhere, rather than entered when the program is running. Some programs need to get their input from a *file* on the computer's hard drive.

For example, if you made a game of Hangman, your program would need a word list from which to choose the secret word. That list of words would have to be stored somewhere, probably in a "word list" file that goes with the program. The program would need to open this file, read the word list, and pick a word to use.

The same thing is true for output. Sometimes the output of a program needs to be stored. All the variables that a program uses are temporary—they're lost when the program stops running. If you want to save some of the information to use later, you have to store it somewhere more permanent, like on the hard drive. For example, if you want to keep a list of high scores for a game, you need to store them in a file so that, next time the program runs, it can read the file and display the scores.

In this chapter, you'll see how to open files and how to *read* and *write* them (*get* information from them and *store* information to them).

What's a file?

Before we start talking about opening, reading, and writing files, we should talk about what a file is.

We said that computers store information in *binary* format, which just uses 1s and 0s. Each 1 or 0 is called a *bit*, and a group of eight bits is called a *byte*. A *file* is a collection of bytes that has a name and is stored on a hard drive, a CD, a DVD, a flash drive, or some other kind of storage.

Files can store many different kinds of information. A file can contain text, pictures, music, computer programs, a list of phone numbers, and so on. Everything that's stored on your computer's hard drive is stored as files. Programs are made of one or more files. Your computer's operating system (Windows, or Mac OS X, or Linux, for example) has many, many files that it needs to run.

Files have the following properties:

- A name
- A type, which indicates what kind of data is in the file (picture, music, text)
- A location (where the file is stored)
- A size (how many bytes are in the file)

Filenames

In most operating systems (including Windows), part of the filename is used to tell you what type of data is in the file. Filenames usually have at least one "dot" (the period symbol) in the name. The part after the dot tells you what kind of file it is. That part is called the *extension*.

Here are a few examples:

- In **my_letter.txt**, the extension is **.txt**, which stands for "text," so this file probably has text in it.
- In **my_song.mp3**, the extension is **.mp3**, which is a kind of sound file.
- In **my_program.exe**, the extension is **.exe**, which stands for "executable." As I mentioned way back in chapter 1, "executing" is another word for running a program. So **.exe** files are usually programs that you can run.
- In **my_cool_game.py**, the extension is **.py**, which usually means a Python program.

In Mac OS X, program files (files that contain a program you can run) have the extension **.app**, which stands for "application," which is another word for "program."

One important thing to know is that you can name a file anything you want and use any extension. You can make a text file (in Notepad, for instance) and call it **my_notes.mp3**. That does *not* make it a sound file. It still has just text in it, so it's really a text file. You have given it a file extension that makes it *look like* it's a sound file, which will probably confuse people and computers. When naming a file, it's a very good idea to use a file extension that matches what kind of file it is.

File locations

Up until now, we have been working with files that are stored in the same location as the program itself. We haven't worried about how to find the file, because it's in the same place as the program.

It's like, when you're in your room, you don't have to worry about how to find your closet—it's right there. But if you're in another room, in another house, or in another city, then finding your closet is more complicated!

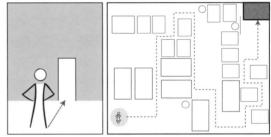

Every file needs to be stored *somewhere*, so in addition to a name, every file has a location. Hard drives and other storage media are organized into *folders* or *directories*. *Folders* and *directories* are two names for the same thing. They're a way of grouping files together. The way the folders or directories are arranged and connected is called a *folder structure* or *directory structure*.

In Windows, each storage media has a letter, like **C** for the hard drive, or maybe **E** for a flash drive. In Mac OS X and Linux, each storage media has a name (for example, **hda** or **FLASH DRIVE**). Each storage unit can be divided up into a number of folders, such as **Music**, **Pictures**, and **Programs**. If you look at it in a file viewer like Windows Explorer, it will look like this:

Folders can also have other folders within them, and those folders can have other folders within them, and so on. Here's an example of three levels of folders:

The first level is **Music**. The next level has **New Music** and **Old Music**, and the next level has **Kind of old music** and **Really old music**.

WORD BOX

> The folders within other folders are called *subfolders*. If you're using the term *directories*, you'd call them *subdirectories*.

When you're trying to find a file or folder in Windows Explorer (or some other file browser), the folders are like branches of a tree. The *root* is the drive itself, like **C:** or **E:**. Each main folder is like a main branch of the tree. The folders within each main folder are like smaller branches, and so on.

But when you need to access files from within a program, the tree idea doesn't quite work. Your program can't click folders and browse around the tree to find individual files. It needs a more direct way to find the file. Fortunately, there's another way to represent the tree structure. If you look in the address bar of Windows Explorer when you click different folders and subfolders, you'll see something that looks like this:

```
E:\Music\Old Music\Really old music\my_song.mp3
```

That's called the *path*. The path is a description of where the file is in the folder structure. This particular path reads like this:

1. Start at the **E:** drive.
2. Go into the folder called **Music**.
3. In the **Music** folder, go into a subfolder called **Old Music**.
4. In the **Old Music** subfolder, go into a subfolder called **Really old music**.
5. In the **Really old music** subfolder, there's a file called **my_song.mp3**.

You can get to any file on your computer using a path like this. That's the way programs find and open files. Here's an example:

```
image_file = "c:/program files/HelloWorld/examples/beachball.png"
```

You can always get to a file using its full pathname. That's the name including all the folder names right down the tree to the root (the drive, like **C:**). The name in this example is a full pathname.

Slash or backslash?

It's important that the slashes (\ and /) go the right way. Windows will accept either a forward slash (/) or a backslash (\) in pathnames, but if you use something like `c:\test_results.txt` in a Python program, the `\t` part will cause a problem. Remember, in chapter 21, we talked about special characters for print formatting, like `\t` for tab? That's why you should avoid the \ character in file paths. Python (and Windows) will treat `\t` as a tab character instead of part of your filename as you intended. Use / instead.

The other option is to use double backslashes, like this:

```
image_file  "c:\\program files\\HelloWorld\\images\\beachball.png"
```

Remember that, if you want to print a \ character, you have to put another one in front of it. It works the same way in filenames. But I recommend you use / instead.

Sometimes you don't need the whole file path. The next section talks about finding a file if you're already partway down the path.

Finding where you are

Most operating systems (including Windows) have the idea of a *working directory*, sometimes called the *current working directory*, or *cwd* for short. This is the directory in the folder tree you're currently working in.

Imagine that you started at the root (**C:**), and you moved down the **Program Files** branch to the **Hello World** branch. Your current location or *current directory* would be **C:/Program Files/ Hello World**.

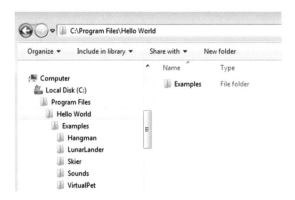

Now, to get to the file called **beachball.png**, you have to go down the **Examples** branch. So your path to get there would be /**Examples/beachball.png**. Because you were already partway down the right path, you only needed the rest of the path to get where you wanted to go.

Remember, in chapter 19 on sound, we opened our sound files as **splat.wav**, and so on? We didn't use a path. That's because I told you to copy the sound files to the same folder where you saved the program. If you looked at it in Windows Explorer, it would look something like this:

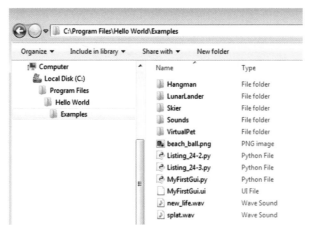

Notice that I have Python files (with the **.py** extension) in the same folder as sound files (with the **.wav** extension). When a Python program is running, its *working directory* is whatever folder the **.py** file is stored in.

If you stored your program in **e:/programs** and ran the program, that program would start with **e:/programs** as its *working directory*. If you have a sound file stored in the same folder, your program only needs the filename to use that file. It doesn't need a path to get there, because it's already there. So you can just do this:

```
my_sound = pygame.mixer.Sound("splat.wav")
```

Notice that you don't need to use the full pathname of the sound file (which would be **e:/programs/splat.wav**). You just use the filename without the path, because the file is in the same folder as the program that's using it.

Enough about paths!

That's all I'm going to say about paths and file locations. The whole topic of folders and directories, paths, working directories, and so on, is one that some people find confusing, and it would take a lot of pages to fully explain it. But this book is about programming, not about operating systems, file locations, or paths, so if you're having trouble with this, maybe you can ask a parent, a teacher, or someone else who knows about computers to help you.

All the other examples in this book that use files have them in the same place as the program, so you don't have to worry about the path or about using full pathnames.

Opening a file

Before you open a file, you need to know what you'll be doing with the file:

- If you'll be using the file as *input* (looking at what's in the file without changing it), you'll open the file for *reading*.
- If you'll be *creating* a brand-new file or *replacing* an existing file with something brand new, you'll open the file for *writing*.
- If you'll be *adding* to an existing file, you'll open the file for *appending*. (Remember from chapter 12 that *append* means to add to something.)

When you open a file, you make a *file object* in Python. (See, I told you that many things in Python are objects.) You make the file object by using the `open()` function with the name of the file, like this:

```
my_file = open('my_filename.txt','r')
```

The filename is a *string*, so it needs quotes around it. The `'r'` part means you're opening the file for reading. You'll learn more about that in the next section.

It's important to understand the difference between the *file object* and the *filename*. The *file object* is what you'll use inside the program to access the file. The *filename* is what Windows (or Linux or Mac OS X) calls the file on the disk.

You do the same thing with people. You have different names that you use in different places. If your teacher's name is Fred Weasley, you probably call him Mr. Weasley. His friends probably call him Fred, and his computer username might be fweasley. With files, there's a name that's used by the operating system to store the file on disk (the filename), and there's a name your program uses when working with the file (the file object).

The two names—the name of the object and the name of the file—don't have to be the same. You can call the object whatever you want. For example, if we have a text file with some notes in it that's called **notes.txt**, we could do this:

```
notes = open('notes.txt', 'r')
```
File object   Filename

Or we could do this:

```
some_crazy_stuff = open("notes.txt", 'r')
```
File object   Filename

Once you have opened the file and created the file object, you don't need the filename any more. You do everything in the program using the file object.

Reading a file

As I mentioned in the last section, you open a file and create a file object using the `open()` function. This is one of Python's built-in functions. To open the file for reading, you use `'r'` as the second argument, like this:

```
my_file = open('notes.txt', 'r')
```

If you try to open a file for reading that does not exist, you'll get an error. (After all, you can't read something that's not there, right?)

Python has a couple more built-in functions for getting information from the file into your program once the file is open. To read lines of text from a file, you can use the `readlines()` method, like this:

```
lines = my_file.readlines()
```

This will read the whole file and make a list, with one line of text in each item of the list. Let's say the **notes.txt** file contained a short list of things we need to do today:

```
Wash the car
Make my bed
Collect allowance
```

We could have used a program like Notepad to create this file. In fact, why don't you make a file like this using Notepad (or your favorite text editor) right now? Call it **notes.txt**, and save it in the same place you save your Python programs. Then close Notepad.

If we open this file with a short Python program and read it, the code might look like this.

Listing 22.1   *Opening and reading from a file*

```
my_file = open('notes.txt', 'r')
lines = my_file.readlines()
print lines
```

The output would be like this (depending on what you put in the file):

```
>>>==================== RESTART ========================
>>>
['Wash the car\n', 'Make my bed\n', 'Collect allowance']
```

The lines of text were read from the file, and they were put into a list, which we called `lines`. Each item in the list is a string containing one line from the file. Notice the `\n` part at the end of the first two lines. These are the *newline* characters that separate the lines in the file. That's where we pressed **Enter** when we were creating the file. If you pressed **Enter** after typing in the last line, there will be a third \n after the third item.

There's one more thing we need to add to the program in listing 22.1. When we're done with the file, we should close it:

```
my_file.close()
```

Why? Why not leave it open so we can access it later?

Well, Carter, if another program needs to use the file and our program hasn't closed it, the other program might not be able to access the file. It's generally a good idea to close files when you're done using them.

Once the file is in your program as a list of strings, you can do whatever you want with it. This list is just like any other Python list, so you can loop through it, sort it, append items, delete items, and so on. The strings are like any other strings, so you can print them, convert them to `int` or `float` (if they contain numbers), use them as labels in a GUI, or do anything else that you'd do with a string.

Reading one line at a time

The `readlines()` method reads all the lines of a file, right up until the end of the file. If you want to read just one line at a time, you can use the `readline()` method, like this:

```
first_line = my_file.readline()
```

This will read just the first line of the file. If you use `readline()` again in the same program, Python remembers where it was. So the second time you use it, you'll get the second line of the file. The next listing shows an example of this.

Listing 22.2 Using `readline()` more than once

```
my_file = open('notes.txt', 'r')
first_line = my_file.readline()
second_line = my_file.readline()
print "first line = ", first_line
print "second line = ", second_line
my_file.close()
```

The output of that program would look like this:

```
>>>================= RESTART ====================
>>>
first line =  Wash the car

second line =  Make my bed
```

The `readline()` method only reads one line at a time, so it doesn't put the results into a list. Each time you use `readline()`, you get a single string.

Going back to the start

If you have used `readline()` a few times and you want to start back at the beginning of the file, you can use the `seek()` method, like this:

```
first_line = my_file.readline()
second_line = my_file.readline()
my_file.seek(0)
first_line_again = my_file.readline()
```

The `seek()` method makes Python go to whatever place in the file you tell it. The number in brackets is the number of bytes from the start of the file. So setting it to 0 takes it right back to the start of the file.

Text files and binary files

All the examples of opening files and reading lines of text so far are assuming one thing: *the file actually has text in it!* Remember that text is just one of the kinds of things you can store in a file. Programmers lump together all other kinds of files and call them *binary files*.

There are two main types of files you can open:

- *Text files*—These have text in them, with letters, numbers, punctuation, and some special characters, like *newlines*.
- *Binary files*—These don't have text in them. They might have music, pictures, or some kind of data, but because they don't have text, they don't have lines either, because there are no *newlines*.

That means you can't use `readline()` or `readlines()` on a binary file. If you try to read a "line" from a **.wav** file, for example, you don't know what you'll get. Most likely, you'll get a whole bunch of gobbledygook that looks like this:

```
>>> f = open('splat.wav', 'r')
>>> print f.readline()
RIFFö▲  WAVEfmt ▶   ☺ ☺ "V  "V   datap▲
ÇÇÇÇÇÇÇÇüÇÇÇÇÇÇÇÇÇÇÇÇÇÇÇÇÇÇ◊ÇÇ◊◊◊◊◊◊Ç◊◊◊◊Ç
ÇÇ◊◊◊ÇÇÇÇÇÇÇÇÇÇÇ◊Ç◊ÇÇÇÇüÇÇÇÇÇÇÇÇÇÇÇÇÇÇÇÇ◊ÇÇÇÇÇüüÇÇÇ◊ÇÇ◊ÇÇÇÇÇ◊◊ÇÇüéééÇzvvy{|Çâ
  çïê}trv|äëïîèå~ut|◊yrqrtxÇîÖℝæäàütvÇÆÄ|mlfWR}jnmpxüêÅ ºfâràó«¼Ö}`ORj◊{hZZg-
  wàëy{äæá-¿ÿézâÿèmWLISjÇàzrvÇüytv~üÇ}yrifjt}äêèêëÄöÉémSCFZlrtyéïö¥ñ¬½-ñ¢ÆÄìÅôòÆ
  ÄÅæ|åÜ¬ÿüpd\UME@;99:>EJMW]YTZfuçòf┌▓║┴─┬─┤┐┌¢ôë~{|{yxzzuiZNG-
  HLSbs◊~wrnf\TPQU]`jvàæÉ◊osÇïôæä}üàëℝ┤
```

There's something that looks like text at the start of the **.wav** file, but then it gets crazy. That's because a **.wav** file doesn't have text in it, it has sound. The `readline()` and `readlines()` methods are only for reading text files.

Most of the time, if you need to use a binary file, you'll be using something like Pygame or some other module to load the file, like we did in chapter 19:

```
pygame.mixer.music.load('bg_music.mp3')
```

In that case, Pygame takes care of opening the file and reading the binary data (which is music in this example).

This book isn't going to cover how to process binary files. But just so you know what it looks like, you can open a binary file by adding a *b* to the file mode, like this:

```
my_music_file = open('bg_music.mp3', 'rb')
```

The `'rb'` part means you're opening the file for *reading* in *binary* mode.

In the past few sections, you have been learning how to get information from a file into your program, which is called *reading* the file. Next you're going to learn about getting information out of your program into a file. This is called *writing* the file.

Writing to a file

If you want to store some information from your program more permanently, you could look at it on the screen and write it down on a piece of paper. But that kind of defeats the purpose of using a computer!

A better idea is to save the information on the hard drive, so that, even when the program isn't running—in fact, even when the computer is turned off—your data is still there and you can get it later. You have done this many, many times already. Every time you save a report for school, a picture, a song, or a Python program, you're storing it to the hard drive.

IN THE GOOD OLD DAYS

Back in my day, all we had was paper! There were no monitors, printers, or even keyboards. You "wrote" your code by punching holes into cards. Then you fed this stack of cards into a big machine that would convert the punched holes into electrical signals the computer could understand. Sometimes it took days to get an answer. Boy, was that painful!

Old computer punch card

As I mentioned earlier, there are two ways you can put things in a file:

- *Writing*—This means starting a new file or overwriting an existing one.
- *Appending*—This means adding to an existing file and keeping what's already there.

To write or append to a file, you first have to open the file. You use the `open()` function, just like we did before, except that the second parameter will be different:

- For reading, you use `'r'` as the file mode:

  ```
  my_file = open('new_notes.txt', 'r')
  ```

- For writing, you use `'w'` as the file mode:

  ```
  my_file = open('new_notes.txt', 'w')
  ```

- For appending, you use `'a'` as the file mode:

  ```
  my_file = open('notes.txt', 'a')
  ```

If you use `'a'` for *append* mode, the filename has to be one that already exists on the hard drive, or you'll get an error. That's because *append* is for adding to an existing file.

Correction! You can open a file for appending if it's not there. It'll just create a new one that's blank!

Carter is right, *again*!

If you use `'w'` for *write* mode, there are two possibilities:

- If the file already exists, whatever is in the file will be lost and replaced with whatever you write there.
- If the file doesn't exist, a new file with that name will be created, and whatever you write will go into the new file.

Let's look at some examples.

Appending to a file

First we'll take the **notes.txt** file that we created earlier and *append* something to it. Let's add another line that says "Spend allowance." If you were looking closely when we did the `readlines()` example, you might have noticed that there's no \n, no *newline*, at the end of the last line. So we need to add one, and then add our new string. To write strings to a file, we use the `write()` method, like this.

Listing 22.3   Using append mode

```
todo_list = open('notes.txt', 'a')        ←——— Opens the file in
todo_list.write('\nSpend allowance')      ←———   append mode
todo_list.close()     ←——— Closes the file    Adds our string to the end
```

When we were reading files, I said you should close the file when you're done. But it's even more important to use `close()` when you're done *writing*. That's because the changes don't actually get saved to the file until you `close()` it.

After you run the program in listing 22.3, open **notes.txt** using Notepad (or any other text editor) and see what's in it. Remember to close Notepad when you're done.

Writing to a file

Now let's try an example of writing to a file using the write mode. We'll open a file that isn't on the hard drive. Type in the program in this listing and run it.

Listing 22.4   Using write mode on a new file

```
new_file = open("my_new_notes.txt", 'w')
new_file.write("Eat supper\n")
new_file.write("Play soccer\n")
new_file.write("Go to bed")
new_file.close()
```

How do you know it worked? Check in the folder where you saved the program from listing 22.4. You should see a file there called **my_new_notes.txt**. You can open this file in Notepad to see what's in it. You should see this:

```
Eat supper
Play soccer
Go to bed
```

You created a text file with this program and stored some text in it. This text is on the hard drive, and it'll stay there forever—or at least as long as the hard drive keeps working—unless you delete it. So you have a way to permanently store data from your programs. Now your programs can leave a permanent mark on the world (or at least on your hard drive). Anything you need to keep when the program stops and the computer is shut off, you can put in a file.

Let's see what happens if we use write mode on a file that's already on the hard drive. Remember our file called **notes.txt**? If you ran the program in listing 22.3, it looks like this:

```
Wash the car
Make my bed
Collect allowance
Spend allowance
```

Let's open this file in write mode and write to it, to see what happens. Here's the code.

Listing 22.5   Using write mode on an existing file

```
the_file = open('notes.txt', 'w')
the_file.write("Wake up\n")
the_file.write("Watch cartoons")
the_file.close()
```

Run this code, and then open **notes.txt** in Notepad to see what it contains. You should see this:

```
Wake up
Watch cartoons
```

The stuff that was in **notes.txt** before is gone. It has been replaced by the new stuff from the program in listing 22.5.

Writing to a file using `print`

In the last section, we wrote to a file using `write()`. You can also use `print` to write to a file. You still have to open the file in write or append mode, but then you can write to the file using `print`, like this:

```
my_file = open("new_file.txt", 'w')
print >> my_file, "Hello there, neighbor!"
my_file.close()
```

The two > symbols (which are sometimes called *chevrons*) are telling `print` to send its output to a file instead of to the screen. This is called *redirecting* output.

Sometimes it's more convenient to use `print` than `write()`, because `print` does things like automatically converting numbers to strings, and so on. You can decide whether to use `print` or `write()` to put text into a file.

Saving your stuff in files: `pickle`

In the first part of this chapter, we talked about reading and writing text files. Text files are one way you can store things to the hard drive. But what if you want to store something like a list or an object? Sometimes the items in the list might be strings, but not always. And what about storing things like objects? You might be able to convert all the object's properties to strings and write them to a text file, but then you'd have to do the opposite to go from the file back to an object. It could get complicated.

Luckily, Python has a way to make storing things like lists and objects easier. It's a Python module called `pickle`. That's kind of a funny name, but think about it: pickling is a way of preserving food so you can use it later. In Python, you "pickle" your data so you can save it on disk and use it later. Makes sense!

Pickling

Let's say we have a list with different kinds of things in it, like this:

```
my_list = ['Fred', 73, 'Hello there', 81.9876e-13]
```

To use `pickle`, first you have to import the `pickle` module:

```
import pickle
```

Then to "pickle" something, like a list, you use the `dump()` function. (That's easy to remember if you think of dumping your pickles into the jar.) The `dump()` function needs a file object, and you know how to make one of those:

```
pickle_file = open('my_pickled_list.pkl', 'w')
```

We open it for *writing* with `'w'` because we're going to be *storing* something in this file. You can pick whatever name and extension you want. I picked **.pkl** as the extension, short for "pickle."

Then we `dump()` our list into the pickle file:

```
pickle.dump(my_list, pickle_file)
```

The whole process looks like this.

Listing 22.6   Using `pickle` to store a list to a file

```
import pickle
my_list = ['Fred', 73, 'Hello there', 81.9876e-13]
pickle_file = open('my_pickled_list.pkl', 'w')
pickle.dump(my_list, pickle_file)
pickle_file.close()
```

You can use this same method to store any kind of data structure to a file. But what about getting it back? That's next.

Unpickling

In real life, once you pickle something, it stays pickled. You can't undo it. But in Python, when you "preserve" some data by pickling it, you can also reverse the process and get your data back the way it was.

The function to "unpickle" something is `load()`. You give it a file object for the file that contains the pickled data, and it gives you back the data in its original form. Let's try it. If you ran the program in listing 22.6, you should have a file called **my_pickled_list.pkl** in the same place where you store your programs. Now try the program in the next listing and see if you get the same list back.

Listing 22.7   Unpickling using `load()`

```
import pickle
pickle_file = open('my_pickled_list.pkl', 'r')
recovered_list = pickle.load(pickle_file)
pickle_file.close()

print recovered_list
```

You should get output that looks like this:

```
['Fred', 73, 'Hello there', 8.1987599999999997e-012]
```

It looks like the unpickling worked! We got back the same items we pickled. The E-notation looks a little different, but it's the same number, at least to 16 decimal places. The difference is from *roundoff error*, which we talked about in chapter 4.

In the next section, we're going to use what we have learned about file input and output to help us make a new game.

Game time again—Hangman

Why do we have a game in the chapter on files? Well, one thing that makes a game of Hangman interesting is having a nice big list of words from which to choose the puzzles. The easiest way to do that is to read it from a file. We'll also use PyQt for this game to show that using Pygame isn't the only way to make graphical games.

I'm not going to explain this program in quite as much detail as some other programs. By now, you should be able to look at the code and figure out how most of it works on your own. I'll just give you a little guidance to help you along.

The Hangman GUI

The main GUI for our Hangman program looks like this:

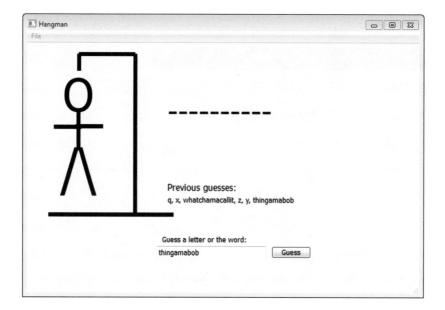

This shows all the parts of the hanged man, but when the program runs, we'll start by hiding all his parts. When the player guesses a wrong letter, we'll reveal a part of the man. If the whole man is drawn, it's *game over*!

When the player guesses a letter, the program checks to see if the letter is in the secret word. If it is, the letter is revealed. In the middle of the window, the player can see everything he's guessed so far. The player can also try to guess the word at any time.

Here's a summary of how the program works.

At the start, the program does these things:

- Loads word list from a file
- Takes newline characters off the end of each line
- Makes all parts of the man invisible
- Picks a word randomly from the word list
- Shows the same number of dashes as there are letters in the secret word

When the player clicks the **Guess!** button, the program does these things:

- Checks whether the guess is a single letter or a word
- If it's a letter:
  - Checks the secret word to see if it contains the letter
  - If the player's guess is right, shows the places where the letter occurs by replacing the dash with the letter
  - If the player's guess is wrong, reveals a part of the man
  - Adds the guessed letter to the **Previous guesses** display
  - Checks to see if the player has completed the word (guessed all the letters)
- If it's a word:
  - Checks to see if the player's guess is correct
  - If it is, shows a dialog saying **You Won!** and starts a new game
- Checks to see if the player is out of turns—if so, shows a dialog saying **You Lost** and shows what the secret word was

Getting words from the word list

This is a chapter about files, so let's look at the part of the program that gets the word list. The code looks like this:

```
f = open("words.txt", 'r')
self.lines = f.readlines()
for line in self.lines:
    line.strip()              ←——— Removes newline
f.close()                           characters
                                    from each line
```

The **words.txt** file is just a text file, so we can read it using **readlines()**. Then, to pick a word from the list, we use the **random.choice()** function, like this:

```
self.currentword = random.choice(self.lines)
```

Revealing the man

There are several ways we could have kept track of which parts of the man are already revealed and which part to reveal next. We decided to use a loop. It looks like this:

```
def wrong(self):
        self.pieces_shown += 1
        for i in range(self.pieces_shown):
            self.pieces[i].setHidden(False)
        if self.pieces_shown == len(self.pieces):
            message = "You lose.  The word was " + self.currentword
            QtGui.QMessageBox.warning(self,"Hangman",message)
            self.new_game()
```

We use `self.pieces_shown` to keep track of how many pieces of the hangman we're showing. If all the pieces are showing, we use a dialog box to tell the player he's lost.

Checking the letter guesses

One of the trickiest parts of this program is checking the player's guessed letter to see if it appears in the secret word. What makes it tricky is that the letter could appear more than once in the word. For example, if the secret word is *lever*, and the player guesses *e*, you have to reveal both the second and fourth letters because they're both *e*.

We have a couple of functions that help us do this. The `find_letters()` function finds all the places a particular letter appears in a word and returns a list of those positions. For example, for the letter *e* and the word *lever*, it would return [1, 3], because the letter *e* appears at index 1 and index 3 in the string. (Remember that the indices start at 0.) Here's the code:

```
def find_letters(letter, a_string):                          Checks where
    locations = []                                           letter appears
    start = 0
    while a_string.find(letter, start, len(a_string)) != -1:
        location = a_string.find(letter, start, len(a_string))
        locations.append(location)
        start = location + 1                    Replaces dashes with letter
    return locations
```

The `replace_letters()` function takes the list from `find_letters()` and replaces the dashes at those positions with the correct letter. In our example (the letter *e* in "lever"), it would replace ----- with -e-e-. It shows the player where the correctly guessed letters appear in the word, and leaves the rest as dashes. Here's the code:

```
def replace_letters(string, locations, letter):
    new_string = ''
    for i in range (0, len(string)):
        if i in locations:
            new_string = new_string + letter
        else:
            new_string = new_string + string[i]
    return new_string
```

Then, when the player makes a letter guess, we use the two functions we just defined, `find_letters()` and `replace_letters()`:

```
if len(guess) == 1:                             Checks if letter
    if guess in self.currentword:               is in word          Checks where
        locations = find_letters(guess, self.currentword)           letter appears
        self.word.setText(replace_letters(str(self.word.text()),
                              locations,guess))
        if str(self.word.text()) == self.currentword:   Checks if no dashes left
            self.win()                                  (which means we won!)
    else:
        self.wrong()
```

Are we guessing a single letter?

Replaces dashes with letter

The total program is about 95 lines of code, plus some blank lines to make things look nice. Listing 22.8 shows the whole program, with some notes explaining the different sections. The code is in the **\Examples\Hangman** folder on your computer if you used the installer, and it's also on the web site. It includes **hangman.py**, **hangman.ui**, and **words.txt**. Remember, as we mentioned in chapter 20, if you are on a Mac, you will need to open **hangman.ui** in Qt Designer and deselect the `nativeMenuBar` property for the `menubar` object.

Listing 22.8   The whole hangman.py program

```python
import sys
from PyQt4 import QtCore, QtGui, uic
import random

form_class = uic.loadUiType("hangman.ui")[0]

def find_letters(letter, a_string):
    locations = []
    start = 0
    while a_string.find(letter, start, len(a_string)) != -1:
        location = a_string.find(letter, start, len(a_string))
        locations.append(location)
        start = location + 1
    return locations
```
Finds letters

```python
def replace_letters(string, locations, letter):
    new_string = ''
    for i in range (0, len(string)):
        if i in locations:
            new_string = new_string + letter
        else:
            new_string = new_string + string[i]
    return new_string
```
Replaces dashes with letters when the player guesses a letter correctly

```python
def dashes(word):
    letters = "abcdefghijklmnopqrstuvwxyz"
    new_string = ''
    for i in word:
        if i in letters:
            new_string += "-"
        else:
            new_string += i
    return new_string
```
Replaces letters with dashes at the start of the program ❶

```python
class MyWidget(QtGui.QMainWindow, form_class):
    def __init__(self, parent=None):
        QtGui.QMainWindow.__init__(self, parent)
        self.setupUi(self)
        self.btn_guess.clicked.connect(self.btn_guess_clicked)
        self.actionExit.triggered.connect(self.menuExit_selected)
        self.pieces = [self.head, self.body, self.leftarm, self.leftleg,
                       self.rightarm, self.rightleg]
```
Connect event handlers

Parts of the man

```
            self.gallows = [self.line1, self.line2, self.line3, self.line4]
            self.pieces_shown = 0
            self.currentword = ""
            f=open("words.txt", 'r')
            self.lines = f.readlines()
            f.close()
            self.new_game()

    def new_game(self):
            self.guesses.setText("")
            self.currentword = random.choice(self.lines)
            self.currentword = self.currentword.strip()
            for i in self.pieces:
                i.setFrameShadow(QtGui.QFrame.Plain)
                i.setHidden(True)
            for i in self.gallows:
                i.setFrameShadow(QtGui.QFrame.Plain)
            self.word.setText(dashes(self.currentword))
            self.pieces_shown = 0

    def btn_guess_clicked(self):
            guess = str(self.guessBox.text())
            if str(self.guesses.text()) != "":
                self.guesses.setText(str(self.guesses.text())+", "+guess)
            else:
                self.guesses.setText(guess)
            if len(guess) == 1:
                if guess in self.currentword:
                    locations = find_letters(guess, self.currentword)
                    self.word.setText(replace_letters(str(self.word.text()),
                                            locations,guess))
                    if str(self.word.text()) == self.currentword:
                        self.win()
                else:
                    self.wrong()
            else:
                if guess == self.currentword:
                    self.win()
                else:
                    self.wrong()
            self.guessBox.setText("")

    def win(self):
            QtGui.QMessageBox.information(self,"Hangman","You win!")
            self.new_game()

    def wrong(self):
            self.pieces_shown += 1
            for i in range(self.pieces_shown):
                self.pieces[i].setHidden(False)
            if self.pieces_shown == len(self.pieces):
                message = "You lose.  The word was " + self.currentword
                QtGui.QMessageBox.warning(self,"Hangman", message)
                self.new_game()
```

Parts of the gallows

Gets word list

Randomly pick a word from the list

Hides the man

Calls the function to replace letters with dashes

Guess a letter

Lets the player guess a letter or word

Guess a word

Display a dialog if player wins

Wrong guess

Reveal another piece of the man

Player lost

```
    def menuExit_selected(self):
        self.close()

app = QtGui.QApplication(sys.argv)
myapp = MyWidget(None)
myapp.show()
app.exec_()
```

For simplicity, our Hangman program uses only lowercase letters. The word list we provide only has lowercase, and the user must enter her guesses in lowercase.

The `dashes()` function ❶ replaces the letters with dashes at the start of a new game. But it doesn't replace punctuation, like apostrophes. So if the word was *doesn't*, the player would see - - - - - ' - .

I encourage you to try creating this program on your own. You can build the GUI in Qt Designer. It doesn't matter if it doesn't look exactly the same as the version I have here. Just make sure you look at the code to see what names to use for the components. The names in the code have to match the names in the **.ui** file.

Type in the code if you can. Run the program and see how it works. And if you think of something different to try, go for it! Have fun, play around with it, and experiment. That's one of the most fun and rewarding parts of programming, and it's how you'll learn the most.

What did you learn?

In this chapter, you learned

- What a file is
- How to open and close files
- Different ways to open a file: reading, writing, and appending
- Different ways to write things to a file: `write()` or `print >>`
- How to use `pickle` to save lists and objects (and other Python data structures) to a file
- A lot about folders (also called directories), file locations, and paths

We also made a Hangman game that used data from a file to get a word list.

Test your knowledge

1 The kind of object in Python that's used to work with files is called a _____.
2 How do you create a file object?
3 What's the difference between a file object and a filename?

4   What should you do with a file when you're done reading or writing it?

5   What happens if you open a file in append mode and then write something to the file?

6   What happens if you open a file in write mode and then write something to the file?

7   How do you start reading the start of a file after you have already read part of it?

8   What `pickle` function is used to save a Python object to a file?

9   What `pickle` method is used to "unpickle" an object—to get it from a pickle file and put it back in a Python variable?

Try it out

1   Make a program to create silly sentences. Each sentence should have at least four parts, like this:

The _____ _____ _____ _____

    (adjective)   (noun)   (verb phrase) (adverb phrase)

For example: "The crazed monkey played a ukulele on the table."

         adjective   noun   verb phrase   adverb phrase

The program should create the sentence by randomly picking an adjective, a noun, a verb phrase, and an adverb phrase. The words will be stored in files, and you can use Notepad to create them. The simplest way to make this program work is to have one file for each of the four groups of words, but you can do it however you want. Here are some ideas to get you started, but I'm sure you'll come up with your own:

- Adjectives: crazed, silly, shy, goofy, angry, lazy, obstinate, purple
- Nouns: monkey, elephant, cyclist, teacher, author, hockey player
- Verb phrases: played a ukulele, danced a jig, combed his hair, flapped her ears
- Adverb phrases: on the table, at the grocery store, in the shower, after breakfast, with a broom

Here's another sample output: "The lazy author combed his hair with a broom."

2   Write a program that asks the user to enter her name, age, favorite color, and favorite food. Have the program save all four items to a text file, each one on a separate line.

3   Do the same as in question #2, but use `pickle` to save the data to a file. (Hint: This will be easy if you put the data in a *list*.)

## CHAPTER 23

Take a Chance—Randomness

One of the most fun things about games is that you never know what will happen. Games are unpredictable. They're *random*. It's this randomness that makes them interesting.

As you have already seen, computers can simulate random behavior. In our number-guessing program (in chapter 1), we used the `random` module to generate a random integer, which the user had to guess. You also used `random` to pick words for the silly sentence program in the "Try it out" section in chapter 22.

Computers can also simulate the random behavior of rolling dice or shuffling a deck of cards. This makes it possible to create computer games with cards or dice (or other randomly behaving objects). For example, almost everyone has tried playing Solitaire on Windows, which is a card game where the program randomly shuffles the cards before each game. Computer Backgammon, which uses two dice, is also very popular.

In this chapter, you'll learn how to use the `random` module to make computer-generated dice and decks of cards that you can play games with. We'll also look at how you can use computer-generated random events to explore the idea of *probability*, which is how likely something is to happen.

What's randomness?

Before we start talking about how to make programs have random behavior, you should understand what "random" really means.

Take the example of flipping a coin. If you toss a coin in the air and let it land, it will land either heads-up or tails-up. For a normal coin, the chances of getting heads are the same as the chances of getting tails. Sometimes you'll get heads, sometimes tails. On any one toss, you don't know what you'll get. Because the outcome of a toss can't be predicted, we say it's *random*. Tossing a coin is an example of a *random event*.

If you toss the coin many times, you'll probably get about the same number of heads as tails. But you can never really be sure. If you toss the coin 4 times, you might get 2 heads and 2 tails. But you could get 3 heads and 1 tail, 1 head and 3 tails, or even 4 heads (or tails) in a row. If you toss the coin 100 times, you might get 50 heads. But you could get 20, 44, 67, or even all 100 tosses coming up heads! That's very unlikely, but it could happen.

The point is that each event is random. Although there might be some pattern to it if you made a lot of tosses, each individual toss has the same chance of coming up heads or tails. Another way to say this is that the coin has no *memory*. So even if you just tossed 99 heads in a row, and you think it's nearly impossible to get 100 heads in a row, the next toss still has a 50 percent chance of being heads. That's what *random* means.

A *random event* is an event with two or more possible outcomes, where you can't predict which outcome will happen. The outcome could be the order of cards in a shuffled deck, or the number of spots that show when you roll the dice, or which side a coin will land on.

Rolling the dice

Almost everyone has played a game using dice. Whether it's Monopoly, Yahtzee, Trouble, Backgammon, or some other game, rolling dice is one of the most common ways to generate a random event in a game.

Dice are very easy to simulate in a program, and Python's `random` module has a couple of ways to do it. One is the `randint()` function, which picks a random integer. Because the number of spots on the sides of a die are integers (1, 2, 3, 4, 5, and 6), rolling a single die could be simulated like this:

```
import random
die_1 = random.randint(1, 6)
```

That gives us a number from 1 to 6, with each number having an equal chance of appearing. This is just like a real die.

Another way to do the same thing is to make a list of the possible results and then use the choice() function to pick one of them. Here's how that would look:

```
import random
sides = [1, 2, 3, 4, 5, 6]
die_1 = random.choice(sides)
```

This would do exactly the same thing as the previous example. The choice() function randomly chooses an item from a list. In this case, the list is the numbers from 1 to 6.

More than one die

What if you want to simulate rolling two dice? If you're going to add up the two dice to get the total, you might think of doing it this way:

```
two_dice = random.randint(2, 12)
```

After all, the total of two dice can be from 2 to 12, right? Well, yes and no. You *will* get a random number between 2 and 12, but not in the same way as adding up two random numbers from 1 to 6. What that code line does is like rolling one big 11-sided die, not two 6-sided dice. But what's the difference? That gets into a topic called *probability*. The easiest way to see the difference is to try it out and see.

Let's roll the dice many times and keep track of how many times each total comes up. We'll do that with a loop and a list. The loop will roll the dice, and the list will keep track of how many times each total comes up. Let's start with the single 11-sided die, as shown in this listing.

Listing 23.1   Rolling a single 11-sided die 1,000 times

```
import random

totals = [0, 0, 0, 0, 0, 0, 0, 0, 0, 0, 0, 0, 0]   ◁——❶  List has 13 items,
for i in range(1000):                                      with index 0 to 12
    dice_total = random.randint(2, 12)
    totals[dice_total] += 1       ◁——❷  Adds 1 to the count
                                          of this total
for i in range (2, 13):
    print "total", i, "came up", totals[i], "times"
```

❶ The list has indexes from 0 to 12, but we won't use the first two, because we don't care about totals 0 or 1—they'll never happen. ❷ When we get a result, we add 1 to that list item. If the total is 7, we add one to totals[7]. So totals[2] is the number of 2s we got, totals[3] is the number of 3s we got, and so on.

If you run this code, you should get something like this:

```
total 2 came up 95 times
total 3 came up 81 times
total 4 came up 85 times
total 5 came up 86 times
total 6 came up 100 times
total 7 came up 85 times
total 8 came up 94 times
total 9 came up 98 times
total 10 came up 93 times
total 11 came up 84 times
total 12 came up 99 times
```

If you look at the totals, you can see that all the numbers came up roughly the same number of times, between 80 and 100. They didn't come up exactly the same number of times because the numbers are random, but they're close, and there's no obvious pattern of some numbers coming up much more often than others. Try running the program a few times to make sure. Or try increasing the number of loops to 10,000 or 100,000.

Now let's try the same thing with two 6-sided dice. The following code does that.

Listing 23.2   Rolling two 6-sided dice 1,000 times

```python
import random

totals = [0, 0, 0, 0, 0, 0, 0, 0, 0, 0, 0, 0, 0]
for i in range(1000):
    die_1 = random.randint(1, 6)
    die_2 = random.randint(1, 6)
    dice_total = die_1 + die_2
    totals[dice_total] += 1

for i in range(2, 13):
    print "total", i, "came up", totals[i], "times"
```

If you run the code in listing 23.2, you should get output that looks something like this:

```
total 2 came up 22 times
total 3 came up 61 times
total 4 came up 93 times
total 5 came up 111 times
total 6 came up 141 times
total 7 came up 163 times
total 8 came up 134 times
total 9 came up 117 times
total 10 came up 74 times
total 11 came up 62 times
total 12 came up 22 times
```

Notice that the highest and lowest numbers came up less often, and the middle numbers, like 6 and 7, came up most often. That's different from what happened with a single 11-sided die. If we do this many more times and then calculate the percentage of times that a certain total occurs, it looks like this:

Result	One 11-sided die	Two 6-sided dice
2	9.1%	2.8%
3	9.1%	5.6%
4	9.1%	8.3%
5	9.1%	11.1%
6	9.1%	13.9%
7	9.1%	16.7%
8	9.1%	13.9%
9	9.1%	11.1%
10	9.1%	8.3%
11	9.1%	5.6%
12	9.1%	2.8%

If we plot a graph of these numbers, it looks like this:

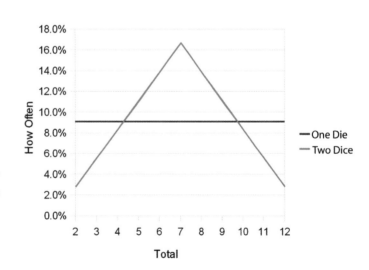

Why are they different? The reason involves the rather large topic of *probability*. Basically, the middle numbers are more likely to come up with two dice because there are more ways the middle totals can happen with two dice.

When you roll two dice, there are many different combinations that can happen. Here's a list of them, with their totals:

1+1 = 2	1+2 = 3	1+3 = 4	1+4 = 5	1+5 = 6	1+6 = 7
2+1 = 3	2+2 = 4	2+3 = 5	2+4 = 6	2+5 = 7	2+6 = 8
3+1 = 4	3+2 = 5	3+3 = 6	3+4 = 7	3+5 = 8	3+6 = 9
4+1 = 5	4+2 = 6	4+3 = 7	4+4 = 8	4+5 = 9	4+6 = 10
5+1 = 6	5+2 = 7	5+3 = 8	5+4 = 9	5+5 = 10	5+6 = 11
6+1 = 7	6+2 = 8	6+3 = 9	6+4 = 10	6+5 = 11	6+6 = 12

There are 36 possible combinations. Now look at how many times each total appears:

- The total 2 appears 1 time.
- The total 3 appears 2 times.
- The total 4 appears 3 times.
- The total 5 appears 4 times.
- The total 6 appears 5 times.
- The total 7 appears 6 times.
- The total 8 appears 5 times.
- The total 9 appears 4 times.
- The total 10 appears 3 times.
- The total 11 appears 2 times.
- The total 12 appears 1 time.

This means that there are more ways to roll a 7 than a 2. For a 7, you can roll 1+6, 2+5, 3+4, 4+3, 5+2, or 6+1. For a 2, the only way to get it is to roll 1+1. So it makes sense that, if we roll the dice a bunch of times, we should expect more 7s than 2s. And that's what we got from our two-dice program.

Using computer programs to generate random events is a really good way to experiment with probability and see what happens over a large number of tries. It would take you a long time to roll a real pair of dice 1,000 times and record the results. But a computer program can do the same thing in a fraction of a second!

Ten in a row

Let's do one more probability experiment before we move on. A few pages ago, we talked about flipping a coin and how likely it would be to get a bunch of heads in a row. Why don't we try an experiment to see how often we get 10 heads in a row? It won't happen very often, so we're going to have to do a lot of coin flips before we see it. Why don't we try 1,000,000! With a real coin, that would take … a long time.

Yeesh. How many more times do I have to flip this thing?

If you could do one coin toss every 5 seconds, that would be 12 per minute, or 720 per hour. If you could do coin tosses for 12 hours a day (after all, you still have to eat and sleep), you could do about 8,640 tosses a day. So it would take about 115 days (about 4 months) to do one million coin tosses. But with a computer, we can do it in seconds. (Okay, maybe a few minutes, because we have to write the program first.)

For this program, in addition to flipping the coin, we have to keep track of when we get 10 heads in a row. One way to do this is to use a *counter*. A counter is a variable used to count something.

We'll need two counters. One will be for the number of heads we have tossed in a row. Let's call it `heads_in_row`. The other is for the number of times we get 10 heads in a row. Let's call it `ten_heads_in_row`. This is what the program will do:

- Whenever we get heads, the `heads_in_row` counter will increase by 1.
- Whenever we get tails, the `heads_in_row` counter will go back to 0.
- When the `heads_in_row` counter reaches 10, we'll increase the `ten_heads_in_row` counter by 1 and set the `heads_in_row` counter back to 0, to start over.
- At the end, we'll print a message saying how many times we got 10 heads in a row.

Here's some code to do this.

Listing 23.3   Looking for 10 heads in a row

```
from random import *
coin = ["Heads", "Tails"]
heads_in_row = 0
ten_heads_in_row = 0
for i in range (1000000):
    if choice(coin) == "Heads":          ⟵——— Flips the coin
        heads_in_row += 1
    else:
        heads_in_row = 0
    if heads_in_row == 10:                    Got 10 heads in a row,
        ten_heads_in_row += 1        ⟵——— increments counter
        heads_in_row = 0

print "We got 10 heads in a row", ten_heads_in_row, "times."
```

When I ran this program, it said

```
We got 10 heads in a row 510 times.
```

I ran the program a few times, and the number was always around 500. That means, in a million coin tosses, we should expect to get 10 heads in a row about 500 times, or about once every 2,000 tosses (1,000,000 / 500 = 2,000).

Creating a deck of cards

Another kind of random event that's used a lot in games is drawing a card. It's random because the deck is shuffled, so you don't know what card is coming next. And every time the deck is shuffled, the order is different.

With dice and coin tosses, we said that every toss has the same probability, because the coin (or die) has no memory. But that's not true with cards. As you draw cards from the deck, there are fewer and fewer cards left (in most games, anyway). That changes the probability of drawing each one of the remaining cards.

For example, when you start with a full deck, the chances of drawing the 4 of Hearts is 1/52, or about 2 percent. This is because there are 52 cards in the deck, and only one 4 of Hearts. If you keep drawing (and haven't drawn the 4 of Hearts yet), when you're halfway through the deck, the chances of getting the 4 of Hearts are 1/26, or about 4 percent. By the time you reach the last card, if you still haven't drawn the 4 of Hearts, the chances of drawing it are 1/1, or 100 percent. It's certain that you'll draw the 4 of Hearts next, because it's the only card left.

The reason I'm telling you all this is to show that, if we're going to make a computer game using a deck of cards, we need to keep track of which cards have been removed from the deck as we go along. One good way to do this is with a list. We can start with a list of all 52 cards in the deck and use the `random.choice()` function to pick cards randomly from the list. As we pick each card, we can remove it from the list (the deck) using `remove()`.

Shuffling the deck

In a real card game, we shuffle the deck, which means we mix up the cards so they're in a random order. That way we can just take the top card, and it'll be random. But with the `random.choice()` function, we're going to pick randomly from the list anyway. We don't have to take the "top" card, so there's no point in "shuffling" the deck. We'll just randomly pick a card from anywhere in the deck. This is like fanning out the cards and saying "Pick a card, any card!" That would be rather time-consuming to do for each person's turn in a card game, but it's very easy in a computer program.

Pick a card, any card!

A card object

We're going to use a *list* to act as our "deck" of cards. But what about the cards themselves? How should we store each one? As a string? An integer? What things do we need to know about each card?

For card games, these are the three things we usually need to know about a card:

- *Suit*—Diamonds, Hearts, Spades, or Clubs.
- *Rank*—Ace, 2, 3, … 10, Jack, Queen, King.

■ *Value*—For the numbered cards (2 through 10), this is usually the same as their rank. For Jack, Queen, and King, it's usually 10, and for the Ace, it can be 1, 11, or some other value, depending on the game.

Rank	Value
Ace	1 or 11
2	2
3	3
4	4
5	5
6	6
7	7
8	8
9	9
10	10
Jack	10
Queen	10
King	10

So we need to keep track of these three things, and we need to keep them together in some kind of container. A list would work, but we'd have to remember which item was which. Another way is to make a "card" object that has attributes like these:

```
card.suit
card.rank
card.value
```

That's what we'll do. We'll also add a couple more attributes called `suit_id` and `rank_id`:

■ `suit_id` is a number from 1 to 4 for the suit, where

1 = Diamonds, 2 = Hearts, 3 = Spades, 4 = Clubs

■ `rank_id` is a number from 1 to 13, where

1 = Ace

2 = 2

3 = 3

…

10 = 10

11 = Jack

12 = Queen

13 = King

The reason for adding these two attributes is so that we can easily use a nested **for** loop to make a deck of 52 cards. We can have an inner loop for the rank (1 to 13) and an outer loop for the suit (1 to 4). The __init__() method for the card object will take the `suit_id` and `rank_id` and create the other attributes of suit, rank, and value. It also makes it easy to compare the rank of two cards to see which has the higher rank.

We should add two more attributes to make our card object easy to use in a program. When the program needs to print the card, it'll want to print something like "4H" or "4 of Hearts." For the face cards, it would be something like "JD" or "Jack of Diamonds." We'll add the attributes `short_name` and `long_name`, so the program can easily print either a short or long description of the card.

Let's make a class for a playing card. The code is shown in the next listing.

Listing 23.4   The `Card` class

```
class Card:
    def __init__(self, suit_id, rank_id):
        self.rank_id = rank_id
        self.suit_id = suit_id

        if self.rank_id == 1:
            self.rank = "Ace"
            self.value = 1
        elif self.rank_id == 11:
            self.rank = "Jack"
            self.value = 10
        elif self.rank_id == 12:
            self.rank = "Queen"
            self.value = 10
        elif self.rank_id == 13:
            self.rank = "King"
            self.value = 10
        elif 2 <= self.rank_id <= 10:
            self.rank = str(self.rank_id)
            self.value = self.rank_id
        else:
            self.rank = "RankError"
            self.value = -1

        if self.suit_id == 1:
            self.suit = "Diamonds"
        elif self.suit_id == 2:
            self.suit = "Hearts"
        elif self.suit_id == 3:
            self.suit = "Spades"
        elif self.suit_id == 4:
            self.suit = "Clubs"
        else:
            self.suit = "SuitError"
        self.short_name = self.rank[0] + self.suit[0]
        if self.rank == '10':
            self.short_name = self.rank + self.suit[0]
        self.long_name = self.rank + " of " + self.suit
```

Creates rank and value attributes

Creates suit attribute

❶ *Performs some error checking*

The error checking in the code ❶ makes sure `rank_id` and `suit_id` are in range and that they are integers. If they aren't, you would see something like "7 of SuitError" or "RankError of Clubs" when displaying the card in a program.

The line that sets the `short_name` simply takes the number or first letter of the rank (6 or Jack) and the first letter of the suit (Diamonds) and puts them together. For the King of Hearts, `short_name` would be KH. For the 6 of Spades, it would be 6S.

Listing 23.4 isn't a complete program. It's just the class definition for our `Card` class. Because this is something we could use over and over in different programs, maybe we should make it a *module*. Save the code in listing 23.4 as **cards.py**.

Now we need to make some instances of cards—in fact, a whole deck would be nice! To test our `Card` class, let's make a program to create a deck of 52 cards and then pick 5 cards at random and display their attributes. Here's some code for that.

Listing 23.5 Making a deck of cards

```
import random
from cards import Card          ◄——— Imports our cards module

deck = []
for suit_id in range(1, 5):
    for rank_id in range(1, 14):                    ❶  Uses nested for loops
        deck.append(Card(suit_id, rank_id))             to make a deck

hand = []
for cards in range(0, 5):                   ❷  Picks 5 cards from the
    a = random.choice(deck)                     deck to make a hand
    hand.append(a)
    deck.remove(a)

print
for card in hand:
    print card.short_name, '=' ,card.long_name, "  Value:", card.value
```

❶ The inner loop goes through each card in the suit, and the outer loop goes through each suit (13 cards * 4 suits = 52 cards). ❷ Then the code picks five cards from the deck and puts them in a hand. It also removes the cards from the deck.

If you run the code in listing 23.5, you should get something like this:

```
7D = 7 of Diamonds   Value: 7
9H = 9 of Hearts   Value: 9
KH = King of Hearts   Value: 10
6S = 6 of Spades   Value: 6
KC = King of Clubs   Value: 10
```

If you run it again, you should get five different cards. And no matter how many times you run it, you should never get the same card twice in one hand.

So now we can make a deck of cards and randomly draw cards from it to add them to a hand. It sounds like we have the basic things we need to make a card game! In the next section, we'll make a card game that you can play against the computer.

Crazy Eights

You might have heard of a card game called Crazy Eights. You might even have played it.

One thing about card games on the computer is that it's difficult to have multiple players. That's because, in most card games, you're not supposed to see the other players' cards. If everyone is looking at the same computer, everybody will see everyone else's cards. So the best card games for playing on the computer are those where you can play with just two players—you against the computer. Crazy Eights is one of those games that works well with two players, so we're going to make a Crazy Eights game where the user plays against the computer.

Here are the rules for our program. It is a game for two players. Each player gets five cards. The rest of the cards are placed face down, and then one card is turned face up to start the discard pile. The object of the game is to get rid of all your cards before anyone else and before the deck runs out:

1. At each turn, a player has to do one of the following:
   - Play a card of the same suit as the up card.
   - Play a card of the same rank as the up card.
   - Play an 8.
2. If the player plays an 8, he can "call the suit," which means he gets to choose the suit that the next player is trying to match.
3. If the player can't play any of his cards, he must pick up a card from the deck and add it to his hand.
4. If a player gets rid of all his cards, he wins that game, and he gets points depending on what the other player has left in his hand:
   - 50 points for each 8
   - 10 points for each face card
   - Face value for every other card
   - 1 point for each Ace

5 If the deck runs out and no one can make a play, the game is over. In that case, both players get points for the other player's remaining cards.

6 You can play up to a certain point total, or just keep playing until you're tired, and the one with the most points wins.

The first thing we should do is modify some of our card objects a bit. The point values in Crazy Eights are mostly the same as what we had before, except for the 8, which is worth 50 points instead of 8 points. We could change the __init__ method in our `Card` class to make 8s worth 50 points, but that would affect every other game that might use the `cards` module. It would be better to make the change in the main program and leave the class definition alone. Here's one way we could do it:

```
deck = []
for suit in range(1, 5):
    for rank in range(1, 14):
        new_card = Card(suit, rank)
        if new_card.rank == 8:
            new_card.value = 50
        deck.append(new_card)
```

Here, before adding the new card to the deck, we check to see if it's an 8. If it is, we set its value to 50.

Now we're ready to start making the game itself. Here are some of the things our program will need to do:

- Keep track of the face-up card.
- Get the player's choice of what to do (play a card or draw a card).
- If the player tries to play a card, make sure the play is valid:
  - The card must be a valid card.
  - The card must be in the player's hand.
  - The card must either match the rank or suit of the face-up card or be an 8.
- If the player plays an 8, ask for the new suit (and make sure the choice is a valid suit).
- Play the computer's turn (more on that shortly).
- Determine when the game is over.
- Count up the points.

In the rest of the chapter, we'll go through these requirements one by one. Some of them will need just a line or two of code, and some will be a bit longer. For the longer ones, we'll create functions that we can call from the main loop.

The main loop

Before we get into the details, let's figure out what the main loop of the program will look like. Basically, we have to alternate turns between the player and the computer until somebody wins or both are blocked. The code will look something like this.

Listing 23.6   The main loop of Crazy Eights

```
init_cards()
while not game_done:                        Player's turn
    blocked = 0                              ╱
    player_turn()              ◁────────────
    if len(p_hand) == 0:       ◁─────────────  Player's hand (p_hand) has
        game_done = True                       no cards left, so player wins
        print
        print "You won!"            Computer's turn
    if not game_done:                  ╱
        computer_turn()       ◁───────
    if len(c_hand) == 0:      ◁─────────────  Computer's hand (c_hand) has
        game_done = True                      no cards left, so computer wins
        print
        print "Computer won!"
    if blocked >= 2:          ◁───── ❶  Both players are blocked,
        game_done = True                  so game ends
        print "Both players blocked.  GAME OVER."
```

Part of the main loop is figuring out when the game is over. It can be over when either the player or the computer is out of cards. It can also be over if neither of them is out of cards but both of them are blocked (that is, they have no valid plays). The `blocked` variable is set in the code for the player's turn (if the player is blocked) and the computer's turn (if the computer is blocked). ❶ We wait until `blocked = 2`, to make sure both player and computer are blocked.

Note that listing 23.6 isn't a complete program, so if you try to run it, you'll get an error. It's just the main loop. We still need all the other parts to make the program complete.

This code is for a single game. If we want to keep playing more games, we can wrap the whole thing in another, outer `while` loop:

```
done = False
p_total = c_total = 0
while not done:
    [play a game... see listing 23.6]
play_again = raw_input("Play again (Y/N)? ")
    if play_again.lower().startswith('y'):
        done = False
    else:
        done = True
```

This gives us the main structure of the program. Now we need to add the individual pieces to do what we need.

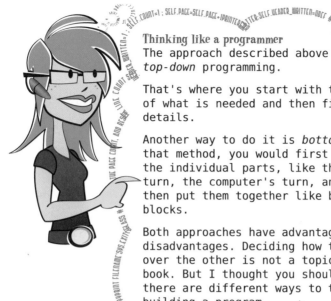

Thinking like a programmer

The approach described above is called *top-down* programming.

That's where you start with the outline of what is needed and then fill in the details.

Another way to do it is *bottom-up*. In that method, you would first create all the individual parts, like the player's turn, the computer's turn, and so on, and then put them together like building blocks.

Both approaches have advantages and disadvantages. Deciding how to choose one over the other is not a topic for this book. But I thought you should know that there are different ways to tackle building a program.

The face-up card

When the hand is first dealt, one card from the deck is turned up to start the discard pile. When any player plays a card, it goes on the discard pile, face up. The card that's showing on the discard pile at any time is called the *up card*. We could keep track of this by making a *list* for the discard pile, the same way we made a list for the "hand" in our test code in listing 23.5. But we don't really care about all the cards in the discard pile. We only care about the last card added to it. So we can just use a single instance of a `Card` object to keep track of it.

When the player or computer plays a card, we'll do something like this:

```
hand.remove(chosen_card)
up_card = chosen_card
```

The active suit

Usually, the active suit (the one the player or computer is trying to match) is the same as the suit of the up card. But there's an exception. When an 8 has been played, the player calls the suit. So if he plays the 8 of Diamonds, he might call Clubs as the suit. That means that the next play must match Clubs, even though a Diamond (the 8 of Diamonds) is showing.

This means we need to keep track of the active suit, because it might be different from the suit that's showing. We can use a variable, `active_suit`, to do this:

```
active_suit = card.suit
```

Whenever a card is played, we'll update the active suit, and when a player plays an 8, he'll choose the new active suit.

The player's turn

When it's the player's turn, the first thing we need to do is get his choice of what to do. He can play a card from his hand (if possible) or draw from the deck. If we were making a GUI version of this program, we'd have the player click the card he wanted to play, or click the deck to draw. But we're making a text-based version of the program, so he'll have to type in a choice, and then we'll have to check what he typed and figure out what he wants to do and whether that input is valid.

To give you an idea of what kind of input the player will need to provide, we'll look at a sample game. The player's input is in **bold**:

```
Crazy Eights

Your hand: 4S, 7D, KC, 10D, QS    Up Card:  6C
What would you like to do?  Type a card name or "Draw" to take a card:  KC
You played the KC (King of Clubs)
Computer plays 8S  (8 of spades) and changes suit to Diamonds

Your hand:  4S, 7D, 10D, QS   Up Card:  8S    Suit:  Diamonds
What would you like to do?  Type a card name or "Draw" to take a card: 10D
You played 10D (10 of Diamonds)
Computer plays QD (Queen of Diamonds)

Your hand:  4S, 7D QS   Up card:  QD
What would you like to do?  Type a card name or "Draw" to take a card: 7D
You played 7D (7 of Diamonds)
Computer plays 9D (9 of Diamonds)

Your hand:  4S, QS   Up card:  9D
What would you like to do?  Type a card name or "Draw" to take a card: QM
That is not a valid card.  Try again:  QD
You do not have that card in your hand.  Try again: QS
That is not a legal play.  You must match suit, match rank, play an 8, or draw a card
Try again: Draw
You drew 3C
Computer draws a card

Your hand:  4S, QS, 3C   Up card:  9D
What would you like to do?  Type a card name or "Draw" to take a card: Draw
```

```
You drew 8C
Computer plays 2D

Your hand:  4S, QS, 3C, 8C   Up card:  2D
What would you like to do?  Type a card name or "Draw" to take a card: 8C
You played 8C (8 of Clubs)
Your hand:  4S, QS, 3C   Pick a suit: S
You picked spades
Computer draws a card

Your hand:  4S, QS, 3C  Up card: 8C   Suit:  Spades
What would you like to do?  Type a card name or "Draw" to take a card: QS
You played QS (Queen of Spades)
   .
   .
   .
```

This isn't a complete game, but you get the idea. The player has to type in things like QS or
Draw to tell the program his choice. The program has to check that what the player typed in
makes sense. We'll use some string methods (from chapter 21) to help us with that.

Displaying the hand

Before we ask the player what he wants to do, we should show him what cards are in his
hand and what the up card is. Here's some code for that:

```
print "\nYour hand: ",
for card in p_hand:
    print card.short_name,
print "  Up card: ",   up_card.short_name
```

If an 8 has been played, we also need to tell him what the active suit is. So let's add a couple
more lines, as shown next.

Listing 23.7   Displaying what's in the player's hand

```
print "\nYour hand: ",
for card in p_hand:
    print card.short_name,
print "  Up card: ", up_card.short_name
if up_card.rank == '8':
    print"  Suit is", active_suit
```

Just like listing 23.6, listing 23.7 is not a complete program. We are still building up the
parts we need to make a complete program. But when the code in listing 23.7 runs (as part
of the complete program), it gives output like this:

```
Your hand:  4S, QS, 3C  Up card: 8C   Suit:  Spades
```

If you wanted to use the long names for the cards instead of the short names, the output would look something like this:

```
Your hand:  4 of Spades, Queen of Spades, 3 of Clubs
Up Card:  8 of Clubs    Suit:  Spades
```

In our examples, we'll use the short names.

Getting the player's choice

Now we need to ask the player what he wants to do and process his response. He has two main choices:

- Play a card
- Draw a card

If he decides to play a card, we need to make sure the play is valid. We said before that we need to check three things:

- Is his choice a valid card? (Did he try to play the 4 of Marshmallows?)
- Is the card in his hand?
- Is the chosen card a legal play? (Does it match the rank or suit of the up card, or is it an 8?)

But if you think about it, his hand can only have valid cards in it. So if we check that the card is in his hand, we don't have to worry about checking whether it is valid. He can't have the 4 of Marshmallows in his hand, because it never existed in the deck.

So let's look at some code that will get the player's choice and validate it. It's shown in listing 23.8.

WORD BOX

Validate means to make sure something is valid, which means it is allowed or makes sense.

Listing 23.8   Getting the player's choice

```
print "What would you like to do? ",
response = raw_input ("Type a card to play or 'Draw' to take a card: " )
valid_play = False
while not valid_play:              ◄——— Keeps trying until player enters something valid
    selected_card = None
    while selected_card == None:          Gets a card the player
        if response.lower() == 'draw':    has in hand, or draws
            valid_play = True
            if len(deck) > 0:
```

```
                        card = random.choice(deck)
                        p_hand.append(card)
                        deck.remove(card)
                        print "You drew", card.short_name
                    else:
                        print "There are no cards left in the deck"
                        blocked += 1
                    return
            else:
                for card in p_hand:
                    if response.upper() == card.short_name:
                        selected_card = card
                if selected_card == None:
                    response = raw_input("You don't have that card. Try again:")

        if selected_card.rank == '8':
            valid_play = True
            is_eight = True
        elif selected_card.suit  == active_suit:
            valid_play = True
        elif selected_card.rank  == up_card.rank:
            valid_play = True

        if not valid_play:
            response = raw_input("That's not a legal play.  Try again: ")
```

Got "draw", so returns to main loop

If "draw", takes card ❶ from deck and adds it to player's hand

Checks if the selected card is in player's hand—keeps trying until it is (or he draws)

Playing an 8 is always legal

Checks if selected card matches up-card suit

Checks if selected card matches up-card rank

(Again, this is not a complete, runnable program.)

❶ At this point, we have a choice that's valid: either drawing or playing a valid card. If the player draws, we add a card to his hand, as long as there are cards left in the deck.

If playing a card, we need to remove the card from the hand and make it the up card:

```
p_hand.remove(selected_card)
up_card  = selected_card
active_suit = up_card.suit
print "You played", selected_card.short_name
```

If the card played was an 8, the player needs to tell us what suit he wants next. Because the `player_turn()` function is getting a bit long, we'll make getting the new suit into a separate function called `get_new_suit()`. The next listing shows the code for this function.

Listing 23.9   Getting the new suit when the player plays an 8

```
def get_new_suit():
    global active_suit
    got_suit = False
    while not got_suit:
        suit = raw_input("Pick a suit: ")
        if suit.lower() == 'd':
            active_suit = "Diamonds"
```

Keeps trying until player enters a valid suit

```
            got_suit = True
        elif suit.lower() == 's':
            active_suit = "Spades"
            got_suit = True
        elif suit.lower() == 'h':
            active_suit = "Hearts"
            got_suit = True
        elif suit.lower() == 'c':
            active_suit = "Clubs"
            got_suit = True
        else:
            print"Not a valid suit.  Try again. ",
    print "You picked", active_suit
```

This is everything we need for the player's turn. In the next section, we'll make the computer smart enough to play Crazy Eights.

The computer's turn

After the player's turn, the computer has to play, so we need to tell the program how to play Crazy Eights. It has to follow the same rules as the player, but the program needs to decide what card to play. We have to specifically tell it how to handle all possible situations:

- Playing an 8 (and picking a new suit)
- Playing another card
- Drawing

To make things a bit simpler, we'll tell the computer to always play an 8 if it has one. This might not be the best strategy, but it's a simple one.

If the computer plays an 8, it must pick the new suit. The easiest way to do that is to count the number of cards of each suit in the computer's hand and pick the suit that it has the most of. Again, this isn't a perfect strategy, but it's one of the simplest to code.

If there's no 8 in the computer's hand, the program will go through all the cards and see which ones are possible plays. Out of these cards, it'll pick the one with the highest value and play that one.

If there's no option to play a card, the computer will draw. If the computer tries to draw and there are no cards left in the deck, the computer is blocked, just like the human player.

Here's the code for the computer's turn, with a few notes of explanation.

Listing 23.10   The computer's turn

```python
def computer_turn():
    global c_hand, deck, up_card, active_suit, blocked
    options = []
    for card in c_hand:
        if card.rank == '8':                        ◄———— Plays an 8
            c_hand.remove(card)
            up_card  = card
            print "  Computer played ", card.short_name
            #suit totals:  [diamonds, hearts, spades, clubs]
            suit_totals = [0, 0, 0, 0]              ◄┐
            for suit in range(1, 5):                 │
                for card in c_hand:                  │  Counts cards in each
                    if card.suit_id == suit:         │  suit; suit with the most
                        suit_totals[suit-1] += 1     │  is the "long suit"
            long_suit = 0
            for i in range(4):
                if suit_totals[i] > long_suit:
                    long_suit = i
            if long_suit == 0:  active_suit = "Diamonds"    ┐
            if long_suit == 1:  active_suit = "Hearts"      │  Makes long
            if long_suit == 2:  active_suit = "Spades"      │  suit the
            if long_suit == 3:  active_suit = "Clubs"       │  active suit
            print "  Computer changed suit to ", active_suit
            return                                  ◄────  Ends computer's
        else:                                               turn; back to
            if card.suit == active_suit:                    main loop
                options.append(card)        ┐
            elif card.rank == up_card.rank:  │  Checks what
                options.append(card)         │  cards are
                                             │  possible plays

    if len(options) > 0:
        best_play = options[0]
        for card in options:                      ┐
            if card.value > best_play.value:       │  Checks which option is
                best_play = card                   │  best (highest value)

        c_hand.remove(best_play)                ┐
        up_card = best_play                      │
        active_suit = up_card.suit               │  Plays card
        print "  Computer played ", best_play.short_name

    else:
        if len(deck) >0:
            next_card = random.choice(deck)     ┐
            c_hand.append(next_card)             │  Draws, because no
            deck.remove(next_card)               │  possible plays
            print "  Computer drew a card"
        else:
            print"  Computer is blocked"         ┐  No cards left in deck—
            blocked += 1                         │  computer is blocked
    print "Computer has %i cards left" % (len(c_hand))
```

We're almost done—just a couple more things to add. You might have noticed that the computer's turn was defined as a function, and we used some global variables in that function. We could also have passed the variables to the function, but using globals works just as well and is more like the real world, where the deck is "global"—anybody can reach over and take a card from it.

The player's turn is also a function, but we didn't show the first part of that function definition. It would look like this:

```python
def player_turn():
    global deck, p_hand, blocked, up_card, active_suit
    valid_play = False
    is_eight = False
    print "\nYour hand: ",
    for card in p_hand:
        print card.short_name,
    print "  Up card: ", up_card.short_name
    if up_card.rank == '8':
        print"  Suit is", active_suit
    print "What would you like to do? ",
    response = raw_input("Type a card to play or 'Draw' to take a card: ")
```

There's just one more thing we need. We have to keep track of who wins!

Keeping score

The last thing we need for our game to be complete is scoring. When a game ends, we need to keep track of how many points the winner gets for the cards remaining in the loser's hand. We should display the points for that game, as well as the total for all games. Once we add those things in, the main loop will look something like this.

Listing 23.11   The main loop with scoring added

```python
done = False
p_total = c_total = 0
while not done:
    game_done = False

    blocked = 0
    init_cards()                        ①   Sets up deck and player
    while not game_done:                         and computer hands
        player_turn()
        if len(p_hand) == 0:                 ◁——— Player wins
            game_done = True
            print
            print "You won!"
            # display game score here
            p_points = 0
```

```
        for card in c_hand:                    Adds points from computer's
            p_points += card.value             remaining cards
        p_total += p_points
        print "You got %i points for computer's hand" % p_points
                                                                    Adds points
    if not game_done:                                               from this game
        computer_turn()                                             to total
    if len(c_hand) == 0:                ←——— Computer wins
        game_done = True
        print
        print "Computer won!"
        # display game score here
        c_points = 0
        for card in p_hand:             Adds points from           Adds points
            c_points += card.value      player's remaining cards   from this game
        c_total += c_points                                        to total
        print "Computer got %i points for your hand" % c_points
    if blocked >= 2:
        game_done = True
        print "Both players blocked.  GAME OVER."
        player_points = 0
        for card in c_hand:                            Both blocked,
            p_points += card.value                     so both get
        p_total += p_points                            points
        c_points = 0
        for card in p_hand:
            c_points += card.value
        c_total += c_points
        print "You got %i points for computer's hand" % p_points    Prints game
        print "Computer got %i points for your hand" % c_points     points
    play_again = raw_input("Play again (Y/N)? ")
    if play_again.lower().startswith('y'):
        done = False
        print "\nSo far, you have %i points" % p_total        Prints total
        print  "and the computer has %i points.\n" % c_total  points so far
    else:
        done = True

print "\n Final Score:"
print "You: %i     Computer: %i" % (p_total, c_total)      Prints final totals
```

❶ The `init_cards()` function (not shown here) sets up the deck and creates the player's hand (5 cards), the computer's hand (5 cards), and the first up card.

Listing 23.11 is still not a complete program, so it will give you an error if you try to run it. But if you have been following along, you have almost the whole program in your editor by now. The complete listing for Crazy Eights is too long to print here (it's about 200 lines of code, plus blank lines and comments), but you can find it in the **\Examples** folder, if you used the book's installer. It's also on the web site (**www.helloworldbook2.com**). You can use IDLE to edit and run this program.

What did you learn?

In this chapter, you learned

- What randomness and random events are
- A little bit about probability
- How to use the `random` module to generate random events in a program
- How to simulate flipping a coin or rolling dice
- How to simulate drawing cards from a shuffled deck
- How to play Crazy Eights (if you didn't already know)

Test your knowledge

1 Describe what a "random event" is. Give two examples.
2 Why is rolling one 11-sided die with numbers from 2 to 12 different from rolling a pair of 6-sided dice, which produce totals from 2 to 12?
3 What are two ways to simulate rolling a die in Python?
4 What kind of Python variable did we use for a single card?
5 What kind of Python variable did we use for a deck of cards?
6 What method did we use to remove a card from the deck when it's drawn, or from a hand when it's played?

Try it out

1 Try the "10 in a row" experiment using the program from listing 23.3, but try different amounts for the "in a row." How often do you get five in a row? How about six, seven, eight, and so on? Do you see a pattern?

Computer Simulations

Have you ever seen a "virtual pet": those little toys with a small display screen and a few buttons for feeding your pet when it's hungry, letting it sleep when it's tired, playing with it when it's bored, and so on? The virtual pet has some of the same characteristics as a real, live pet. That's an example of a computer simulation—the virtual pet device is a tiny computer.

In the last chapter, you learned about random events and how to generate them in a program. In a way, that was a kind of simulation. A *simulation* is where you create a computer model of something from the real world. We created computer models of coins, dice, and decks of cards.

In this chapter, you'll learn more about using computer programs to simulate the real world.

Modeling the real world

There are many reasons to use a computer to simulate or model the real world. Sometimes it isn't practical to do an experiment because of time, distance, danger, or other reasons. For example, in the last chapter we simulated flipping a coin a million times. Most of us don't have time to do that with a real coin, but a computer simulation did it in seconds.

Sometimes scientists want to figure out "What if … ?" What if an asteroid smashed into the Moon? You can't make a real asteroid smash into the Moon, but a computer simulation can tell us what would happen. Would the Moon zoom off into space? Would it crash into Earth? How would its orbit change?

When pilots and astronauts are learning to fly planes and spacecraft, they can't always practice on the real thing. That would be very expensive! (And would *you* want to be the passenger of a student pilot?) So they use simulators, which give them all the same controls as the real plane or spacecraft to practice on.

In a simulation, you can do many things:

- Try an experiment or practice a skill without having any equipment (except your computer) and without putting anyone in danger
- Speed up or slow down time
- Do many experiments at once
- Try things that would be costly, dangerous, or impossible in the real world

The first simulation we're going to do is one involving gravity. We're going to try to land a spacecraft on the Moon, but we only have a certain amount of fuel, so we have to be careful how we use our thrusters. This is a very simple version of an arcade game called Lunar Lander that was popular many years ago.

Lunar Lander

We'll start with our spacecraft some distance above the Moon's surface. The Moon's gravity will start to pull it down, and we'll have to use the thrusters to slow its descent and make a soft landing.

At right you can see what the program will look like.

The small grey bar on the left side is the throttle. You drag it up or down with the mouse to control the thrust of the engines. The fuel gauge tells you how much fuel you have left, and the text gives you information on your velocity, acceleration, height, and thrust.

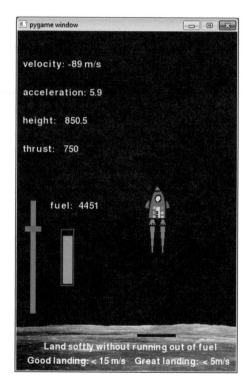

Simulating the landing

In order to simulate a spacecraft landing, you have to understand how the force of gravity and the force of the spacecraft's engine balance against each other.

For our simulation, we'll assume the force of gravity is constant. That's not quite true, but as long as the spacecraft isn't too far from the Moon, gravity is very nearly constant—close enough for our simulation.

WORD BOX

The word *velocity* means almost the same thing as *speed*, except that velocity includes a direction, and speed doesn't. For example, "fifty miles an hour" describes a speed, while "fifty miles an hour due north" describes a velocity. Many people use the word *speed* when they really mean *velocity*, and vice versa. In our program, we need to know whether the spaceship is going up or down, so we will use velocity.

Acceleration means how fast the velocity is changing. Positive acceleration means the velocity is increasing, and negative acceleration means the velocity is decreasing.

The force of the engines depends on how much fuel we're burning. Sometimes it'll be greater than the force of gravity, sometimes less. When the engines are off, their force is 0, and we're left with only the force of gravity.

To get the total or *net* force on the spacecraft, we just add the two forces. Because they're in opposite directions, one will be positive and one will be negative.

Once we have the net force on the spacecraft, we can figure out its speed and position with a formula.

Our simulation will have to keep track of the following things:

- The spacecraft's height above the Moon, and its velocity and acceleration.
- The mass of the spacecraft (which changes as we use up fuel).
- The thrust, or force, of the engines. The more thrust we use, the faster we'll burn fuel.
- The amount of fuel on the spacecraft. As we burn fuel with our thrusters, the spacecraft will get lighter, but if we run out of fuel, there will be no more thrust.
- The force of gravity on the spacecraft. That depends on the size of the Moon, and the mass of the spacecraft and fuel.

Pygame returns

We'll use Pygame again to make this simulation. The Pygame clock tick will be our unit of time. For every tick, we'll check the net force on the spacecraft and update the height, velocity, acceleration, and fuel remaining. Then we'll use that information to update the graphics and text.

Because the animation is very simple, we won't use a sprite for the spaceship. But we'll use one for the throttle (the grey rectangle), because that makes it easy to drag it with the mouse. The fuel gauge is just a couple of rectangles drawn with Pygame's `draw.rect()` method. The text is made with `pygame.font` objects, just like we did for PyPong.

The code will have sections that do the following:

- Initialize the game—set up the Pygame window, load the images, and set some initial values for the variables
- Define the sprite class for the throttle
- Calculate the height, velocity, acceleration, and fuel consumption
- Display the information
- Update the fuel gauge
- Display the rocket flames (which change size depending on the thrust)
- Blit everything to the screen, check for mouse events, update the throttle position, and check if the ship has landed—this will be the main Pygame event loop
- Display "Game Over" and final stats

Listing 24.1 shows the code for Lunar Lander, and you can find it as **Listing_24-1.py** in the **\Examples\LunarLander** folder or on the website (**www.helloworldbook2.com**). The graphics (the spaceship and moonscape) are there too. Have a look at the code and the notes, and make sure you understand how everything works. Don't worry about the height, velocity, and acceleration formulas. You'll learn about all that in high school physics, pass the exam, and then soon forget it (unless you go to work for NASA). Or maybe this program will help you remember!

Listing 24.1   Lunar Lander

```
import pygame, sys

pygame.init()
screen = pygame.display.set_mode([400,600])
screen.fill([0, 0, 0])
ship = pygame.image.load('lunarlander.png')
moon = pygame.image.load('moonsurface.png')
ground  = 540
start = 90
clock = pygame.time.Clock()
ship_mass = 5000.0
fuel = 5000.0
velocity = -100.0
gravity = 10
height = 2000
thrust = 0
delta_v = 0
y_pos = 90
held_down = False
```

Landing pad
is y = 540

Initializes
program

```
class ThrottleClass(pygame.sprite.Sprite):
    def __init__(self, location = [0,0]):
        pygame.sprite.Sprite.__init__(self)
        image_surface = pygame.surface.Surface([30, 10])
        image_surface.fill([128,128,128])
        self.image = image_surface.convert()
        self.rect = self.image.get_rect()
        self.rect.left, self.rect.centery = location
```

Sprite class
for the
throttle

```
def calculate_velocity():
    global thrust, fuel, velocity, delta_v, height, y_pos
    delta_t = 1/fps
    thrust = (500 - myThrottle.rect.centery) * 5.0
    fuel -= thrust /(10 * fps)
    if fuel < 0:  fuel = 0.0
    if fuel < 0.1:  thrust = 0.0
    delta_v = delta_t * (-gravity + 200 * thrust / (ship_mass + fuel))
    velocity = velocity + delta_v
    delta_h = velocity * delta_t
    height = height + delta_h
    y_pos = ground - (height * (ground - start) / 2000) - 90
```

Tick is one frame of
Pygame loop

Calculates
height, velocity,
acceleration, fuel

Turns throttle sprite
y-position into thrust amount

Subtracts fuel
depending on thrust

Physics formula

Converts height
into Pygame
y-position

```
def display_stats():
    v_str = "velocity: %i m/s" % velocity
    h_str = "height:    %.1f" % height
    t_str = "thrust:    %i" % thrust
    a_str = "acceleration: %.1f" % (delta_v * fps)
    f_str = "fuel:    %i" % fuel
    v_font = pygame.font.Font(None, 26)

    v_surf = v_font.render(v_str, 1, (255, 255, 255))
    screen.blit(v_surf, [10, 50])
    a_font = pygame.font.Font(None, 26)
    a_surf = a_font.render(a_str, 1, (255, 255, 255))
    screen.blit(a_surf, [10, 100])
    h_font = pygame.font.Font(None, 26)
    h_surf = h_font.render(h_str, 1, (255, 255, 255))
    screen.blit(h_surf, [10, 150])
    t_font = pygame.font.Font(None, 26)
    t_surf = t_font.render(t_str, 1, (255, 255, 255))
    screen.blit(t_surf, [10, 200])
    f_font = pygame.font.Font(None, 26)
    f_surf = f_font.render(f_str, 1, (255, 255, 255))
    screen.blit(f_surf, [60, 300])
```

Displays
stats using
font objects

```
def display_flames():
    flame_size = thrust / 15
    for i in range (2):
        startx = 252 - 10 + i * 19
        starty = y_pos + 83
        pygame.draw.polygon(screen, [255, 109, 14], [(startx, starty),
                            (startx + 4, starty + flame_size),
                            (startx + 8, starty)], 0)
```

Draws flame
triangles

Displays rocket
flames using
two triangles

```
def display_final():
    final1 = "Game over"
    final2 = "You landed at %.1f m/s" % velocity
    if velocity > -5:
        final3 = "Nice landing!"
        final4 = "I hear NASA is hiring!"
    elif velocity > -15:
        final3 = "Ouch!  A bit rough, but you survived."
        final4 = "You'll do better next time."
    else:
        final3 = "Yikes!  You crashed a 30 Billion dollar ship."
        final4 = "How are you getting home?"
    pygame.draw.rect(screen, [0, 0, 0], [5, 5, 350, 280],0)
    f1_font = pygame.font.Font(None, 70)
    f1_surf = f1_font.render(final1, 1, (255, 255, 255))
    screen.blit(f1_surf, [20, 50])
    f2_font = pygame.font.Font(None, 40)
    f2_surf = f2_font.render(final2, 1, (255, 255, 255))
    screen.blit(f2_surf, [20, 110])
    f3_font = pygame.font.Font(None, 26)
    f3_surf = f3_font.render(final3, 1, (255, 255, 255))
    screen.blit(f3_surf, [20, 150])
    f4_font = pygame.font.Font(None, 26)
    f4_surf = f4_font.render(final4, 1, (255, 255, 255))
    screen.blit(f4_surf, [20, 180])
    pygame.display.flip()
```

Displays final stats when game is over

```
myThrottle = ThrottleClass([15, 500])
running = True
while running:
    clock.tick(30)
    fps = clock.get_fps()
    if fps < 1:  fps = 30
    if height > 0.01:
        calculate_velocity()
        screen.fill([0, 0, 0])
        display_stats()
        pygame.draw.rect(screen, [0, 0, 255], [80, 350, 24, 100], 2)
        fuelbar = 96 * fuel / 5000
        pygame.draw.rect(screen, [0,255,0],
                [84,448-fuelbar,18, fuelbar], 0)
        pygame.draw.rect(screen, [255, 0, 0],
                [25, 300, 10, 200],0)
        screen.blit(moon, [0, 500, 400, 100])
        pygame.draw.rect(screen, [60, 60, 60],
                [220, 535, 70, 5],0)
        screen.blit(myThrottle.image, myThrottle.rect)
        display_flames()
        screen.blit(ship, [230, y_pos, 50, 90])
        instruct1 = "Land softly without running out of fuel"
        instruct2 = "Good landing: < 15m/s   Great landing: < 5m/s"
        inst1_font = pygame.font.Font(None, 24)
        inst1_surf = inst1_font.render(instruct1, 1, (255, 255, 255))
```

Creates throttle object

Start of main Pygame event loop

Fuel gauge outline

Fuel amount

Throttle slider

Moon

Landing pad

Thrust handle

Ship

Draws everything

```
        screen.blit(inst1_surf, [50, 550])
        inst2_font = pygame.font.Font(None, 24)                    Draws
        inst2_surf = inst1_font.render(instruct2, 1, (255, 255, 255))   everything
        screen.blit(inst2_surf, [20, 575])
        pygame.display.flip()

    else:                    ←——— Game Over. Print final score.
        display_final()

    for event in pygame.event.get():
        if event.type == pygame.QUIT:
            running = False
        elif event.type == pygame.MOUSEBUTTONDOWN:        Checks for
            held_down = True                              mouse drag
        elif event.type == pygame.MOUSEBUTTONUP:          of throttle
            held_down = False
        elif event.type == pygame.MOUSEMOTION:
            if held_down:
                myThrottle.rect.centery = event.pos[1]
                if myThrottle.rect.centery < 300:         Updates
                    myThrottle.rect.centery = 300         throttle
                if myThrottle.rect.centery > 500:         position
                    myThrottle.rect.centery = 500
pygame.quit()
```

Give the program a try. Maybe you'll find out you're a good spaceship pilot! If you think it's too easy, you can modify the code to make gravity stronger, make the ship heavier (more massive), give yourself less fuel, or set a different starting height or velocity. You're the programmer, so you can decide how the game should work.

The Lunar Lander simulation is mostly about gravity. In the rest of the chapter, we'll talk about another important factor in simulations—time. And we'll make a simulation that requires keeping track of time.

Keeping time

Time is an important factor in many simulations. Sometimes you want to speed up time, or make things happen faster than in the real world, so you don't have to wait so long to find out what happens. Sometimes you want to slow things down, so you can get a better look at things that normally happen faster than you can see. And sometimes you want the program to keep *real time*—to act just like it would in the real world. In all cases, you need some kind of clock to measure time in your program.

Every computer has a clock built in that you can use to measure time. You have already seen a couple of examples of using and measuring time:

- In chapter 8, we used the `time.sleep()` function to make a countdown timer.

■ In our Pygame programs, we have used both Pygame's `time.delay` and `clock.tick` functions to control the animation speed or frame rate. We also used `get_fps()` to check how fast the animation was running, which is a way of measuring time (the average time for each frame).

So far, we have always kept track of time while the program was running, but sometimes you need to keep track of time even when the program is not running. If you made a Virtual Pet program in Python, you wouldn't want to leave it running all the time. You'd want to play with it for a while, and then stop and come back to it later. While you were away, you'd expect your pet to get tired or hungry, or to go to sleep. So the program needs to know how much time has passed since the last time it ran.

One way to do this is for the program to save a little piece of information—the current time—to a file just before it shuts down. Then, next time it starts up, it can read the file to get the previous time, check the current time, and compare the two to see how much time has passed since the program last ran.

Python has a special kind of object for working with times and dates. You're going to learn a bit about Python's date and time objects in the next section.

WORD BOX

When you save the current time to a file for reading back later, that's called a *timestamp*.

Time objects

Python's date and time object classes are defined in their own `datetime` module. The `datetime` module has classes for working with dates, times, and the difference or *delta* between two dates or times.

WORD BOX

The word *delta* means "difference." It's a letter of the Greek alphabet, and it looks like this: Δ (a triangle).

Letters of the Greek alphabet are often used in science and math as a shorthand for certain quantities. Delta is used for a difference between two values.

The first kind of object we'll use is a `datetime` object. (Yes, the class has the same name as the module.) The `datetime` object includes the year, month, day, hour, minute, and second. You create one like this (follow along in interactive mode):

```
>>> import datetime
>>> when = datetime.datetime(2012, 10, 24, 10, 45, 56)
```

Module name   Class name

Let's see what we have:

```
>>> print when
2012-10-24 10:45:56
```

We have created a **datetime** object, called **when**, which contains date and time values.

When creating a **datetime** object, the order of the parameters (the numbers in brackets) is year, month, day, hour, minute, second. But if you can't remember that, you can put them in any order you want, as long as you tell Python which one is which, like this:

```
>>> when = datetime.datetime(hour=10, year=2012, minute=45, month=10,
                             second=56, day=24)
```

There are some other things you can do with **datetime** objects. You can get the individual pieces like year, day, or minute. You can also get a formatted string of the date and time. Try these in interactive mode:

```
>>> print when.year
2012
>>> print when.day
24
>>> print when.ctime()
Wed Oct 24 10:45:56 2012
```

Gets individual parts of datetime object

Prints string version of date and time

A **datetime** object has both the date and the time. If you only care about the date, there's also a **date** class that only has the year, month, and day. If you only care about the time, there's a **time** class that only has the hour, minute, and second. Here's what they look like:

```
>>> today = datetime.date(2012, 10, 24)
>>> some_time = datetime.time(10, 45, 56)
>>> print today
2012-10-24
>>> print some_time
10:45:56
```

Just like with the **datetime** object, you can pass the parameters in a different order if you specify which is which:

```
>>> today = datetime.date(month=10, day=24, year=2012)
>>> some_time = datetime.time(second=56, hour=10, minute=45)
```

There's also a way to break up a **datetime** object into a **date** object and a **time** object:

```
>>> today = when.date()
>>> some_time = when.time()
```

And you can combine a `date` and a `time` to make a `datetime` object by using the `combine()` method of the `datetime` class in the `datetime` module:

```
>>> when = datetime.datetime.combine(today, some_time)
```

   Module name   Class name   Method

Now that you have seen what a `datetime` object is and some of its properties, we'll look at how you can compare two of them to find the difference between them (how much time has passed between one and the other).

Difference between two times

Quite often in simulations, you need to know how much time has passed. For example, in a Virtual Pet program, you might need to know how much time has passed since the pet was fed so you can figure out how hungry it is.

The `datetime` module has an object class that will help you figure out the difference between two dates or times. The class is called `timedelta`. Remember that *delta* means "difference." So a `timedelta` is a difference between two times.

To create a `timedelta` and figure out the difference between two times, you just subtract them, like this:

```
>>> import datetime
>>> yesterday = datetime.datetime(2012, 10, 23)
>>> tomorrow = datetime.datetime(2012, 10, 25)
>>> difference = tomorrow - yesterday          Gets the
                                               difference of the
>>> print difference          Tomorrow and     two dates
2 days, 0:00:00               yesterday are 2
>>> print type(difference)    days apart
<type 'datetime.timedelta'>                    Difference is a
                                               timedelta object
```

Notice that, when we subtracted the two `datetime` objects, what we got wasn't another `datetime`, but rather a `timedelta` object. Python does that automatically.

Small pieces of time

Up to now, we have been looking at time measured in whole seconds. But the time objects (`date`, `time`, `datetime`, and `timedelta`) are more precise than that. They can measure down to the microsecond, which is one millionth of a second.

To see this, try out the `now()` method, which gives you the current time of your computer's clock:

```
>>> print datetime.datetime.now()
2012-10-24 21:25:44.343000
```

Notice how the time doesn't just have seconds, it has fractions of a second:

```
44.343000
```

On my computer, the last three digits will always be 0 because my operating system's clock only goes to milliseconds (thousandths of a second). But that's plenty precise enough for me!

It's important to know that, although it looks like a float, the seconds are actually stored as a number of seconds (an integer) and a number of microseconds (an integer): 44 seconds and 343,000 microseconds. To make this into a float, you need a little formula. Assuming you have a `time` object called `some_time`, and you want the number of seconds as a float, here's what the formula looks like:

```
seconds_float = some_time.second + some_time.microsecond / float(1000000)
```

The `float()` function is used to make sure you don't get caught by the integer-division gotcha.

You can use the `now()` method and a `timedelta` object to test your typing speed. The program in listing 24.2 displays a random message, and the user has to type the same message in. The program times how long it takes to type it in and then calculates the typing speed. Give it a try.

Listing 24.2   Measuring time differences—typing speed test

```
import time, datetime, random          ◁——— Uses time module for
                                             the sleep() function
messages = [
    "Of all the trees we could've hit, we had to get one that hits back.",
    "If he doesn't stop trying to save your life he's going to kill you.",
    "It is our choices that show what we truly are, far more than our abilities.",
    "I am a wizard, not a baboon brandishing a stick.",
    "Greatness inspires envy, envy engenders spite, spite spawns lies.",
    "In dreams, we enter a world that's entirely our own.",
    "It is my belief that the truth is generally preferable to lies.",
    "Dawn seemed to follow midnight with indecent haste."     Uses time module for
    ]                                                         the sleep() function

print "Typing speed test. Type the following message. I will time you." ◁
time.sleep(2)
print "\nReady..."
time.sleep(1)                                                 Prints instructions
print "\nSet..."
time.sleep(1)
print "\nGo:"
```

```
message = random.choice(messages)        ⟵—— Picks message from list
print "\n " + message
start_time = datetime.datetime.now()     ⟵—— Starts clock
typing = raw_input('>')
end_time = datetime.datetime.now()       ⟵—— Stops clock          Calculates
diff = end_time - start_time                                      elapsed time
typing_time = diff.seconds + diff.microseconds / float(1000000)   ⟵
cps = len(message) / typing_time       For typing speed,
wpm = cps * 60 / 5.0            ⟵————— 1 word = 5 characters
print "\nYou typed %i characters in %.1f seconds." % (len(message),
                        typing_time)
print "That's %.2f chars per sec, or %.1f words per minute" %(cps, wpm)
if typing == message:                         Displays results with
    print "You didn't make any mistakes."     print formatting
else:
    print "But, you made at least one mistake."
```

There's one more thing you should know about **timedelta** objects. Unlike **datetime** objects, which have year, month, day, hour, minute, second (and microseconds), a **timedelta** object only has days, seconds, and microseconds. If you want the months or years, you have to calculate them from the number of days. If you want minutes or hours, you have to calculate them from the seconds.

Saving time to a file

As we mentioned at the start of the chapter, sometimes you need to save a time value to a file (on the hard disk) so it can be saved even when the program isn't running. If you save the **now()** time whenever a program finishes, you can check the time when the program starts again and print a message like this:

```
It has been 2 days, 7 hours, 23 minutes since you last used this program.
```

Of course, most programs don't do that, but some programs need to know how long they have been idle, or not running. One example is a Virtual Pet program. Just like the virtual pet keychains that were popular a few years ago, you might want the program to keep track of time even when you're not using it. So, for example, if you end the program and then come back to it two days later, your virtual pet should be very hungry! The only way for the program to know how hungry the pet should be is for it to know how much time has passed since the last time the virtual pet was fed. That includes the time the program was shut down.

There are a couple of ways you could save the time to a file. You could just write a string to the file, like this:

```
timeFile.write ("2012-10-24 14:23:37")
```

Then, when you want to read the timestamp, you 'll use some string methods like `split()` to break the string up into the various parts, like day, month, year and hour, minute, second. That should work just fine.

The other way is to use the `pickle` module, which you saw in chapter 22. The `pickle` module lets you save any kind of variable to a file, including objects. Because we'll be using `datetime` objects to keep track of time, it should be quite easy to use `pickle` to save them to a file and read them back again.

Let's try a very simple example that prints a message saying when the program was last run. It will need to do these things:

- It will look for a pickle file and open it. Python has a module called **os** (short for "operating system") that can tell us if the file exists. The method we'll use is called `isfile()`.
- If the file exists, we'll assume that the program has run before, and we'll find out when it last ran (from the time in the pickle file).
  - Then we'll write a new pickle file with the current time.
- If this is the first time the program has run, there will be no pickle file to open, so we'll display a message saying we created a new pickle file.

The following listing has the code. Try it and see how it works.

Listing 24.3   Saving time to a file using `pickle`

```
import datetime, pickle        Imports datetime, pickle,
import os                      and os modules

first_time = True                          Checks if the pickle file exists
if os.path.isfile("last_run.pkl"):
    pickle_file = open("last_run.pkl", 'r')        Opens pickle file for
    last_time = pickle.load(pickle_file)           reading (if it exists)
    pickle_file.close()                    Unpickles the datetime object
    print "The last time this program was run was ", last_time
    first_time = False
                                           Opens (or creates) the
                                           pickle file for writing
pickle_file = open("last_run.pkl", 'w')
pickle.dump(datetime.datetime.now(), pickle_file)
pickle_file.close()                               Pickles the datetime
if first_time:                                    object of the current time
    print "Created new pickle file."
```

Now we have all the pieces we need to make a simple Virtual Pet program, which we'll do in the next section.

Virtual Pet

We're going to make a very simplified Virtual Pet program, which, as we indicated, is a kind of simulation. You can buy virtual-pet toys (like a keychain with a small screen). There are also websites like Neopets and Webkinz, which are forms of virtual pets. All of these, of course, are simulations as well. They mimic the behavior of a living thing and get hungry, lonely, tired, and so on. To keep them happy and healthy, you have to feed them, play with them, or take them to the doctor.

Our virtual pet will be a lot simpler and less realistic than the ones you can buy or play online, because I just want to give you the basic idea, and I don't want the code to get too complicated. But you could take our simple version and expand or enhance it as much as you want.

Here are the features our program will have:

- The pet will have four different activities that you can do: feed it, walk it, play with it, or take it to the doctor.

- The pet will have three stats that you can monitor: hunger, happiness, and health.

- The pet can be awake or asleep.

- The pet will get hungrier over time. You can reduce hunger by feeding.
- The pet will get hungry more slowly when it is asleep.
- If the pet is asleep and you do any activity, it will wake up.
- If the pet gets too hungry, its happiness will decrease.
- If the pet gets very, very hungry, its health will decrease.
- Walking the pet will make both its happiness and health increase.

- Playing with the pet will make its happiness increase.
- Taking the pet to the doctor will make its health increase.
- The pet will have six different graphics:
    - One for sleeping
    - One for being awake but doing nothing
    - One for walking
    - One for playing
    - One for eating
    - One for going to the doctor

The graphics will use some simple animation. In the next few sections, you'll see how this all goes together in a program.

The GUI

Carter and I have created a PyQt GUI for our Virtual Pet program. It has buttons (actually icons on a toolbar) to do the activities. It has progress bars for the vital stats. As you can see, there's also a place to show the graphic of what the pet is doing.

Notice that the title bar of the window says **Virtual Pet**. How do you set the window title? Create a new form in the Qt Designer application, and click the **MainWindow** object in the Object Inspector. Then, in the Property Editor, find the property called **windowTitle**, and change it to **Virtual Pet** (or whatever you want to show in the title bar).

The group of buttons for the activities is a type of PyQt widget called *Toolbar*. The toolbar has *actions* in it just like a menu does, but the difference with a toolbar is that each action has an *icon* associated with it.

To add a toolbar, right-click the main window and select **Add Toolbar**. This creates the toolbar at the top of the window, but it will be very small. Find the toolbar in the Object Inspector, click it, and then look in the Property Editor for the **minimumSize** property. Set the minimum size to **100** for width and **50** for height.

To add actions (icons) to the toolbar, click the **Action Editor** tab at lower right in Qt Designer. Right-click anywhere in the Action Editor pane, and pick New. You'll get a dialog box for adding a new action. The only thing you have to type in is the **Text**, and Qt Designer will fill in the object name. Then find the little box in the middle with three dots (…), and click the down-arrow to the right of it. Pick **Choose File**, and pick the image file you want to use for the toolbar button.

There's one last step to adding the new toolbar icon. Once you've created the new action, you'll see it in the list in the Action Editor. Now you have to drag it onto the toolbar. When you do that, the graphic you picked for the new action will appear as a new icon on the toolbar. Qt Designer will automatically scale the image so it fits on the toolbar.

The health meters are a widget type called **Progress Bar**. The main graphic is a **Push Button** (like we have used before) with its properties set in a certain way so it doesn't look like a regular button, but instead displays an image.

The extra bits of text are **Label** widgets.

You can create a GUI like this using the PyQt Designer. Or you can load the one we made (from the examples folder) into Qt Designer and examine the widgets and their properties.

The algorithm

To be able to write the code for the Virtual Pet program, we need to be more specific about the behavior of the pet. Here's the algorithm we'll use:

- We'll divide the pet's "day" into 60 parts, which we'll call *ticks*. Each tick will be 5 seconds of real time, so the pet's "virtual day" will be 5 minutes of our time.

- The pet will be awake for 48 ticks, and then it will want to sleep for 12 ticks. You can wake it up, but it might be grumpy!
- Hunger, happiness, and health will be on a scale of 0 to 8.
- When awake, hunger increases 1 unit for every tick, and happiness decreases 1 unit for every 2 ticks (unless walking or playing).
- When sleeping, hunger increases 1 unit for every 3 ticks.
- When eating, hunger decreases 2 units for every tick.
- When playing, happiness increases 1 unit for every tick.
- When walking, happiness and health increase 1 unit for every 2 ticks.
- When at the doctor, health increases 1 unit for every tick.
- If hunger goes to 7, health decreases 1 unit for every 2 ticks.
- If hunger goes to 8, health decreases 1 unit for every tick.
- If awakened while sleeping, happiness decreases by 4 units.
- While the program isn't running, the pet is either awake (doing nothing) or asleep.
- When the program restarts, we'll count how many ticks have passed, and update the stats for each tick that passed.

These might seem like a lot of rules, but they're actually pretty easy to code. In fact, you might even want to add a few more behaviors of your own to make it more interesting. The code, with some explanations, is coming right up.

Simple animation

You don't always need Pygame to do animation. You can do some simple animation in PyQt by using something called a *timer*. A timer is something that creates an *event* every so often. Then you write an *event handler* to make something happen when the timer goes off. This is just like writing an event handler for a user action, like clicking a button, except that the timer event is generated by the program, not by the user. The type of event a timer generates when it expires is a *timeout* event.

Our Virtual Pet GUI will use two timers: one for the animation and one for the ticks. The animation will update every half second (0.5 seconds), and the tick will happen every 5 seconds.

When the animation timer goes off, we'll change the image of the pet that's being displayed. Each activity (eating, playing, and so on) will have its own set of images for the animation, and each set will be stored in a list. The animation will cycle through all the images in the list. The program will figure out which list to use depending on what activity is happening.

Try, try again

We'll be using another new thing in this program. It's called a `try-except` block.

If a program is going to do something that could cause an error, it's nice to have some way to catch the error and deal with it, instead of having the program just stop. A `try-except` block does that.

For example, if you try to open a file and the file doesn't exist, you'll get an error. If you don't handle this error, the program will stop at this point. But maybe you want to ask the user to reenter the filename, in case she made a typo. A `try-except` block lets you catch the error and keep going.

Here's what it looks like, using the example of opening a file:

```
try:
    file = open("somefile.txt", "r")
except:
    print "Couldn't open the file.  Do you want to reenter the filename?"
```

The thing that you want to try (that might cause an error) goes in the `try` block. In this case, it's trying to open a file. If that happens without an error, the `except` part is skipped.

If the code in the `try` block causes an error, the code in the `except` block runs. The code in the `except` block tells the program what to do if there was an error. You can think of it this way:

```
try:
    to do this (don't do anything else...)
except:
    if there was an error, then do this
```

The `try-except` statements are Python's way of doing what's generally called *error handling*. Error handling lets you write code where things can go wrong—even things that would normally stop your program—so that your program will still work. We're not going to talk about error handling in any more detail in this book, but I wanted to show you the basics, because you'll see it in the Virtual Pet code.

Let's look at the code, which is shown in listing 24.4. The notes will explain most of what's going on. This one is a bit long, so if you don't feel like typing it all in, you can find it in the **\Examples\VirtualPet** folder (if you ran the book's installer). It can also be downloaded from the book's website (**www.helloworldbook2.com**). The PyQt UI file and all the graphics are there, too. Try running it, and then look at the code and make sure you understand how it works.

Listing 24.4   VirtualPet.py

```python
import sys, pickle,datetime
from PyQt4 import QtCore, QtGui, uic

formclass, baseclass = uic.loadUiType("mainwindow.ui")

class MyForm(baseclass, formclass):
    def __init__(self, parent=None):
        QtGui.QMainWindow.__init__(self, parent)
        self.setupUi(self)
        self.doctor = False
        self.walking = False
        self.sleeping = False
        self.playing = False
        self.eating = False
        self.time_cycle = 0
        self.hunger = 0
        self.happiness  = 8
        self.health = 8
        self.forceAwake = False
        self.sleepImages = ["sleep1.gif","sleep2.gif","sleep3.gif",
                            "sleep4.gif"]
        self.eatImages = ["eat1.gif", "eat2.gif"]
        self.walkImages = ["walk1.gif", "walk2.gif", "walk3.gif",
                           "walk4.gif"]
        self.playImages = ["play1.gif", "play2.gif"]
        self.doctorImages = ["doc1.gif", "doc2.gif"]
        self.nothingImages  = ["pet1.gif", "pet2.gif", "pet3.gif"]

        self.imageList = self.nothingImages
        self.imageIndex = 0

        self.actionStop.triggered.connect(self.stop_Click)
        self.actionFeed.triggered.connect(self.feed_Click)
        self.actionWalk.triggered.connect(self.walk_Click)
        self.actionPlay.triggered.connect(self.play_Click)
        self.actionDoctor.triggered.connect(self.doctor_Click)

        self.myTimer1 = QtCore.QTimer(self)
        self.myTimer1.start(500)
        self.myTimer1.timeout.connect(self.animation_timer)

        self.myTimer2 = QtCore.QTimer(self)
        self.myTimer2.start(5000)
        self.myTimer2.timeout.connect(self.tick_timer)

        filehandle = True
        try:
            file = open("savedata_vp.pkl", "r")
        except:
            filehandle = False
        if filehandle:
            save_list = pickle.load(file)
            file.close()
```

Initializes values

Lists images for animations

Connects event handlers for toolbar buttons

Sets up timers

Tries to open pickle file

← Reads from pickle file, if open

```
        else:
            save_list = [8, 8, 0, datetime.datetime.now(), 0]
        self.happiness = save_list[0]
        self.health    = save_list[1]
        self.hunger    = save_list[2]
        timestamp_then = save_list[3]
        self.time_cycle = save_list[4]

        difference = datetime.datetime.now() - timestamp_then
        ticks = difference.seconds / 50
        for i in range(0, ticks):
            self.time_cycle += 1
            if self.time_cycle == 60:
                self.time_cycle = 0
            if self.time_cycle <= 48:
                self.sleeping = False
                if self.hunger < 8:
                    self.hunger += 1
            else:
                self.sleeping = True
                if self.hunger < 8 and self.time_cycle % 3 == 0:
                    self.hunger += 1
            if self.hunger == 7 and (self.time_cycle % 2 ==0) \
                            and self.health > 0:
                self.health -= 1
            if self.hunger == 8 and self.health > 0:
                self.health -=1
        if self.sleeping:
            self.imageList = self.sleepImages
        else:
            self.imageList = self.nothingImages

    def sleep_test(self):
        if self.sleeping:
            result = (QtGui.QMessageBox.warning(self, 'WARNING',
"Are you sure you want to wake your pet up?  He'll be unhappy about it!",
                    QtGui.QMessageBox.Yes | QtGui.QMessageBox.No,
                    QtGui.QMessageBox.No))

            if result == QtGui.QMessageBox.Yes:
                self.sleeping = False
                self.happiness -= 4
                self.forceAwake = True
                return True
            else:
                return False
        else:
            return True

    def doctor_Click(self):
        if self.sleep_test():
            self.imageList = self.doctorImages
            self.doctor = True
            self.walking = False
            self.eating = False
            self.playing = False
```

Annotations:

- *Uses default values if pickle file not open* (points to `save_list = [8, 8, 0, datetime.datetime.now(), 0]`)
- *Pulls individual values out of list* (points to the `self.happiness` through `self.time_cycle` assignments)
- *Checks how long since last run* (points to the `difference` / `ticks` lines)
- *Awake* (points to `if self.time_cycle <= 48:`)
- *Sleeping* (points to `else:`)
- *Simulates all ticks that happened during down time*
- *Uses correct animation—awake or sleeping*
- *Type of dialog*
- *Buttons to show*
- *Default button*
- *Checks if pet is sleeping before doing an action*
- *The doctor button event handler*

```
    def feed_Click(self):
        if self.sleep_test():
            self.imageList = self.eatImages
            self.eating = True
            self.walking = False
            self.playing = False
            self.doctor = False
```

The feed button
event handler

```
def play_Click(self):
    if self.sleep_test():
        self.imageList = self.playImages
        self.playing = True
        self.walking = False
        self.eating = False
        self.doctor = False
```

The play button
event handler

```
def walk_Click(self):
    if self.sleep_test():
        self.imageList = self.walkImages
        self.walking = True
        self.eating = False
        self.playing = False
        self.doctor = False
```

The walk button
event handler

```
def stop_Click(self):
    if not self.sleeping:
        self.imageList = self.nothingImages
        self.walking = False
        self.eating = False
        self.playing = False
        self.doctor = False
```

The stop button
event handler

```
def animation_timer(self):
    if self.sleeping and not self.forceAwake:
        self.imageList = self.sleepImages
    self.imageIndex += 1
    if self.imageIndex >= len(self.imageList):
        self.imageIndex = 0
    icon = QtGui.QIcon()
    current_image = self.imageList[self.imageIndex]
    icon.addPixmap(QtGui.QPixmap(current_image),
            QtGui.QIcon.Disabled, QtGui.QIcon.Off)
    self.petPic.setIcon(icon)
    self.progressBar_1.setProperty("value", (8-self.hunger)*(100/8.0))
    self.progressBar_2.setProperty("value", self.happiness*(100/8.0))
    self.progressBar_3.setProperty("value", self.health*(100/8.0))
```

The animation timer
(every 0.5 sec)
event handler

Updates
pet's image
(animation)

```
def tick_timer(self):        ←——   Start of main 5 sec
    self.time_cycle += 1              timer event handler
    if self.time_cycle == 60:
        self.time_cycle = 0
    if self.time_cycle <= 48 or self.forceAwake:
        self.sleeping = False
    else:
        self.sleeping = True
    if self.time_cycle == 0:
        self.forceAwake = False
```

Checks if
sleeping
or awake

```
                    if self.doctor:
                self.health += 1
                self.hunger += 1
            elif self.walking and (self.time_cycle % 2 == 0):
                self.happiness += 1
                self.health += 1
                self.hunger += 1
            elif self.playing:
                self.happiness += 1
                self.hunger += 1
            elif self.eating:
                self.hunger -= 2
            elif self.sleeping:
                if self.time_cycle % 3 == 0:
                    self.hunger += 1
            else:
                self.hunger += 1
                if self.time_cycle % 2 == 0:
                    self.happiness -= 1
            if self.hunger > 8:  self.hunger = 8
            if self.hunger < 0:  self.hunger = 0
            if self.hunger == 7 and (self.time_cycle % 2 ==0) :
                self.health -= 1
            if self.hunger == 8:
                self.health -=1
            if self.health > 8:  self.health = 8
            if self.health < 0:  self.health = 0
            if self.happiness > 8:  self.happiness = 8
            if self.happiness < 0:  self.happiness = 0
            self.progressBar_1.setProperty("value", (8-self.hunger)*(100/8.0))
            self.progressBar_2.setProperty("value", self.happiness*(100/8.0))
            self.progressBar_3.setProperty("value", self.health*(100/8.0))

    def closeEvent(self, event):
        file = open("savedata_vp.pkl", "w")
        save_list = [self.happiness, self.health, self.hunger, \
                    datetime.datetime.now(), self.time_cycle]
        pickle.dump(save_list, file)
        event.accept()

    def menuExit_selected(self):
        self.close()

app = QtGui.QApplication(sys.argv)
myapp = MyForm()
myapp.show()
app.exec_()
```

Adds or subtracts units depending on activity

Makes sure values are not out of range

Updates progress bars

Saves status and timestamp to pickle file

Line-continuation character

The `sleep_test()` function uses a PyQt "warning message" dialog box. A couple of parameters tell it which buttons to show and which one of those buttons is the default. The notes in listing 24.4 explain this. When the dialog pops up (when you try to wake your pet), it looks like this:

Don't worry if you don't understand all this code. You can learn more about PyQt on your own if you want. A good place to start is the PyQt website: **www.riverbankcomputing.co.uk/ software/pyqt/intro**.

In this chapter, we have only scratched the surface of what can be done with computer simulations. You have seen the basic ideas of simulating real-world conditions, like gravity and time, but computer simulations are widely used in science, engineering, medicine, finance, and many other fields. Many of them are very complex and take days or weeks to run even on the fastest computers. But even the little virtual pet on your friend's keychain is a kind of simulation, and sometimes the simplest simulations are the most interesting.

What did you learn?

In this chapter, you learned

- What computer simulations are and why they're used
- How to simulate gravity, acceleration, and force
- How to keep track of and simulate time
- How to save timestamps to a file using `pickle`
- A bit about error handling (`try-except`)
- How to use timers to generate periodic events

Test your knowledge

1 List three reasons computer simulations are used.
2 List three kinds of computer simulations that you have seen or that you know of.
3 What kind of object is used to store a difference between two dates or times?

Try it out

1. Add an "out of orbit" test to the Lunar Lander program. If the ship goes out the top of the window, and the velocity exceeds +100m/s, stop the program and display a message like this: "You have escaped the Moon's gravity. No landing today!"

2. Add an option for the user to play Lunar Lander again after landing the ship, without having to restart the program.

3. Add a **Pause** button to the Virtual Pet GUI. This should stop or "freeze" time for the pet, and it should stay frozen even when the program is not running. (Hint: This means you probably need to save the "paused" state in the pickle file.)

Skier Explained

In Chapter 10, you typed in a Skier game (hopefully!) and ran it. There were some notes in the code, but we didn't give any other explanation. Typing in code and running it, even if you don't completely understand it, can be a great way to learn programming in general or learn a particular language.

But now that you know more about Python, maybe you're a little curious about how the Skier program works. In this chapter, we're going to go through it in detail.

The skier

First we'll program the skier. When you played the Skier program, you probably noticed that the skier only moves back and forth across the screen. He doesn't move up and down. The illusion of skiing "down" the hill is created by the scenery (trees and flags) scrolling up past him.

There are five different images for the skier going down the hill: one for going straight down, two for turning left (a little and a lot), and two for turning right (a little and a lot). At the start of the program, we made a list of these images, and we put them in the list in a certain order:

```
skier_images = ["skier_down.png",
                "skier_right1.png", "skier_right2.png",
                "skier_left2.png", "skier_left1.png"]
```

You'll see why this order matters soon.

To keep track of which way the skier is facing, we use a variable called `angle`. This has values from -2 to +2, as follows:

- -2 = Turning sharp left
- -1 = Turning a little left
- 0 = Going straight down
- +1 = Turning a little right
- +2 = Turning sharp right

(Note that *right* and *left* refer to screen right and left, as we see them, not the skier's right and left.)

We use the value of `angle` to know which image to use. In fact, we can directly use the value of `angle` as the index to the list of images:

- `skier_images[0]` is the one where he's going straight down.

- `skier_images[1]` is the one where he's turning a little right.

- `skier_images[2]` is the one where he's turning sharp right.

Now comes the tricky part. Remember in Chapter 12, when we talked about lists, that we said that a negative list index will wrap around and start counting backward from the end of the list? So, in this case

- `skier_images[-1]` is the one where he is turning a little left (this would usually be called `skier_images[4]`).

- `skier_images[-2]` is the one where he is turning sharp left (this would usually be called `skier_images[3]`).

Now you can see why we arranged the images in the list in that specific order:

- `angle` = +2 (turning sharp right) = `skier_images[2]`
- `angle` = +1 (turning a little right) = `skier_images[1]`
- `angle` = 0 (going straight down) = `skier_images[0]`
- `angle` = -1 (turning a little left) = `skier_images[-1]` (also known as `skier_images[4]`)
- `angle` = -2 (turning sharp left) = `skier_images[-2]` (also known as `skier_images[3]`)

We make a class for the skier, which is a Pygame `Sprite`. The skier is always 100 pixels from the top of the window, and we start him in the center of the window, left-to-right, which is at x=320, because the window is 640 pixels wide. So his initial position is [320, 100]. The first part of the skier class definition looks like this:

```
class SkierClass(pygame.sprite.Sprite):
    def __init__(self):
        pygame.sprite.Sprite.__init__(self)
        self.image =
    pygame.image.load("skier_down.png")
        self.rect = self.image.get_rect()
        self.rect.center = [320, 100]
        self.angle = 0
```

We make a class method to turn the skier, which changes `angle`, loads the correct image, and also sets the skier's speed. The speed has both x and y components. We only move the skier sprite left and right (x-speed). But the y-speed determines how fast the scenery scrolls by (how fast he goes "down" the hill). When he is going straight down, his downward speed is faster; and when he is turning, his downward speed is slower. The formula for speed looks like this:

```
speed = [self.angle, 6 - abs(self.angle) * 2]
```

The `abs` in that line of code gets the *absolute value* of `angle`. That is, we ignore the sign (+ or -). For downward speed, we don't care which direction the skier is turning, we just need to know how much he is turning.

The whole method for turning looks like this:

```
def turn(self, direction):
        self.angle = self.angle + direction
        if self.angle < -2:  self.angle = -2
        if self.angle >  2:  self.angle =  2
        center = self.rect.center
        self.image = pygame.image.load(skier_images[self.angle])
        self.rect = self.image.get_rect()
        self.rect.center = center
        speed = [self.angle, 6 - abs(self.angle) * 2]
        return speed
```

We also need a method to move the skier back and forth. This makes sure he doesn't go past the edge of the window:

```
def move(self, speed):
        self.rect.centerx = self.rect.centerx + speed[0]
        if self.rect.centerx < 20:  self.rect.centerx = 20
        if self.rect.centerx > 620: self.rect.centerx = 620
```

We use the arrow keys to steer the skier left and right, so we'll add our Pygame initialization and event loop code, which gives us a working program that only has the skier. This is shown in the following listing.

Listing 25.1   Building the Skier game—skier only

```python
import pygame, sys, random

skier_images = ["skier_down.png",
                "skier_right1.png", "skier_right2.png",
                "skier_left2.png", "skier_left1.png"]

class SkierClass(pygame.sprite.Sprite):
    def __init__(self):
        pygame.sprite.Sprite.__init__(self)
        self.image = pygame.image.load("skier_down.png")
        self.rect = self.image.get_rect()
        self.rect.center = [320, 100]
        self.angle = 0

    def turn(self, direction):
        self.angle = self.angle + direction
        if self.angle < -2:  self.angle = -2
        if self.angle >  2:  self.angle =  2
        center = self.rect.center
        self.image = pygame.image.load(skier_images[self.angle])
        self.rect = self.image.get_rect()
        self.rect.center = center
        speed = [self.angle, 6 - abs(self.angle) * 2]
        return speed

    def move(self, speed):
        self.rect.centerx = self.rect.centerx + speed[0]
        if self.rect.centerx < 20:  self.rect.centerx = 20
        if self.rect.centerx > 620: self.rect.centerx = 620

def animate():
    screen.fill([255, 255, 255])
    screen.blit(skier.image, skier.rect)
    pygame.display.flip()

pygame.init()
screen = pygame.display.set_mode([640,640])
clock = pygame.time.Clock()
skier = SkierClass()
speed = [0, 6]

running  = True
while running:
    clock.tick(30)
    for event in pygame.event.get():
        if event.type == pygame.QUIT: running = False
        if event.type == pygame.KEYDOWN:
```

Different images for the skier depending on his direction

Don't let the skier turn more than +/-2

Move the skier left and right

Redraw the screen

Check for keypresses

Main Pygame event loop

```
            if event.key == pygame.K_LEFT:
                speed = skier.turn(-1)
            elif event.key == pygame.K_RIGHT:
                speed = skier.turn(1)
        skier.move(speed)
        animate()

  pygame.quit()
```

Left arrow turns left

Right arrow turns right

Main Pygame event loop

If you run listing 25.1, you'll see just the skier (no score, no obstacles), and you'll be able to turn him left and right.

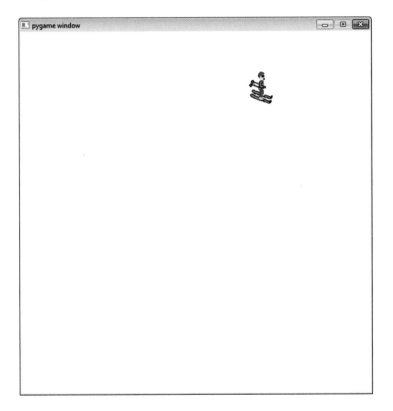

The obstacles

The next thing we'll do is figure out how to make the obstacles—the trees and flags. For this part, to keep things simple, we're going to start from scratch again—no skier, just the obstacles. We'll put the skier code together with the obstacle code at the end.

The window for the skier game is 640 x 640 pixels. To keep things simple and prevent having obstacles too close together, we divide the window into a 10 x 10 grid. There are 100 spaces on the grid. Each space on the grid is 64 x 64 pixels. Because our obstacle sprites aren't that big, there will be some space between them even if they're in adjacent spaces on the grid.

Creating individual obstacles

First we need to create individual obstacles. We make a class for that, which we call `ObstacleClass`. Just like the skier, this is a Pygame `Sprite`:

```
class ObstacleClass(pygame.sprite.Sprite):
    def __init__(self, image_file, location, type):
        pygame.sprite.Sprite.__init__(self)
        self.image_file = image_file
        self.image = pygame.image.load(image_file)
        self.rect = self.image.get_rect()
        self.rect.center = location
        self.type = type
        self.passed = False
```

Creating a map of obstacles

Let's now create a single screen's worth of obstacles—enough to fill one 10 x 10 grid, which fills the 640 x 640 pixel screen. We randomly sprinkle 10 obstacles (flags and trees) in the 100 squares of the grid. Each obstacle can be either a flag or a tree. We could end up with 2 flags and 8 trees, 7 flags and 3 trees, or any combination that adds up to 10. They're randomly chosen. The locations on the grid are also random.

The only thing we have to watch out for is that we don't try to put two obstacles in the same location. So we keep track of what locations we have used. The variable `locations` is a list of the locations we have already used. When placing a new obstacle in a particular location, we first check if there is already one in that location:

```
def create_map():
    global obstacles
    locations = []
    for i in range(10):                                       ← 10 obstacles per screen
        row = random.randint(0, 9)
        col = random.randint(0, 9)
        location  = [col * 64 + 32, row * 64 + 32 + 640]      ← (x, y) location of the obstacle
        if not (location in locations):                        ← Make sure we don't get 2 obstacles in the same location
            locations.append(location)
            type = random.choice(["tree", "flag"])
            if type == "tree": img = "skier_tree.png"
            elif type == "flag":  img = "skier_flag.png"
            obstacle = ObstacleClass(img, location, type)
            obstacles.add(obstacle)
```

> Hey, why did the y position have an extra 640 pixels added to it?

Good eye, Carter! When the game starts, we don't want the screen to be full of obstacles. We want it to start out blank, and have the obstacles begin to appear from the bottom. So, we create each screenful of scenery "below" the bottom of the window. To do that, we add 640 (the height of our window) to each obstacle's y-value.

When the game starts, we want the obstacles to start scrolling up. To do that, we change each obstacle's y-position. How much we change it depends on the skier's apparent speed down the hill. We put that in a method called `update()`, which is part of `ObstacleClass`:

```
def update(self):
    global speed
    self.rect.centery -= speed[1]
```

The variable `speed` is the skier's speed, which is a global variable. `speed` has both the skier's x and y speed, so we use index [1] to get just the y (vertical) speed.

As our first screenful of obstacles makes it all the way onto the screen, we need to create more of them, another screenful, at the bottom. How do we know when that is? We have a variable called `map_position` that keeps track of how far the scenery has scrolled up. We do that in the main loop:

```
running = True
  while running:
      clock.tick(30)
      for event in pygame.event.get():
          if event.type == pygame.QUIT: running = False

      map_position += speed[1]

      if map_position >= 640:
          create_map()
          map_position = 0
```

Keep track of how far the map has scrolled up

If it has scrolled all the way onto the screen, create a new screenful of obstacles

We have the `animate()` function, just like in our skier-only code, to redraw everything.

All together, the obstacle-only code looks like this.

Listing 25.2   Building the skier game—obstacles only

```python
import pygame, sys, random

class ObstacleClass(pygame.sprite.Sprite):
    def __init__(self, image_file, location, type):
        pygame.sprite.Sprite.__init__(self)
        self.image_file = image_file
        self.image = pygame.image.load(image_file)
        self.rect = self.image.get_rect()
        self.rect.center = location
        self.type = type
        self.passed = False

    def update(self):
        global speed
        self.rect.centery -= speed[1]

def create_map():
    global obstacles
    locations = []
    for i in range(10):
        row = random.randint(0, 9)
        col = random.randint(0, 9)
        location = [col * 64 + 32, row * 64 + 32 + 640]
        if not (location in locations):
            locations.append(location)
            type = random.choice(["tree", "flag"])
            if type == "tree": img = "skier_tree.png"
            elif type == "flag":  img = "skier_flag.png"
            obstacle = ObstacleClass(img, location, type)
            obstacles.add(obstacle)

def animate():
    screen.fill([255, 255, 255])
    obstacles.draw(screen)
    pygame.display.flip()

pygame.init()
screen = pygame.display.set_mode([640,640])
clock = pygame.time.Clock()
speed = [0, 6]
obstacles = pygame.sprite.Group()
map_position = 0
create_map()

running = True
while running:
    clock.tick(30)
    for event in pygame.event.get():
        if event.type == pygame.QUIT: running = False
```

Class for obstacle sprites
(trees and flags)

10 obstacles
per screen

Create one "screen" of
obstacles: 640 x 640

Prevent 2 obstacles
in the same place

Redraw
everything

Initialize everything

Main loop

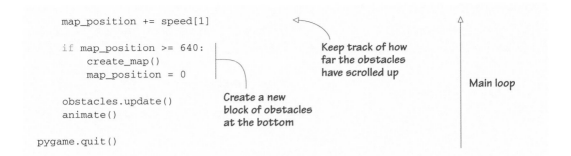

```
    map_position += speed[1]

    if map_position >= 640:
        create_map()
        map_position = 0

    obstacles.update()
    animate()

pygame.quit()
```

Keep track of how far the obstacles have scrolled up

Create a new block of obstacles at the bottom

Main loop

If you run listing 25.2, you should see trees and flags scrolling up the screen.

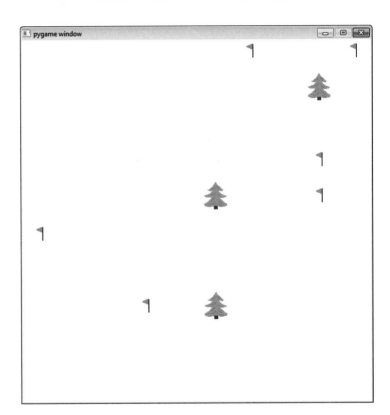

What happens to the obstacles after they scroll off the top of the screen?

That's a good question, Carter. With our current code, they just keep going up, above the top of the window, with their y positions getting more and more negative. If the game runs for a long time, we end up creating a large number of obstacle sprites. This could actually cause our program to slow down or run out of memory at some point. So we need to clean up a bit.

In the `update()` method for the obstacle class, we add a test to see if the obstacle has gone off the top of the screen. If it has, we get rid of it. Pygame has a built-in method for doing this, called `kill()`. The new `update()` method looks like this:

```
def update(self):
    global speed
    self.rect.centery -= speed[1]
    if self.rect.centery < -32:
        self.kill()
```

Check if the sprite is past the top of the screen

Get rid of it

Now we're ready to put the skier and the obstacles together:

- We need both `SkierClass` and `ObstacleClass`.
- Our `animate()` function needs to draw both the skier and the obstacles.
- Our initialization code needs to create the skier and the initial map.
- The main loop needs to include both the skier key event handling and the creation of new blocks of obstacles.

Basically, this is a combination of listing 25.1 and listing 25.2. The result is shown in listing 25.3.

Listing 25.3   Skier and obstacles together

```
import pygame, sys, random

skier_images = ["skier_down.png", "skier_right1.png", "skier_right2.png",
                "skier_left2.png", "skier_left1.png"]

class SkierClass(pygame.sprite.Sprite):
    def __init__(self):
        pygame.sprite.Sprite.__init__(self)
        self.image = pygame.image.load("skier_down.png")
        self.rect = self.image.get_rect()
        self.rect.center = [320, 100]
        self.angle = 0

    def turn(self, direction):
        self.angle = self.angle + direction
        if self.angle < -2:  self.angle = -2
        if self.angle >  2:  self.angle =  2
        center = self.rect.center
        self.image = pygame.image.load(skier_images[self.angle])
        self.rect = self.image.get_rect()
        self.rect.center = center
        speed = [self.angle, 6 - abs(self.angle) * 2]
        return speed

    def move(self, speed):
        self.rect.centerx = self.rect.centerx + speed[0]
        if self.rect.centerx < 20:  self.rect.centerx = 20
        if self.rect.centerx > 620: self.rect.centerx = 620
```

Skier code

```
class ObstacleClass(pygame.sprite.Sprite):
    def __init__(self, image_file, location, type):
        pygame.sprite.Sprite.__init__(self)
        self.image_file = image_file
        self.image = pygame.image.load(image_file)
        self.rect = self.image.get_rect()
        self.rect.center = location
        self.type = type
        self.passed = False

    def update(self):
        global speed
        self.rect.centery -= speed[1]
        if self.rect.centery < -32:
            self.kill()

def create_map():
    global obstacles
    locations = []
    for i in range(10):
        row = random.randint(0, 9)
        col = random.randint(0, 9)
        location  = [col * 64 + 32, row * 64 + 32 + 640]
        if not (location in locations):
            locations.append(location)
            type = random.choice(["tree", "flag"])
            if type == "tree": img = "skier_tree.png"
            elif type == "flag":  img = "skier_flag.png"
            obstacle = ObstacleClass(img, location, type)
            obstacles.add(obstacle)

def animate():
    screen.fill([255, 255, 255])
    obstacles.draw(screen)
    screen.blit(skier.image, skier.rect)
    pygame.display.flip()

pygame.init()
screen = pygame.display.set_mode([640,640])
clock = pygame.time.Clock()
points = 0
speed = [0, 6]
skier = SkierClass()
obstacles = pygame.sprite.Group()
create_map()
map_position = 0

running = True
while running:
    clock.tick(30)
    for event in pygame.event.get():
        if event.type == pygame.QUIT: running = False

        if event.type == pygame.KEYDOWN:
            if event.key == pygame.K_LEFT:
```

Obstacle code

Redraw skier and obstacles

Create skier

Initialize everything

Create obstacles

Main loop

```
                    speed = skier.turn(-1)
            elif event.key == pygame.K_RIGHT:
                    speed = skier.turn(1)
        skier.move(speed)

        map_position += speed[1]

        if map_position >= 640:
            create_map()
            map_position = 0

        obstacles.update()
        animate()

    pygame.quit()
```

Main loop

If you run listing 25.3, you'll be able to steer the skier down the hill, and you'll see the obstacles scrolling past. You'll also notice that the skier's speed, both left-right and down the hill, depends on which way he's turned. We're getting close.

The last two pieces we need are these:

- To detect when the skier hits a tree or picks up a flag
- To keep track of the score and display it

You saw how to do collision detection in chapter 16. The code in listing 25.3 already puts the obstacle sprites into a sprite group, so we can use the `spritecollide()` function to detect when the skier sprite hits a tree or flag sprite. Then we need to figure out which it is (a tree or a flag), and do the right thing:

- If it's a tree, change the skier's image to the "crash" image, and deduct 100 points from the score.

- If it's a flag, add 10 points to the score, and remove the flag from the screen.

The code to do that goes in the main loop, and it looks like this:

```
hit =  pygame.sprite.spritecollide(skier, obstacles, False)        Check for
    if hit:                                                        collisions
        if hit[0].type == "tree" and not hit[0].passed:
            points = points - 100                          Hit a tree


            skier.image = pygame.image.load("skier_crash.png")    Show the "crashed"
            animate()                                             image for a second
            pygame.time.delay(1000)
            skier.image = pygame.image.load("skier_down.png")     Continue
            skier.angle = 0                                       skiing down
            speed = [0, 6]                    Remember that we
            hit[0].passed = True             already hit this tree

        elif hit[0].type == "flag" and not hit[0].passed:     Got a flag
            points += 10
            hit[0].kill()           Remove the flag
```

The variable `hit` tells us which obstacle sprites the skier sprite collided with. It's a list, but in our case it has only one item, because the skier can only collide with one obstacle at a time. So the obstacle the skier collided with is `hit[0]`.

The `passed` variable is used to indicate that a tree has been hit. This ensures that, when the skier continues skiing down the hill, he doesn't immediately hit the same tree again.

Now we need to display the score. This takes only three more lines of code. In the initialization section, we create a `font` object, which is an instance of Pygame's `Font` class:

```
font = pygame.font.Font(None, 50)
```

In the main loop, we render the `font` object with the new score text:

```
score_text = font.render("Score: " +str(points), 1, (0, 0, 0))
```

And in the `animate()` function, we display the score in the upper-left corner:

```
screen.blit(score_text, [10, 10])
```

That's all we need. If you put this all together, you'll end up with the code from chapter 10, in listing 10.1. Only now you understand it a lot better. Understanding how Skier works should help you when you're thinking about and developing your own games.

What did you learn?

In this chapter, you learned

- How all the parts of the Skier program work
- How to create a scrolling background

Try it out

1 Try modifying Skier so that it gets harder as the game goes on. Here are some suggestions for things to try:

   - Make the speed increase as the game goes on.
   - Add more trees farther down the hill.
   - Add "ice," which makes turning more difficult.

2 The SkiFree program that was the inspiration for Skier had an Abominable Snowman that randomly appeared and chased the skier. If you're up for a real challenge, try adding something like that to the Skier program. You'll have to find or create a new sprite image and figure out how to modify the code to get the behavior you want.

## CHAPTER 26

Python Battle

In this book, we've covered how to make your own games. One thing we haven't talked about yet, however, is game artificial intelligence (AI). Almost every game since Pac-Man has had some form of artificial intelligence that attacks the player, and this chapter will show you how to make one yourself.

Python Battle

The AIs we're going to make in this chapter will be part of a game called Python Battle. Python Battle is a simple game with simple rules. On each turn, you may move forward, turn to face a different direction, or attack. When one bot attacks another, the bot that gets attacked loses one "health point." The first bot to lose all its health points loses the game. Bots can only attack the square directly in front of them.

But Python Battle has one twist: it's a game played by robots. You have to code a strategy, or AI, to control your bot, and then run Python Battle to see how well it does against another AI. Of course, the AI code, and Python Battle itself, are written in Python.

Note that Python Battle should be included on your computer if you ran our book's installer. I've included three AI programs for you to try out: CircleAI (drives in circles around the playing field), RandomAI (moves and turns randomly), and NullAI (doesn't do anything). Let's try running them against each other to see who wins.

Running Python Battle

Follow these steps:

1. Make sure the AI scripts you want to use are in the same folder as **PythonBattle.py**.
2. Run **PythonBattle.py**.
3. You'll see a prompt:

   ```
   Enter red AI:
   ```

   Enter the name of the AI script you want to use. Leave the **.py** extension off the end. For example, if you wanted to test **CircleAI.py**, you would type `circleai`.
4. Do the same for the blue AI.
5. Watch the battle to see who wins!
6. Close the Pygame window at the end.

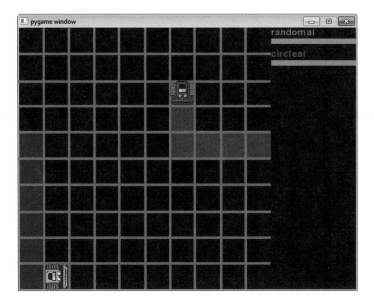

The rules of the game

Now that you've watched a few Python Battles, let's take a closer look at how the game works. Every turn, a robot can do one of six things:

- Go forward one space
- Go backward one space
- Turn left
- Turn right

- Attack the space directly in front of it
- Stay still

In addition, a robot can look at the board any time it wants. The goal of the game is to successfully attack an enemy 10 times.

While you were watching CircleAI and RandomAI play against each other, did you notice the red and blue squares? When a robot drives over a square, that square turns the same color as the bot (red or blue). After 1,000 turns, if neither robot has attacked the other, or if the robots are tied in health points, whoever has the most squares in their color wins.

Creating a Python Battle Robot

Let's make a robot to try to beat CircleAI and RandomAI. The first step in making a robot is to come up with a strategy. For our first Python Battle Robot, we should probably start with a simple strategy:

1. If I'm facing the enemy, I should attack him.
2. If I'm facing a wall, I should turn around.
3. Otherwise, I should drive forward.

Although this isn't the most advanced strategy, it might just beat CircleAI. If it doesn't, we can always go back and tweak it a bit.

The second step is to start coding the robot. Create a new Python file (I'm going to call mine **better_than_circleai.py**), and type in this code:

```
class AI:
    def __init__(self):
        pass
    def turn(self):
        pass
```

This is the basic code that all robots must start from. The __init__() function is called when the AI is created at the start of the game. The turn() function is called every round, and it decides what the robot does. The class has to be called AI, or Python Battle won't know where to find your AI code.

The next step in coding the robot is to add the code that makes the bot carry out our strategy. You'll be using these functions to make the robot move around:

- `self.robot.lookInFront()`
- `self.robot.turnRight()`
- `self.robot.turnLeft()`

- `self.robot.goForth()`
- `self.robot.attack()`

These methods have to be called `self.robot.xx()` because `self` refers to the AI, not the robot that the AI controls, and the AI object isn't actually moving around or attacking. The AI object is just responsible for telling the robot what to do, and the robot object takes care of doing the moving and attacking.

Let's start writing the `turn()` method. Remove the `pass`, and add this to your code:

```
self.robot.goForth()
```

If you test the robot now, you can see it tries to go forward every turn. This quickly causes it to hit the wall of the playing field. If the opponent gets in the way, the robot simply stops moving. You can fix this using `self.robot.lookInFront()`. This function returns `"bot"` if there's a robot directly in front that you can attack. Change the `turn()` function so that it looks like this:

```
if self.robot.lookInFront() == "bot":
    self.robot.attack()
else:
    self.robot.goForth()
```

Now, if something gets in the way of your robot, the robot attacks. But if the robot hits a wall, it still stops. `self.robot.lookInFront()` returns `"wall"` if you're up against a wall. Add this to your `turn()` function, between `self.robot.attack()` and `else`:

```
elif self.robot.lookInFront() == "wall":
    self.robot.turnRight()
```

Now, if you run the code, the robot starts going in circles! When it hits a wall, it turns right, and when it hits the next wall it turns right again, and so on. You want the bot to turn all the way around when it hits a wall, and it takes two right turns to turn all the way around. So, when the robot hits a wall, it needs to make a right turn. Then, on the next round, it needs to turn right again. Basically, you need the bot to remember that it's in the middle of a U-turn. You can do this by giving the AI a new property (a variable) to keep track of what it's doing. Let's add a new line to the __init__() function:

```
self.currentlyDoing = "forward"
```

This will tell the robot that when it starts, it needs to go forward. When the robot is in the middle of a U-turn, you can change this to say `"turnRight"` to remind the robot that it needs to turn right. After modifying the `turn()` function, the final code looks like this.

Listing 26.1 The completed robot AI

```
class AI:
    def __init__(self):
        self.currentlyDoing = "forward"
    def turn(self):
        if self.robot.lookInFront() == "bot":
            self.robot.attack()
        elif self.robot.lookInFront() == "wall":
            self.robot.turnRight()
            self.currentlyDoing = "turnRight"
        elif self.currentlyDoing == "turnRight":
            self.robot.turnRight()
            self.currentlyDoing = "forward"
        else:
            self.robot.goForth()
```

If you run this, you might notice that the AI has some flaws. Let's try to make changes so our robot beats CircleAI.

A more complicated robot

Our first robot was pretty simple, and it didn't win against CircleAI. In order to beat all the other robots, we'll need a really good strategy. A really good strategy is more than "drive in circles until the enemy goes in front of me." A really good strategy requires using every command available. Most of all, a really good strategy requires a lot of thought as to how it's going to work.

There are a few methods I didn't mention in the last section, which could help us on our quest to create a winning strategy:

- `self.robot.goBack()`—Pretty self-explanatory: the robots can move backward.
- `self.robot.checkSpace(space)`—Lets you look at any space on the board. `self.robot.checkSpace((3,3))`, for example, tells you what is on space (3,3). If there's nothing there, it returns `"blank"`. Otherwise, it returns `"bot"` (if the enemy is there), `"me"` (if your robot is there), or `"wall"` (if the space is out of bounds).
- `self.robot.locateEnemy()`—Gives you the position and direction of the enemy.
- `self.robot.position`—Gives you your own position.
- `self.robot.rotation`—Gives you your own direction.
- `self.robot.calculateCoordinates(direction, distance, position)`—Explained later. First, we need to understand how the coordinate system in Python Battle works.

The coordinate system

In Python Battle, the coordinate system goes from (1,1) to (10,10). It starts from the top-left, just like Pygame. Walls surround the playing field in every direction. We can use `self.robot.position` to find the position of the robot in the coordinate system.

Directions

Directions are stored as a number from 0–3. 0 is up (North), 1 is right (East), 2 is down (South), and 3 is left (West). When the robot turns right, it adds 1 to its direction. When it turns left, it subtracts 1 from its direction. It's that simple. We can use `self.robot.rotation` to find the robot's direction.

calculateCoordinates()

The `calculateCoordinates()` function take three parameters: `distance`, `direction`, and `position`. Basically, it finds the coordinates of the space that is `distance` squares from `position` in `direction`. For example, `calculateCoordinates(2,3,(5,5))` finds the space that's two squares to the left (left is direction 3) of square (5,5).

Now we can come up with a strategy. I'm going with a straightforward one:

1 Go in the direction of the enemy.
2 Attack when possible.

Let's start with some of the basic code from the previous robot:

```python
class AI:
    def __init__(self):
        pass
    def turn(self):
        if self.robot.lookInFront() == "bot":
            self.robot.attack()
```

This code will handle the second part of our strategy: "attack when possible." Now we need to code the first part. Let's add this code to the `turn()` function:

```python
else:
    self.goTowards(self.robot.locateEnemy()[0])
```

This will call the method of our `AI` class called `self.goTowards()` with the enemy's position as the argument. The `self.robot.locateEnemy()` method returns a list containing the enemy's position and rotation. If you run this code, it won't work because we haven't defined `self.goTowards()` yet. Let's start to define it now:

```python
def goTowards(self, enemyLocation):
    myLocation = self.robot.position
    delta = (enemyLocation[0]-myLocation[0],
            enemyLocation[1]-myLocation[1])
```

You start by finding the delta, or difference, between the target location and your robot's location. Next, you need to figure out which direction you need to be facing to face the enemy bot:

```python
if abs(delta[0]) > abs(delta[1]):
    if delta[0] < 0:
        targetOrientation = 3
    else:
        targetOrientation = 1
else:
    if delta[1] < 0:
        targetOrientation = 0
    else:
        targetOrientation = 2
```

Face left

Face right

Face up

Face down

Now you have to go in that direction. If you're already facing in that direction, it's easy:

```python
if self.robot.rotation == targetOrientation:
    self.robot.goForth()
```

Otherwise, you need to figure out which way to turn. First, you figure out how many left turns you would need to make in order to be facing the correct direction:

```python
else:
    leftTurnsNeeded = (self.robot.rotation - targetOrientation) % 4
```

Next, you have to turn the right way. If it would take more than two left turns to face where you need to, you can instead just turn right once:

```python
if leftTurnsNeeded <= 2:
    self.robot.turnLeft()
else:
    self.robot.turnRight()
```

Here's the full code for the robot.

Listing 26.2   A more complicated robot

```
class AI:
    def __init__(self):
        pass
    def turn(self):
        if self.robot.lookInFront() == "bot":
            self.robot.attack()
        else:
            self.goTowards(self.robot.locateEnemy()[0])
    def goTowards(self, enemyLocation):
        myLocation = self.robot.position
        delta = (enemyLocation[0]-myLocation[0], enemyLocation[1]-myLocation[1])
        if abs(delta[0]) > abs(delta[1]):
            if delta[0] < 0:
                targetOrientation = 3          Face left
            else:
                targetOrientation = 1              Face right
        else:
            if delta[1] < 0:             Face up
                targetOrientation = 0
            else:                          Face down
                targetOrientation = 2
        if self.robot.rotation == targetOrientation:
            self.robot.goForth()
        else:
            leftTurnsNeeded = (self.robot.rotation - targetOrientation) % 4
            if leftTurnsNeeded <= 2:
                self.robot.turnLeft()
            else:
                self.robot.turnRight()
```

Let's try this on CircleAI. Surely all our hard work has paid off and allowed us to finally defeat it! Save the AI as **morecomplicatedai.py**, and run PythonBattle again:

```
>>>
Enter red AI: circleai
Enter blue AI: morecomplicatedai
    .
    .
    .
Red wins with 10 health!
```

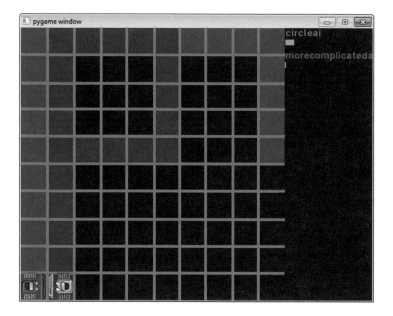

What?!
CircleAI
won again!

I guess we'll need to revise our strategy a little in order to beat CircleAI. CircleAI is so hard to beat because it's hard to hit. If you try to attack it from the side or back, it will run away before your robot can hit it more than once. Also, because it hugs the wall, there's only one side you can attack it from. If you try to attack it from the front, it will most likely get the first hit and thus win the game. Even if it's not the most advanced strategy, CircleAI is really tough to beat.

It's probably possible to devise an AI that can beat CircleAI consistently, but that's if you know CircleAI is the AI you're going up against. If you don't know what the other player is using as a strategy for their AI, it's even trickier!

What did you learn?

In this chapter, you learned

- How games use AI to make enemies smart
- How to make your own AI as part of PythonBattle

Try it out

1 Revise my strategy, and try to come up with a robot that beats CircleAI.

What's Next?

This is the end of *Hello World! Computer Programming for Kids and Other Beginners.* If you've read the whole book and tried the examples, you should have a good basic understanding of programming and some fun things you can do with it.

This chapter will give you some places to look for more information on programming. There are some resources for programming in general, for Python in particular, for game programming, and a few other things.

How you decide to learn more about programming depends on what you want to do with it. You have a start with Python, and many of the things you've learned from this book are general programming ideas and concepts that will transfer to other computer languages. How and what you learn depends on the direction you want to go: games? web programming? robotics? (Robots need software to tell them what to do.)

For younger programmers

For younger readers, if you've enjoyed learning programming with Python, you might also enjoy trying a different approach. Squeak Etoys is a programming "language" for kids that's almost entirely graphical. You write almost no code, and you make programs by creating graphical objects and modifying their properties and actions. Behind the scenes, your graphical objects are turned into code in a language called Smalltalk. You can find out more about Etoys at **squeakland.org**.

Another language that looks similar to Squeak is Scratch. Scratch also lets you make programs with drag-and-drop, similar to Squeak. Scratch programs can also be shared on the web. Scratch is available at **scratch.mit.edu**.

Python

There are many places to learn more about Python. The online Python documentation is very complete, but it can be a bit hard to read. It includes a Language Reference, a Library Reference, a Global Module Index, and a Tutorial by Guido van Rossum, who created Python. You can find it here: **docs.python.org**.

Many books have been written about more advanced Python. In fact, there are so many that I can't recommend just one or two. It depends on your tastes, your learning style, and the particular things you want to do with Python. But I'm sure that if you want to go further with Python, you'll be able to find the right books for you.

Mailing lists are also useful. You can post a message, and other users will do their best to answer it. Most of the lists have archive pages where you can read or search older messages to see if someone has already asked your question.

Game programming and Pygame

If making games is what you want to do, many books are available on the subject—too many to list here. You'll probably want to learn about something called OpenGL, which is short for Open Graphics Language. This is a graphics system that many games use. OpenGL is available in Python by using a module called PyOpenGL, and there are several books about it.

If Pygame caught your interest, there are a few places you can look to find out more. The Pygame site, **pygame.org**, has many examples and tutorials.

If you really want to do game programming with Pygame, you can check out a couple of very good resources. One is the Pygame mailing list. I have found it very helpful. You can find out about it at **pygame.org/wiki/info**. The mailing-list address is **pygame-users@seul.org**.

If you want to have accurate physics in your game, you can use a library called PyMunk. PyMunk is based around something called Chipmunk Physics. Chipmunk lets you create circles, lines, and shapes in a 2D world. Then it simulates basic physics forces like gravity and friction acting on those shapes. PyMunk is available from **pymunk.org**.

Other game programming (non-Python)

If you're interested in making games, you might want to look at the Unity game engine. Unity encompasses several things, including a 3D game engine, a physics engine, and ways to write scripts. One of the languages you can use for scripting is called Boo, which has a lot of similarities to Python.

Some games that you might already play let you write code to extend the game. For example, Roblox (**www.roblox.com**) lets you write code in a language called Lua. You can get mods for Minecraft (**www.minecraft.com**) that let you write code in Lua or Java. (By the way, the popular game Angry Birds is written in Lua.)

Keep it BASIC

One thing you might notice if you look for books at the library is that quite a few programming books for kids were written in the 1980s, and many of them use a language called BASIC, which was very popular back then. (You can still get versions of BASIC for modern computers.) These books tend to have lots of games in them. Something that might be fun to try is to take a game from one of the old BASIC books and try to rewrite it using Python. You could use Pygame or PyQt to help with graphics if you need to. I guarantee you'd learn a *lot* by doing that!

Mobile apps

If you're interested in making apps for the iPhone or Android phones, there are a couple of ways to do it. You can write iPhone apps using HTML5 and CSS using a tool called PhoneGap (**phonegap.com**). If you do it that way, you can also easily port the app to another phone operating system (like Android or Blackberry OS). The other way is to write native iPhone code using a language called Objective-C and a library called Cocoa Touch. The editor you use for this is called Xcode, and it only runs on Mac OS X. Apps for Android are mostly written in Java, but you can use libraries like PhoneGap to program in other languages.

Look around

There are many, many other topics to explore and resources that can help you in different areas of programming in general and Python in particular. You can always check at your library or bookstore for books that have information on a topic you're interested in. You can also do a web search on the topic to see if there are online tutorials or Python modules to help do what you want to do.

Python can take you a long way, but to do some specific things you may need a different language, like C, C++, Java, JavaScript (different from Java), or another one. If so, you'll want to find a book or other resource that teaches you that specific language. There are so many different ones out there that I can't give you much advice on that subject.

Whatever you do, have fun with programming! Keep learning, exploring, and experimenting. The more you learn about programming, the more interesting it gets!

Variable Naming Rules

Here are the rules for variable names (also called identifiers):

- They must begin with either a letter or an underscore character. Following that, you can use an unlimited sequence of letters, numbers, or underscore characters.
- The letters can be uppercase or lowercase, and case matters. In other words, `Ax` is not the same as `aX`.
- The numbers can be any of the digit characters from 0 to 9 inclusive.

Aside from letters, numbers, and the underscore character, no other characters can be used. Spaces, punctuation, and other characters are not allowed in variable names:

```
~ ` ! @ # $ % ^ & * ( ) ; - : " ' < > , . ? / { } [ ] + = /
```

The only special character that's allowed is the underscore character. In case you don't know what that is, here are a couple of examples:

- `first_number = 15`
- `student_name = "John"`

The character between `first` and `number` is the underscore. There's also one between `student` and `name`. Programmers sometimes use an underscore to separate two words in the name of a variable. Because spaces aren't allowed in variable names, they use the underscore instead.

I recommend that you not use the underscore character at the beginning or end of a variable name unless you know exactly why you're using it. In some situations, using the underscore character at the beginning or end of an identifier has a special meaning. So avoid this:

- `_first_number = 15`
- `student_name_ = "John"`

Here are some examples of valid variable names:

- `my_answer`
- `answer23`
- `answer_23`
- `YourAnswer`
- `Your2ndAnswer`

Here are some examples of invalid variable names:

- `23answer` (Variable names can't start with a number.)
- `your-answer` (The hyphen character isn't allowed.)
- `my answer` (Spaces aren't allowed.)

Differences Between Python 2 and 3

Throughout the book, we have mentioned several differences between Python 2 and Python 3. The book uses Python 2, but we also want you to know how to recognize Python 3 code and make your code compatible with Python 3 if you want to. This appendix only talks about the Python 2 to 3 differences in the parts of Python that we have covered in this book. (For example, Python 3 handles Unicode strings differently, but because we didn't talk about Unicode, we won't talk about the Python 3 Unicode changes.)

With that in mind, here are some of the ways Python 3 is different from Python 2.

print

In Python 3, `print` is a function. That means instead of writing

```
print "Hello, World!"
```

you need to write

```
print("Hello, World!")
```

There are some other differences related to this. You can't just put a comma at the end to make output from the next `print` appear on the same line, as you did in Python 2:

```
print "Hello",
print "World!"
```

Instead, in Python 3 you have to do this:

```
print("Hello", end=" ")
print("World! ")
```

There are other things you can do with the **end** argument, but they're rarely used. You can look them up in the Python 3 documentation if you want.

You might have noticed that the code coloring on **print** is different in Python 3 than in Python 2. That's because in Python 2, **print** is a keyword, but in Python 3, **print()** is a function.

input()

In Python 3, the function that used to be called **raw_input()** in Python 2 is now called simply **input()**. This is the function that returns a string and doesn't try to do any evaluation of the input string (for example, converting it to an **int** or **float**).

The function that was called **input()** in Python 2, which does try to evaluate the input (convert it to a number if possible), doesn't exist in Python 3.

That means instead of writing this (in Python 2)

```
your_name = raw_input("Enter your name: ")
```

you have to write (in Python 3)

```
your_name = input("Enter your name: ")
```

And instead of writing (in Python 2)

```
age = input("Enter your age: ")
```

you have to write (in Python 3)

```
age = int(input("Enter your age: "))
```

Integer division

The third major change in Python 3 is how it handles integer division. Remember the "integer division gotcha" we talked about in chapter 2? That's where you get this (in Python 2):

```
>>> print 5/2
2
```

Python 2 does *floor division* by default. Python 3 does *floating-point division* by default. So in Python 3 you get

```
>>> print(5/2)
2.5
```

If you want floor division in Python 3, you can get that by using a double slash, like this:

```
>>> print(5//2)
2
```

The modulus operator (%) to get the remainder in integer division works the same in Python 3 as in Python 2:

Python 2:

```
>>> print 5%2
1
```

Python 3:

```
>>> print(5%2)
1
```

range()

In Python2, the **range()** function returns a list. But in Python 3, **range()** returns a *range object*. For purposes of looping, a range object in Python 3 works basically the same way as a list in Python 2. But if you try to print it, you don't see the individual values in the range:

Python 2:

```
>>> print range(5)
[0, 1, 2, 3, 4]
```

Python 3:

```
>>> print(range(5))
range(0, 5)
```

Python 2 to 3 conversion

There is a tool called **2to3** that attempts to automatically convert Python 2 code to Python 3 code. If you're running Python 3, you can try it on some of the listings in this book. Many of them will likely work. But we haven't tested `2to3` on the code in this book, so we can't guarantee it will work for all the listings.

Even though Python 3 is the latest version of Python, Python 2 is still widely supported. Because lots and lots of people have written Python 2 code that doesn't work in Python 3, many companies and users have continued to use Python 2. Many modules haven't been updated, and some modules might not ever be updated. There are many more resources for Python 2 code than there are for Python 3, and that is one of the reasons we've decided to stick to Python 2 in this book. But if you want to try using Python 3 in your own programming projects, we wish you the best of luck.

Answers to Self-Test Questions

Here are the answers to the "Test your knowledge" and "Try it out" questions at the end of each chapter. Of course, there's sometimes more than one right answer, especially with the "Try it out" questions, but you can use these answers to see if you're on the right track.

Chapter 1: Getting Started

Test your knowledge

1. In Windows, start IDLE by opening the Start menu, and, under the Python 2.7 entry, select the **IDLE (Python GUI)** entry. In Mac OS X, click **IDLE** in the Dock if you have added the application to the Dock, or double-click **IDLE.app** in the **Python 2.7** folder in the **Applications** folder. In Linux, it depends on which window manager you're using, but usually there is some sort of Applications or Programs menu. Note that in Linux, many people don't use IDLE—they just run Python from the Terminal and use an editor like vi or emacs to edit their code.

2. `print` displays some text in the output window (the IDLE shell window, in our first examples).

3. The symbol for multiplication in Python is * (the asterisk symbol).

4. When you run a program, IDLE displays this line:

   ```
   >>> ======================= RESTART =======================
   ```

5. "Executing" a program is another way to say "running" a program.

Try it out

1. `>>> print 7 * 24 * 60` (7 days in a week, 24 hours in a day, 60 minutes in an hour). You should get 10,080 as the answer.

2. Your program should look something like this:

```
print "My name is Warren Sande."
print "My birth date is January 1, 1970."
print "My favorite color is blue."
```

Chapter 2: Remember This—Memory and Variables

Test your knowledge

1. You tell Python that a variable is a string by putting quotes around it.

2. The question was, "Can you change the value that is assigned to a variable?" That depends what you mean by "change." If you do this,

    ```
    myAge = 10
    ```

    then you can do

    ```
    myAge = 11
    ```

    You have changed what is assigned to `myAge`. You have moved the `myAge` tag to a different thing: you moved it from 10 to 11. But you didn't actually change the 10 into an 11. So it's more correct to say that you can "reassign the name to a different value," or "assign a new value to the variable," rather than "change the value of the variable."

3. No, `TEACHER` is not the same as `TEACHEr`. Because variable names are case-sensitive, the last letter of the two variable names makes them different.

4. Yes, `'Blah'` and `"Blah"` are the same. They are both strings, and in this case, Python doesn't care which kind of quotes you use, as long as the opening and closing quotes around the string match.

5. No, `'4'` is not the same as 4. The first one is a string (even though it has only one character) because it has quotes around it. The second one is a number.

6. Answer b. `2Teacher` is not a correct variable name. Variable names in Python can't start with a number.

7. "10" is a string because it has quotes around it.

Try it out

1. In interactive mode, you would do something like this:

    ```
    >>> temperature = 25
    >>> print temperature
    25
    ```

2   You could do either of these:

```
>>> temperature = 40
>>> print temperature
40
```

or

```
>>> temperature = temperature + 15
>>> print temperature
40
```

3   You would do something like this:

```
>>> firstName = "Fred"
>>> print firstName
Fred
```

4   Using variables, your "minutes per day" program would look something like this:

```
>>> DaysPerWeek = 7
>>> HoursPerDay = 24
>>> MinutesPerHour = 60
>>> print DaysPerWeek * HoursPerDay * MinutesPerHour
10080
```

5   To see what would happen if there were 26 hours in the day, you would do this:

```
>>> HoursPerDay = 26
>>> print DaysPerWeek * HoursPerDay * MinutesPerHour
10920
```

Chapter 3: Basic Math

Test your knowledge

1   Python uses the * (asterisk) symbol for multiplication.

2   Python would say that 8 / 3 = 2. Because 8 and 3 are both integers, Python 2 gives the answer rounded down to the nearest integer. (Note that in Python 3, you would get 2.66666666667, because Python 3 doesn't do "floor division" on integers by default like Python 2 does.)

3   To get the remainder, use the Modulus operator: 8 % 3.

4   To get the decimal answer for 8 / 3, change one of them into a decimal number: 8.0 / 3 or 8 / 3.0. (Note that in Python 3, you get the decimal answer automatically.)

5   What's another way of calculating 6 * 6 * 6 * 6 in Python? 6 ** 4.

6   17,000,000 in E-notation would be written as 1.7e7.

7   4.56e-5 is the same as 0.0000456.

Try it out

1 Here are some ways to solve these problems. You might have come up with a different way to do the same thing.

a) Calculate how much each person should pay at the restaurant:

```
>>> print 35.27 * 1.15 / 3
>>> 13.5201666667
```

Rounding this off, each person should pay $13.52.

b) Calculate the area and perimeter of a rectangle:

```
length = 16.7
width = 12.5
Perimeter = 2 * length + 2 * width
Area = length * width
print 'Length = ', length, ' Width = ', width
print "Area = ", Area
print "Perimeter = ", Perimeter
```

Here's a sample run of the program:

```
Length = 16.7 Width = 12.5
Area = 208.75
Perimeter = 58.4
```

2 Here's a program to convert temperatures from Fahrenheit to Celsius:

```
fahrenheit = 75
celsius  = 5.0/9 * (fahrenheit - 32)
print "Fahrenheit  = ", fahrenheit, "Celsius =", celsius
```

3 Calculate the time it will take to drive a certain distance at a given speed:

```
distance = 200
speed = 80.0
time = distance / speed
print "time =", time
```

(Remember to make at least one of the numbers in the division a decimal, unless you want the answer to be rounded down to an integer.)

Chapter 4: Types of Data

Test your knowledge

1 The `int()` function always rounds down (to the next integer closest to zero on the number line).

2 In the temperature-conversion program, would these have worked?

```
cel = float(5 / 9 * (fahr - 32))
cel = 5 / 9 * float(fahr - 32)
```

Try them and see what happens:

```
>>> fahr = 75
>>> cel = float(5 / 9 * (fahr - 32))
>>> print cel
0.0
```

Why didn't it work?

Remember that everything inside the parentheses is done first. So it goes like this:

```
75 - 32 = 43
```

Then

```
5 / 9 = 0
```

Because it goes from left to right, `5 / 9` gets done first. Because 5 and 9 are both integers, Python does integer division and rounds the answer down. Because the answer is less than 1, it gets rounded down to 0. Then

```
0 * 43 = 0
```

Then

```
float(0) = 0.0
```

By the time it got to `float()`, it was too late—the answer was already 0! The same goes for the second equation.

3 You can "trick" `int()` into rounding off instead of rounding down by adding 0.5 to the number you pass to `int()`.

Here's an example (in interactive mode):

```
>>> a = 13.2
>>> roundoff = int(a + 0.5)
>>> roundoff
13
>>> b = 13.7
>>> roundoff = int(b + 0.5)
>>> b
14
```

If the original number is less than 13.5, `int()` gets a number less than 14, which rounds down to 13.

If the original number is 13.5 or greater, `int()` gets a number equal to or greater than 14, which rounds down to 14.

Try it out

1 You can use `float()` to convert a string to a decimal number:

```
>>> a = float('12.34')
>>> print a
12.34
```

But how do you know that this is a number and not a string? Let's check the type:

```
>>> type(a)
<type 'float'>
```

2 You can use `int()` to convert a decimal number to an integer:

```
>>> print int(56.78)
56
```

The answer got rounded down.

3 You can use `int()` to convert a string to an integer:

```
>>> a = int('75')
>>> print a
75
>>> type(a)
<type 'int'>
```

Chapter 5: Input

Test your knowledge

1 With this code,

```
answer = raw_input()
```

if the user types in **12**, **answer** contains a string. That's because `raw_input()` always gives you a string.

Try it in a short program and see:

```
print "enter a number: ",
answer = raw_input()
print type(answer)

>>> ============== RESTART ==============
>>>
enter a number: 12
<type 'str'>
>>>
```

So `raw_input()` gives you a string.

Remember that in Python 3, `raw_input()` is simply called `input()`.

2   To get `raw_input()` to print a prompt message, put some text in quotes inside the parentheses, like this:

```
answer = raw_input("Type in a number: ")
```

3   To get an integer using `raw_input()`, use `int()` to convert the string you get from `raw_input()`. You can do it in two steps, like this:

```
something = raw_input()
answer = int(something)
```

Or you can do it in a single step, like this:

```
answer = int(raw_input())
```

4   This is very similar to the previous question, except you use `float()` instead of `int()`.

Try It Out

1   Your instructions in interactive mode should look something like this:

```
>>> first = 'Warren'
>>> last = 'Sande'
>>> print first + last
WarrenSande
```

Oops! There's no space. You can either add a space at the end of your first name

```
>>> first = 'Warren '
```

or try this:

```
>>> print first + ' ' + last
Warren Sande
```

Or you could just use a comma, like this:

```
>>> first = 'Warren'
>>> last = 'Sande'
>>> print first, last
Warren Sande
```

2   The program should look something like this:

```
first = raw_input('enter your first name: ')
last = raw_input('enter your last name: ')
print 'Hello,', first, last, 'how are you today?'
```

3   The program should look something like this:

```
length = float(raw_input ('length of the room in feet: '))
width = float(raw_input ('width of the room in feet: '))
area = length * width
print 'The area is', area, 'square feet.'
```

4   You can add a few lines to the program from #C:

```
length = float(raw_input ('length of the room in feet: '))
width = float(raw_input ('width of the room in feet: '))
cost_per_yard = float(raw_input ('cost per square yard: '))
area_feet = length * width
area_yards = area_feet / 9.0
total_cost = area_yards * cost_per_yard
print 'The area is', area_feet, 'square feet.'
print 'That is', area_yards, 'square yards.'
print 'Which will cost', total_cost
```

5   The program should look like this:

```
quarters = int(raw_input("How many quarters? "))
dimes = int(raw_input("How many dimes? "))
nickels = int(raw_input("How many nickels? "))
pennies = int(raw_input("How many pennies? "))
total   = 0.25 * quarters + 0.10 * dimes + 0.05 * nickels + 0.01 * pennies
print "You have a total of: ", total
```

Chapter 6: GUIs—Graphical User Interfaces

Test your knowledge

1   To bring up a message box with EasyGui, use **msgbox()**, like this:

```
easygui.msgbox("This is the answer!")
```

2 To get a string as input using EasyGui, use an **enterbox**.

3 To get an integer as input, you can use an **enterbox** (which gets a string from the user) and then convert it to an **int**. Or you can use an **integerbox**.

4 To get a float from the user, you can use an **enterbox** (which gives you a string) **and** then use the **float()** function to convert the string to a float.

5 A default value is like an "automatic answer." Here's one way you might use a default: if you were writing a program where all the students in your class had to enter their name and address, you might have the name of the city where you live as the default city in the address. That way, the students wouldn't have to type it in unless they lived in a different city.

Try it out

1 Here is a temperature-conversion program using EasyGui:

```
# tempgui1.py
# EasyGui version of temperature-conversion program
# converts Fahrenheit to Celsius
import easygui

easygui.msgbox('This program converts Fahrenheit to Celsius')
temperature  = easygui.enterbox('Type in a temperature in Fahrenheit:')
Fahr = float(temperature)
Cel = (Fahr - 32) * 5.0 / 9
easygui.msgbox('That is ' + str(Cel) + ' degrees Celsius.')
```

2 Here is a program that asks for your name and the parts of your address and then displays the whole address. For this one, it helps to know how to force a *newline*. A newline makes the following text start on a new line. To do this, you use **\n**. This is explained in chapter 21, but here is a preview:

```
# address.py
# Enter parts of your address and display the whole thing
import easygui
name = easygui.enterbox("What is your name?")
addr = easygui.enterbox("What is your street address?")
city = easygui.enterbox("What is your city?")
state = easygui.enterbox("What is your state or province?")
code = easygui.enterbox("What is your postal code or zip code?")

whole_addr  = name + "\n" + addr + "\n" + city + ", " + state + "\n" + code

easygui.msgbox(whole_addr, "Here is your address:")
```

Chapter 7: Decisions, Decisions

Test your knowledge

1   The output would be

```
Under 20
```

Because **my_number** is less than 20, the test in the **if** statement is **true**, so the block following the **if** (in this case, just a single line) is executed.

2   The output would be

```
20 or over
```

Because **my_number** is greater than 20, the test in the **if** statement is **false**, so the code in the block following the **if** is not executed. The code from the **else** block is executed instead.

3   To check if a number is greater than 30, but less than or equal to 40, you would use something like this:

```
if number > 30  and  number <= 40:
    print 'The number is between 30 and 40'
```

You could also do this:

```
if 30 < number <= 40:
    print "The number is between 30 and 40"
```

4   To check for the letter *Q* in uppercase or lowercase, you could do something like this:

```
if answer == 'Q' or answer == 'q':
    print "you typed a 'Q' "
```

Notice that the string we printed uses double quotes, but there are single quotes inside it, around the *Q*. In case you were wondering how to print quote marks, that's one way to do it: use the other kind of quote marks to enclose your string.

Try it out

1   Here is one answer:

```
# program to calculate store discount
# 10% off for $10 or less, 20% off for more than $10
item_price = float(raw_input ('enter the price of the item: '))
if item_price <= 10.0:
    discount = item_price * 0.10
```

```
else:
    discount = item_price * 0.20
final_price = item_price - discount
print 'You got ', discount, 'off, so your final price was', final_price
```

I didn't worry about rounding off the answer to two decimal places (cents) or about displaying the dollar sign.

2 Here is one way to do it:

```
# program to check age and gender of soccer players
# accept girls who are 10 to 12 years old
gender = raw_input("Are you male or female? ('m' or 'f') ")
if gender  == 'f':
    age = int(raw_input('What is your age? '))
    if age >= 10 and age <= 12:
        print 'You can play on the team'
    else:
        print 'You are not the right age.'
else:
    print 'Only girls are allowed on this team.'
```

3 Here is one answer:

```
# program to check if you need gas.
# Next station is 200 km away
tank_size = int(raw_input('How big is your tank (liters)? '))
full = int(raw_input ('How full is your tank (eg. 50 for half full)?'))
mileage = int(raw_input ('What is your gas mileage (km per liter)? '))
range = tank_size * (full / 100.0) * mileage
print 'You can go another', range, 'km.'
print 'The next gas station is 200km away.'
if range <= 200:
    print 'GET GAS NOW!'
else:
    print 'You can wait for the next station.'
```

To add a 5-liter buffer, change the line

```
range = tank_size * (full / 100.0) * mileage
```

to

```
range = (tank_size - 5) * (full / 100.0) * mileage
```

4 Here is a simple password program:

```
password  = "bigsecret"
guess  = raw_input("Enter your password: ")
if guess == password:
    print "Password correct. Welcome"
    # put the rest of the code for your program here
else:
    print "Password incorrect. Goodbye"
```

Chapter 8: Loop the Loop

Test your knowledge

1 The loop would run five times.

2 The loop would run three times, and the values would be as follows: i = 1, i = 3, i = 5.

3 `range(1, 8)` would give you [1, 2, 3, 4, 5, 6, 7].

4 `range(8)` would give you [0, 1, 2, 3, 4, 5, 6, 7].

5 `range(2, 9, 2)` would give you [2, 4, 6, 8].

6 `range (10, 0, -2)` would give you [10, 8, 6, 4, 2].

7 You use `continue` to stop the current iteration of a loop and jump ahead to the next iteration.

8 A `while` loop ends when the condition being tested is `false`.

Try it out

1 Here is a program to print a multiplication table of the user's choice using a `for` loop:

```
# program to print multiplication table up to 10
number = int(raw_input('Which table would you like? '))
print 'Here is your table:'
for i in range(1, 11):
    print number, 'x', i, '=', number * i
```

2 Here is the same multiplication table using a `while` loop:

```
# program to print mult table (while loop)
number = int(raw_input('Which table would you like? '))
print 'Here is your table:'
i = 1
while i <= 10:
    print number, 'times', i, '=', number * i
    i = i + 1
```

3 Here is the multiplication table with a user-defined range:

```
# program to print multiplication table
# user inputs how high they want it to go
number = int(raw_input('Which table would you like? '))
limit = int(raw_input('How high would you like it to go? '))
print 'Here is your table:'
for i in range(1, limit + 1):
    print number, 'times', i, '=', number * i
```

Notice in the `for` line that the second thing in `range()` includes a variable, not just a number. You will learn more about that in chapter 11.

Chapter 9: Just for You—Comments

Try it out

1 Here's a sample of some comments I would add to the temperature-conversion program:

```
# tempconv1.py
# program to convert a Fahrenheit temperature to Celsius
Fahr = 75
Cel = (Fahr - 32) * 5.0 / 9   #decimal division, not integer
print "Fahrenheit = ", Fahr, "Celsius = ", Cel
```

Chapter 10: Game Time

Try it out

1 Did you try typing in the program and running it? Don't forget to put the graphics in the same folder as the program.

Chapter 11: Nested and Variable Loops

Test your knowledge

1 You can make a variable loop in Python by putting a variable in the **range()** function, like this

```
for i in range(numberOfLoops)
```

or

```
for i in range(1, someNumber)
```

2 To make a nested loop, put a loop in the body of another loop, like this:

```
for i in range(5):
    for j in range(8):
        print "hi",
    print
```

This code will print "hi" eight times on a line (the inner loop), and do five lines of that (the outer loop).

3 There will be 15 stars printed.

4   The output from the code will look like this:

```
*   *   *
*   *   *
*   *   *
*   *   *
*   *   *
```

5   For a four-level decision tree, there are 2**4 or 2 * 2 * 2 * 2 possible choices. That's 16 possible choices, or 16 paths through the tree.

Try it out

1   Here is a countdown timer program that asks the user where to start:

```
# Countdown timer asks the user where to start
import time
start = int(raw_input("Countdown timer:  How many seconds? ", ))
for i in range (start, 0, -1):
    print i
    time.sleep(1)
print "BLAST OFF!"
```

2   Here is a version that prints a row of stars beside each number:

```
# Countdown timer asks the user where to start
# and prints stars beside each number

import time
start = int(raw_input("Countdown timer:  How many seconds? ", ))
for i in range (start, 0, -1):
    print i,
    for star in range(i):
        print '*',
    print
    time.sleep(1)
print "BLAST OFF!"
```

Chapter 12: Collecting Things Together—Lists

Test your knowledge

1   You can add something to a list using `append()`, `insert()`, or `extend()`.

2   You can remove something from a list using `remove()`, `pop()`, or `del`.

3   To get a sorted copy of the list, you can do either of these:

■   Make a copy of the list, using slices: `new_list = my_list[:]`. Then sort the new list: `new_list.sort()`.

■   Use the `sorted()` function: `new_list = sorted(my_list)`.

4   You find out whether a certain value is in a list by using the `in` keyword.

5   You find out the location of a value in a list by using the `index()` method.

6   A tuple is a collection that is like a list, except that you can't change it. Tuples are immutable (unchangeable), whereas lists are mutable (changeable).

7   You can make a list of lists in several ways:

   ▪ By using nested square brackets:

   ```
   >>> my_list = [[1, 2, 3], ['a', 'b', 'c'], ['red', 'green', 'blue']]
   ```

   ▪ By using `append()`, and appending a list:

   ```
   >>> my_list = []
   >>> my_list.append([1, 2, 3])
   >>> my_list.append(['a', 'b', 'c'])
   >>> my_list.append(['red', 'green', 'blue'])
   >>> print my_list
   [[1, 2, 3], ['a', 'b', 'c'], ['red', 'green', 'blue']]
   ```

   ▪ By making individual lists and then combining them:

   ```
   >>> list1 = [1, 2, 3]
   >>> list2 = ['a', 'b', 'c']
   >>> list3 = ['red', 'green', 'blue']
   >>> my_list = [list1, list2, list3]
   >>> print my_list
   [[1, 2, 3], ['a', 'b', 'c'], ['red', 'green', 'blue']]
   ```

8   You get a single value from a list of lists by using two indexes (or indices):

   ```
   my_list = [[1, 2, 3], ['a', 'b', 'c'], ['red', 'green', 'blue']]
   my_color = my_list[2][1]
   ```

   The answer would be `'green'`.

9   A dictionary is a collection of key-value pairs.

10 You can add an item to a dictionary by specifying the key and value:

   ```
   phone_numbers['John'] = '555-1234'
   ```

11 To look up an item in a dictionary by its key, you can use an index:

   ```
   print phone_numbers['John']
   ```

Try it out

1 Here is a program that will get five names, put them in a list, and then print them out:

```
nameList = []
print "Enter 5 names (press the Enter key after each name):"
for i in range(5):
    name = raw_input()
    nameList.append(name)

print "The names are:", nameList
```

2 Here is a program that will print the original list and a sorted version:

```
nameList = []
print "Enter 5 names (press the Enter key after each name):"
for i in range(5):
    name = raw_input()
    nameList.append(name)

print "The names are:", nameList
print "The sorted names are:", sorted(nameList)
```

3 Here is a program to print only the third name in the list:

```
nameList = []
print "Enter 5 names (press the Enter key after each name):"
for i in range(5):
    name = raw_input()
    nameList.append(name)

print "The third name is:", nameList[2]
```

4 Here is a program to allow the user to replace a name in the list:

```
nameList = []
print "Enter 5 names (press the Enter key after each name):"
for i in range(5):
    name = raw_input()
    nameList.append(name)
print "The names are:", nameList
print "Replace one name. Which one? (1-5):",
replace = int(raw_input())
new = raw_input("New name: ")
nameList[replace - 1] = new
print "The names are:", nameList
```

5   Here is a program to allow the user to create a dictionary with words and definitions:

```
user_dictionary = {}
while 1:
    command = raw_input("'a' to add word,  'l' to lookup a word,  'q' to quit ")

    if command == "a":
        word = raw_input("Type the word: ")
        definition = raw_input("Type the definition: ")
        user_dictionary[word] = definition
        print "Word added!"

    elif command == "l":
        word = raw_input("Type the word: ")
        if word in user_dictionary.keys():
            print user_dictionary[word]
        else:
            print "That word isn't in the dictionary yet."

    elif command == 'q':
        break
```

Chapter 13: Functions

Test your knowledge

1   You use the `def` keyword to create a function.
2   You call a function by using its name with parentheses.
3   You pass arguments to a function by putting the arguments in the parentheses when you call the function.
4   There is no limit to the number of arguments a function can have.
5   The function sends information back to the caller using the `return` keyword.
6   After a function is finished running, any local variables are destroyed.

Try it out

1   The function is just a bunch of `print` statements:

```
def printMyNameBig():
    print "  CCCC        A         RRRRR  TTTTTTT  EEEEEE  RRRRR  "
    print " C    C      A A        R    R    T     E       R    R "
    print "C          A   A        R    R    T     EEEE    R    R "
    print "C          AAAAAAA      RRRRR     T     E       RRRRR  "
    print " C    C   A       A     R    R    T     E       R    R "
    print "  CCCC   A         A    R    R    T     EEEEEE   R     R"
```

The program that calls it could look like this:

```
for i in range(5):
    printMyNameBig()
```

2 Here's my example for printing addresses with seven arguments:

```
# define a function with seven arguments
def printAddr(name, num, street, city, prov, pcode, country):
    print name
    print num,
    print street
    print city,
    if prov !="":
        print ", "+prov
    else:
        print ""
    print pcode
    print country
    print

#call the function and pass seven arguments to it
printAddr("Sam", "45", "Main St.", "Ottawa", "ON", "K2M 2E9", "Canada")
printAddr("Jian", "64", "2nd Ave.", "Hong Kong", "", "235643", "China")
```

3 No answer, just try it.

4 The function to add up change should look like this:

```
def addUpChange(quarters, dimes, nickels, pennies):
    total  = 0.25 * quarters + 0.10 * dimes + 0.05 * nickels + 0.01 * pennies
    return total
```

The program that calls it would look like this:

```
quarters = int(raw_input("quarters: "))
dimes = int(raw_input("dimes: "))
nickels = int(raw_input("nickels: "))
pennies = int(raw_input("pennies: "))

total  = addUpChange(quarters, dimes, nickels, pennies)

print "You have a total of: ", total
```

Chapter 14: Objects

Test your knowledge

1 To define a new object type, you use the `class` keyword.

2 Attributes are the "things you know" about an object. They are variables contained in an object.

3 Methods are the actions you can do to an object. They are functions contained in an object.

4 A class is just a definition or blueprint for an object. An instance is what you get when you make an object from the blueprint.

5 The name `self` is usually used as the instance reference in an object method.

6 Polymorphism is the ability to have two or more methods with the same name on different objects. The methods can behave differently depending on which object they belong to.

7 Inheritance is the ability of objects to acquire attributes and methods from their "parents." The "child" class (which is called a subclass or derived class) gets all the attributes and methods of the parent and can also have attributes and methods that are not shared with the parent.

Try it out

1 A class for a bank account might look like this:

```
class BankAccount:
    def __init__(self, acct_number, acct_name):
        self.acct_number = acct_number
        self.acct_name = acct_name
        self.balance = 0.0

    def displayBalance(self):
        print "The account balance is:", self.balance

    def deposit(self, amount):
        self.balance = self.balance + amount
        print "You deposited", amount
        print "The new balance is:", self.balance

    def withdraw(self, amount):
        if self.balance >= amount:
            self.balance = self.balance - amount
            print "You withdrew", amount
            print "The new balance is:", self.balance
        else:
            print "You tried to withdraw", amount
            print "The account balance is:", self.balance
            print "Withdrawal denied. Not enough funds."
```

And here's some code to test it and make sure it's working:

```
myAccount = BankAccount(234567, "Warren Sande")
print "Account name:", myAccount.acct_name
print "Account number:", myAccount.acct_number
myAccount.displayBalance()

myAccount.deposit(34.52)
myAccount.withdraw(12.25)
myAccount.withdraw(30.18)
```

2 To make an interest account, make a subclass of `BankAccount`, and create a method to add interest:

```
class InterestAccount(BankAccount):
    def __init__(self, acct_number, acct_name, rate):
        BankAccount.__init__(self, acct_number, acct_name)
        self.rate = rate

    def addInterest (self):
        interest = self.balance * self.rate
        print "adding interest to the account,", self.rate * 100, "percent"
        self.deposit (interest)
```

Here's some code to test it:

```
myAccount = InterestAccount(234567, "Warren Sande", 0.11)
print "Account name:", myAccount.acct_name
print "Account number:", myAccount.acct_number
myAccount.displayBalance()
myAccount.deposit(34.52)
myAccount.addInterest()
```

Chapter 15: Modules

Test your knowledge

1 Some of the advantages of using modules are

- You can write some code once and use it in many programs.
- You can use modules that other people have written.
- Your code files are smaller, so it's easier to find things in your code.
- You can use only the parts (modules) you need to do the job.

2 You create a module by writing some Python code and saving it in a file.

3 When you want to use a module, you use the `import` keyword.

4 Importing a module is the same as importing a namespace.

5 The two ways to import the time module so that you have access to all the names in the module are

```
import time
```

and

```
from time import *
```

Try it out

1 To write a module, just put the code for your "big name" function in a file—something like **bigname.py**. Then, to import the module and call the function, do something like this:

```
import bigname
bigname.printMyNameBig()
```

Or you could do this:

```
from bigname import *
printMyNameBig()
```

2 To bring `c_to_f()` into the main program's namespace, you can do this

```
from my_module import c_to_f
```

or this:

```
from my_module import *
```

3 A short program to print five random integers from 1 to 20 would look like this:

```
import random
for i in range(5):
    print random.randint(1, 20)
```

4 A short program that prints out a random decimal number every 3 seconds for 30 seconds would look like this:

```
import random, time
for i in range(10):
    print random.random()
    time.sleep(3)
```

Chapter 16: Graphics

Test your knowledge

1 The RGB value [255, 255, 255] makes the color white.

2 The RGB value [0, 255, 0] makes the color green.

3 To draw rectangles, you use the Pygame method `pygame.draw.rect()`.

4 To draw lines joining a number of points together (like connect-the-dots), you use the `pygame.draw.lines()` method.

5 The term *pixel* is short for "picture element," and it means one dot on the screen (or paper).

6 In a Pygame window, location [0, 0] is the upper-left corner.

7 In the diagram, location [50, 200] is at letter B.

8 In the diagram, location [300, 50] is at letter D.

9 The `blit()` method is used to copy images in Pygame.

10 To move or animate an image, use these two steps:

- Erase the image from its old location.
- Draw the image in its new location.

Try it out

1 Here is a program that draws a few different shapes on the screen. You can also find it as **TIO_CH16_1.py** in the **\answers** folder and on the web site:

```
import pygame, sys
pygame.init()
screen=pygame.display.set_mode((640, 480))
screen.fill((250, 120, 0))
pygame.draw.arc(screen, (255, 255, 0), pygame.rect.Rect(43, 368, 277, 235),
    -6.25, 0, 15)
pygame.draw.rect(screen, (255, 0, 0), pygame.rect.Rect(334, 191, 190, 290))
pygame.draw.rect(screen, (128, 64, 0), pygame.rect.Rect(391, 349, 76, 132))
pygame.draw.line(screen, (0, 255, 0), (268, 259), (438, 84), 25)
pygame.draw.line(screen, (0, 255, 0), (578, 259), (438, 84), 25)
pygame.draw.circle(screen, (0, 0, 0), (452, 409), 11, 2)
pygame.draw.polygon(screen, (0, 0, 255), [(39, 39), (44, 136), (59, 136),
    (60, 102), (92, 102), (94, 131), (107, 141), (111, 50), (97, 50), (93,
    86), (60, 82), (58, 38)], 5)
pygame.draw.rect(screen, (0, 0, 255), pygame.rect.Rect(143, 90, 23, 63), 5)
pygame.draw.circle(screen, (0, 0, 255), (153, 60), 15, 5)
clock = pygame.time.Clock()
pygame.display.flip()

running = True
while running:
    clock.tick(60)
```

```
        for event in pygame.event.get():
            if event.type == pygame.QUIT:
                running = False
            elif event.type == pygame.KEYDOWN and event.key == pygame.K_ESCAPE:
                running = False
    pygame.quit()
```

2 To replace the beach ball image with a different one, just replace the filename in this line

```
    my_ball = pygame.image.load('beach_ball.png')
```

with a different filename for a different graphic.

3 In listing 16.16, change

```
    x_speed = 10
    y_speed = 10
```

to something else, like

```
    x_speed = 20
    y_speed = 8
```

4 To make the ball bounce off an "invisible" wall, change the line in listing 16.16 from

```
    if x > screen.get_width() - 90  or  x < 0:
```

to this:

```
    if x > screen.get_width() - 250  or  x < 0:
```

This makes the ball reverse direction before it gets to the edge of the window. You can do the same thing for the "floor" with the y-coordinates.

5 Here's what listing 16.6 looks like with the `display.flip` moved inside the `while` loop, and with a delay added:

```
import pygame, sys, random
pygame.init()
screen = pygame.display.set_mode([640,480])
screen.fill([255, 255, 255])
for i in range (100):
    width = random.randint(0, 250)
    height = random.randint(0, 100)
    top = random.randint(0, 400)
    left = random.randint(0, 500)
    pygame.draw.rect(screen, [0,0,0], [left, top, width, height], 1)
    pygame.display.flip()
    pygame.time.delay(30)
```

You should be able to see each rectangle appear individually, because we have slowed down the program and are refreshing the display after each rectangle is drawn. If you do this to the sine wave programs, you can see each point in the sine wave being plotted.

Chapter 17: Sprites and Collision Detection

Test your knowledge

1 Rect collision detection means detecting when two graphical objects are touching or overlapping by using a rectangle around the objects.

2 Pixel-perfect collision detection uses the true outline of the graphical object to do collision detection. Rect collision detection uses a rectangle around the object to determine collisions. Pixel-perfect collision detection is more accurate and realistic, but it also takes more code, which slows things down a bit.

3 You can keep track of a number of sprite objects together by using either a regular Python list or a Pygame Sprite group.

4 You can control the speed of animation (frame rate) in your code either by adding delays between each frame or by using `pygame.time.Clock` to get a specific frame rate. You can also change how far (how many pixels) the object moves in each frame.

5 Using the delay method is less accurate because it doesn't take into account how long the code itself takes for each frame, so you don't know exactly what frame rate you'll get.

6 You can find out what frame rate your program is running at by using `pyg-ame.time.Clock.get_fps()`.

Chapter 18: A New Kind of Input—Events

Test your knowledge

1 Two kinds of events that a program can respond to are keyboard events and mouse events.

2 The piece of code that deals with an event is called an *event handler*.

3 Pygame uses the `KEYDOWN` event to detect keys being pressed.

4 The `pos` attribute tells you where the mouse is located when the event happens.

5 To get the next available event number for user events, use `pygame.USEREVENT`.

6 To create a timer, use `pygame.time.set_timer()`.

7 To display text in a Pygame window, use a `font` object.

8   These are the three steps to use a font object:
- Create a font object.
- Render the text, creating a surface.
- Blit this surface to the display surface.

Try it out

1   Why does the ball behave strangely when it hits the side of the paddle instead of the top? Because you have a collision, so the code tries to reverse the ball's y-direction (make it go up instead of down). But because the ball is coming in from the side, it's still "colliding" with the paddle, even after reversing direction. The next time through the loop (one frame later), it reverses direction again, so it's going down again, and so on. A simple way to fix this is to always set the ball to go "up" (a negative y-speed) when it collides with the paddle. It's not perfect, because it means even if the ball hits the side of the paddle, it will bounce up—not too realistic! But it solves the problem of the ball bouncing around in the paddle. If you want a more realistic solution, it will require a bit more code. You would probably need to add something where you check which edge of the paddle the ball has collided with before "bouncing" it.

2   An example of some code that adds randomness to the program is posted on the web site as **TIO_CH18_2.py**.

Chapter 19: Sound

Test your knowledge

1   Types of files used for storing sound include Wave (**.wav**), MP3 (**.mp3**), Ogg Vorbis (**.ogg**), and Windows Media Audio (**.wma**).

2   The `pygame.mixer` module is used for playing music.

3   You set the volume for Pygame sound objects using the `set_volume()` method of each sound object.

4   You set the volume of background music using `pygame.mixer.music.set_volume()`.

5   To make music fade out, use the `pygame.mixer.music.fadeout()` method. Use the number of milliseconds (thousandths of a second) of fade time as an argument. For example, `pygame.mixer.music.fadeout(2000)` will fade out the sound in 2 seconds.

Try it out

1   The code for a number-guessing program with sound is on the web site, as **TIO_CH19_1.py**.

Chapter 20: More GUIs

Test your knowledge

1. Three names for the graphical elements of a GUI are *control*, *widget*, and *component*.
2. The letter that you press (along with **Alt**) to get into a menu is called a *hot key*.
3. Qt Designer files need to end in **.ui**.
4. Types of components you can include in a GUI using PyQt include button, check box, progress bar, list, radio button, spin box, slider, text field, image, label, and several others. See the **Widget Box** in Qt Designer to view the whole list.
5. To make a widget do something, it needs to have an event handler.
6. The & (ampersand) character is used to define a hot key in Qt Designer.
7. The content of a spin box in Qt Designer is always an integer.

Try it out

1. A version of the number-guessing program using Qt Designer is posted on the web site as **TIO_CH20_1.py** and **TIO_CH20_1.ui**.
2. To fix the spinner problem, select the spin box widget in Qt Designer. In the Property Editor, change the `minimum` and `maximum` properties. The `minimum` property should be something like –1000, and the `maximum` can be something very large like 1000000.

Chapter 21: Print Formatting and Strings

Test your knowledge

1. If you have two separate `print` statements, and you want everything to print on the same line, put a comma at the end of the first `print` statement, like this:

```
print "What is",
print "your name?"
```

2. To add extra blank lines when you print something, you can add extra `print` statements with nothing in them, like this:

```
print "Hello"
print
print
print
print "World"
```

Or you can print newline characters, \n, like this:

```
print "Hello\n\n\nWorld"
```

3   To line things up in columns, use the tab character, \t.

4   To make a number print in E-notation, use the format string %e or %E, like this:

```
>>> number = 12.3456
>>> print '%e' % number
1.234560e+001
```

Try it out

1   The program would look like this:

```
name = raw_input("What is your name? ")
age = int(raw_input("How old are you? "))
color = raw_input("What is your favorite color? ")

print "Your name is", name,
print "you are", age, "years old,",
print "and you like the color", color
```

2   The code to line up the times table using tabs would look like this:

```
for looper in range(1, 11):
    print looper, "\ttimes 8 =\t", looper * 8
```

Notice the \t in front of the word **times** and after the = sign.

3   Here is a program to print the fractions of 8:

```
for i in range(1, 9):
    fraction = i / 8.0
    print str(i) + '/8 = %.3f' % fraction
```

The first part, **print str(i) + '/8 =**, prints the fraction. The last part, **%.3f' %**
fraction, prints the decimal number with three decimal places.

Chapter 22: File Input and Output

Test your knowledge

1   The kind of object in Python that's used to work with files is called a *file object*.

2   You create a file object by using the **open()** function, which is one of Python's built-in functions.

3   A *filename* is the name used to store the file on the disk (or on other storage, like a flash drive). A *file object* is the thing used to work with files in Python. The name of the file object does not have to be the same as the filename on the disk.

4   When a program is done reading or writing a file, the program should close the file.

5   If you open a file in append mode and write something to it, the information you write gets added (appended) to the end of the file.

6   If you open a file in write mode and then write something to the file, everything that was in the file is lost and is replaced with the new data.

7   To reset the read point of a file back to the beginning, use the `seek()` method, with an argument of 0, like this:

```
myFile.seek(0)
```

8   To save a Python object to a file using `pickle`, you use the `pickle.dump()` method, with the object you want to save and the filename as arguments, like this:

```
pickle.dump(myObject, "my_pickle_file.pkl")
```

9   To unpickle or retrieve an object from a pickle file, use the `pickle.load()` method, with the pickle file as an argument, like this:

```
myObject = pickle.load("my_pickle_file.pkl")
```

Try it out

1   Here is a simple program to create silly sentences:

```python
import random

noun_file = open("nouns.txt", 'r')
nouns = noun_file.readline()
noun_list = nouns.split(',')
noun_file.close()

adj_file = open("adjectives.txt", 'r')
adjectives = adj_file.readline()
adj_list = adjectives.split(',')
adj_file.close()

verb_file = open("verbs.txt", 'r')
verbs = verb_file.readline()
verb_list = verbs.split(',')
verb_file.close()

adverb_file = open("adverbs.txt", 'r')
adverbs = adverb_file.readline()
adverb_list = adverbs.split(',')
adverb_file.close()
```

```
noun = random.choice(noun_list)
adj = random.choice(adj_list)
verb = random.choice(verb_list)
adverb = random.choice(adverb_list)

print"The", adj, noun, verb, adverb + '.'
```

The word files should just be lists of words separated by commas.

2 Here is a program that saves some data in a text file:

```
name = raw_input("Enter your name: ")
age = raw_input("Enter your age: ")
color = raw_input("Enter your favorite color: ")
food = raw_input("Enter your favorite food: ")

my_data = open("my_data_file.txt", 'w')
my_data.write(name + "\n")
my_data.write(age + "\n")
my_data.write(color + "\n")
my_data.write(food)

my_data.close()
```

3 Here is a program that saves some data using the `pickle` module:

```
import pickle

name = raw_input("Enter your name: ")
age = raw_input("Enter your age: ")
color = raw_input("Enter your favorite color: ")
food = raw_input("Enter your favorite food: ")

my_list = [name, age, color, food]

pickle_file = open("my_pickle_file.pkl", 'w')
pickle.dump(my_list, pickle_file)

pickle_file.close()
```

Chapter 23: Take a Chance—Randomness

Test your knowledge

1 A *random event* is something that happens (an "event") where you don't know ahead of time what the outcome will be. Two examples are flipping a coin (you don't know if it will come up heads or tails) and rolling a pair of dice (you don't know what numbers will come up on the dice).

2 Rolling an 11-sided die is different from rolling two 6-sided dice because, with an 11-sided die, all numbers from 2 to 12 have an equal probability of coming up. With two 6-sided dice, some numbers (totals of the two dice) will come up more often than others.

3 Here are two ways to simulate rolling a die in Python:

```
import random
sides = [1, 2, 3, 4, 5, 6]
die_1 = random.choice(sides)
```

and

```
import random
die_1 = random.randint(1, 6)
```

4 To represent a single card, we used an object.

5 To represent a deck of cards, we used a list. Each item in the list was one card (an object).

6 To remove a card from a deck or a hand, we used the **remove**() method for lists, like this: **deck.remove**() or **hand.remove**().

Try it out

1 Just try it and see what happens.

Chapter 24: Computer Simulations

Test your knowledge

1 Computer simulations are used for a number of reasons:
- To save money (to do experiments that would be too expensive to do in the real world).
- To protect people and equipment (to do experiments that would be too dangerous in the real world).
- To try things that simply aren't possible in the real world (like making a big asteroid crash into the Moon).
- To speed up time (to make an experiment go faster than it would in the real world). This is good for studying things that take a long time, like glaciers melting.
- To slow down time (to make an experiment go slower than it would in the real world). This is good for studying things that happen very fast, like electrons zipping down a wire.

2 You can list any kind of computer simulations you can think of. These could be games, math or science programs, or even weather forecasts (which are created by using computer simulations).

3 A `timedelta` object is used to store the difference between two dates or times.

Try it out

The programs for this section are quite long—too long to print in the book. You can find them all on the web site:

1 **TIO_CH24_1.py**—Lunar Lander with out-of-orbit check

2 **TIO_CH24_2.py**—Lunar Lander with play-again option

3 **TIO_CH24_3.py**—Virtual Pet GUI with **Pause** button

Chapter 26: Python Battle

Try it out

1 This is a basic robot that beats CircleAI:

```
class AI:
    def __init__(self):
        self.isFirstTurn = True
    def turn(self):
        if self.isFirstTurn:
            self.robot.turnLeft()
            self.isFirstTurn = False
        elif self.robot.lookInFront() == "bot":
            self.robot.attack()
        else:
            self.robot.doNothing()
```

This robot's strategy is to wait for CircleAI to come around the board and attack when CircleAI reaches it. I created it using my knowledge of how CircleAI works, and it wouldn't win against other robots. As I said in the chapter, it would be much, much harder to make a robot that wins every time, even when it doesn't know what robot it's battling against.

List of Code Listings

451

Index